Diversity and Design

Diversity and Design explores how design—whether of products, buildings, landscapes, cities, media, or systems—affects diverse members of society. Fifteen case studies in television, marketing, product design, architecture, film, video games, and more illustrate the profound, though often hidden, consequences design decisions and processes have on the total human experience. The book not only investigates how gender, race, class, age, disability, and other factors influence the ways designers think, but also emphasizes the importance of understanding increasingly diverse cultures and, thus, averting design that leads to discrimination, isolation, and segregation.

With over 140 full-color illustrations, chapter summaries, discussion questions and exercises, *Diversity and Design* is a valuable tool to help you understand the importance of designing for all.

Beth Tauke is Associate Professor of Architecture at the University at Buffalo—State University of New York, USA.

Korydon Smith is Associate Professor of Architecture at the University at Buffalo—State University of New York, USA, and the editor of *Introducing Architectural Theory*.

Charles Davis is Assistant Professor at the University of North Carolina at Charlotte, in North Carolina, USA.

"We needed a book that introduces students to issues of diversity in design practice; this edited volume fills that gap. Fifteen engaging chapters argue that diversity can be an end product of a creative process that promotes social and economic inclusion. This volume places design at the center of emancipatory and progressive social practices and encourages designers and students of designed artefacts, environments, and systems to think of the social impact of their practices."

Arijit Sen, Associate Professor of Architecture, University of Wisconsin–Milwaukee, USA

"All design has hidden consequences. This anthology is a welcome addition to the literature exploring the role of designers in helping to create a more inclusive society."

Jeremy Myerson, Helen Hamlyn Professor of Design, Royal College of Art, UK

"*Diversity and Design* provides evidence of the profound but often unintended consequences of design decisions across a diverse spectrum of users and range of scales from video games and everyday-use products to architectural environments. The 15 case studies that comprise the book's chapters illustrate how a range of factors and user characteristics influence designers' thinking. Through content, discussion questions, and exercises, the book provides excellent tools for design instructors to better illustrate ways to avoid unintentional discrimination and segregation with design."

Lynne M. Dearborn, Associate Professor, University of Illinois at Urbana–Champaign, USA

"This book is a new interpretation and overview of the social issues that have been finding their way into education and practice for the last 50 years. Beth Tauke and colleagues have provided the overview necessary to take an array of perspectives and put them into a coherent and well-organized structure [allowing] educators and practitioners to continue to evolve toward a greater understanding of the continual emerging complexity in the global culture for which we are designing."

Craig Vogel, Director of the Center of Design, Research and Innovation
at the University of Cincinnati, Ohio, USA

Diversity and Design
Understanding Hidden Consequences

Edited by
Beth Tauke, Korydon Smith,
and Charles Davis

Routledge
Taylor & Francis Group

NEW YORK AND LONDON

First published 2016
by Routledge
711 Third Avenue, New York, NY 10017

and by Routledge
2 Park Square, Milton Park, Abingdon, Oxon OX14 4RN

Routledge is an imprint of the Taylor & Francis Group, an informa business

Library of Congress Cataloging in Publication Data
Diversity and design : understanding hidden consequences / [edited by] Beth Tauke,
Korydon Smith and Charles L. Davis.
pages cm
Includes bibliographical references and index.
1. Design--Human factors. 2. Design--Social aspects. I. Tauke, Beth, editor. II. Smith,
Korydon H., 1977- editor. III. Davis, Charles L., II, editor.
NK1520.D59 2015
745.4--dc23
2015003522

ISBN: 978-1-138-02316-1 (hbk)
ISBN: 978-1-138-02317-8 (pbk)
ISBN: 978-1-315-77579-1 (ebk)

Acquisition Editor: Wendy Fuller
Editorial Assistant: Grace Harrison
Production Editor: Christina O'Brien

Typeset in Avenir
by Saxon Graphics Ltd, Derby

Contents

Part 2 Gender and Sexuality

Part 3 Age and Ability

Acknowledgments

A text on diversity and design requires input from many people with diverse points of view. We are grateful for the ongoing, lively debates with colleagues that inspired this project, the designers who have taken on diversity issues as a primary focus, and those from underrepresented groups who have influenced the practice of design. In addition, we express our appreciation to the many students who have contributed to and inspired the conceptual underpinnings of our work.

Implementation of this project required the creativity and dedication of many people. First, we are most appreciative of Megan Basnak, Design Research Associate at the Center for Inclusive Design and Environmental Access (IDeA) and steward of this book, for her assistance, organizational skills, wisdom, conscientiousness, commitment, patience, humor, and too-long-to-list set of positive qualities. We thank the University of North Carolina at Charlotte Research Assistant Emily Dallmeyer, who assisted with several chapters. We thank the researchers and staff of the IDeA Center for their continual feedback and encouragement. In particular, we are grateful to Dr. Edward Steinfeld, Director of the IDeA Center, for supporting our efforts and urging those in the inclusive design communities to more fully incorporate diversity issues into their missions.

Robert Shibley, Dean of the School of Architecture and Planning, and Omar Khan, Chair of the Department of Architecture, at the University at Buffalo—State University of New York gave Beth Tauke and Korydon Smith the time to work on this manuscript, and, since 2002, have supported a university general education course on diversity and design, which, in great part, has contributed to the concept of this book. Ken Lambla, Dean of the College of Arts and Architecture at the University of North Carolina at Charlotte, and Chris Jarrett, Director of the Department of Architecture, granted Charles Davis travel support and research assistance for this project.

We thank the Routledge editorial team for shepherding us through the editorial and production process. In particular, we appreciate Wendy Fuller's guiding feedback in the conceptualization of the work and Grace Harrison's chaperoning of the development and completion of the book.

Finally, there are those people for whom mere thanks are not enough. Beth Tauke thanks Jean La Marche for his gentle encouragement, incisive reviews, and sage counsel. Korydon Smith thanks Julie Haase-Smith for her tremendous patience and generosity (a true gift to the world), and Eston and Khale for their spirit, wit, and early-morning breakfast conversations (and hugs). Charles Davis thanks Jeehyun Lim for critical insight into debates on diversity within the humanities at a critical time during this project.

This book was, in part, developed under a grant from the Department of Education, National Institute on Disability and Rehabilitation Research (NIDRR) grant number H133E100002. However, those contents do not necessarily represent the policy of the Department of Education, and you should not assume endorsement by the federal government.

Figures

Closing the Gap between the Designer and the Recipients of Design

Sina Mossayeb, Global Systems Design Lead, IDEO

Few people think about it or are aware of it, but there is nothing made by human beings that does not involve a design decision somewhere.

(Bill Moggridge, Co-Founder, IDEO)

In 1991, British designers Bill Moggridge and Mike Nuttall, along with Stanford d.school founder David Kelley, co-founded IDEO, continuously ranked among the world's most innovative companies. Moggridge described his life work as being driven by his interest in people and their relationship to things. Bill, Mike, David, and a team of young designers, ethnographers, and engineers in California set out to rethink what it meant to do good design work. Their focus was on design methods—the way designers make decisions. IDEO called this approach to innovation "human-centered design."

At its core, human-centered design is about empathizing with people before designing for them. Human-centered designers suggest that it is not enough for a designer to consider important questions like: "Is this design idea technologically feasible?" or "Is this design idea viable for the market?" At IDEO, we argue that designers benefit most from starting with a more central question: "Who are we designing for and is this what they want or need?" By starting with people, you get human-centered design, but you also get more innovative, higher-quality design.

When designing to solve for a human problem or fill an opportunity gap, designers need to look at what people say and do, as well as understand and connect with what they are feeling and thinking. They also need context about those people. Some needs are universal, but how we express those needs and how we want those needs met vary across cultures and groups.

On one project, my team was interviewing Sally, a mother of two, who described herself as "organized." When we arrived at her home, the place was a mess—toys sprawled on the floor, clothes in a big pile, and dishes unwashed in the sink. If we had not visited her home and, instead, had based our knowledge solely on the survey, we would not have understood the subtleties at play. In discussions with her, we realized what she meant by "organized" was "knowing where things were" and not necessarily having things tidy. She took out a stack of papers from a drawer and showed us the insurance she recently purchased. To Sally, being "organized" was also about feeling "safe." She cared less about visual clutter and sought security through an organized life.

Consider, as well, something that is seldom discussed: the diversity among those designing. Designers often talk about their point of view when addressing a design problem. Truly, what they are talking about is their view, not the *point* from which they are viewing. That *point* includes their experiences, their context, and all the other stuff that influences beliefs and perspectives—personality, gender, age, etc.—and it influences how the designer approaches the problem or opportunity at hand.

I have been part of several design teams that could not be more different, whether that diversity is in the team members' craft, discipline, depth or breadth of experience, ideology, temperament, ethnic and cultural background, gender, or sexual orientation. I have worked on several projects where we put together interdisciplinary teams that (ideally) address the complexity of the design challenge—whether that is improving the employee experience for frontline staff or designing attractive packaging for a line of supplements for people with the metabolic disorder Phenylketonuria. So, when IDEO talks about diversity, we are talking about both the diversity of the design team and the diversity of the recipients of the design. When setting out to design, we reflect on the diversity of the design team: Who are we? What is our background? What context and views do we bring to this design brief? And we think about those for whom we are designing: Who are they? What experiences do they have? How do they feel, what do they think, and what is their everyday life like? What do they want or need?

It is then that we can confidently take on a bold design prompt: "How might *we* design _____ for *them*?"

An important development in the process of human-centered design has been the idea of co-creation. Instead of thinking, "I'm designing this *for* them," IDEO designers shift toward a more inclusive and collaborative, "I'm designing *with* them." Beyond observations and empathy exercises—like going into the homes of people, hanging out for a weekend with them, spending hours shadowing people at work, and so forth—what if you posed the design brief directly to people and had them solve it? Invite them to brainstorm ideas with you. Facilitate their involvement in sketching a prototype of what they think would be an ideal way to engage their children in learning, of vitamin packaging to suit their needs, or of the desirable layout of a playground.

As a design student or beginning professional, you can build your ideas from human-centered research. You can take your prototype out into the world and have people interact with it—then make revisions, get more feedback, and make further revisions—before finalizing it. The design will be much improved and most likely more relevant to those for whom you are designing.

A colleague of mine designed a transportable mosquito net for workers who travel through the rainforests of Southeast Asia. The design was durable, lightweight, and efficient—a really great piece of work. But, when his team took the prototype out into villages and showed people, the team received disturbing reactions. The people did not want to use it for sleeping, not because the net did not work but because it looked exactly like netted coffins they used to use. How could the designers have anticipated that without engaging the cultural context of those for whom they were designing?

In this book, there are many case studies that raise questions about human-centered design. As you read, consider how those designing came to their conclusions. What was the makeup of the design team? What processes did they use and how did it affect the end product? What were the unintended consequences of that process?

I have often found that the further I get from the insights drawn from those for whom I am designing, the more unreliable, ineffective, and inelegant the outcome. So, I wonder, in the case of failed designs, what role did the designers' *points* of view play in the outcome? Did they take time to understand the values, beliefs, and lived experiences of diverse end-users? Did they use participatory methods to co-create with them? Did they put themselves in their shoes? Human-centered design is itself not free of limitations or unintended consequences. Yet it is a process that beckons us to move beyond our assumptions and self-perceived expertise. Notwithstanding each person's inherent traits and biases, the goal is to lessen the gap between the designer and the recipients of the design.

Introduction

Beth Tauke, Korydon Smith, and Charles Davis

> *If we cannot now end our differences, at least we can help make the world safe for diversity.*
> (John F. Kennedy, 35th President of the United States)

> *Design shapes the way we live. So it ought to serve everyone.*
> (Eva Maddox, Co-Founder, Archeworks)

While the case can be made for many populations—ethnic minorities, women, or people with disabilities—children are among the most underrepresented groups in design. Most of the world is designed by and for adults. Children have little say in what gets designed, almost no voice in the design process, and no active recourse for products, buildings, and cities that fail to meet their needs or preferences. Children's museums are the rare exception. Even elementary schools are more frequently designed from adult perspectives—teachers, administrators, and parents—than from the vantage point of kids. Rarer still is our critical questioning of the *immediate consequences* of design on children and the *residual effects* on their transition into adulthood. How does school design affect educational attainment? How does toy design affect children's perceptions of themselves? How does media design affect a kid's opinions about gender, race, or religion? How does the design of a city impact a child's long-term physical and mental health?

Even the history of children is "a marginal subject." Children "leave fewer historical sources than adults, and their powerlessness makes them less visible than other social groups," despite their relevance in major discourses such as immigration, slavery, and war.[1] Leaving children out of history and out of design—effectively off the list of recognized groups or issues, e.g., racism, gender inequality, etc.—both inhibits their development and restricts society's advancement. In contrast, incorporating historical narratives of children expands and enriches our understanding of society. Likewise, recognizing the physical, cognitive, and emotional needs of children broadens and deepens the methods and impacts of design for other social groups.

Children provide a resounding example. They have, on average, less physical ability and less education than adults. They have little economic power and almost no political power. These factors both lead to and exacerbate their marginal status in design and society. As this book illustrates, however, design impacts all social groups: young and old; black, white, and multiracial; lesbian, gay, bisexual, transgender, and heterosexual. Design is never neutral. Design— positive or negative, overt or hidden—affects physical health, impacts emotional well-being, and governs social interaction. Design influences how we see ourselves, how we see others, and how others see us.

In parallel, the demographics and values of a society affect all of the design professions—from interior design to urban planning, from industrial design to architecture, and from media design to systems design. Larger, wealthier, and more politically powerful groups, "the majority," shape the ordinances that form our cities and towns. They drive which products are designed, manufactured, and sold, and at what prices. They provide the backdrop against which commercial and political messages are interpreted as conventional or innovative, agreeable or offensive. The minority (in number and/or power), conversely, has less influence, but is not without agency. A two-part strategy is needed: (1) uncovering the hidden consequences that dominant groups and prevailing design paradigms have on marginalized groups and (2) revealing and infusing the capacities of disenfranchised groups into the popular ethos and mainstream design processes, i.e., recognizing and integrating a minority group's capacities into everyday social and design practices.

Design and diversity—two social forces that shape our identities and our material world—can no longer be separate fields of study. As such, this book, *Diversity and Design*, focuses on the changing nature of society, and examines the rich diversity of cultural experiences and their associated design issues. Using case studies, contributors to this book discuss ways in which physical and media environments affect various populations and, reciprocally, the ways diverse populations have affected the designed world. Cases uncover instances of design discrimination as well as exemplars of emancipation (freedom). To that end, the book has three pairs of specific objectives:

- to introduce readers to various design disciplines and their relevant histories, and to introduce readers to various diversity groups and their relevant histories
- to raise awareness of the impacts that design decisions have had on diverse populations, and to raise awareness of the impacts that diverse populations have had on design decisions
- to analyze the social impacts of designed artifacts, environments, and systems; and to critically examine the social impacts of design processes and practices.

Building upon the traditions of feminism, critical race theory, inclusive design (design for disability), and other emancipatory paradigms, we assert that designers can no longer exclusively design in their own image. San Francisco-based graphic designer, Joshua Brewer, for example, asserted that "you are not your user." Brewer added: "Socrates said, 'Know thyself.' I say, 'Know thy users.' And guess what? They don't think like you do."[2] Designers must actively consider the perspectives of "the other" in both general and specific terms. Renowned philosopher Martin Heidegger, for example, proposed that the very idea of communication itself, the exchange of words and symbols, presupposes the desire to hear or understand "the other" and is a fundamental aspect of being human.[3] This drive to know "the other"—to see or understand differences—is a subject in many disciplines, but more recent in design.

Encyclopedist Denis Diderot, in his "Letter on the Blind for the Use of Those Who See," engaged the idea of "the other" by taking the reader on an unusual journey of the visual from the perspective of the tactile. Sight, Diderot's blind man concludes, "is a kind of touch which extends to distant objects." Presenting "the other" through a set of comparisons or metaphors moves both parties, the blind man and the sighted man, beyond themselves into a space of greater understanding.[4]

Psychoanalyst Jacques Lacan presented the idea of "the other" through his concept of the mirror-stage. Lacan argued that the basic nature of difference emerges at the moment when one recognizes her/his reflection as a distinct entity in a mirror for the first time. We recognize ourselves outside of our bodies, the same as others do, yet awkwardly and self-consciously so, awaiting the promise of a unified, integrated *self-and-other*.[5]

Seeking out, knowing, and becoming "the other" is a common theme in many books, films, and television series—*Avatar*, *Star Trek*, *Beauty and the Beast*, *West Side Story*, *Big*, *The Merchant of Venice*, *The Little Prince*, and *To Kill a Mockingbird*, along with Facebook, online gaming, and other media. Despite its popularity in mainstream media, taking on the tasks of actively seeking difference and knowing "the other" typically is not part of mainstream education or design. But design for "the other"—what we might term "empathic design"—is essential to the study and practice of design (ethically and economically). Indeed, in the same way that certain IQ tests have grown obsolete due to their cultural biases and limited definitions of intelligence, some design fields and techniques, even some designers themselves, will face obsolescence (becoming "design-o-saurs") if they continue to focus on a shrinking or narrowly defined majority.[6]

Defining Diversity

Diversity is a global issue, but particularly relevant in multicultural places like the United States. The meaning of the term *diversity* has shifted several times in the U.S. during the postwar period, a history that holds global lessons.

According to Jodi Melamed, Professor of English and Africana Studies, intellectuals and activists of the 1960s considered diversity to be the natural end product of multiculturalism, the public coexistence of various cultural traditions.[7] A distinct quality of early calls for diversity was their legal and economic character. Moving beyond the mere inclusion of social minorities, these policies sought to provide underrepresented groups with the institutional tools required to redress the inequalities that kept them from living better lives. This practical ethos fueled legislative efforts in the U.S. to inaugurate social programs such as affirmative action, the Voting Rights Act, and the near passage of the Equal Rights Amendment. On American college campuses, faculty members and students worked together to establish academic departments that enabled underrepresented groups to recover, record, and preserve their histories.

By the late 1970s and early 1980s, however, the meaning and spirit of diversity had changed. A more conservative political environment gave birth to an alternative model of inclusion that no longer invested in large-scale social programs for uplifting poor and marginalized communities. Instead, time and money were spent on promoting fewer, but extremely well-placed examples of women and minority successes. The biographies of celebrities such as Will Smith and Michael Jordan, or entrepreneurs such as Oprah Winfrey and Barbara Walters, led many to believe that anyone could achieve success if they worked hard enough. Such sentiments elevated individual achievements over the amelioration of institutional barriers. While many political and corporate institutions added non-discrimination clauses to their mission statements, and even experimented with quotas for hiring women and minority candidates, the prospects for social mobility for working- and middle-class women and minorities declined. By 2010, the likelihood of poor Americans raising their living standard above that of their parents was lower than it was in the 1960s. The radicals of the 1960s learned that diversity (as an endpoint of multiculturalism) was not as simple as making discrimination illegal. In an ironic twist of events, Americans have learned to celebrate individual differences just as improving the lives of underrepresented groups has become more difficult to accomplish.

As the philosopher Charles Taylor noted, personal identity formation is indelibly linked to the visual representation of diversity; without images of "people like us" in the public sphere, it is hard to imagine ourselves contributing to society.[8] In tandem with these positive effects, however, the visual representation of diversity can also mask continuing patterns of inequality. Such a situation is summarized in Walter Benn Michaels' polemical book, *The Trouble with Diversity: How We Learned to Love Identity and Ignore Inequality*.[9] If the link between diversity and economic uplift is broken, *diversity* loses much of its progressive meaning.

In an attempt to reverse the growing irrelevance of diversity in public life, the editors of this book have attempted to revive the socially progressive spirit that marked the late 1960s and early 1970s. Toward this end, we consider diversity to be the end product of a creative process that promotes social and economic inclusion. *Diversity*, as an end point rather than a static list of characteristics, requires that we do more than celebrate our individual identities or recognize an "other" as distinct from the "self." It requires us to be actively engaged in building a more just and inclusive society, whether we are personally affected by discrimination or not. Our definition of diversity also establishes the conceptual basis for treating design as a material form of *social praxis*.[10] We encourage anyone reading this book—students, scholars, and designers—to couple their intellectual recognition of "the other" with the critical tools and strategies required to redress social inequality. This is no easy task. It means that we must understand the specific conditions that influence "the other" in our society and work at extending the forms of agency they already possess.

The essays included in this volume actively build upon academic traditions that examine specific aspects of "the other," while demonstrating how design can be used strategically to extend practical and political concerns. For example, one historical movement implicit in several chapters is critical race theory, which analyzes the ways that laws supported discrimination in the eighteenth, nineteenth, and twentieth centuries. Derrick Bell, Cheryl Harris, and Kimberlé Crenshaw inaugurated this field of study by exposing the legal codes that reproduced majority ownership of minority peoples and their lands, even without the conscious efforts of these groups.[11] Several chapters in this volume expose the ways that competing land-use claims are ultimately issues of group affiliation within physical spaces. The naming of spaces has legal implications that legitimize the cultural and historical claims used to orient future actions. Such a perspective opens the way to see that even the aesthetic decisions of designers are political acts.

In addition to these racial discourses, several essays in this book build upon the writings of feminist scholars, such as Judith Butler, which consider gender and sexuality to be the result of "gender performances" instead of a rigid product of biological characteristics.[12] This perspective provides women and lesbian, gay, bisexual, and transgender (LGBT) individuals with greater agency in everyday and professional life. The postcolonial critiques of Edward Said, Homi Bhabha, and Gayatri Spivak have also paved the way for considering the role of empire building in shaping of so-called "Western" and "non-Western" spaces and cultures.

Of course, it is impossible to be comprehensive in our coverage of diversity issues. This work, however, provides the conceptual tools and strategies for discovering parallel examples.

Defining Design

Like diversity, design is a vast subject, "too complex a matter to be summarized in less than a [full] book."[13] In this text, nevertheless, the term *design* is considered in both professionally focused and culturally expansive ways. Design is, first, considered as a set of professional disciplines in which the members have acquired specific knowledge and skills necessary to design media, products, buildings, cities, environments, systems, and services.

More important, design also is considered a basic component of humanity. Walter Gropius, founder of the Bauhaus, contended "that design is neither an intellectual nor a material affair, but simply an integral part of the stuff of life, necessary for everyone in a civilized society."[14] Likewise, if we accept Michael Shannon's notion that "design is the fundamental creative activity with which we direct our lives, and collectively, the earth's transformation from its original, natural state into our human-made world," then *we all are designers*.[15]

Although humans have been designing at every scale for thousands of years, the term *design* did not emerge until the 1540s, approximately the same time the term *architecture* appeared.[16] Design was not a named profession until after the industrial revolution. Prior to this time, those with titles such as artisan, craftsperson, and engineer did what we think of as design. Formalizing design as a profession, in part, was a result of the German Bauhaus curriculum, which combined architecture, the applied arts (crafts), and the fine arts into a core set of studies. This eminent school removed the barriers between these fields and encouraged architects, craftspeople, and artists to integrate industrialization into their work. It promoted a connection between art and industry, paving the way for the professionalization of design.

The design professions addressed in this book include graphic design, industrial (or product) design, interior design, architecture, urban design, landscape architecture, and systems design. While there are organizations and publications that solidify each profession as its own entity, the many shifts, overlaps, merging of specialties, and appearance of new ones, make design more fluid than the design disciplines suggest. The intent here is not to focus on each discipline but to critique the various design professions by looking at their impacts through case studies. Whether it is the acknowledgment of marginalized populations through the design of memorials or the empowerment of children through ergonomic fit, design is regarded as a political activity that influences people on global, civic, and individual levels, and affects social and power relationships.

So, who develops our products, visuals, and environments?

In the U.S., the average graphic designer is an able-bodied, white female who works in an urban area.[17] The average web designer is a 37-year-old white male who works in an urban area.[18] The average product designer is an able-bodied, white male who works in an urban area.[19] The average interior designer is an able-bodied, 42-year-old white female who works in an urban area.[20] The average architect is an able-bodied, white male over the age of 40 who works in an urban area.[21] The average landscape architect is an able-bodied, white male over the age of 40 who works in an urban area.[22] The average planner is an able-bodied, white male under the age of 50 who works in an urban area.[23]

These statistics are similar in other Western industrialized nations, and the litany sends a potent message. Those who are highly underrepresented in the design professions include seniors, children, non-Caucasians, those with physical or cognitive disabilities, rural inhabitants, and those who are economically disadvantaged. A more diverse pool of design professionals would better address the needs of more people, especially those who currently are not considered in the design process. What difference might this make? Would a 72-year-old man with diminished vision design the typical cell phone used today? Would a low-income teen design sneakers that no one in his neighborhood could afford? Would a woman who had been attacked design a dimly lit dead-end stairwell in a public building?

The concern about the lack of underrepresented groups in the design professions extends similar worries about medicine, law, and other professions. Underrepresented groups are participants in and recipients of design. It is, therefore, important that design practices recruit and include people from all groups, particularly those who are, in some way, marginalized. Simultaneously, more inclusive design processes are needed, fostering work that resonates with a broader population and contains meaning for more people. With this, design becomes a primary catalyst for social justice and cultural change.[24]

While these idealistic notions are encouraging, it is important to remember that the consequences of considering social justice as a fundamental component of design have yet to be fully determined. Very few design practices focus on diversity issues. This is, in part, because design choices often are driven by economic profit. Given the pressures of a business, finding time to explore and understand diversity issues is outside standard practices. Moreover, making design decisions that ensure sensitivity to and enrichment for others involves broadmindedness—a willingness to explore ideas and ways of being other than your own. This mindset transforms design from something mostly about shape and form to something that is more about experience. It follows, then, that this broader view requires intellectual and economic investments. It is important, therefore, to tie these investments to greater profitability and/or improved quality of life.

What is important here is that diverse participation in the design process, from both professionals and public citizens alike, yields diverse and more equitable results. At the very least, understanding the cultural context reduces the likelihood of suffering hidden social, health, or economic costs. (Consider, for instance, the failings of the mosquito net discussed in the foreword to this book.) Inclusive processes help designers to make critically sound and socially conscious choices in complex situations. It fosters actions that: (1) take the viewpoints, needs, and desires of underrepresented populations into consideration, (2) relate various languages, systems, cultures, and diversity groups, and (3) broaden and deepen the equity and accessibility of our digital, visual, and physical environments. Reducing the "distance" between designers and the many populations they serve is perhaps the single most important charge to the design professions today.

Design also might be thought of as a basic life skill, a way for us to examine our relationship to the world and take informed action. As such, all of us need to be able to critically analyze it. *Time Magazine*'s 2006 person of the year supports this concept. The award went to "You." As editor Lev Grossman stated, "It's about the *many* wresting power from the *few* … and how that will not only change the world, but also change the way the world changes."[25]

As such, it is essential for designers to work within a questioning framework that integrates marginalized groups and peripheral points of view. Most important, examining the consequences of an expanded social agenda provokes questions about how to take action in ever-changing conditions—conditions that ultimately move toward diversity in design. Throughout this book, we emphasize that a socially minded study of design moves us from supporters of the status quo to arbiters of change.

Diversity and Design: The Themes and Case Studies in this Volume

A variety of viewpoints come forth in each case study, resulting, collectively, in the presentation of dozens of concepts. Taken together, *Diversity and Design* provides four cross-cutting themes: (1) revealing unintended consequences, (2) pluralizing voices and canons, (3) empowering underserved groups, and (4) promoting identity development.

Revealing Unintended Consequences

Design critic Ralph Caplan wrote, "Imagining consequences is as important as anything else designers learn to do."[26] He used the example of the leaf blower to make his point. Designers were focused on ergonomic fit and blowing force, but forgot about the noise. They failed to imagine that people might blow leaves off their decks at seven o'clock in the morning, waking and annoying neighbors in the process.

While the oversights of leaf-blower designers might irritate people, other unintended consequences of design are more serious. One of the worst design decisions regarding human aid involves food-ration packets and cluster munitions in Afghanistan. Both were the same canary-yellow color and similar in size. Both contained black sans-serif text written in English. The Humanitarian Daily Rations package held a 2,000 calorie meal. The cluster munitions package held a BLU-97 bomb "capable of killing anyone within a 50-meter radius and severely injuring anyone within 100 meters from the detonation."[27] Some Afghanis, both adults and children, who could not read English, confused the two packages; the results were devastating.

There are many reasons why designers fail to consider consequences. They might lack essential knowledge, make errors, hold biases, focus too narrowly, overreact, put immediate interests over long-term interests, disregard conflicting agendas, make assumptions, and/or ignore contexts. Designers cannot anticipate all consequences of their work. Nonetheless, more thoughtful design processes can help to eliminate many undesirable outcomes.

While this theme runs throughout the book, it is most thoroughly discussed in chapter 14, "Packaging Panic: The Design Consequences of the Tylenol Murders." Beth Tauke uses the 1982 Tylenol murders to show how focusing on immediate concerns rather than longer-term issues can result in unintended consequences. This case is used to demonstrate what design teams did not consider in their processes: functionality for underrepresented populations, evolving consumer attitudes, possible injuries, and additional non-biodegradable waste.

Older people feel the fallout when the execution of public housing plans neglect context in chapter 11, Mary Jane Carroll's "(Re)forming Regent Park: When Policy Does Not Equal Practice." Although the redevelopment project was based on a sound set of policies, shifts during design and implementation caused residents to be segregated not only by income but also by age.

Developers neglected to consider the pitfalls of isolating seniors in a high rise far from basic amenities, such as grocery stores and public transportation.

In chapter 13, conflicting agendas of security and access cause difficulties for well-meaning designers of public amenities. Jo-Anne Bichard, in "ExcLOOsion: How Design is Failing Sanitary Provision," discusses research into the challenges people face regarding public toilets. She shows how designers' focus on preventing negative behaviors in restrooms, e.g., drug use or vandalism, takes prominence over physical access and functionality. In this case, the unintended consequence is that people with disabilities either have difficulty or are altogether excluded from using public toilets. The chapter also illustrates how a design-anthropology approach aids designers in developing a deeper understanding of users' encounters with design.

Pluralizing Voices and Canons

Between the mid-1980s and the early 1990s, a series of debates ensued in American colleges that have come to be known as the "canon wars."[28] These debates were about the ultimate purpose of a liberal arts education in contemporary society. For the ranking traditionalists, such as University of Chicago Professor Allan Bloom, the purpose of the liberal arts was to provide American citizens with a basic understanding of the classical works of literature and philosophy that defined Western society since the Greeks.[29] A rising tide of revisionists, however, such as Cornell University Professor Martin Bernal, challenged the European and male bias of the Western canon, which, he and colleagues contended, no longer reflected the diversity of an ever-changing global society.[30]

Over time, as the revisionists persisted, university curricula expanded the voices included in the canon. The foundation of Western society was no longer restricted to the historical contributions of "great white men," but expanded to include women, minorities, and non-Western figures. In addition, the basic toolkit of college students shifted from the rote memorization of principles in classical texts to critical modes of inquiry and interpretation. With these new tools, it became possible for many more people to see themselves contributing to historical change.

Contributing to the pluralizing of the canon inaugurated nearly three decades ago, the contributors of this volume demonstrate several complementary ways of reinterpreting the past. In chapter 6, Despina Stratigakos exposes the gender politics of Germany's architectural profession in the late nineteenth and early twentieth centuries. Using the modern architect Otto Bartning's essay, "Should Women Build?" as a prompt, Stratigakos communicates how controversial the idea of female professionalism was at the time. Her use of photography to contextualize Emilie Winkelmann and Fia Wille's self-presentations as architects, mothers, and advocates visualizes the challenges women faced as professionals, a struggle that remains in the profession of architecture today.

In chapter 4, "Chinese Puzzle: Shifting Spatial and Social Patterns in Shanghai *Shikumen* Architecture," Peter Wong examines the material effects of international trade on building cultures of eighteenth-, nineteenth-, and twentieth-century China. Wong examines the historical buildings that European businessmen first constructed to accommodate their migrations into Shanghai's business district. While the spatial organization of these structures was based on Western architectural models, their similarities to Chinese rural structures enabled them to be easily adopted by local workers. Wong notes the multicultural nature of these social environments, tracing the critical function of the central stairway in enabling Chinese families to adjust to modernization.

In two chapters of this volume, the concept of storytelling is employed as a critical means of reinterpreting the social histories of racial and ethnic minorities. In contrast to scholars who rely on a paper archive to understand the past, these scholars treat the physical landscape as a material archive.[31] Walter Hood and Megan Basnak, in "Diverse Truths: Unveiling the Hidden Layers of the *Shadow Catcher* Commemoration" (chapter 2), outline the role of storytelling in the design of the *Shadow Catcher* memorial on the University of Virginia's campus. Instead of presenting us with a perfect reconstruction of the African American past, Walter Hood develops a landscape for constructing a story of the past that extends into the present. The project marks the physical boundaries of the archaeological remnants on the site without determining how a visitor should feel about the past. In this sense, every visitor is encouraged to catch a glimpse of the shadows that previously marked the site while interpreting the contemporary significance of the university's role in the slave trade of the antebellum South. In chapter 3, Patsy Eubanks Owens, Maggie La Rochelle, and Jennifer L. McHenry develop the concept of "Landscape Stories" as a means to recover the lost histories of ethnic groups in the United States. Their study of Japanese, Punjabi, and Polish farmers who lived in California's Northern Sacramento Valley helps us to visualize the patterns of everyday life that get lost in time. As they note, these lost histories are more than just stories of the past; these histories provide the means for memorializing the contributions of historical groups in the present.

In addition to the more popular subjects of revisionist histories, such as women and racial minorities, this volume examines the problematic ways that persons with disabilities are presented in the public realm. In chapter 12, "Victims and Heroes: Exhibiting Difference in Trafalgar Square," Korydon Smith examines the furor that arose in London's Fourth Plinth Project. In a physical setting usually reserved for the most heroic of national figures, such as generals and statesmen, Marc Quinn's nude statue of a disabled, female protagonist presented a political critique of who constitutes the "common man" in the United Kingdom. The heroic display of this figure in a public space forced people to confront their presuppositions regarding what forms of humanity should be celebrated in public spaces.

Empowering Underserved Groups

In *Lysistrata*, Greek playwright Aristophanes tells the story of a woman who convinces the women of Greece to work together to end the Peloponnesian

War. Lysistrata and her sisters agree to refuse sex with their husbands until all the men agree to cease fighting and sign a peace treaty. This classic play addresses the theme of empowerment in a comedic way. Leyma Gbowee might be considered a modern-day Lysistrata. Gbowee convinced hundreds of Liberian women to act together to end the country's civil war. Her group, The Women of Liberia Mass Action for Peace launched public protests against Liberian dictator Charles G. Taylor and his rebel warlords. Like Lysistrata and her collaborators, The Women of Liberia, too, held a sex strike. They also staged peaceful sit-ins that disrupted daily life. Dressed in all white, the women sat in an open field in suburban Monrovia until Taylor agreed to develop a peace treaty. Later, when negotiations for the treaty started breaking down, they locked arms in a human chain and prevented anyone from leaving the room until an agreement was reached. Gbowee's group was a primary force in driving out Taylor and bringing peace to Liberia.

Empowerment is "a multi-dimensional social process that helps people gain control over their lives."[32] It relies on the belief that power can change and expand. Empowerment and its counterpart, disempowerment, are relational concepts linked to power structures. In "Repositioning Power: An Alternate Approach to Podium Design" (chapter 10), Kathryn H. Anthony examines the typical podium and reveals the disempowering characteristics inherent in its design. In this case study, because of poor fit between human bodies and the podium, some speakers, especially those of short stature, are disadvantaged. She remedies this problem with a team approach to design an inclusive, empowering podium.

Mark Addison Smith, in chapter 8, confronts the theme of empowerment by exploring the hegemonic dynamics in restroom graffiti. In "Overwriting Hate: The Queer Writing on the Bathroom Wall," one person's homophobic text on the bathroom wall of a truck stop is transformed by another artist into a coded language for queer empowerment and identity reclamation.

In chapter 5, "Architects at War: Designing Prison Cities for Japanese American Communities," Lynne Horiuchi reveals the sudden disempowerment of Japanese Americans. In 1942, between 110,000 and 120,000 people of Japanese heritage who lived in the U.S. were confined. In some cases, architects working for the U.S. Farm Security Administration designed prison camps for Japanese American architects who worked with them. This troubling power shift between colleagues personalized a larger cultural change taking place across the nation as a result of wartime attitudes.

Empowerment requires attitudinal change in individuals and groups in order to stimulate action. Visual messages are one of the most effective ways to bring about change, and they are an essential component of advocacy campaigns. In chapter 7, Maya Indira Ganesh and Gabi Sobliye present visual persuasion techniques that capture the attention of viewers, call their opinions in question, and, ultimately, inspire action. In "Communicating Gender: The Challenges of Visualizing Information for Advocacy," they offer several case studies on gender and sexual identity, and demonstrate a proactive approach that is both data-driven and visual. They do not claim to empower people per se, but provide strategies and opportunities for people to take action.

Promoting Identity Development

A fundamental role of college education is to foster character and identity development, to bolster self-awareness and self-confidence. This also is one of the central, but often-overlooked, roles of design. Coupled with a vision toward heightened aesthetic pleasure and innovation, the mission of many design professions is to ensure health, safety, and welfare. But seldom do designers ask: How does this product, building, city, system, or graphic I am designing nurture or impede identity development? Personal identity and its constituent parts—gender, race, language, personality, etc.—is more commonly ascribed to education and upbringing than to design. Design, nevertheless, plays an important mediating role in the way one sees herself/himself and others.

This theme re-emerges throughout the book, and appears within many of the chapters already mentioned. The theme of identity development first appears in the opening chapter, "No Longer Just a Dream: Commemorating the African American Experience on the National Mall." Here, Charles Davis compares two distinct design approaches—*mimesis*, lifelike or figural representation of a person or event, and *abstraction*, non-pictorial, geometric, and material expressions—for two historical markers in Washington, D.C., USA: a sculpture of Dr. Martin Luther King, Jr., and the Smithsonian's National Museum of African American History and Culture. The projects communicate racial identity in highly divergent ways, illustrating, on the one hand, that the histories of a given group are varied and, on the other, that the means of communicating those histories is not singular.

Just as there is more than one way to discuss and express racial history, there are many possibilities for designing and constructing housing to the meet the needs and preferences of society. Housing is, perhaps, the most significant contributor to identity in the built environment, as homes provide (or deny) a means of self-expression via the colors, materials, and objects we choose. Housing serves as a place to explore (or represses) the most intimate of personal feelings, values, beliefs, and aspirations. In chapter 9, "Designing LGBT Senior Housing: Triangle Square, Carefree Boulevard, and BOOM," Carl Matthews, Jennifer Webb, and Caroline Hill explore the challenges and biases that LGBT older adults face in both healthcare and housing.

Likewise, through Craig Vogel, Linda Dunseath, and Lori E. Crosby's "iTransition: Promoting Healthcare Independence for Teens with Chronic Illness" (chapter 15), we learn that new technologies and systems can provide support and freedom at key moments in life. This case illustrates how teenagers, who are particularly vulnerable to social stigmas and isolation, can better manage chronic disease as they enter the autonomy of adulthood with the assistance of well-designed systems.

From Awareness to Action

As citizens and designers, who do we think about, or include, and who do we not think about, or exclude?

Design affects all members of society. The decisions that designers make about media, products, buildings, transportation systems, and urban/regional planning have profound, though often hidden, consequences on both individuals and collectives. Design innovations can foster freedom, but they also can have caustic effects: discrimination, disease, and segregation.

Designers have been slow to respond to demographic shifts, designing for only a narrow segment of the population. Moreover, most recipients of design—from passive citizens to active consumers—are only tacitly aware of how the design of media, products, buildings, and environments impacts their own and others' physical and psychosocial well-being.

Learning about diversity has become a core mission of public education at all levels. It is now a fundamental piece of design education. It follows, then, that the coupled study of diversity and design is essential to anyone involved in the making and inhabiting of the built world—as advocates, consumers, and citizens.

This book equips students of all disciplines and the next generation of designers, patrons, and activists with a foundational knowledge of diversity and design issues across categories. As you read each case study, we encourage you to think across social groups and design disciplines, not merely about the group or profession explicitly discussed in the case. How do discussions of gender and sexuality relate to discussions of race and ethnicity? How do themes in product design compare to opportunities and challenges in landscape architecture?

One of these broad themes is that diversity and design are not about *eliminating* biases. Design processes always have consequences; designed things always have consequences. "To design is to transform" … the natural environment, the built world, society.[33] The challenge is to *recognize* and *manage* the biases—personal preferences, biography, education, etc.—that influence the way you think and act as a citizen or designer.

Finally, we put forth one last challenge. Whether you are a first-year interior design student, an upper-level student in disability studies, an early-career filmmaker, a second-term humanities student, or an experienced designer or scholar: seek to become a "citizen-designer." Use the questions the authors raise throughout this book to broaden your awareness. Use the cases to reflect on your own values and actively transform your thinking. Then consider how you might apply your skills and knowledge to build capacity in a group for which there are few advocates. Utilize what you learn, through this book and through these experiences, to improve health and well-being across groups. Learn from the triumphs and mistakes of history; learn from triumphs and mistakes you make as a student, designer, or advocate; and expand the vision of what design and society can achieve.

Notes

1   Steven Mintz, *Huck's Raft: A History of American Childhood* (Cambridge, MA: Harvard University Press, 2004), vii.

2   Joshua Brewer, "You Are Not Your User," *52 Weeks of UX*, February 12, 2010, accessed November 30, 2014, http://52weeksofux.com/post/385981879/you-are-not-your-user.

3   Martin Heidegger, *On the Way to Language,* trans. Peter D. Hertz (New York: Harper & Row, 1971), 17–22.

4   Denis Diderot, "Letter on the Blind for the Use of Those Who See," (1749), *Diderot's Early Philosophical Works,* trans. Margaret Jourdain (Chicago: Open Court Publishing, 1916), 72.

5   See: Jean La Marche, "Self and Surface: The Mirror of Architecture," *The Person-Environment Theory Series* (Berkeley, CA: Center for Environmental Design Research, University of California, 1993), 4; and Paul Ricoeur, *Oneself as Another,* trans. Kathleen Blamey (Chicago: University of Chicago Press, 1992).

6   For a discussion on the history and limitations of IQ tests, see: James R. Flynn, "Cultural Distance and the Limitations of IQ," in *Cultural Diversity and the Schools, Vol. 1: Education for Cultural Diversity: Convergence and Divergence*, ed. James Lynch, Celia Modgill, and Sohan Modgill (London: Routledge, 1992), 343–360.

7   Jodi Melamed, *Represent and Destroy: Rationalizing Violence in the New Racial Capitalism* (Minneapolis: University of Minnesota Press, 2011).

8   Charles Taylor, "The Politics of Recognition," in *Multiculturalism: Examining the Politics of Recognition*, ed. Amy Gutman (Princeton, NJ: Princeton University Press, 1994), 25–74.

9   Walter Benn Michaels, *The Trouble with Diversity: How We Learned to Love Identity and Ignore Inequality* (New York, NY: Henry Holt, 2006).

10 Philosophers and social scientists have used the term *praxis* to refer to practices and techniques that embody the social and cultural ideals of a people. Dalibor Vesely and Alberto Perez Gomez use the term *technē* to refer to a similar concept used in classical Greek society.

11 Kimberlé Crenshaw has edited a critical reader on this movement entitled *Critical Race Theory: The Key Writings that Formed the Movement* (New York, NY: New Press, 1996). Other texts include Derrick Bell's *Faces at the Bottom of the Well: The Permanence of Racism* (New York, NY: Basic Books, 1993), and Cheryl Harris' essay "Whiteness as Property," *Harvard Law Review* 106, no. 8 (June 1993): 1707–1791.

12 Judith Butler's theory of gender performativity can be found in the book *Gender Trouble: Feminism and the Subversion of Identity* (New York, NY: Routledge, 1990).

13 Bryan Lawson, *How Designers Think: The Design Process Demystified*, 4th ed. (Amsterdam: Elsevier, 2005), 33.

14 Walter Gropius, *Scope of Total Architecture* (New York: Collier Books, 1962), 20.

15 Michael J. Shannon, "Educating the Designer," *Design Issues* 7, no. 1 (1990): 29–41.

16 The etymology of design is as follows: **design** (v.), 1540s, from Latin *designare* "mark out, devise, choose, designate, appoint," from *de-* "out" (see *de-*) + *signare* "to mark," from *signum* "a mark, sign" (see *sign* (n.)). Originally in English with the meaning now attached to *designate*, many modern uses of *design* are metaphoric extensions. Also: **design** (n.), 1580s, from Middle French *desseign* "purpose, project, design," from Italian *disegno*, from *disegnare* "to mark out," from Latin *designare* "to mark out" (see *design* (v.)). *Online Etymology Dictionary*, accessed November 2, 2014. www.etymonline.com/index.php?term=design&allowed_in_frame=0. **Disegno**, from the Italian word for drawing or design, carries a more complex meaning in art, involving both the ability to make the drawing and the intellectual capacity to invent the design. From the Renaissance this ability to invent, or create, put the artist on a footing with God, the ultimate Creator, and was a means of raising the status of

painting from craft to art. "Glossary," The National Gallery, accessed November 2, 2014, www.nationalgallery.org.uk/paintings/glossary/disegno.

17   Richard Grefe, "What the U.S. Census Says about the Design Workforce," *AIGA Insight*, November 3, 2011, accessed July 21, 2015, www.aiga.org/what-the-us-census-says-about-the-design-workforce/.

18   "Findings from the A LIST APART Survey, 2011," *A List Apart Magazine*, 2012, http://archive.aneventapart.com/alasurvey2011/00.html2011; based on an average of 15,000 respondents for each question.

19   Kate Rockwood, "Forget 'Shrink It and Pink It': The Femme Den Unleashed," *Fast Company Magazine*, October 2009, accessed July 21, 2015, www.fastcompany.com/1353548/forget-shrink-it-and-pink-it-femme-den-unleashed.

20   "Employed Persons by Detailed Occupation and Age, 2012 Annual Averages," Spreadsheet, Distributed by the American Society of Interior Designers, 2012.

21   "Table 5d. Employed Architects by Worksite: 2006–2010," Spreadsheet, Distributed by National Endowment for the Arts, http://arts.gov/artistic-fields/research-analysis/data-profiles/data-profile-1/dp1-nea-tables-eeo-2006-2010-data.

22   "2010 ASLA Membership Survey Results: Executive Summary," American Society of Landscape Architects, 2011, http://asla.org/uploadedFiles/CMS/About__Us/Leadership/Leadership_Handbook/Meeting_Agenda_Books/2011_EXC_Calls/ExCom%20Con%20Call%20Agenda%2001-11-11.pdf.

23   "American Planning Association 2012 Salary Survey," American Planning Association, 2012.

24   Beth Tauke and Alex Bitterman, "F001: Feature: Diversity in Design: The Journal of Inclusive Design Education," *Diversity in Design* 1, no. 1 (2004), accessed November 13, 2014, http://ap.buffalo.edu/idea/diversityindesign/currentfea.htm.

25   Emphasis added.

26   Ralph Caplan, "Consequences," in *Cracking the Whip: Essays on Design and Its Side Effects* (New York, NY: Fairchild Publications, 2006), 73–77.

27   Richard Stupart, "Seven Worst International Aid Ideas," *Matador Network*, February 17, 2012, accessed November 2, 2014, http://matadornetwork.com/change/7-worst-international-aid-ideas/.

28   For a summary of the canon wars see Rachael Donadio's essay "Revisiting the Canon Wars" in the *New York Times*, September 16, 2007.

29   For an example of the traditional defense of the Western canon, see Allan Bloom's *The Closing of the American Mind* (New York, NY: Simon and Schuster, 1987).

30   For an example of a critique of the Western canon, see Martin Bernal's *Black Athena: The Afroasiatic Roots of Classical Civilization* (New Brunswick, NJ: Rutgers University Press, 1987). This text was key in spiriting a broader recognition of the African and Asian roots of classical Greek civilization.

31   A pioneering example of this type of scholarship can be found in Kendrick Ian Grandison's essay "From Plantation to Campus: Progress, Community, and the Lay of the Land in Shaping the Early Tuskegee," *Landscape Journal* 15, no. 1 (1996): 6–32.

32   Nanette Page and Cheryl E. Czuba, "Empowerment: What Is It?" *Journal of Extension* 37, no. 5 (1999), accessed July 21, 2015, www.joe.org/joe/1999october/comm1.php.

33   This is an excerpt from graphic designer Paul Rand's book *Design Form and Chaos* (New Haven, CT: Yale University Press, 1993) and the statement, "To design is to transform prose into poetry."

Part 1 | Race and Ethnicity

Editors' Introduction to Chapter 1

If design is a material form of social praxis, then what role might cultural history play in its creation? When do material form and cultural history intersect with one another during the design process, and what is affected when technique and meaning converge? This case study explores these questions by examining the racial politics of representing the African American experience in two commemorative sites on the National Mall: the Martin Luther King Jr. Memorial and the Smithsonian National Museum of African American History and Culture. As a public space that aspires to represent the cultural ideals of a nation, the Mall resonates with both individual and collective notions of citizenship. In turn, the memorials constructed for this space influence the notion of what it means to be "American." The challenge for a designer in this context is to select the appropriate means of communicating such ephemeral ideals to a public audience.

In this chapter, Charles Davis argues, "The techniques artists employ to design commemorative spaces on the Mall are not free of meaning, but are conditioned by the cultural traditions they inherit. These cultural histories delimit the ways one can use form to interpret contemporary meaning, which, in turn, demands that an artist consciously manages the cultural implications of employing specific techniques." In line with this thesis, he compares the cultural meanings associated with the architectural tradition of *mimesis* (the pursuit of beauty through the imitation of nature) employed in the MLK Memorial, with the subsequent tradition of *abstraction* (the technique of composing physical objects with simple geometries and a minimal material palette) employed in the Smithsonian Museum. While each principle suggests a clear method for creating art, their cultural associations intersect with African American history in distinct ways, accessing different sets of values, perspectives, and experiences.

In the classical tradition of mimesis, the concept of beauty was constituted by the visual means an artist used to represent the inner character of their subjects. In time, the anthropological study of human character introduced scientific racisms that visually codified racial aptitude in art. In light of this history, the decision to construct a 30-foot statue of Martin Luther King Jr. directly engages with the historical representation of black character in Western art. By contrast, the modern architectural tradition of abstraction emerged from a desire to invent an international language of art that was based on pure geometry. In their efforts to situate architectural forms into specific cultural contexts, many architects synthesized the monolithic character of their works with regional art forms by making formal references to indigenous techniques. The design for the Smithsonian Museum extends this artistic tradition by making references to North African religious cult forms and African American folk-art practices in the composition of its roof structure. Such a form expresses the multiple sources of African culture that coexist in the United States.

As you read this chapter, challenge yourself to speculate on the hidden implications of each designer's approach. What is really at stake when one decides which style, structure, or materials to use in a memorial project? And, if technique and meaning are as integrated as the author suggests, then what role can architectural history play in the design process?

Chapter 1

No Longer Just a Dream

Commemorating the African American Experience on the National Mall

Charles Davis

Introduction

In a metaphorical sense, the National Mall operates as a stage where Americans can perform their roles as citizens of the United States. They become literal actors in the public sphere when gathering on the Mall for peaceful assembly, whether it is to contemplate the nation's history via the museums and artifacts collected there, or to protest the limits of American freedom through political rallies and other gatherings. In addition, the buildings, memorials, and monuments situated on the Mall behave as rhetorical actors that provide material reminders of our shared cultural history. The concrete elements of the Mall and its visitors are constantly engaged in an imaginary conversation over the appropriate interpretation of national values. As monuments concretize the values that citizens of the past believed should be upheld, present citizens reflect upon and reform these social values through new acts of protest, civic engagement, and monumentalism. This historical exchange has resulted in the design and construction of two commemorative sites in the new millennium that preserve the African American experience for future visitors. This case study outlines the role of racial politics in the creation of sculpture, architecture, and public space on the National Mall. I argue that the techniques artists employ to design commemorative spaces are not free of cultural meaning, but are inherently conditioned by the cultural traditions inherited from the past. These cultural histories limit the ways a designer can use form to interpret contemporary meaning, which, in turn, demand that an artist consciously manages the cultural implications of employing specific techniques.

The 1963 March on Washington for Jobs and Freedom is a premier example of the types of political rallies that have been staged on the National Mall. The postwar activities of leaders such as Martin Luther King Jr., A. Philip Randolph, and Bayard Rustin clearly articulated the moral failures that racial discrimination represented for American democracy. However, in the 1950s, most of these protests took place within the American South where racial tensions were historically most intransigent. Once the strategy of peaceful protest gained momentum in the South, it was implemented at a broader scale. By the time it reached the Mall, its message had reached thousands of people; not only was it heard by the thousands of volunteers directly participating in these protests, but also it was seen and heard by tens of thousands viewing these events from their television screens, newspaper photographs, or those listening to radio programs announcing these problems to the world. During this march, the Mall operated once again as a stage for enacting a national conversation, this time about the inalienable rights of black Americans. In addition to speaking to the world, black volunteers made a plea to the nation to preserve the most enduring values of democracy. They stood in proximity to the statue of Abraham Lincoln situated in the Lincoln Memorial, and metaphorically spoke to George Washington in the form of the Washington Monument captured in many of the period's photographs. In light of this, we cannot under-estimate the power that black volunteers held at this moment. The high visibility of black bodies on the Mall exposed the conspicuous absence of visual repre-sentations of minorities in this symbolic space. Before 1960, representations of African Americans on the National Mall were visible but modest. As an example, *Harper's Magazine* produced illustrations in the nineteenth century that depicted the black slaves leased by Southern plantation holders to construct the U.S. Capitol Building, and ornamental reliefs existed in small monuments depicting the agricultural products of Africa, or statues referencing freed slaves by the 1880s and 1890s.[1]

Within this artistic context, a concrete structure entirely dedicated to the African American experience is a major statement of inclusion within the National Mall. The first commemorative project of this nature was the Martin Luther King Jr. (MLK) Memorial, which began as a design competition in 2005 and opened to great fanfare in 2009. A second commemorative project, the Smithsonian's National Museum of African American History and Culture (SNMAAHC) also began as a design competition in 2009.

While almost everyone agrees on the value of preserving the African American experience for future generations, the form and content of this effort has provoked serious debate. The question of which artistic forms and materials are most appropriate for commemorating this past has proven a difficult question for the sculptors, architects, and urban planners involved. At least two distinctive artistic traditions have influenced the designs of the above-mentioned projects. The first is the Beaux-Arts traditions that dominated late nineteenth- and early twentieth-century federal construction during the period now called the "American Renaissance."[2] This approach was marked by a return to and revision of neo-classical European aesthetic traditions on American soil. The second artistic tradition was the rise of abstract modernism that emerged in the postwar period as legislators adopted a new official building style for federal construction. As architectural tastes changed, the symbolic purpose of the Mall also shifted; initially a space of respite and leisure, the Mall quickly became a symbolic core for the nation after the turn of the twentieth century. A brief examination of this history will provide some background into the forces that generally condition a designer's choices when creating commemorative spaces for the Mall.

The Literal and Representational Functions of the National Mall

The National Mall currently is formed by an uninterrupted central axis that stretches across the heart of Washington, D.C. As an urban spatial form, the Mall is essentially a vast public lawn that stretches from the foot of the Capitol Building to the steps of the Lincoln Memorial. The Frenchman Pierre Charles L'Enfant was commissioned to design a public space for the Capitol in 1792, and his initial designs emulated French and British landscape conventions by providing a rambling pastoral escape from the bustling metropolis beyond. As a romantic landscape, the Mall was constantly in danger of being broken up to accommodate municipal functions that seemed more pressing for an ever-expanding capital. This pressure for change only increased as the aesthetic appreciation for pleasure gardens waned in the late nineteenth century. As early as 1816, the architect Benjamin Latrobe wanted to place a national university immediately across from the Washington Monument, which would have materialized one aspect of L'Enfant's initial plan for the capital.[3] In 1841, Robert Mills proposed to subdivide the Mall with major vehicular thoroughfares to provide access to and from satellite branches of the Smithsonian Museum. None of these changes ever took shape. Instead, a permanent public lawn was secured with the adoption of the 1901 McMillan Commission Plan. This plan employed a modern conception of urban space that geometrically balanced building masses and spatial voids in

▼ Figure 1.1

McMillan Commission Plan of the National Mall in Washington, D.C. (c.1901).

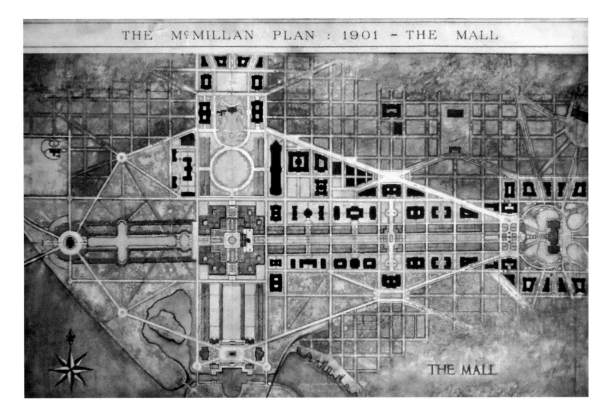

order to structure the viewer's experience of the capital. In contrast to the restricted spaces that characterized less democratic regimes, the Mall allowed everyday people access to the most centralized and unifying space of the Capitol. In this sense, the people of the republic served as one of the decorative elements of the plan. By the end of the twentieth century, the physical integrity of the Mall remained intact even as new construction projects began.

The spatial organization of the McMillan Plan ties together buildings and spaces designed in many different styles, including the above-mentioned neo-classical and modernist styles. Traces of each artistic tradition can be found in the design of the MLK Memorial and the Smithsonian Museum of African American History and Culture, although one approach tends to dominate in each case. The project team for the MLK Memorial employs a monumental approach to space that incorporates a 30-foot statue of the slain civil rights leader. Within the context of the Mall, this heroic depiction of a black, male subject diversifies the racial and ethnic characters used to illustrate American life. The naturalism of Martin Luther King Jr.'s facial expression also becomes an explicit factor of the design. The *mimetic*, or imitative strategy used to capture his inner character, dates back to Beaux-Arts sculptural practices popularized in the nineteenth century. Artists trained in French academies learned to imitate the lines of natural forms, and, in the case of heroic subjects, they strived to emulate Greek and Roman ideals of beauty. Americans trained in these academies brought this style of sculpture back home to depict heroic national subjects. The mannered poses American sculptors applied to their artworks exaggerated the noble qualities of their subjects by emulating the virtuous characteristics of classical precedents while maintaining a realistic likeness of contemporary figures. This realism reflected the belief that human nature was an extension of organic nature, and universal laws of order served as the basis for artistic beauty.

In 1840, the American artist Horatio Greenough created a statue of George Washington that was patterned after the Greek god Zeus. While Washington's physical stature and pose mimics the perpetual youth of its divine precedent, his head exposes the baldness of old age that exemplifies the wisdom required of a great leader. Another example of the Beaux-Arts style of representation is Daniel Chester French's pensive statue of Abraham Lincoln, which is now the most famous aspect of the Lincoln Memorial. French's depiction of Lincoln, loosely based from a life-cast of the president taken shortly after his death, emulates the repose of Greek and Roman statuary at a grand scale. Its solemnity reflects the sorrow and shame the country suffered after Lincoln's assassination, and its scale reflects the grand ideals for which he gave his life in order to preserve a political union between abolitionist and slave-holding states. The importation of the Beaux-Arts style marked the growing maturity of American public taste, although some period architects objected to an over-reliance on European traditions in order to invent an American style.[4] The design of heroic statues today can be interpreted as a revival of these historical practices, and the selection of minority subjects in these cases are an explicit attempt to situate nonwhite peoples within the Beaux-Arts artistic tradition. The statue of King elevates the physiognomic depiction of black subjects by reflecting mimetic

▲ Figure 1.2

Enthroned Washington in marble, by Horatio Greenough (1840).

▶ Figure 1.3

African Venus in bronze, by Frenchman Charles Cordier (1851).

ideals of beauty into the contemporary landscape. The heroic display of black figures was not always considered an appropriate subject for representing national history. Historical statuary in France was a category reserved for depicting national leaders and celebrated men, and most of these were of European descent. Charles Cordier was one of a few French sculptors to include heroic black figures in his artistic oeuvre, and this was in part predicated by a desire to visually represent the ethnographic variety contained within the French Empire. Cordier studied real-life models, including Seïd Enkess, a freed slave living in France after the abolition of slavery in 1848.

The modernist tradition that emerged in 1920s Europe offers a different influence for African American commemorative sites on the National Mall. This approach to form evolved in the interwar and postwar periods before being adopted as the official style for federal construction projects in the 1950s and 1960s. The transformation of public taste in this period introduced new artistic standards to the American public, including the reduction of mimetic statuary in favor of sculptural depictions of abstract geometrical forms that only

◀ Figure 1.4

Daniel Chester French in his
sculpture studio (c.1920).

ambiguously referenced literal objects found in nature. Modern artists experimented with the representational limits of abstraction, which not only reformed
the limits of mimetic representation, but also reflected some of the social reor-
ganizations caused by European modernization. For example, art historians
have documented the influence of abstract African art on major European
painters who observed foreign objects obtained from colonial territories.[5] In
addition to Pablo Picasso's and George Braque's cubist technique for abstracting
the lines found within African masks, the French-Swiss architect Le Corbusier
transposed the spare adobe walls and trabeated structural frames of Turkish and
Moorish vernacular housing into the house-machines that catapulted him to
fame.[6] These spare, geometrical dwellings include the famous Villa Savoye of
1929. Le Corbusier substituted the wooden structures of older forms with
modern materials, but kept what he considered the *primitive* simplicity and
functionality of these vernacular precedents. While modern artists looked to
traditional forms for inspiration, their abstract techniques allowed them to simultaneously index multiple historical traditions; African, European and American
folk-art forms were coherently combined into new works of modern art. In such
cases, abstraction was a fundamental means of creating art that appealed to an
international audience since they did not borrow directly from one historical
tradition or time period. Though this position has been criticized for its contributions to exploiting the historical traditions and labor of colonial subjects, it
continues to exert a strong influence over contemporary designers who wish to
translate the material cultures of global communities into an idiom accepted in
the Euro-American world.

The Mimetic Principles of Statuary at the MLK Memorial

Bonnie Fisher and Boris Dramov were the lead designers for the winning competition entry for the Martin Luther King Jr. Memorial. Fisher and Dramov served as the head principles for the ROMA Design Group, an architecture and landscape architecture firm located in San Francisco, California. Their final design situated a 30-foot statue of Martin Luther King Jr. within an open plaza bound by a bisected crescent earth berm made of black marble and concrete. Inside of this crescent is a series of quotations taken from the speeches King delivered during his career as a civil rights activist. In order to relate the human rights ideals of this movement with the larger aspirations of American democracy, the ROMA design team placed the King statue on an imaginary axis between Abraham Lincoln and Thomas Jefferson, two representative presidents in the nation's struggle with black civil rights. By tracing this line, one can interpret Lincoln's sacrifice as paving the way for King's, because both figures gave their lives. Following this imaginary axis to its end point, both Lincoln and King face Jefferson and challenge those like him who did not more energetically respond to the plight of poor, black citizens. This is apt, as Jefferson opposed slavery but could not bring himself to advocate integration, nor was he able to free most of his own slaves as promised in his will after his death.[7] This rhetorical drama preserves the historical fight for civil rights in the United States, from the legal abolition of slavery to the protest movements of the 1960s.

▼ Figure 1.5

Competition model completed by ROMA group (c.2005–06).

The topography leading up to the King Memorial rises into two mounds of earth that become symmetrical masses of craggy rock, 30-feet in height. Fisher and Dramov identified these paired rock masses as the "Mountain of Despair" after a line found in King's famous "I Have a Dream" speech. They consulted with the historian Clayborne Carson to identify the specific line that became a central aspect of the final design. As one walks through the compressed opening, another rock mass can be seen sitting within the pedestrian courtyard in the crescent. On the face of this "Rock of Hope" that was dislodged from the previous "Mountain of Despair" is carved the figure of Dr. King, who is looking intently across the water's edge toward the Jefferson Memorial. This aspect of the design established a sound basis for a living monument to the Civil Rights Movement. The ROMA Group not only looked to memorialize King's sacrifice by creating a physical dialogue between his statue and those of historical leaders, but also they created a series of aediculae mounted atop the crescent berm surrounding his statue to commemorate the many volunteers that made the Civil Rights Movement a success. In this sense, the winning proposal was a hybridization of a monument to a movement and a memorial to its most prominent leader. Several of the smaller spaces atop the berm were to be fitted with plaques dedicated to a few well-known individuals such as Rosa Parks, Bayard Rustin, and others, while leaving a few empty spaces for future contributors to the movement. These empty spaces formally suggest that the Civil Rights Movement is not one to be consigned to history, but one that will continue to evolve in the future.

King's demand for the legal recognition of minority civil rights was symbolically represented by the presence of a promissory note held in his hands, which was initially going to be accompanied by a quote from King's 1963 speech inscribed onto the side of his statue:

> When the architects of our republic
> wrote the magnificent words of the
> Constitution and the
> Declaration of Independence,
> they were signing a promissory note
> to which every American was a full heir.
> This note was the promise that all men,
> yes, black men as well as white men,
> would be guaranteed the "inalienable Rights
> of Life, Liberty, and the pursuit of Happiness."

28 August 1963
Washington, D.C.

This promissory note was never installed, however, because Congressional committees believed it established a confrontational stance between King (a private citizen) and Jefferson (a U.S. President). As a result, changes were implemented to minimize any distractions from King's message of peace and non-violent confrontation. These included debating the expression on King's face when complaints were levied against the sculptor, Chinese artist Lei Yixin, for creating a portrait of King that was too confrontational.[8] In an effort to capture King's likeness and character, Yixin studied hundreds of photographs to determine the physiognomy of the final statue. After further Congressional meetings, it was decided that the expression captured by a 1963 photograph of King standing in front of Mahatma Gandhi conveyed the appropriate message.

What effects might softening the statue's gaze have on its overall message? In one respect, this new facial expression suggests that peaceful protest is the primary message of King's legacy. In a more practical sense, it means that this strategy is the only form of resistance one can take against direct physical oppression.[9] The biblical proverb of "turning the other cheek" is transformed into a single-option strategy for redressing inequality. In addition, the crucial balance that King attained between peaceful protest, stubborn resolve, and resistance to adversity is potentially elided with the Congressional committee's preference for a peaceful looking statue. The final memorial also eliminated the upper-story aediculae dedicated to other contributors to the Civil Rights Movement, which strongly suggests the defense of minority rights was closed with King's sacrifice. These design changes potentially limit our understanding of the Civil Rights Movement and King's outsized role in this populist narrative. Instead of recognizing the thousands of anonymous volunteers who helped promote unpopular change in a reticent democratic republic, we are left with the impression that powerful individuals are necessary to affect change. The final quotes etched into the side of the King statue do nothing to inspire participatory action from the contemporary viewer either; they simply preserve an official historical narrative of one man's heroic efforts: "Out of the Mountain of Despair, a Stone of Hope."

A historical explanation of King's evolving positions on non-violent protest and the collective nature of the Civil Rights Movement has been exiled to a small pavilion adjacent to the site where history books and other memorabilia are sold. It is in the pages of these academic books, and not on the book of stone preserved for public consumption, where one can investigate the institutional challenges African Americans faced to expose the limits of democracy. As W.J.T. Mitchell described in his essay "Violence in Public Art," the role of official monuments is generally to preserve a sanitized version of historical events that reinforces the power and benevolence of the State.[10] Monuments and memorials that challenge this official function are generally considered too contentious, as the example of Maya Lin's modernist solution for the Vietnam Memorial attests.[11]

Abstraction in the Smithsonian National Museum of African American History and Culture

An international design competition jury selected the final design for the Smithsonian National Museum of African American History and Culture. The six finalists were all internationally recognized architectural firms, with most headquartered in North America and the United Kingdom.[12] The winning entry was created by a team headed by Tanzanian-born British architect David Adjaye,

with The Freelon Group, Davis Brody Bond and SmithGroup serving as the architects of record. The composition of this team, with a lead designer of African descent and an African American architect of record, is unique for projects constructed on the National Mall. Adjaye is a strong proponent of a neo-modernist architectural aesthetic that combines the rationalism and functionalism of modern architecture with select infusions of global cultural traditions, including Yoruban courtly artifacts. Like Le Corbusier of the early twentieth century, Adjaye looks to the formal characteristics of vernacular art as inspiration for the abstract monumental forms of his public architecture.[13] This process is not intended to make his architectural forms "African" in any direct way, but their quotation of folk-art forms allows his designs to simultaneously resonate with African, African American, and European cultural traditions.[14]

This type of formal synthesis is manifest in the design of the corona, or triple-stacked crown Adjaye uses to cap the Smithsonian Museum on the Mall. This perforated copper form wraps around the glass perimeter of the upper stories, emulating the crowns used by African kings to denote their status. Crowning the building not only recalls the remote past of African royalty, but also celebrates the cultural achievements of the African diaspora in the United States, a gesture that has been postponed since African American leaders first lobbied for a museum in Congress in 1900.[15] The final material for this

CHAPTER 1 Charles Davis

architectural feature was selected because of the facility with which African tribes learned to master copper from an early date. In addition, the filigreed ornamental patterns that perforate the copper facing to permit views of the Mall beyond is a visual reference to the ornamental ironwork that decorated the porches and verandas of African American homes in Charleston and New Orleans.[16] In order to create a dialogue between the corona of the museum and the space of the Mall, the design team decided to match the seventeen-degree pitch of the Washington Monument in the angle of the canted walls surrounding the upper stories. The Washington Monument is an obelisk. Designed in 1833 and finished in 1884, this "Washington Pyramid" harkens back to the period of Egyptian revivalism in the United States.[17] During the nineteenth century, Egyptian art was a popular neo-classical style because it was considered to be the foundation of Greek and Etruscan culture. This historical image was fitting for representing George Washington's position in American history as one of the founding fathers of the United States.

The visual dialogue maintained between the Smithsonian Museum and the Washington Monument is dramatized in an early perspective drawing created by the design team. This view, taken from a second-story terrace above the main entryway of the museum, juxtaposes the skyward point of the Washington Monument with the earthbound corona of the Smithsonian. Adjaye considers this elevated space to be another parallel to the front porches found on historical African and African American house forms. Archaeological research has recovered the historical migration routes of freed slaves that led the porch archetypes of the shotgun house typology from Haiti to New Orleans in the 1830s and 1840s.[18] By the 1880s, this housing type had become the basis for developer housing throughout the Southeast, with many European and African Americans embellishing such designs with new artistic flourishes. Thus, with the use of abstraction, Adjaye and his team combine the historical fragments of indigenous African, Haitian, and African American folk-art forms into a single object. The collection of this museum will be composed of objects taken from all periods of African diasporic history, including African and Caribbean folk-art, the material culture of slaves in the Americas, and the official records of leaders and participants in the Civil Rights Movement. The curators of this collection have taken contributions from prominent African Americans such as Oprah Winfrey and Harvard Professor Henry Louis Gates Jr., as well as solicited more anonymous artifacts from the basements and attics of everyday citizens. In the end, this space will serve as a living museum to African American history, which will enable people in the present to reflect upon the past, now and in the future.

It is important to note that not everyone celebrates Adjaye's aesthetic solution for the Smithsonian Museum. Jack Travis, an African American architect with a professional practice in New York City, consulted on the creation of an alternative scheme for the 2006 Smithsonian Museum competition with Antoine Predock and Associates. He has publicly critiqued the Adjaye team's competition design, not so much for its use of abstractions (which is also important to Travis' work), but because the façade's perforated copper corona fails to visualize the racial traumas and struggles minorities have faced in the United States.[19] For Travis and many others heavily influenced by the message of race

▲ Figure 1.7

View from southern terrace
toward the Washington
Monument.

consciousness popularized by the black social movements of the postwar period, any museum on African American history is a unique opportunity to publicly acknowledge the complex and tortured legacy of racism and slavery that is unique to black people living in the United States. While the African American experience cannot be reduced to the legacy of racism and slavery, it is difficult to fully understand the origins and character of black art without recognizing the institutional challenges that conditioned its emergence. For these reasons, Travis makes a clear distinction between jazz music and blues music in American history; while jazz can represent the hybridization of a wide range of musical traditions, the subset of blues is more viscerally expressive of the pain and agony of the traumas imposed by anti-black racism in the United States.[20]

Adjaye's choice to visually express the pan-African reach of African American history is compelling considering the contemporary influence of globalization, including the new impact of rapidly modernizing African cities.[21] In the field of art, contemporary artists are reinterpreting the historical meaning of "blackness" so that it no longer exclusively refers to the abject, negative racial categories of the past.[22] However, in an era marked by a rise in post-racial ideologies in the United States, Adjaye's approach potentially exacerbates the notion that minorities have finally "made it" and racism is officially a thing of the past. Such attitudes have contributed to the repeal of the very affirmative action laws that the Civil Rights Movement helped inaugurate in the 1960s. Despite the election of the first African American President in 2008, troubles with racism, rampant unemployment, and police brutality continue to plague black citizens in the new millennium. This historical context should reinforce the high stakes of commemorative architecture. In the end, striking a balance between celebrating the achievements of the historical black diaspora and visually expressing the institutional limits placed upon minorities living in the U.S. context is more than an issue of proper technique—it is an issue of cultural meaning.

Epilogue

It is important to contemplate the range of cultural meanings that are associated with the use of architectural techniques. Following the logic of this argument, it is impossible to make a clear distinction between the past and the present in contemporary design; one is continuously influenced by historical traditions, and new designs continually remake history in the present. Conceptualizing design as a mutual conversation between the past and the present is a fruitful way of engaging with the limits of artistic traditions. Such an approach enables the designer to achieve their creative goals in a way that remains sensitive to historical and cultural contexts. The examples of the Martin Luther King Jr. Memorial and the Smithsonian National Museum of African American History and Culture demonstrate the relative benefits and perils of using mimesis and abstraction to represent black cultural history on the National Mall. However, over the course of a career, a designer's tasks are likely to exceed the small niche of commemorative spaces. Public artists, architects, and urban planners will have to employ a broad range of aesthetic approaches to shape the built environment beyond the Mall. Consciously managing the conceptual relationships that exist between form and meaning will enrich our collective interpretation of the past, but that management will require a designer to directly embrace cultural history.

Discussion Questions and Explorations

Descriptive

1. Draw a diagram of the National Mall that isolates the public lawn where people can meet for formal or informal assembly. This part of the Mall stretches from the foot of the Capitol building (on the east) to the foot of the Lincoln Memorial (on the west), with the Washington Monument standing in between. Do not fill in any of the places where people cannot walk. Be sure to color in the pedestrian sections of the Mall in green.

2. Draw another diagram of the National Mall that isolates the locations of architectural buildings and hard landscape elements adjacent to the public lawn. Do not fill in any of the pathways to and from these spaces, but do indicate where the buildings are located along the Mall. Be sure to color in these sections of the Mall in black.

Analytical

1. Think about the different African American publics that are addressed with the Martin Luther King Jr. Memorial and the Smithsonian National Museum of African American History and Culture. What definition of "African American" do you think best suits the historical scope and biographical nature of the MLK Memorial? And how does the definition of "African American" change with the pan-African historical scope of the Smithsonian Museum? What do these two definitions teach us about the power of labels when creating a commemorative design?

2. Compare and contrast David Adjaye's design for the Smithsonian Museum with Maya Lin's design for the Museum of the Chinese in America. Discuss the architectural tools each architect uses to visualize a particular ethnic group's experience. Do you think Maya Lin has used a mimetic or an abstract approach to her design? Explain your answer.

3. Explain why the Martin Luther King Jr. Memorial omits the accomplishments of other African American leaders such as Marcus Garvey or Malcolm X. How did the goals of these social movements align with and differ from Dr. King's message or the goals of the Civil Rights Movement more generally? Why do you think these figures were not included in the King Memorial, which was originally designed to commemorate a broad number of activists dedicated to civil rights? Do you think Garvey or Malcolm X will ever be recognized in a monument or memorial situated on the Mall?

4. Review the style of all the major buildings populating the National Mall and indicate whether they employ mimetic or abstract formal techniques. Do you notice a preference for one technique over the other in the overall plan? Which do you prefer? Explain your answer.

Speculative

1. Redesign the MLK Memorial so that it does not make use of a literal statue of Martin Luther King Jr. How can you communicate the importance of King's contribution without literally representing him in this space? Do you think removing his statue diminishes the rhetorical power of the memorial?

2. Examine the overall design for the National Museum of the American Indian on the National Mall. Describe what aspects of this design employ mimetic and abstract principles. What relationship do you think exists between the overall form of this design and the cultural meaning that is communicated by its different spaces, materials, and orientation to the Mall?

Notes

1   Historians have revealed the contrasting historical assessments of the Capitol building and the Lincoln Memorial. The former was completed with slave labor, while the latter was dedicated to the U.S. President remembered for freeing the slaves with an executive order during the Civil War. See Scott Sandage, "A Marble House Divided: The Lincoln Memorial, the Civil Rights Movement, and the Politics of Memory, 1939–1963," in *Race and the Production of Modern American Nationalism*, edited by Reynolds J. Scott-Childress (New York: Garland Publishers, 1999).

2   Richard Guy Wilson, "Expressions of Identity," in *The American Renaissance, 1876–1917* (New York: Pantheon Books, 1979), 10–25.

3   See Michael J. Lewis' essay "The Idea of the American Mall," in *The National Mall: Rethinking Washington's Monumental Core*, edited by Nathan Glazer and Cynthia R. Field (Baltimore, MD: Johns Hopkins University Press, 2008), 15–18.

4   Louis Sullivan was one such architect, who debated Daniel Burnham during the construction of the Columbian Exposition in Chicago, IL, about the appropriate use of historical styles. Burnham's reliance on European ornament can be contrasted with Sullivan's use of purely invented geometrical forms in his Transportation Building of 1893–94. See Robert Twombly, *Louis Sullivan: His Life and Works* (Chicago: University of Chicago Press, 1986).

5   A noteworthy example was Alfred Barr's recognition of the influence of what he called "Negro Sculpture" on the development of Cubism at the 1936 "Cubism and Abstract Art" show at the Museum of Modern Art.

6   See Michael North's *The Dialect of Modernism: Race, Language and Twentieth Century Literature* (Oxford: Oxford University Press, 1998), and Adolf Max Vogt's *Le Corbusier: The Noble Savage: Toward an Archaeology of Modernism* (Cambridge, MA: MIT Press, 2000).

7   According to historical records, nearly 200 slaves were sold upon Jefferson's death to pay for debts he accrued in his lifetime. See Lucia C. Stanton's *Slavery at Monticello* (Charlottesville, VA: Thomas Jefferson Memorial Foundation, 1996). For a history of Jefferson's personal relations with slaves, including his mistress Sally Hemings, see Annette Gordon-Reed's *The Hemingses of Monticello: An American Family* (New York: W. W. Norton, 2008).

8   A political controversy emerged surrounding the selection of Lei Yixin, a Chinese sculptor, to complete the statue of Martin Luther King Jr. Many black artists voiced their opinion that an African American sculptor would make a better choice, especially given the limited opportunities provided to such artists in the past. See Ariana Eunjung Cha's article "A King Statue 'Made in China'?" in the *Washington Post*, August 15, 2007.

9   Historians have compared King's position on peaceful protest to those taken by more radical black and student movements of the 1960s, including those advocated by the Student Nonviolent Coordination Committee, Congress on Racial Equality, and the Black Panther Party. The latter group was an outgrowth of discontent on the lack of legislative victories obtained for working-class African Americans. In addition to free lunch programs and other social programs, they have become infamous for advocating the open carrying of arms to defend oneself from police brutality and other forms of overt violence. See Dean E. Robinson's *Black Nationalism in American Politics and Thought* (Cambridge: Cambridge University Press, 2001), 51–69.

10 W.J.T. Mitchell, "The Violence of Public Art: 'Do the Right Thing'," *Critical Inquiry* 16, no. 4 (Summer 1990), 880–899.

11 Maya Lin's struggles have been documented in several sources including documentaries, interviews, and academic essays. See Frieda Lee Mock's documentary *Maya Lin: A Strong, Clear Vision* (New Video Group, 2003). Also, see Marita Sturken's book *Tangled Memories: The Vietnam War, the AIDS Epidemic, and the Politics of Remembering* (Berkeley: University of California Press, 1997), 44–84. It is also important to note that the MLK Memorial also employed Lin's use of polished black granite to record inscriptions. This adoption reveals how conventional Lin's technique has become over time.

12 The six finalists included the British architectural firm Norman Foster & Partners; the Canadian firm Moshe Safdie and Associates; the American firms Moody Nolan with Antoine Predock Associates and Diller Scofidio and Renfro; Devrouax & Purnell Architects/Planners with Pei Cobb Freed & Partners Architects; and the David Adjaye team.

13 Peter Allison, ed., *David Adjaye: Making Public Buildings* (London: Thames & Hudson, 2006).

14 Philip Freelon, the architect of record, has a steady history of designing local museums that commemorate African American culture. These projects include the Museum of the African Diaspora in Los Angeles, California (2005); the Reginald F. Lewis Museum of Maryland African American History and Culture in Baltimore, Maryland (2005); the Harvey Gantt Center for African American History and Culture in Charlotte, North Carolina (2009); and the International Civil Rights Center and Museum in Greensborough, North Carolina (2010). This last project preserved and expanded the location of the first sit-in staged by black college students at the then Woolworth's Department Store in 1960, which initiated a larger public protest of racial segregation in private eating establishments in the state.

15 See Randy Kennedy's article in the *New York Times* titled "Architects Chosen for Black History Museum," April 14, 2009.

16 J. Michael Welton, "Phil Freelon, Lead Architect of the Smithsonian's African American Museum," *The Washington Post*, February 18, 2012.

17 Scott Trafton, *Egypt Land: Race and Nineteenth Century American Egyptomania* (Durham, NC: Duke University Press, 2004), 144–146.

18 The African origins of shotgun house typology are most strikingly covered by two essays by John Michael Vlach in the 1970s. See John Michael Vlach, "The Shotgun House: An African American Legacy," in *Common Places: Readings in American Vernacular Architecture*, edited by Dell Upton and John Michael Vlach (Athens: University of Georgia Press, 1986), 58–78.

19 There are many occasions when Travis has publicly presented questions to David Adjaye regarding the meaning of his designs. One can be heard during the question and answer session presented at Columbia University commemorating the release of Mabel Wilson's *Negro Building: Black Americans in the World of Fairs and Museums* (Berkeley: University of California Press, 2012) on October 1, 2012. This exchange can be heard on the following link: www.youtube.com/watch?v=a-3Yps9Qs8w (accessed September 11, 2014).

20 Ibid., listen to Travis' comments after the 50-minute mark during the question and answer portion of the program.

21 Lagos has captured the imagination of several prominent architects, including David Adjaye and Rem Koolhaas. These interests are reflected in a series of recent publications and documentaries. See Koolhaas' essay on Lagos in *Lagos: How It Works* (Baden: Lars Muller Publishers, 2007) and Adjaye's ethnographic catalogue of modern African vernacular architecture in *African Metropolitan Architecture* (New York, NY: Rizzoli International Publications, 2007).

22 For a discussion of blackness in contemporary art, see Pauline de Souza's essay "Implications of Blackness in Contemporary Art," in Amelia Jones' edited volume *A Companion to Contemporary Art Since 1945* (Malden, MA: Blackwell Publishing, 2006), 356–377.

Editors' Introduction to Chapter 2

Designers of cities, buildings, and landscapes make hundreds, if not thousands, of decisions on any given project—everything from what materials to use to the overall form or concept one is seeking to impart. Design decisions are complex and interrelated, as architects and landscape architects negotiate cost parameters, structural and material limitations, human and environmental factors, and legal constraints. Throughout the process of design and construction, there is a constant reconciliation of technical, aspirational, and ethical issues, and, at each step, there are a multitude of paths forward, each with a resultant set of opportunities and consequences.

Historians confront a similar challenge. The history of an event or life can be told from various perspectives—the person/people who lived it, the closely affiliated people who witnessed it, or more distant outsiders. Likewise, a history can be organized or sequenced in a variety ways—chronological, reverse chronological, thematic, etc. Historians also have the difficult job of selecting which details to highlight and which to suppress, which to include and which to exclude. Histories of the everyday are particularly challenging, as folk histories are often overlooked and the documentation or records are often fractured.

Architecture and landscape architecture with a historical focus have the compounded difficulty of the historian and the designer. Design in a historical context must choose both the concepts used and the stories told, especially for projects in controversial cultural, geographic, or historical settings (burial sites and archaeological sites being two clear examples). Landscape architecture carries this challenge in a particularly weighty manner, as the most basic materials of the discipline—earth, water, and sky—carry profound metaphorical meanings.

The landscape architect must ask: What story or stories do I choose to tell about the history of the people and the land? What materials do I employ to tell those stories? Reciprocally, what stories do I diminish or exclude; what materials do I diminish or exclude? These questions were central to the design of *Shadow Catcher*, part of a cultural heritage site on the University of Virginia campus.

In the case study that follows, Walter Hood and Megan Basnak discuss the "diverse truths" that surround heritage sites with hidden and controversial histories. In the case of *Shadow Catcher*, designed by Hood, the history of slavery and black sovereignty in the United States is brought together with four disparate truths: Thomas Jefferson's internationally renowned campus plan, lesser-known historical figures, the burial practices and mythologies of ancient Africa, and a contemporary American university. The case illustrates how design for the everyday and design for commemoration can be integrated, leading to a more compelling commentary on that which is sacred and that which is mundane. As you read, think about your own life history and the culture that surrounds you, and how this personal and cultural history connects to the personal and cultural histories of the past. How does landscape architecture mediate these near and distant histories? More precisely, consider how landscape architecture (and art) tell stories that are simultaneously universal and highly specific—how an under-told story of African American history is portrayed in built form and interpreted by society today.

Chapter 2

Diverse Truths

Unveiling the Hidden Layers of the *Shadow Catcher* Commemoration

Walter Hood and Megan Basnak

Introduction

In the summer of 1993, while excavating a portion of the University of Virginia campus for parking lot expansion, contractors discovered twelve grave shafts in an area known during the late nineteenth century as "Canada." Researchers discovered that Canada, a small community of free African Americans, many of whom worked for the University of Virginia, fell within what is now the university's South Lawn.

Archaeologists later identified the graves as belonging to a cemetery for African Americans who served as laborers during periods of construction on the campus and provided various services including laundering for university employees.[1] One of the workers, Catherine "Kitty" Foster, a free, land-owning African American woman, worked as a seamstress for university faculty during the late 1800s. At the time of the discovery, the general public knew very little about the university's unique historical connection with both free and enslaved African Americans.[2] As a result, finding the grave shafts catalyzed an ongoing effort to recognize their contributions to the university. Amidst discussion of implementing landscape plans for the newly planned South Lawn Project in 2004, university officials proposed a park at the site of Kitty Foster's homestead to commemorate this often-overlooked group in the historical University of Virginia population. The university selected Hood Design Studio, along with a team of landscape architects and designers from the Office of Cheryl Barton, to design the proposal for the newly planned site. In this chapter, we will examine this work as well as a few others from Hood Design Studio that exemplify a culturally focused design practice.

▼ Figure 2.1

Location of the South Lawn within the current University of Virginia campus.
Diagram by Megan Basnak.

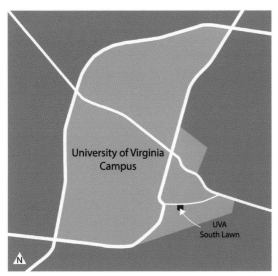

Culturally Focused Practice

A culturally focused design practice affords designers the opportunity to immerse themselves in the community and cultivate meaningful relationships. In the landscape architecture field, a profession often mistakenly viewed as only focused on plant science and horticulture-related issues, this translates into the ability to explore and influence larger issues such as environmental justice. Environmental justice, "the fair treatment and meaningful involvement of all people regardless of race, color, national origin, or income with respect to issues, laws, and regulations concerning the environment," is rooted in the act of acknowledging and building upon individual realities.[3] Inevitably, both designers and clients bring their individual biases to each project. These biases may come through in a number of ways including the design process, design style, and even the design solution. Recognition of cognitive biases, one's tendency to "make systematic decisions in certain circumstances based on cognitive factors rather than evidence," is the first step to bringing justice to the work.[4] In practice, it is not always easy to be honest about the realities that exist and sometimes pursuing this form of truth forces one to go against the larger goals of a project. Overcoming the tendency to do or believe things because others do or believe the same, also known as the "bandwagon effect," and understanding that local cultures are more complex than they first appear are the initial steps to recognizing the diverse realities in one's work.[5]

Triad of Investigations

In a culturally focused practice, designers often base work on a triad of investigations: (1) the everyday and mundane, (2) commemoration, and (3) life ways. A community's culture is replete with the everyday and mundane actions of people that make up the human experience. People are conditioned to the familiar, including actions such as trips to the grocery store, walking the dog, and driving to work. The objects that facilitate these actions are ubiquitous and often go unnoticed.[6] Despite their ordinariness, these elements often are where people and governments spend the most money. Take, for example, the freeway part of urban and suburban infrastructure. Artists and designers typically do not view freeways as an opportunity for artistic expression. Projects such as Hood Design Studio's *Splashpad Park* in Oakland, California, attempt to change this view.

The Everyday and Mundane

Splashpad Park, a once vacant traffic island bounded by an interstate and streets, is now a bustling pedestrian plaza that plays host to farmers' markets and reconnects pedestrians to the greater Lake Merritt park system in Oakland, California. The layering of plants and different surface materials such as brick, crushed granite, and grass create different "rooms" for various activities. A cultural practice conscious of the everyday and mundane recognizes these

Hood Design Studio, *Splashpad Park*, Oakland, CA.
Photo by Hood Design Studio.

objects and spaces as opportunities, and transforms them into public sculptures that embrace and validate the everyday patterns and rituals of neighborhoods.[7] A series of small walkways throughout the site not only link pedestrians to the nearby commercial corridor, but also invite them into and through a number of experiences including a wood-paved gathering area illuminated by lights from below. While these elements contribute to the acknowledgment and appreciation of the often-overlooked space beneath freeways, they also pay homage to what once occupied the space before and after the construction of the freeway. For instance, a serpentine wall acknowledges the previous existence of a fountain, a section of old curb defines the edge of a pre-existing street, and a large planting of dogwoods references the area's past existence as a wetland.[8] These intentional references to the past all become part of the larger act of commemorating the once forgotten.

Commemoration

Defined as "something that is intended to honor an important event or person from the past," commemoration, the second leg of the triad, is an attribute incorporated into many projects designed by those with culturally focused practices.[9] In order to overcome cognitive biases held by designers, commemoration also must look to the culture of places in which projects occur to

▲ Figure 2.3

Hood Design Studio, *Witness Walls*, Nashville, TN.
Rendering by Hood Design Studio.

understand what is most important to the people. American historian Michael Kammen identified the notion that "societies in fact reconstruct their pasts rather than faithfully record them, and they do so with the needs of contemporary culture clearly in mind—manipulating the past in order to mold the present."[10] One can bring truth to remembrance by emphasizing the importance of the past in how the present, and eventually the future, is constructed.[11] This effort is particularly evident in *Witness Walls*, a recent commission to Hood Design Studio for the Metropolitan Nashville Arts Commission (Metro Arts) in Nashville, Tennessee. Although many people know Nashville as "Music City," very few know it for its role at the center of the Civil Rights Movement during the 1960s. Some of the nation's first sit-ins occurred in Nashville, beginning in February 1960, and the actions of many citizens during that time greatly influenced the early progress of the movement.

Communities have collective and individual past, present, and future identities. As a result, the process of returning one's mindset to the community's origins through commemoration is complex and indeterminate.[12] In the case of *Witness Walls*, the design uses fragmented walls to remember the contributions of everyday people to the early progress of the Civil Rights Movement. Images of historic moments, gleaned from photographs in the collection of the Nashville Public Library's Civil Rights Reading Room, are etched into the concrete walls.[13] Located on the west side of the Metro Nashville Courthouse, the proposed project also incorporates period music associated with civil rights, further recognizing the city's past life. *Witness Walls* commemorates everyday people and their actions to tell an important story, one that is relative and relevant to the particular culture in which the story is told.

Life Ways

At the core of a culturally focused practice is the third leg of the triad of investigations, acknowledgment of a community's life ways. The "life-ways" approach begins with the acknowledgment that within communities people live in specific ways that are important.[14] In order to effectively acknowledge life ways, designers must first understand where one's power lies. Definitions of power vary, including "the capacity or ability to direct or influence the behavior of others or the course of events," and "the capacity of something to affect the emotions or intellect strongly."[15] Power also comes in various forms ranging from the most well known such as economic and political to lesser considered forms such as social and historical.[16] For designers, power lies in their media. They are able to use media to validate, challenge, or normalize people's ways of life. For example, in 2012, a community organization formed with the mission of rehabilitating the first opera house in the San Francisco Bay area, dating back to the late 1800s. Initial city plans for reusing the theater, which locals historically valued as the place in which they could go to experience the arts, included incorporating a community garden and other types of "social reform"-based initiatives. Many of these initiatives had little to do with what the residents envisioned for the future of the building. In response, residents, many of whom were African American, attended meetings and voiced concerns echoing the sentiment that the proposed use of the facility as a community garden made them feel as if it were a plantation. In the end, the city allowed them to get rid of the chickens and the garden and remake their opera house into something cultural, something significant.

The Bayview Opera House scenario exemplifies why everyone, particularly designers, need to be careful in how they make decisions for each other. In the case of Bayview, city leaders assumed those living in the neighborhood wanted to "return to their agrarian roots." They neglected to understand that many of the African Americans living in the Bayview neighborhood did not come from

▼ Figure 2.4

Hood Design Studio, Bayview Opera House, San Francisco, CA. *Rendering by Hood Design Studio.*

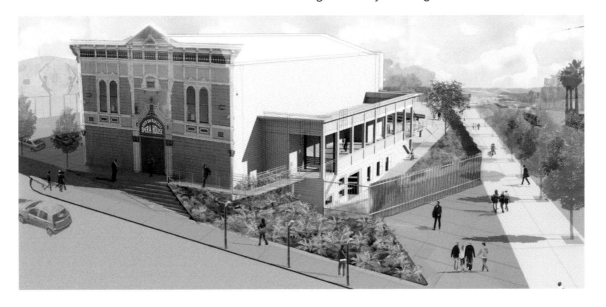

the traditionally assumed slavery background. Leaders failed to take the time to understand how diverse the diaspora truly was in different areas of the United States. There are many other examples in the design field where this same thing happens—normative values dictated by the few overcome the individual ways of life of the majority. As a result of normative reform, many people, along with their ways of life, are dismissed and forgotten. To avoid this form of dismissal, culturally focused practitioners connect with members of the community in an effort to better understand their history and ways of life. The *Shadow Catcher*, on the University of Virginia campus, exemplifies this willingness to understand in order to tell a story true to its origins.

The *Shadow Catcher*: Writing the Story, Not Telling the Narrative

The University of Virginia, located in the foothills of the Blue Ridge Mountains in the city of Charlottesville, Virginia, encompasses 3,411 acres of land across all of its campuses.[17] When Thomas Jefferson founded the university in 1819, it was the first nonsectarian university in the United States founded on the mission of educating leaders in practical affairs and public service.[18] Prior to 2010, when traversing the university's main campus, one could easily see the Jeffersonian influence in the design and construction of many of the campus's most notable buildings.[19] Presentations of the university's history to both the public and students often focused on Jefferson and the realization of his vision of a university to "educate the common man" in order to eliminate ignorance, which he believed to be the enemy of freedom.[20] Not so visible, both physically on the campus and in written form detailing the history of the university, was the unique relationship during its formative years between the university and both freed and enslaved African Americans. Until 2010, a small slate memorial plaque installed in 2007 in the brick pavement near the university's iconic Rotunda building served as the only evidence of this relationship.

Canada

In the nineteenth century, the state of Virginia's unique geographical location between the slave-owning states of the south and the free states of the north allowed for its African American population to be representative of the beliefs of both the north and south. Both free and enslaved African Americans populated cities and towns throughout the state of Virginia, the University of Virginia being no exception. Records from the summer of 1817 are the earliest evidence of the university employing the work of slaves. Throughout the university's construction process, slaves hauled and dressed timber, molded and fired bricks, and completed other tasks that contributed to the erection of university buildings. While many of the African Americans who worked on the construction of buildings during the university's formative years were enslaved, some were free. Free African American contractors provided services such as hauling building materials, making clothes for enslaved laborers, and washing and cooking for the university's white contractors.[21] As the university shifted from a period of construction to welcoming students to campus, both enslaved and free African Americans continued to provide services to the university community. Although students could not bring their slaves to campus, university administration allowed faculty to bring slaves to reside with them on university grounds. The university itself held as many as 100 or more slaves at any given time, and the slave-to-student ratio consistently averaged one slave for every 20 students.[22]

During periods of university construction, most free African Americans contracted to do work stayed within the campus limits. Once the university opened, many families moved to land surrounding the university, most often to areas bordering the southernmost extents of the campus grounds. These households often consisted of family members who supplied various services to university staff such as laundering and seamstress work. Institutional and county records document this small residential area of free, land-owning or renting African Americans as Canada. Likely named after the United States' neighbor to the north that abolished slavery in 1834, Canada housed only four families during the early years of the university's existence between 1825 and 1870.[23] One of those families included that of university seamstress, Catherine "Kitty" Foster.

The Foster Family

Prior to 1830, little is known about the history of Catherine "Kitty" Foster. In 1833, she purchased a 2⅛-acre tract of land adjacent to the University of Virginia in the Canada neighborhood. At the time, a free African American landowner was quite rare; rarer yet was a free African American woman landowner. Like Kitty, many of her children and grandchildren worked in service capacities for the university. Upon her passing, Kitty Foster's children subdivided her property and family members constructed new structures on the newly formed lots. Over time, Kitty's family subdivided the property several times over and, by 1907, all but one of Kitty's grandchildren sold their portions of the property to white land developers. In 1921, Kitty's great-grandchildren sold the last of the property to a white developer.[24] At some point during the time in which the Fosters occupied the land parcel, the family formed a burial ground in the western half of the property where they laid their family members to rest.

University Discoveries

As white landowners reacquired land parcels in Canada, the land area that once housed Catherine "Kitty" Foster and other free African American families went through a process known as *gentrification*. Gentrification is the renewal and rebuilding that accompanies the influx of middle-class or affluent people into deteriorating areas that often displaces poorer residents.[25] In 1916, a local Charlottesville newspaper, *Daily Progress*, documented the process in an article titled "Pest Hole Clean Up" stating:

What has for 60 years or more been regarded as a public nuisance and plague spot, is about to receive a thorough cleaning up and made to "blossom like the rose." This ugly place, located directly opposite the University, on the Fry's Springs trolley line, has been observed by passers-by for generations with abhorrence as they have noticed the filthy, ramshackled buildings, pig pens and piles of junk full of offensive odors. The property has recently been purchased by Mr. Albert E. Walker and others, whose intention it is to transform the present horrid mess into a beautiful grove, with gardens and lawns. The entire neighborhood is to undergo a decided change, and what with the new chemical building of the University, now in the course of construction [Cobb Hall], the handsome new University gates and new rustic station of the railway company, the place will be one of real beauty.[26]

Some white landowners even went as far as writing racial clauses into their deeds prohibiting the future lease or sale of the property to African Americans. It was not until the late twentieth century that the university acquired the parcels of land in and around the former Canada neighborhood.[27]

During the process of grading the site located on the university's South Lawn for parking lot expansion in 1993, University of Virginia construction crews discovered a series of unmarked graves that, after continued archaeological excavation, were identified to be part of a 20- by 25-foot cemetery.

▼ Figure 2.5

Brick paving revealed during archaeological investigation of Foster Homestead site. *Photo by M. Drake Patten.*

Archaeologists identified the location of the cemetery, based on a deed search, as overlapping a land parcel previously occupied by the family of Catherine "Kitty" Foster. Subsequent to this discovery, 15 years of university-funded archaeological research proceeded at the site, leading to the discovery of further artifacts from the Foster family. Findings included a "central residential structure with dug paneled cellar, brick chimney base, hard surfaced circulation and work areas surrounding the residence, a brick-lined well, and intact cultural deposits containing a wide-ranging domestic assemblage."[28] In 2005, archaeologists completed additional work at the site in preparation for the future construction of the university's multi-phased South Lawn Project. Further excavation of the area found additional unmarked graves near those originally attributed to the Foster family. In total, archaeologists found 32 grave sites in an area 40 feet long by 47 feet wide.[29]

Commemorating the Forgotten

▼ Figure 2.6

University plaque recognizing the contributions of free and enslaved men and women to the university.
Photo by University of Virginia Magazine.

The discoveries made during archaeological studies on the University of Virginia campus reignited greater public interest in the university's unique historical relationship with both free and enslaved African Americans. In 2007, based on the recommendation of the university's Board of Visitors, crews installed a slate memorial plaque in a brick-paved area located under the south terrace of the

campus's iconic Rotunda building. At the time of the plaque's installation, it served as the first evidence of public acknowledgment on the university's behalf of the contributions made by both free and enslaved African American workers to the design and construction of the university. The plaque reads, "In honor of the several hundred women and men, both free and enslaved, whose labor between 1817 and 1826 helped to realize Thomas Jefferson's design for the University of Virginia." At the time of installation, members of the University of Virginia community felt that the plaque failed to sufficiently acknowledge contributions made by enslaved laborers due in part to its easily overlooked location on the campus grounds.[30]

While planning for the South Lawn expansion continued after 2005, discussions regarding the Foster site also continued because the site fell directly within the bounds of the proposed project. The project forced the university to acknowledge its past relationship to slavery and, after much discussion, university officials determined that preservation of the Kitty Foster site would become a central part of the South Lawn addition. According to the university, "The decision to retain the historic freed-person's home site and adjacent African American burial ground to create an interpretive public park in commemoration was viewed as a positive step. The move unified the vision of the South Lawn Project to the overarching history of the University itself, creating cultural ties that are essential."[31]

The Freedom to Tell the Truth

As part of the master plan for the South Lawn addition, university officials commissioned a ten-acre landscape encompassing the new series of academic buildings. Within that area, officials included a one-acre commemorative site acknowledging the Kitty Foster Homestead and the neighborhood, Canada. Hood Design Studio used traditional African American cultural mythology referencing the myth of the "Flash of the Spirit" to guide the design of the commemorative proposal. According to the myth, when individuals leave the planet, they need a flash of light to take them to heaven.[32] In this regard, the design of the site intervention had to include light to create a connection between the ground (symbolic of the past) and the sky (symbolic of the future). This notion guided the design of *Shadow Catcher*.

Shadow Catcher is one part of the more expansive design for the Kitty Foster Homestead site. The site sets itself apart from the neo-classical formality of Jefferson's plan by creating a series of experiences that draw upon ephemeral qualities of landscape including light and a freedom of movement mimicking how one might move through the site. The "informality" of the site design, compared to its very formal campus surroundings, alludes to the historical relationship between Canada and the university.[33] Although distinctly different in organization, the design maintains a clear connection between the site and surrounding campus in two ways: (1) the inclusion of a horizontal surface of plantings and (2) by continuing trees from the new site into the South Lawn courtyard.[34] Central to the site is a polished aluminum frame in the shape of the

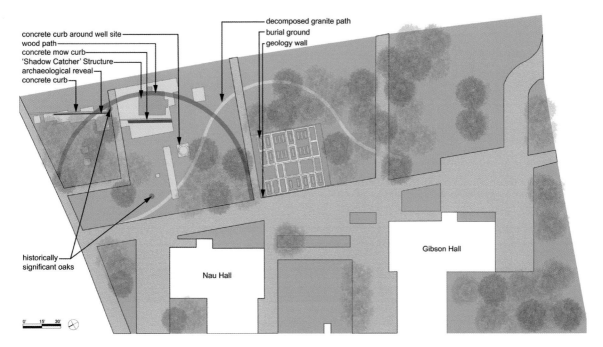

concrete curb around well site
wood path
concrete mow curb
'Shadow Catcher' Structure
archaeological reveal
concrete curb

decomposed granite path
burial ground
geology wall

historically
significant oaks

Nau Hall

Gibson Hall

0' 15' 30'

▲ Figure 2.7

Foster Homestead site plan.
Redrawn from original plan created by Hood Design Studio.

Foster house. This frame is embedded in a 40-by-40 foot polished aluminum grid work designed to resemble the division of an archaeological dig site and is used as a means to transfer the scale of the Foster house, sections of which still exist below the ground, to a structure above one's head.

The frame, lifted approximately 12 feet off the ground by a lightweight steel structure, not only generously reflects light due to its material quality, but also casts a shadow onto the ground. Instead of demarcating the ground, the structure demarcates space overhead, allowing light to filter through and create the markings on the ground. This effect gives an almost dream-like quality of light as one moves throughout the space.[35] The south-facing site of *Shadow Catcher* provides for continuously changing light throughout the day, allowing for different experiences for visitors who experience the structure at different times. The significant increase in depth of the steel members used to represent the outline of the house from those used to create the grid allows the cast shadows to grow and shrink throughout the day.[36]

In addition to *Shadow Catcher*, the design for the Kitty Foster site also includes several "reveals" allowing visitors to view ruins from the Foster Homestead. Unlike ruins found in Rome that are left exposed to the elements, the ruins found at the Kitty Foster site are made of masonry and stone more than a hundred years old, which may deteriorate if left out to the elements for any significant period of time. As a result, the design incorporates clear protective barriers over the exposed areas, allowing them to remain visible while still protected from the elements.

Adjacent to the Foster Homestead is the Foster burial ground. Archaeological studies conducted at the site were not able to identify those interred in each grave; as a result, the design intervention avoids identifying individual sites

▲ Figure 2.8

The polished aluminum grid of the *Shadow Catcher* represents the outline of the Foster house embedded in a grid work typical of archaeological dig sites.
Photo by Marcus Brooks.

◀ Figure 2.9

Revealed ruins of the Foster Homestead.
Photo by Benjamin P. Ford, Rivanna Archaeological Services, LLC.

▲ Figure 2.10

Depressions in the ground represent the hallowed burial ground that lies below.

Photo by Marcus Brooks.

and instead highlights the fact that the area is hallowed ground. Visits by the design team to several cemeteries in the surrounding community to observe different burial practices yielded an interesting realization that the composition of soils in the region allows for the ground to settle and create depressions as bodies continue to decompose below the surface. Reflecting this discovery, the burial ground, surrounded by a stone wall set high on a plinth, is visible only as a series of depressions in the ground. The locations of the depressions do not necessarily correspond with actual burial plots; instead, they serve as a representation of the hallowed ground without having to disturb the interred remains below. The polarity between the openness of the burial ground and the density of the adjoining campus contributes to the powerful effect that it has on those visiting. The design gives visitors the opportunity to "occupy" a homestead once occupied a hundred years ago. It is not a site frozen in time; instead, the site continues to be a part of the community.[37]

Both *Shadow Catcher* and the Foster burial ground include multiple voices and points of view to tell the story of Kitty Foster and her neighbors. A cultural understanding of the site opened doors that allowed the design to tell these stories without having to define the narrative. These interpretations leave open the opportunity for others to develop their personal interpretive meanings of the site.

Conclusion: Designing for Diverse Truths

The design for the Kitty Foster site tells a story that allows visitors to ponder multiple truths not only as they relate to Kitty Foster and her life, but also to the University of Virginia's relationship with both free and enslaved African Americans. Because the design comes from a culturally focused practice that acknowledges the various histories of this site, visitors can get caught in any number of interpretations. These individual truths are what Greek philosopher Protagoras and the doctrine on relativism described, saying, "Of all things, the measure is man, of things which are, that they are, of things which are not, that they are not."[38] Landscape architecture gives designers the opportunity to tell a story and affords the public an opportunity to explore and realize truths relevant to their lives. Designers cannot always anticipate the consequences of their work—good, bad, or otherwise—but if they get out of the way and acknowledge others' voices, something new emerges, something that acknowledges voices from those who experience the work. This interaction is one of the most beautiful things about design; one piece of work can stir the emotions of so many in so many different ways.

The *Shadow Catcher*'s ordinariness is what allows it to take on different meanings to different people. Imagine moving through the site as one would have done during the late nineteenth century, and viewing artifacts used in everyday life. What was it like to live there at the time? How do the shadows and reflections allude to that life? How do they provoke questions about our connections to those lives? Occupying such a small, insignificant space surrounded by the large, monumental structures of the campus gives a small preview of how one might have felt living in Canada. When one approaches a project through the life lens of others, an alternative way of designing is facilitated, one with the potential to overcome biases and make work that is more relevant to more people.

Discussion Questions and Explorations

Descriptive

1.   Describe how Walter Hood's culturally focused practice differs from most landscape design and/or architecture practices today.
2.   Describe how Bayview residents felt about the government's official plans for using the Bayview Opera House.

Analytical

1. How does Walter Hood's "Triad of Investigations" apply to the *Shadow Catcher* project? Are all three types of investigation apparent in the final design?
2. Identify some of the potential unintended consequences of Walter Hood's *Shadow Catcher* and the causes of those consequences.

Speculative

1. Define gentrification as it is used in this chapter. How do you think the sequence of events related to Kitty Foster and the site of her home would have been different had gentrification of the area not occurred?
2. Select something that is memorialized in landscape on your campus or in your city. Use Hood's "Triad of Investigations" to design a new landscape intervention. What would your intervention represent/commemorate? How would it be represented?

Notes

1 Carolyn Dillard, "Out of the Shadows: Event to Commemorate Kitty Foster and Canada Community," news release, March 31, 2011, accessed September 4, 2014, https://news.virginia.edu/content/out-shadows-event-commemorate-kitty-foster-and-canada-community.
2 Meghan Saunders Faulkner, "Slavery at the University of Virginia: A Catalogue of Current and Past Initiatives," accessed September 4, 2014, www.virginia.edu/vpdiversity/documents/SlaveryatUVA_FAULKNER_001.pdf.
3 "Environmental Justice," Environmental Protection Agency, accessed September 5, 2014, www.epa.gov/environmentaljustice/.
4 "Bias," The Baumann Foundation, accessed September 8, 2014, www.beinghuman.org/theme/bias.
5 Andrew Colman, "Bandwagon Effect," in *Oxford Dictionary of Psychology* (New York: Oxford University Press, 2003), 77.
6 Walter Hood, "Developing a Cultural Practice," *Frameworks* (2014), accessed September 5, 2014, http://ced.berkeley.edu/frameworks/2013/developing-a-cultural-practice/.
7 Ibid.
8 Deborah Bishop, "Design 101: The People's Park," *Dwell* (2009), accessed September 5, 2014, www.dwell.com/design-101/article/peoples-park.
9 "Commemoration," Merriam-Webster.com, accessed September 5, 2014, www.merriam-webster.com/dictionary/commemoration.
10 Michael Kammen, "Introduction," in *Mystic Chords of Memory: The Transformation of Tradition in American Culture* (New York: Random House, 1991), 3.
11 Hood, "Developing a Cultural Practice."
12 Ibid.
13 Jennifer Cole, "Artist/Educator Walter Hood Selected to Create Civil Rights Art in Public Square Park," news release, March 18, 2014, accessed September 5, 2014,

www.nashville.gov/News-Media/News-Article/ID/2664/ARTISTEDUCATOR-WALTER-HOOD-SELECTED-TO-CREATE-CIVIL-RIGHTS-ART-IN-PUBLIC-SQUARE-PARK.aspx.

14 Hood, "Developing a Cultural Practice."

15 *"Power, N.1,"* Oxford English Dictionary, accessed September 4, 2014, www.oxford-dictionaries.com/definition/english/power.

16 Herbert Goldhamer and Edward A. Shils, "Types of Power and Status," *American Journal of Sociology* 45, no. 2 (1939): 171–182.

17 "University of Virginia Fact Book," ed. University of Virginia (2014), 18, accessed September 4, 2014, www.virginia.edu/factbook/uvafactbook2014.pdf.

18 Web Communications Office, "Founding of the University," University of Virginia, accessed September 8, 2014, www.virginia.edu/uvatours/shorthistory/.

19 As a self-taught architect, Thomas Jefferson favored the neo-classical style in much of his work. The neo-classical style is heavily influenced by the architecture of Classical Greece and Rome. With clear geometries and a focus on planar qualities, Jefferson's "Jeffersonian Classicism" style is visible throughout the University of Virginia campus. To learn more about Thomas Jefferson and the neo-classical influence on the design of the University of Virginia, see the University of Virginia's Design Guide & Material Palette at http://officearchitect.virginia.edu/pdfs/Design%20Guide_Updated%202013.pdf.

20 "Thomas Jefferson's Plan for the University of Virginia: Lessons from the Lawn," U.S. Department of the Interior National Park Service, accessed September 8, 2014, www.nps.gov/nr/twhp/wwwlps/lessons/92uva/92uva.htm.

21 Benjamin Ford, "Kitty Foster Site—Virginia Department of Historic Resources PIF Resource Information Sheet," ed. Virginia Department of Historic Resources (2014), accessed September 8, 2014, www.dhr.virginia.gov/registers/Cities/Charlottesville/104-5140_Foster_Site_PIF_Form_FINAL_4%2021%202014.pdf.

22 Brendan Wolfe, "Unearthing Slavery at the University of Virginia," *Virginia*, Spring (2013), accessed September 9, 2014, http://uvamagazine.org/articles/unearthing_slavery_at_the_university_of_virginia.

23 Ford, "Kitty Foster Site—Virginia Department of Historic Resources PIF Resource Information Sheet."

24 Ibid.

25 "Gentrification," Merriam-Webster.com, accessed September 9, 2014, www.merriam-webster.com/dictionary/gentrification.

26 "Pest Hole Clean Up," *Daily Progress* (Charlottesville, VA), 1916, quoted in Ford, "Kitty Foster Site—Virginia Department of Historic Resources PIF Resource Information Sheet."

27 Ford, "Kitty Foster Site—Virginia Department of Historic Resources PIF Resource Information Sheet."

28 Ibid.

29 Ibid.

30 Faulkner, "Slavery at the University of Virginia: A Catalogue of Current and Past Initiatives."

31 "Case Studies," *Grounds Plan,* University of Virginia Office of the Architect (2008), 66, accessed September 9, 2014, www.officearchitect.virginia.edu/GroundsPlanWebsite/GPNEW/Introduction/GPHome.html.

32 Walter Hood, *University of Virginia Art & Sciences Magazine*, 2007, accessed September 9, 2014, http://magazine.clas.virginia.edu/x10017.xml.

33 Ibid.

34 Ibid.

35   Ibid.

36   Ibid.

37   Ibid.

38   The relativism doctrine states that no absolutes exist and holds that all truth is relative. To learn more about relativism and Protagoras' theory of truth, see: W.L. Reese, "Relativism, Truth," in *Dictionary of Philosophy and Religion: Eastern and Western Thought* (Atlantic Highlands, NJ: Humanities Press, 1980), 487; 588–589.

Editors' Introduction to Chapter 3

What is a story? The dictionary tells us that a story is a simple account of events, but this is merely a description of what it does. In a more expansive sense, a story provides us with a concrete form for reflecting upon our thoughts, memories, and experiences. A story can consist of imagined events, or it can provide documentation of historical situations or happenings. Regardless of its origins, however, a successful story captures its readers by providing a common basis for understanding a particular phenomenon. A precious few are even able to spur such thoughts into present actions. In this case study, Patsy Eubanks Owens, Maggie La Rochelle, and Jennifer L. McHenry outline a strategy for developing stories of the past that galvanize community action in the present. Their concept of "Landscape Stories" compels the landscape architect to develop a historical narrative for the past that sifts through and interprets the culture and material of underrepresented groups.

In effect, these stories allow historical subjects to speak directly through the physical remnants of the past, even when these traces are seemingly mundane or are, otherwise, overlooked by the casual observer.

A storied approach to landscape architecture studies a group's experiences, physical world, and agency on their terms. Cultures preserve (and transform) their ways of life in a variety of manners. While some cultures build physical structures, others mark their presence by celebrating annual festivals, producing temporary artworks, or creating oral histories of the past. Music and poetry are ephemeral, but they are no less cultural for not being physical; they merely require an alternative means of study. At times, a street sign might be all that is left of the past. Recognizing the range of social phenomena that occur in a place becomes even more important when a cultural group does not have complete control over the spaces they inhabit. The colonial territories of Africa, Asia, and South America, collectively, provide a clear example, as social and political control was not free and equal among the populace. If we did not know that French bureaucrats singled out the preservation of local palaces to promote local tourism while tearing down other forms of culture, we might assume that the princely courts of Northwest Africa were the only Arab enclaves to thrive during French colonialism. This would mask the reality that many other Arab cultures were forced to live in an ever-vanishing present that left few physical traces in the landscape.

Owens, La Rochelle, and McHenry bring our attention to the many international cultures that have thrived in the Northern Central Valley of California, including Japanese, Punjabi, and Portuguese farmers. Recognizing and preserving these cultures has become political, as local tax dollars are earmarked to promote tourism and other development in the region. Which cultural groups are celebrated, and which ones are consigned to history? When answering this question, cultural history becomes more than a simple story of the past; it is an opportunity to elicit economic investment in one's way of life.

Chapter 3

Landscape Stories

Unearthing the Culture of Agricultural Communities in the Central Valley

Patsy Eubanks Owens, Maggie La Rochelle, and Jennifer L. McHenry

In 2010, a group of residents and business owners were gathered in a large meeting room of the Fletcher Farms Community Center in the unincorporated area known as Florin. This area was once a town famous for its large Japanese American population and the strawberries and grapes they and others grew. The question at hand was how to revive the area and improve pedestrian access while building on the community's rich agricultural history. One attendee suggested a statue of Japanese farmers would be a good addition to the plan. A resident asserted that a statue of Japanese farmers was not going to be placed in her town and the idea was quickly dropped and abandoned. No further references to the cultural history of Florin were made. Today, the only obvious evidence of a significant Japanese American population remaining is an old Buddhist temple.

Introduction

This chapter provides a look at how commonplace landscapes can inform our understandings of the cultural history of a place. Through examples of the manifestation of ethnicity and cultural history in the physical environments of three California communities—Florin, Thornton, and Yuba City—we examine how the presence of immigrant populations engaged in agricultural practices starting in the late 1800s is still visible or how it is hidden. We discuss landscape clues to these histories, including signs, structures, and fields, which are often overlooked by current residents, yet tell powerful stories of the settlement and struggles of early inhabitants. We discuss the importance of searching through archives and talking with residents to gain a fuller and richer understanding of the stories the landscapes begin to reveal.

Florin's story is one that captures the important role of Japanese farmers, particularly in strawberry and grape growing, before and after this population's internment during World War II. Portuguese settlers in California played an important role in the cattle and dairy industry; the small town of Thornton hosts prime examples of the influence this cultural group has had on public space and recreation activities including a still functioning bullfighting arena. Lastly, Yuba City settlers included young Punjabi men who eventually married Mexican American women. The presence of these successful peach farmers is still evident in local place names and festivals.

The stories of ethnic identification and cultural influence on the physical environment told in these three communities are played out across many other agricultural communities around the globe. However, education typically does little in the way of teaching students about the intersections between place and people: Why does your community look the way it does? Why did people settle where they did? How might our contemporary decisions impact how people feel about where they live? The lesson we share here is the intentionality and ability to look for cultural messages in our contemporary landscapes to inform planning and design processes. We call this purposeful interpretation of the past the creation of landscape stories.

The stories of these communities are unique but provide insight into the impact that cultural background can have on the current places we now occupy. The ability to read one's physical landscape with cultural sensitivity enables us to see our landscapes as the layered, multicultural sites that they are. When members of the community, as well as designers and planners, are able to read the landscape with this sensitivity, they can better include the cultural history of a place in current decision-making processes.

A Methodology for Learning to Read Cultural and Ethnic Signs in Landscapes

Designers, particularly landscape architects, often begin a design process by examining the natural, physical, and cultural aspects of a site. This site analysis is often focused on the current conditions, and limited effort is given to understanding the history of the site or the community in which it is located. While looking for environmental and physical constraints, opportunities, and challenges in the landscape are important tasks, understanding the cultural context is also essential.[1] Whose stories are told and whose are hidden? It is important for those who participate in the place-making process to find the stories embedded in the landscape by looking carefully not only at a specific project site, but also at the surrounding community and context.

In order to unearth the stories embedded within any place or landscape, time must be spent in the field observing and questioning. Three core methods for beginning to piece together the complexities of any place are: (1) slow, deliberate, well-planned transportation routes with frequent lengthy stops for observation; (2) field journaling, including notes on observations as well as sketches and photos; and (3) follow-up with research of both current-day information as well as archives.[2]

There are a number of ways to discover the layers of meaning in a place. Grady Clay suggests *transecting*, that is, traveling a line through a town by starting at one edge and working one's way through the center of the city to the opposite edge, and observing as much as possible along the route. This method can give an overall idea of a place and is especially useful for the first visit to a large town or city.[3]

Another method is to choose any relatively straight route and stop at every mile to make observations. Similar to Grady Clay's transect, this regular series of stopping points affords the opportunity to make in-depth observations without looking for anything in particular. Another variation is to travel several radial routes out from the center of a place, or to travel a few concentric circles around the center of the place. The exact method and routes should respond to the area under study.

The observation routes for these three case studies were selected following an examination of local maps and an initial exploration by car. Main routes with radiating locations off those routes were chosen. In many places—Yuba City being a prime example—the area is too large to see what is important by simply choosing a path and walking or cycling it. While walking is the best way to discover the hidden stories within landscapes, exploring an entire community in this fashion is typically not feasible. Once the primary routes through each community were identified, observations were conducted at frequent stopping points. Specific buildings and landscape features were noted on field observation maps for each community and they accompany the following sections.

Observations at each stopping point were recorded through journals and sketches. Journals allow for the notation of details, observations, and questions. The benefit of using a journal while observing is in the act of contemplating what is seen while putting pen to paper. This contemplation is an act of meaning making in which the observer tries to figure out what exactly he or she is seeing, how it might link with information already known, or what knowledge might need to be gathered from other sources.

Sketches and photographs were a key component of these landscape observations, and served as useful references after the fieldwork was completed. Regardless of skill level, sketching encourages the observer to notice details that are not obvious through photography. The deliberate act of capturing a place through drawing focuses the observer—enabling her to see things she did not expect and things that might have been overlooked. Photographs can help as place markers and reminders for future research of particular sites in addition to capturing key signs, structures, images, and scenes.

It is important to remember that both sketching and photography, as well as the story the observer builds or "uncovers," are symbolic representations of the landscape story that *the observer* is telling. By this measure, what gets included in landscape representations contributes powerfully to the content of the landscape story being told. What does not get included also matters. After a visit is finished, consider asking: Do these photos and sketches accurately represent what I saw? What is missing? What story, or whose story, am I telling with these images?

Once the fieldwork was completed, other resources were consulted in an effort to confirm impressions and answer outstanding questions and

Study sites—Yuba City, Florin, and Thornton.
Image by Jennifer L. McHenry.

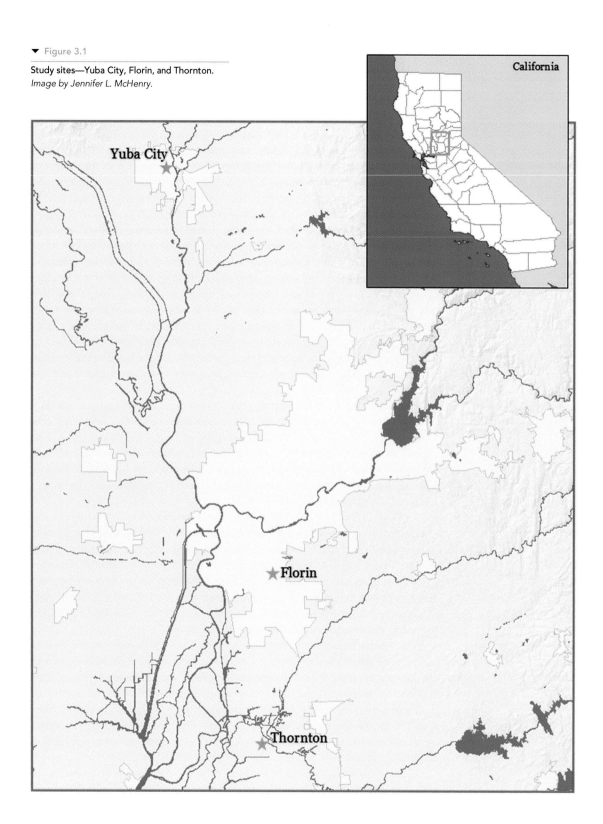

assumptions. Community archives, historical societies, library sources, and residents were consulted in an effort to tease out the full story regarding what was "read" in the landscape observations. This research helped to expose some extraordinary, and frequently hidden or ignored, stories. Often, we did not see important elements of the cultural landscape during the first visit. Multiple visits, with additional background research, helped us move beyond looking for what we expected to see, and into being able to see new and different elements of culture in place.

The Communities

Yuba City, Florin, and Thornton all lie within the Great Central Valley of California. Many people have images of California that include beaches, deserts, Spanish missions overlooking the ocean, and pine-covered mountains once filled with gold miners seeking their fortunes in the streams and rocks. However, Yuba City, Florin, and Thornton are located in a region of California that is best known for its rich agriculture.

From an airplane, the expansive valley is a patchwork of green, yellow, and brown fields surrounding small towns and sprawling metropolitan regions. Driving along any major freeway in the Central Valley during summer might provide views of orchards, vineyards, and fields filled with tomatoes, cotton, corn, and brilliant heavy-headed sunflowers as well as large feed lots filled with beef and dairy cattle. The sides of the freeways are often littered with ripe red tomatoes and occasionally onions and garlic, which managed to escape the backs of trucks on their way to canneries.

Each of these communities got its modern-day start at the beginning of California's history as a U.S. state in the 1850s. All were agricultural towns providing food for the surrounding towns and beyond. The role of the Gold Rush in attracting initial settlement is also considerable. At different times and for different reasons each place became a locus for immigrant communities who participated in the predominant agriculture of that area. The Punjabi in Yuba City, Japanese in Florin, and an ethnically diverse set of immigrants in Thornton including Portuguese settlers came to California as laborers and took up jobs working in agricultural fields to feed California's rapidly growing population.

Unfortunately, fear of a growing permanent population of Chinese and other Asian groups caused the passage of exclusionary laws in the state. The California Alien Land Act of 1913 prevented Asian immigrants from becoming citizens and without citizenship they could not own land. East Indians were not included in the exclusionary practice until the *1923 U.S. v. Thind* Supreme Court decision, which ruled "Hindus were declared ineligible for citizenship because they were not 'free white persons'."[4] The Immigration Act of 1917 stopped all Asian immigration except from Japan. Many Punjabi men circumvented the land ownership law by marrying women from Mexico while the Japanese families purchased land in the name of their eldest American-born child. Despite this discrimination, all three groups became successful in their agricultural pursuits, and left their mark on the communities in which they lived and farmed.

Yuba City

Yuba City (population 65,569) is approximately 40 miles north of Sacramento and the county seat of Sutter County. The city was established in 1849 as a distribution center to serve the Gold Rush prospectors. Located along the Feather River and between San Francisco and the Gold Country, Yuba City, and its neighbor Marysville to the east, were important trade centers during this time. Today, the primary employers in the area are the healthcare and retail industries; agriculture also plays an important role.[5]

In the early 1900s, many immigrants spurred by economic, social, and political uncertainties at home arrived in the Yuba City area from the Punjab Province of India. The majority were Sikhs who worked as agricultural laborers. They had the intention of earning money and returning to India or bringing their families to join them. However, the 1917 Immigration Act prevented the immigration of South Asians, so the family members left in India could not join those already in the U.S.[6]

Additionally, in 1923, the application of California's Alien Land Law to the South Asian population prevented them from owning or leasing agricultural land. It was during this time and into the 1930s that many Punjabi men stopped waiting to be reunited with Punjabi brides and began marrying Mexican women. The Mexican women were granted U.S. citizenship and land was put into their names or the names of their children.[7]

The passage of the Luce-Celler Bill in 1946 gave those of Asian Indian descent the right to become citizens and led to a surge of immigration from the Punjab region. The passage of the 1965 Immigration Act, which supported the reunification of families, further fueled the growth. Between 1947 and 1985, the Asian Indian population in the U.S. increased more than thirtyfold.[8]

With the increase in new Punjabi immigrants, including traditional brides, Sikhs already living in the U.S. began to return to more traditional practices such as orthodox religion and arranged marriages. Additionally, they were adept at using their family networks for economic and corporate goals. Approximately 4,000 Asian Indians lived in Sutter and Yuba Counties in 1975.[9] The Sikh farmers in the area gained prominence in landholdings and in establishing an important peach industry, as well as other crops such as plums, pears, almonds, and walnuts.

Yuba City features its diverse population on its website, proclaiming, "The very diverse population of Yuba City is a source of pride for its citizens." Approximately 28 percent of the population is Hispanic, 6 percent multirace, 17 percent Asian, and 47 percent white.[10] The prominence of the Punjabi population in the Yuba City area is evident in local festivals and businesses. The Punjabi population in the Yuba–Sutter area has grown to be one of the largest in the United States and one of the largest Sikh populations outside of India. Each year on the first Sunday of November, thousands of Sikhs from throughout the world attend the Sikh parade in Yuba City.

Yuba City field
observation map.
Image by Jennifer L. McHenry.

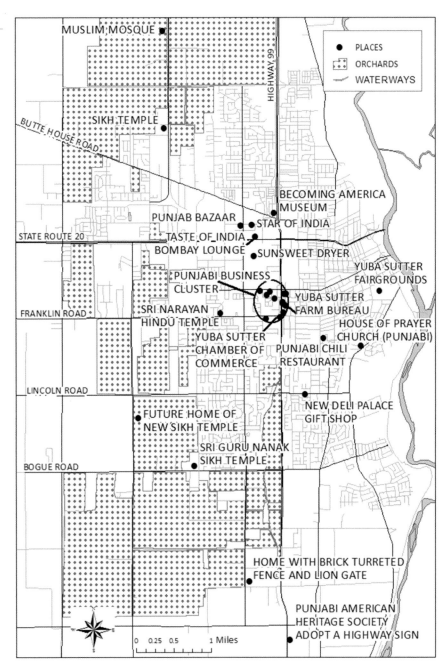

Yuba City

Observations and Discussion

When approaching Yuba City from the south, the first hint of the Punjabi presence is an "Adopt a Highway" sign on the outskirts that credits a Punjabi organization. An unobservant motorist could easily miss this sign and, in turn, miss one of the few obvious indications along the main thoroughfare of the Asian Indian influence in the community. Upon closer inspection, however, some notable visual impacts on the landscape can be found.

The long-standing and vital impact of this populace on the agricultural aspects of this community is most notable and noticeable. An introductory stop at the local Chamber of Commerce immediately confirmed this; after describing that we were working on a research project examining the cultural influences on California agricultural communities, we were told we should talk to someone at the Farm Bureau about the role of the Punjabi because they are "big" in the area and active in the Farm Bureau. While traversing the gridded rural roads, the fruit tree orchards that the Punjabi farmers established and still operate are prevalent.

Homes are often located adjacent to the road and, in many instances, the properties are framed by ornate fencing and gates and demarcated by cypress trees. Our presumption, which was later confirmed by interviews, was that Punjabi families owned these properties.[11] We learned that the use of lions in ornamentation is popular since the Punjabi word for lion is Singh. Singh is the name that the religious founder gave to all Sikh men in 1699 and is still commonly used as a middle name.[12]

Situated among the farms and homes, we also discovered three Sikh temples: one a well-established *gurdwara*, another smaller temple, and the third under development.[13] The first is located on a large property that is completely enclosed by a wall and fencing, but with large open gates. The facility houses community rooms as well as worship areas. The exterior includes a new, almost complete, rose garden labyrinth for strolling, and a shaded area where men gather for conversation. The newest temple is less obvious in that it is located in a renovated home. It was only after seeing a sign announcing this as the future home of the temple, and talking to a few gentlemen on site, that we understood the use of the property.

Along with the residential and religious indications of the Sikh population, we discovered a discrete shopping area just off the main highway consisting of several independent stores housing more traditional Indian products such as clothing, jewelry, and food. In addition to this cluster of shops, many other Asian Indian businesses are scattered throughout the town.

We saw little physical historical evidence of the Punjabi population during our landscape transect observations. There are no buildings dating to the early days of their arrival that tell the story of their early living conditions nor historical signs that mark important events, but there is significant indication of their current place in the community. The story told is one of strong and important roles for this cultural group. The city's economic development manager described the community as a mix and "just the way we are." Several public officials are of Punjabi descent including the current mayor who is believed to be the first elected Punjabi mayor in the U.S.

▲ Figure 3.3

Ornate fencing and gate (a family of lions is shown on the gate).
Photo by Jennifer L. McHenry.

▼ Figure 3.4

A well-established Sikh *gurdwara*.
Photo by Patsy Eubanks Owens.

▲ Figure 3.5

Punjabi American Festival booths.
Photo by Patsy Eubanks Owens.

Observations conducted at the annual Punjabi American Festival, however, indicated more of a cultural separation. Of the more than 10,000 attendees, all appeared to be of Asian Indian heritage except for the authors and a few political invitees. The event featured film screenings, political speeches, music, and dance exhibitions, along with booths filled with saris, henna tattoos, and Indian food. According to a statement made by one of the men during our earlier conversation at the temple, the Sikh parade that is held each fall is more traditional and includes ten days of free food and a parade, whereas the Punjabi American Festival is a "concert-like" event, and "you have to pay." The economic development manager indicated that the majority of the fall parade attendees are also Asian Indian although everyone is invited to attend.

Thornton

The tiny town of Thornton (population 1,131 in 2010) sits between modern-day Interstate 5 and the Mokelumne River in San Joaquin County.[14] It is situated on the northeastern edge of the Sacramento Delta, and just a few miles south of the confluence of the undammed Cosumnes River and the Mokelumne River, which flow from the Sierra Nevada to San Francisco Bay. Breezes from the Delta blow through the mature oaks, vineyards, orchards, dairies, and cattle ranches around Thornton, stirring the dense, quiet heat that marks this portion of the Central Valley in the summertime.

▲ Figure 3.6

Mature valley oaks shade grazing cattle just outside of Thornton.
Photo by Maggie La Rochelle.

Formerly named New Hope, the town of Thornton has its historical origins in the 1850s as part of the influx of settlers for the Gold Rush. Most people in the area at the time lived a few miles away in Mokelumne City at the convergence of the Cosumnes and Mokelumne rivers upstream. However, when a flood ruined most of Mokelumne City in 1862, survivors and residents packed up and moved to the small settlement of New Hope about three miles away, and more importantly on higher ground off-river.[15]

New Hope grew and was renamed Thornton in 1909 after Arthur Thornton, a local landowner who established a ranch in New Hope around 1855. To attract business to the city, Thornton allowed right-of-way to the Western Pacific railroad through his land, and advocated for right-of-way through the rest of the locale—the new station there was, in turn, named after him, and the town followed suit five years later.[16] Thornton's elementary school, however, still bears the name of New Hope Elementary, and a few feet down the street, New Hope Road runs east to west on the northern edge of town.

The river's natural meandering and seasonal winter flooding influence much of the town's history. Thornton and adjacent towns are surrounded by rich, loamy-soiled farmland as a function of this regular flooding activity, and large parcels were and are still used for producing fruit for canning and fresh sales, raising beef and dairy cattle, and, more frequently now, wine grapes.

Thornton's tiny size has led to relatively little extant cultural historical information until very recently. Charlotte Cameron's 2014 book *History of Thornton*, compiled from much of her own historical collection over the years as a long-time resident on the Cameron-Barber Ranch in Thornton, focuses predominantly on the lives of six early settlers and their families and the town's historic buildings and structures. According to Cameron, settlement in the 1850s first attracted an ethnically diverse group of immigrants from various European countries including Portugal, Italy, Switzerland, and the Netherlands.[17]

Indeed, in contrast to the exclusionary attitudes toward immigrants that were pervasive in many areas of California and the U.S. in the early 1900s, early maps, promotion materials, and conversation with local historians suggest that San Joaquin County planners and residents were more open to those who intended to settle and partake in the agricultural production of the region, regardless of ethnicity.[18] Local residents today express positive attitudes toward the cultural diversity of the town. According to the 2010 Census, approximately 68 percent of Thornton's residents today report being of Hispanic or Latino descent.

Thornton's landscape story takes not only the history of the farming, dairy, and cattle industries into account, but also the history of a diverse population of Chinese and European immigrants, and, more recently, Mexican and Filipino immigrants. In addition to its history of family ranches and farms, the town's physical markers acknowledge the diversity and integration that marks its history, linking the official story of the past to the small yet vibrant cultural life of the present.

Thornton field observation map.
Image by Jennifer L. McHenry.

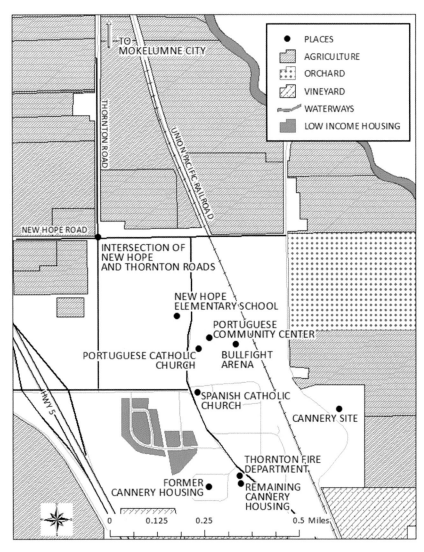

Thornton

Observations and Discussion

Thornton's largest and most notable physical attraction is the presence of a large, still operating bullfighting arena. The arena is managed by the Our Lady of Fatima Society, a community organization that also manages a Portuguese Event Hall and the Thornton Community Hall on the same property. Portuguese Halls—simply, community halls most often used by Portuguese American people—in fact pepper the towns of the Central Valley, acting as cultural landmarks and sites of activity.

FRANK GARCIA & SONS DAIRY
209-685-8540
23867 ROAD 60
TULARE, CA 93274

Cabral Farms
CUSTOM FARMING
RIPPING · DISCING
PHONE
209-744-1805
PAGER
209-775-9850
10035 PRINGLE AVE. GALT CA 95632

JOHN TOLEDO & SON
DAIRY
In Memory of John Toledo

FRANK PIMENTE
DAIRY

▲ Figure 3.8

Advertisements of family ranches and dairies line the uppermost bleachers of Thornton's bullfighting arena.
Photo by Patsy Eubanks Owens.

Perhaps the biggest community event in the region, and certainly in Thornton, is an annual Portuguese Our Lady of Fatima Celebration—residents call it "The Festa"—held over several days in October, which includes parades with local livestock, bullfights, dancing, a free meal for attendees, and the naming of a young lady as Queen. The Festa is attended by thousands of people—more than the town's permanent population.

However, little connection can be found between Thornton's history of immigration and settlement and the strong role of the Portuguese American community in current local culture. Walking around, one notes the prominence of the arena, Events Hall, and church in the town, yet further research yields that most residents are from culturally diverse backgrounds, and that Thornton's Portuguese American population is very small as compared with surrounding larger towns Galt and Lodi. It remains a mystery, or for more research by local planners and historians, as to why Thornton was chosen as the site for the arena.

Upon further research, the stories of many people in Thornton appear to be linked strongly to the cannery that operated from 1928 to 2000, and less to the dairy and cattle industry as a main source of local vocation. "Almost everybody in Thornton can say they worked there at one time or another," Cameron shared.[19] The cannery's most recent owner, Tri-Valley Growers, Inc. filed for bankruptcy in 2000. In 2006, the site and some of the old cannery buildings were repurposed as Plant #235 of Universal Forest Products, Inc. (UFP).

However, UFP employees and residents of Thornton share that most employees at UFP live in surrounding areas and not in Thornton itself, and geographically there is little porousness between the town and cannery site, the latter being located across the railroad tracks from the rest of local development. (See Figure 3.7). A northern entrance to the site has additionally been filled and blocked with a tall concrete wall.

The effect is one of separation of the town from the site of its historic employer, though the plant is adjacent to the town and still holds a number of historic buildings. No commemorative content to mark the cannery's long presence and history in Thornton is present today. Further, Thornton's downtown currently hosts only a few remaining operating businesses after what residents describe as a vibrant, healthy string of hotels, restaurants, and shops in the 1940s and 1950s closed down slowly over time.

Significantly, the largest residential tracts in Thornton today are adjoining county-run farmworker and Section 8 housing complexes. This housing for agricultural workers and their families is an important historic link; it replaced an original complex of cannery-owned farmworker housing. This original cannery housing consisted of small metal, one-room structures, four of which are still standing, rusted, and overgrown in the oak woods behind the current fire department. These little shacks still hold a considerable level of popularity and often attract visitors, as they and the schoolhouse in which the fire department is located are both purported to be haunted.

▼ Figure 3.9

Original cannery-owned farmworker housing.
Photo by Maggie La Rochelle.

Cameron states that many working-class families got their start in this company housing, eventually saving enough money to buy land and build homes of their own. The history of this housing, its links to the main employer of the area for the better part of a century, and its links to a story of the American Dream—in which people work the land, advance themselves, and eventually put down physical and cultural roots on their own plots of land—appear to be focal points of Thornton's landscape story.

Past and current farmworker housing in Thornton appears to be a very important symbol of the town's *raison d'être*. Meanwhile, the bullfighting arena, New Hope school, library, and local churches symbolize other pieces of its community character with community and monetary investment. Though a broad sewerage infrastructure and poor water quality present significant barriers to redevelopment, Thornton certainly still holds numerous sites of community activity, broad-based resident pride, proximity to a large employer with which the town could be reconnected, and signs of important regional and cultural history still visible in local sites and structures.

Florin

Florin, which began as an agricultural community early in California's history, sits just over five miles southeast of downtown Sacramento. The area took off

◀ Figure 3.10

Japanese American children in Florin just before the internment. *Photo by Dorothea Lange; WRA Courtesy of The Bancroft Library, University of California Berkeley, WRA no. C-575.*

Florin field observation map.
Image by Jennifer L. McHenry.

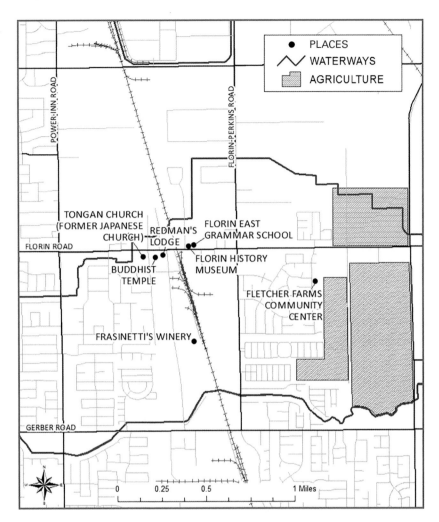

Florin

agriculturally in the 1850s when James Rutter developed the "Florin flame" Tokay grape. With good soil and a very high water table, agriculture thrived in the area, and the landscape developed into an expanse of windmills, fields, and vineyards. Eventually, a railroad stop was placed in the growing town and grapes and strawberries were shipped to cities around the nation.

Originally, the farmers were all of European descent and hired workers were mainly Chinese laborers. However, beginning in the 1890s, Japanese migrant workers began to participate in agricultural labor and became successful at their work.[20] The Japanese Americans stayed despite the challenges to citizenship and land ownership, and, by the 1920s and 1930s, they had become a major part of the community in Florin, and were well known as successful grape and strawberry farmers.[21]

Their success and thriving community came to an abrupt end with the bombing of Pearl Harbor in 1941. As the strawberries began to ripen in the spring of 1943, the town was divided into four quarters based on the railroad and Florin Road, and the Japanese Americans in each quarter were shipped out to a different internment camp.

When the entire Japanese population was removed from Florin and interned in camps across the west, the booming strawberry and grape businesses shifted to new places. Most of the interned Japanese farmers returned to ruined farms with no hope of the success they had previously experienced.[22] Three families found a generous man, Mr. Robert Fletcher, to run their farms before leaving. His help allowed them to maintain successful farms, and return to money in their accounts. Fletcher gave up his job as an agricultural inspector to manage these farms, and after the war continued farming on land he purchased nearby.[23] The town of Florin never regained its agricultural strength and was soon a part of Sacramento County's unincorporated area, surrounded by suburban and industrial developments.

Observations and Discussion

Florin today is a complicated patchwork of industrial, suburban, rural, and commercial land uses with a core of rundown historic buildings where the town once thrived. Florin Road cuts through the middle, with four lanes of traffic and no sidewalks, encouraging drivers to speed past without even realizing they are driving through a historic town. The dominant buildings are a dilapidated two-story lodge bearing the initials I.O.R.M. for the Improved Order of Red Men and an old 1920s building which houses a tractor parts store. The railway station no longer exists, and there is no indication within the landscape that it ever existed.

East of the railroad tracks on the north side of Florin stands a cluster of well-maintained historic buildings painted grey. The Florin Historical Society and their museum occupy one and the other is a building whose sign indicates it was once the Florin East Grammar School, a formerly segregated school for Japanese children. The latter now functions as a therapeutic recreation center. Behind these buildings sits the "Olde Florintown Park." The museum's plaque briefly recounts Florin's history including James Rutter and his grapes, the dominance of strawberries, and the little known Frasinetti's Winery that still operates less than a half-mile away. No suggestion of a Japanese population is alluded to in any of this documentation. In the center of the old town, surrounded by chain-link fence and flanked by two historic Protestant church buildings, sits the campus of a Buddhist temple with a turn-of-the-century building facing Florin Road and two newer buildings behind it.

The story of Robert Fletcher and his generosity to the Japanese families he aided is memorialized in nearby suburbs that include a street and community center named after the Fletcher family. The rapid suburbanization of the area in the decades following the war led to a neglect of Florin in general. As the suburbs have filtered down to lower-income families, the population surrounding the old town has shifted from mostly white to a mix of Latino, African American, and Asian as well as white residents.

▲ Figure 3.12

The original Buddhist temple of Florin now houses the Kendo Dojo while a newer structure nearby houses the congregation and its activities.

Photo by Jennifer L. McHenry.

Census data does not show any significant population of Japanese Americans left in Florin.[24] Unfortunately their story and past presence is not only neglected, but also perhaps hidden in the renovation of the Japanese children's school and the neglect of what was the Japanese Methodist church. Whether due to an inability to acknowledge this painful story in Florin or a general neglect of the history in policy and design decisions, the story of this landscape is mostly hidden.

Recently, the town has been given special planning status as a historic preservation district, and efforts have been underway to change the image of the town from a blink along the commuter's path to a destination worth visiting. In this effort, windmills have been placed at either end of the town, Olde Florintown Park was built, and the county is currently making road improvements and adding sidewalks. However, in all of these efforts, hardly a nod has been made to the former Japanese Americans who played such a vital role in the success of Florin. While the Buddhist temple remains a landmark of the small town, little else remains of the Japanese presence.

If the story of the Japanese Americans is avoided, the Florin landscape tells a half-story. The Japanese are yet again excluded, and their contributions are hidden to those in the surrounding diverse communities and those who might decide to visit this future destination.

▲ Figure 3.13 (a) and (b) ◀

Fletcher Farm Community Center and street sign.
Photos by Jennifer L. McHenry.

Conclusion

While discovering and reading landscape stories provides one way to unearth histories of cultural diversity in everyday physical environments, translating these stories into local planning and design decisions that take such diversity into account presents a much bigger challenge. There is always the risk, especially given a history of social exclusion, that attempting to honor or make visible diverse cultural histories—for example, by erecting memorials or plaques, or even an entire site as in Florin—without a well-developed understanding of local histories and the involvement of all stakeholders in the planning process might end up tokenizing or reifying social exclusions rather than symbolizing inclusion in an authentic, publicly supported way through design.

Common site analysis methodologies used by designers and planners are generally insufficient for getting to the deeper stories that help us understand how places and people work together. Without a critical methodology for reading these spaces, we run the risk of overlooking the layered, multicultural nature of the everyday landscape. The graphic in Figure 3.14 compares a typical methodology that skims the surface of a community to a critical cultural landscape analysis that digs deeper into the multilayered and often hidden stories.

Designers and planners have the power to choose how deeply they engage in critical observation. One might choose to gloss over portions of local history due to time constraints or political aversion, but we argue that this critical work is both necessary and beneficial to community health and design in the long term. The vitality of a community exists in the stories of what has happened and happens there. For full vitality and lasting projects, we advocate for a full landscape story.

Finally, cultural groups in any place are seldom monolithic. This is especially true over time. Present-day planning that honors and incorporates historic landscape stories into design projects requires committed processes of inclusive discourse among many different residents. A dedicated political process is necessary in order to come to thoughtful agreement on how to honor and incorporate various histories of place—especially if those histories are painful or unjust—and to build support for new projects. Knowing and understanding

▼ Figure 3.14

A critical cultural landscape analysis.
Diagram by Patsy Eubanks Owens.

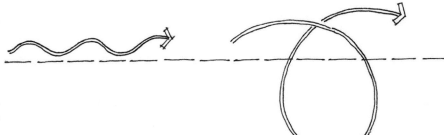

Visible landscape elements – physical evidence

Less visible elements – cultural influences

TYPICAL PHYSICAL ANALYSIS   CRITICAL CULTURAL ANALYSIS

cultural histories of places can be a starting point for local residents and planners to engage in meaningful processes of design for local, urban, and regional planning.

Discussion Questions and Explorations

Descriptive

1. Describe the methods that were used to understand or interpret these landscapes. For example, what were the types of clues that informed our understanding of the cultural influences in these communities?
2. Describe the unique qualities of the physical environments that are a result of the ethnic groups that live/lived in these communities.

Analytical

1. Describe an outdoor space in each of these three communities. Discuss why they are different from one another and why their physical characteristics are a result of cultural influences.
2. Think about the community where you grew up. Describe and discuss any evidence of cultural influence on the physical environment in that community.

Speculative

1. Imagine you are designing an urban plaza for one of the communities discussed in this case study. Describe how you would learn about the cultural history of the community and how this would inform your design.
2. Design an exercise for a beginning landscape architecture or urban design course that would teach students how to "read" a landscape. What is some of the community-based evidence that you would ask them to obtain? How would you ask them to share this information?

Notes

1   Richard H. Schein, "A Methodological Framework for Interpreting Ordinary Landscapes: Lexington, Courthouse Square," *Geographical Review* 99, no. 3 (2009): 377–402; Pierce Lewis, "The Monument and the Bungalow," *Geographical Review* 88, no. 4 (1998): 507–527.
2   Karl Raitz, "Field Observation, Archives, and Explanation," *Geographical Review* 91, no. 1–2 (2001): 121–131.
3   Grady Clay, *Close-Up: How to Read the American City* (Chicago: University of Chicago Press, 1980).

4   Bruce La Brack, *The Sikhs of Northern California: 1904–1975* (New York: AMS Press, 1988), 70.

5   "Yuba City at a Glance," accessed April 24, 2013, www.yubacity.net/community/yuba-city-at-a-glance.html.

6   La Brack, *The Sikhs of Northern California*, 55.

7   In actuality, the Cable Act of 1922 took away the woman's citizenship when she married an ineligible alien; however, records of property ownership indicate that this law was either unknown or overlooked in this region; Karen Leonard, "Punjabi Farmers and California's Alien Land Law," *Agricultural History* 59, no. 4 (1985): 549–562, accessed April 22, 2014, www.jstor.org/stable/3743757.

8   Margaret Gibson, "Punjabi Orchard Farmers: An Immigrant Enclave in Rural California," *International Migration Review* 22, no. 1 (1988): 28–50, accessed April 22, 2014, www.jstor.org/stable/2546395.

9   La Brack, *The Sikhs of Northern California*, 272–285.

10 U.S. Census Bureau, "2010 Census Data," accessed March 19, 2015, www.census.gov/2010census/.

11 Darin Gale, Yuba City, Economic Development Manager, interview by P.E. Owens, Yuba City California, September 25, 2014.

12 Anonymous, interview by P.E. Owens, Yuba City, California, October 3, 2014.

13 The *gurdwara* serves as a social institution as well as a religious center. La Brack, *The Sikhs of Northern California*, 126–136.

14 U.S. Census.

15 Charlotte Cameron, *History of Thornton* (Galt, CA: Galt Area Historical Society, 2014).

16 Erwin G. Gudde, *California Place Names: The Origin and Etymology of Current Geographical Names* (Berkeley: University of California Press, 1949); "Thornton, California," Galt Area Historical Society. Last modified March 17, 2006, www.galthistory.org/history/thornton/.

17 Charlotte Cameron, Galt Area Historical Society, interview by Maggie La Rochelle, Thornton, California, July 16, 2014.

18 The opening lines of an early San Joaquin Chamber of Commerce Agricultural Map (c.1915) begin: "San Joaquin County's invitation is not limited to the homeseeker, the man who will abide, welcome as he is," before going on to cite the region's other tourist attractions—a surprisingly accepting message for the time. The map language also boasts, "Perhaps the most pleasing and significant feature of the region is the constant recurrence of prosperous and well-ordered homes in their fresh garden settings." Map Library, University of California, Davis.

19 Cameron, interview.

20 Harry A. Millis, "Japanese Farming: Some Community Observations," in *The Japanese Problem in the United States* (New York: Macmillan Company, 1915), 152–182.

21 Mary Tsukamoto and Elizabeth Pinkerton, *We the People; A Story of Internment in America* (Elk Grove, CA: Laguna Publishers, 1988), 51–54.

22 Joanne Iritani, "Oral History Interview with Mary Tsuruko Tsukamoto," Florin Japanese American Citizens League and Oral History Program (Sacramento: California State University, 1996), 2–33.

23 Iritani, "Oral History Interview," 2–33.

24 U.S. Census.

Editors' Introduction to Chapter 4

Imitating historical architectural styles is no shortcut to understanding the social and political contexts of a particular culture. All of this imagery must be understood within the historical context of its making. A simple example of this can be found in the importance that monumental gateways have accrued in Chinatowns around the world. While these gates have become a positive aesthetic marker of cultural difference in metropolitan areas from New York City to San Francisco and Montreal to Melbourne, they were derided as symbols of alien cultures as late as the nineteenth century. It was only with the rise of multiculturalism and global tourism that they became desirable symbols of cultural diversity. As time progressed, local tourism played a major role in the historical repetition of this type of imagery; Chinese businessmen learned to produce the types of environments that their customers were willing to associate with the past. The presence of these architectural details now expresses the desire of local customers to enjoy Chinese culture more than it exemplifies an authentic expression of Chinese life.

The following case study examines the ways that material forms come to be associated with the values and cultural patterns of racial and ethnic groups. Peter Wong analyzes the historical origins and development of *lilong* (community lane) housing in nineteenth- and twentieth-century China, which was often identified by its *shikumen* (stone gate) architectural detailing. By the 1850s, European businessmen successfully exported *lilong* prototypes to Shanghai to accommodate the white ethnic immigrants who moved overseas to conduct business. Over time, however, these settlements came to be occupied by rural Chinese workers moving to the city. While these housing developments were based on European prototypes, the organization of these spaces emulated prominent features of rural Chinese dwellings. In the long run, the foreign origins of *lilong* housing did not present insurmountable challenges to local assimilation.

The local acceptance of *lilong* housing forms presents us with a unique opportunity to reflect upon the social and cultural factors that contributed to the longevity of these spaces. What complementary relationships emerged between the physical infrastructures of these developments and the social processes that took place within them that contributed to their acceptance? Is it reasonable to suggest that local workers would have adopted any housing stock that was cheap and readily available, or did *lilong* housing offer special features that enabled them to accommodate modern life in China? In order to answer these questions, Wong moves beyond a simple stylistic accounting of *lilong* housing to investigate the social patterns that activated its interior spaces. He compels us to think of architecture as something that captures more than form and style, but constitutes a physical medium that provides the backdrop for social and cultural happenings to take shape.

A social conception of architecture compels us to associate the material aspects of vernacular forms with the cultural processes responsible for making them relevant in each time period. The historical development of *lilong* housing dramatically illustrates the active and dynamic processes that are required to form long-lasting associations between local communities and physical structures. As you read the following case study, compare and contrast the ways that European settlers and local Chinese families adapted themselves to *lilong* housing.

Chapter 4

Chinese Puzzle

Shifting Spatial and Social Patterns in Shanghai *Shikumen* Architecture

Peter Wong

Sorting Pieces

Urbanism in modern Shanghai resembles many expanding Eastern and Western cities in the first decade of the new millennium. Tall buildings pierce the ground, squeezing sidewalk space between bright storefront displays and noisy street edges. Signage and brands compete for pedestrian eye-time accompanied by smells of traditional soup dumplings or Kentucky Fried Chicken. Yet if one slows to observe the gaps between buildings, evidence can be found of an older city hidden inside the block. Small gatehouses—thresholds between the city streets and these interior realms—are managed by guards who monitor flows of pedestrians entering narrow lanes that connect to a network of low-scale residences.

▶ Figure 4.1

Huai Hai Village, Shanghai, 1924.
Photomosaic by Peter Wong.

Also known as *longtang* or *lilong* (translated as "community lanes"), these pedestrian thoroughfares were important in forming a residential architecture unique to Shanghai from the 1850s to the 1940s. Like a wood puzzle, the arrangement of lanes, housing, and small courtyards created interlocking patterns that governed community life in many neighborhoods in the city. The architecture from this urban layout became synonymous with the *lilong* name, but was frequently referred to as *shikumen* architecture, because of the stone walls and gates that became the notable features of the residences that bordered these lanes.[1]

The history of *lilong* residential architecture is rich and well documented. This chapter traces how that architecture became an important record of cultural and community change from the mid-nineteenth to the mid-twentieth centuries as Shanghai underwent various social, economic, and political changes. *Lilong* and *shikumen* architectures were originally Western forms of worker housing commonly found in the industrialized cities of Britain, Europe, and America in the 1850s. Their arrival in Shanghai helped solidify a Western presence with the promise of lucrative real estate ventures and the establishment of off-shore business colonies that would take advantage of Asian markets, labor, and goods. They became homes for both foreign as well as Shanghainese residents, and therefore present a clear example of how design is continuously challenged (and made) by diverse interests, competing influences, and cross-cultural inhabitants. *Shikumen* residential architecture in Shanghai helped to create a unique experience of urban life that could not be found elsewhere.

Brief Account of the *Shikumen* House

The Shanghai *shikumen* house originated as a developer's model of housing under the British and French Concessions arising from a resolution of the First

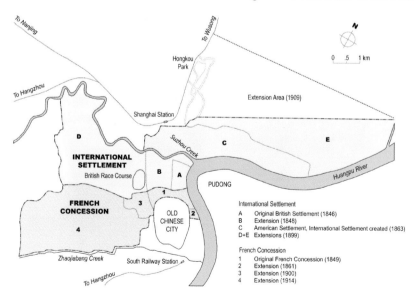

◀ Figure 4.2

Map of Shanghai foreign settlements from 1846 to 1914. *Drawing derived from a map by Lu Hanchao.*

▶ Figure 4.3

Typical Shanghai urban block
in the International Settlement.
The housing pattern depicts a
late-*shikumen* cluster of houses.
Drawing by Peter Wong.

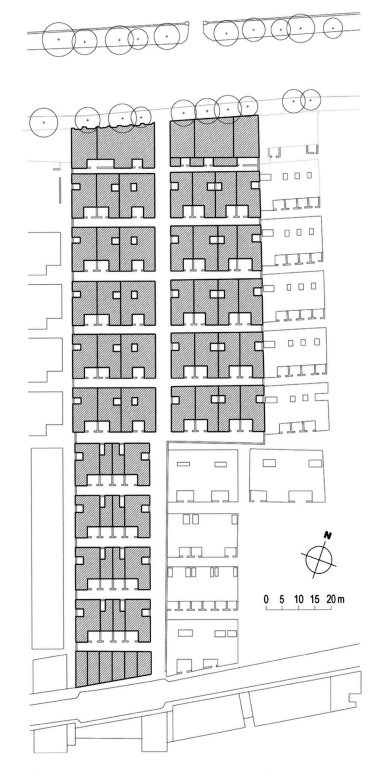

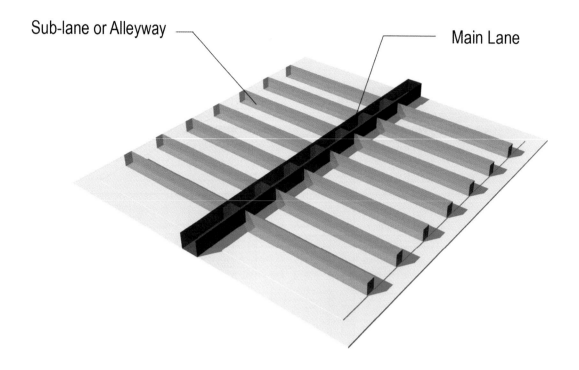

Sub-lane or Alleyway —   — Main Lane

Opium War. Under the 1842 Treaty of Nanking, foreign interests negotiated complete and long-term control of Shanghai districts for business purposes as well as for the building of housing for foreign nationals moving to the city.[2] At first, these blocks were developed for American, British, and French residents. It soon became clear, however, that foreigners alone could not fill the districts. This led to negotiations with local government to house Chinese migrants moving into the city from rural provinces to undertake factory work and commercial labor. *Lilong* developments were considered a valuable and sound investment for foreign investors as the population of Shanghai rose, and capital was to be had from the selling and renting of *lilong* villages.

The persistence of this architectural type provided an easy way of repeating sound labor practices, capitalizing on local building traditions, and creating a dense fabric of residences that could be marketed to both the Western population and a Chinese audience accustomed to living in housing that shared similarities with the water towns outside Shanghai.[3]

Early-*shikumen* (1879–1910) versions were constructed as five-bay (five-*jian*) or three-bay dwellings. The configurations of these early urban houses were very similar in morphology to the rural country houses of the Anhui Province in the region west of Shanghai. The orientation of living spaces was directed to the south while service spaces were situated to the north. Located between these houses were uncovered alleyways that accessed cooking and storage, often with second-story areas to house additional family members. Early versions of these multi-bay houses were constructed as post and beam wood structures in the tradition of rural village types built by local carpenters that provided a

▲ Figure 4.4

Block diagram showing primary lanes and sub-lanes/alleys.
Drawing by Peter Wong.

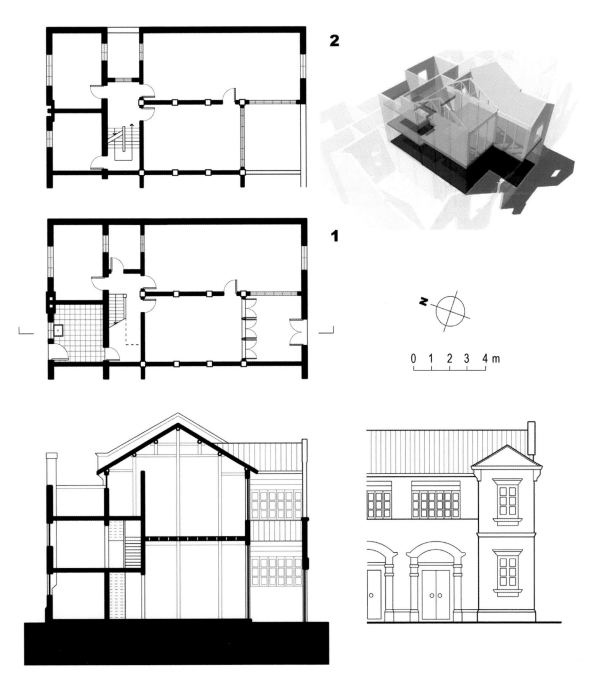

▲ Figure 4.5

Late-*shikumen* house: section,
front (stone gate) façade, plans,
and volume diagram. Note the
different heights of the southern
and northern rooms.
Drawing by Peter Wong.

ready source of labor. Masonry infill between these timbers and party walls provided lateral stability, and also kept sparks from skipping between adjacent dwellings in the event of a fire.

Late-*shikumen* (1910–1930) architecture was characterized by a two or one-and-a-half bay module to create an even denser grain of urban housing. During this time, we also see three-story units that increased the population density of the concession districts. The size of these houses would average between 1,800 and 2,500 square feet.

The *lilong* house (1920–1940) paralleled late-*shikumen* architecture, but was constructed mainly of masonry walls and concrete floors reflecting more modern building techniques. The masonry wall and stone gate of the courtyard were often replaced with a low garden wall or wrought iron fences allowing an unrestricted view of the lane. By 1930, *lilong* housing could be found in both attached and detached villa variations. Both foreign and Chinese developers sought the lucrative possibilities of this era of construction. Variations were rich, and the type was often repeated in both grandiose as well as humble versions according to the class and income of the homebuyer.

As Chinese families moved into these dwellings, it was common to rent north rooms in the home to students and artists. This was the first instance of the *shikumen* being occupied by more than one family. The kitchen was shared, and access to the house was altered to accommodate the coming and going of additional residents.

By the 1940s, *lilong* housing and its neighborhoods made up more than 50 percent of the urban fabric in Shanghai. Though the urban type remained

▼ Figure 4.6

Diagrammatic model of a late-*shikumen* house showing the varied floor heights and complexity of space.
Model and photograph by Peter Wong.

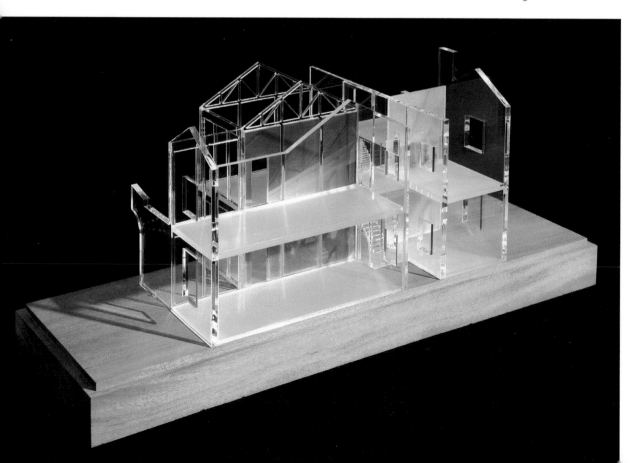

resistant and strong, the 1949 Communist Revolution brought dramatic changes as the government began to assign families to existing housing. It was not uncommon for a single house to accommodate as many as five or six families, each living in one room, with as many as 20 people per house. These modifications significantly changed the interiors of the *lilong* as well as the social and living patterns in the lanes themselves.

East + West

The typological architecture of worker housing from a dense urban British and European model served as the type-form for most *lilong* developments. The overall layout placed public interior spaces to the south and service parts of the program to the north. This arrangement of south to north distribution of the housing elements provided the fundamental arrangement that served as the basic patterning of the lane, sub-lanes, and ultimately the layout of the block. Hence, most of the major streets running east–west in the city served as the entrance points in the urban fabric.

Exterior courtyards and light wells for appropriate light and ventilation were a main spatial feature of these houses. British versions of the type often offered exterior spaces, in particular, the courtyard, which allowed families to plant vegetable gardens. When settling the North American South, for example, the British general and planner James Oglethorpe drew up a plan for Savannah, Georgia, that featured houses with adjacent gardens in a military-style camp arranged around a central square. This open space not only reinforced the idea of self-reliance, but also reflected a layout that could be easily defended.[4]

The provision of an exterior yard was also sympathetic to the patterns of life found in the traditional Chinese house. Though the courtyard in *shikumen* architecture was too small for agricultural purposes, it did serve to provide essential domestic needs such as clothes washing and drying, meal preparation, and other daily uses. These similarities in the spatial planning and arrangement of the house helped anchor both Asian and Western needs, leading to the durability of the *shikumen* type.

Resistant to the influence of architectural pattern books, the *shikumen* represents a more natural development of architecture, space, and culture. On the one hand, it offered comfortable yet familiar spaces for foreigners. A clear rendition of public parlor and private living quarters was customary for Westerners. The separation of family and daily rituals was comparable to European dwelling standards. Kitchen and private services were allocated to a subservient position in the house, and most hygienic and personal needs could be hidden from general family activities. On the other hand, this dense arrangement also suited traditional Chinese, who were familiar with perimeter-wall architecture that protected the patriarchal organization of the interior spaces.

Artisan practices also contributed to the confluence of the type. Design features of the interior were performed by local tradespeople. Details and ways of construction reflected a knowledge of Chinese construction in early-*shikumen*

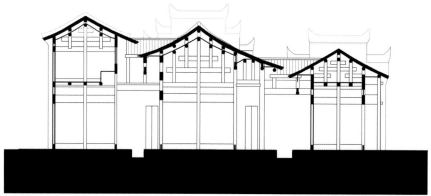

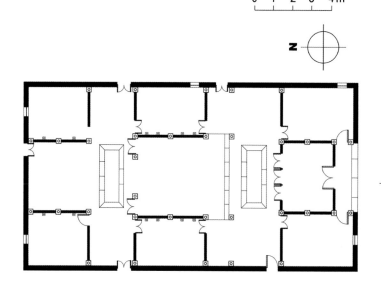

Plan and section of an Anhui Province rural house depicting masonry perimeter walls and two courtyards of increasing privacy (from south to north). The photograph shows the first courtyard in context.
Drawing and photomosaic by Peter Wong.

0 1 2 3 4 m

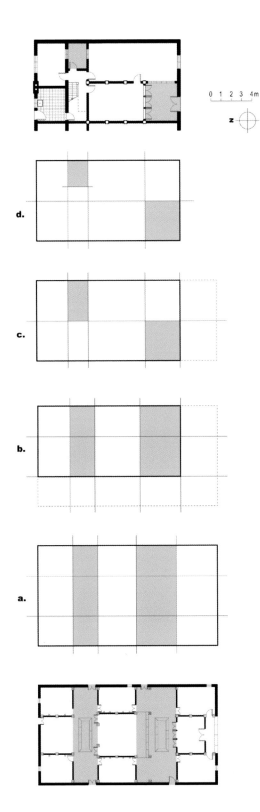

houses. Living spaces for entertaining and social functions were often outfitted with the most fashionable Western finishes. At the same time, the remainder of the house's fittings and equipment were given over to tradespeople, furniture craftsmen, cabinet makers, and finishers that spoke of a local character. For example, one might find modern wallpaper in the guest parlor and other formal areas of the house while the kitchens, stair halls, and service rooms had traditional Chinese joinery and other artisan details.

Stone construction (stone gates in particular) encouraged the use of local building materials and labor. At the same time, the durability of these materials was also part of the defensive requirements of the house during a time when the Chinese still feared civil unrest from aggressors.[5] The stark opacity of brick party walls between houses added further defense from fire threat, and, at the same time, restricted direct interaction between side-by-side neighbors.

A Two-Sided Puzzle

The social life of *shikumen* and *lilong* housing presents a special circumstance different than most urban settlements. Due to their small dimensions, the lanes encourage public interaction between residents in these neighborhoods. Often no wider than 15 to 20 feet, interior block lanes are designed for pedestrians rather than vehicles. Lane housing also functions as a place for walking, sitting, and play. In many instances, there are small stands set up to sell food and other items as well as haircuts and various services. The alleys branching off the main lane become even more intimate, with residents cooking, washing clothes, or talking with their neighbors. But it is the structures of the alleys themselves that reveal the secret of the rich social conditions inherent in all *lilong* settlements.

Unlike the Western arrangement of streets, which present their public faces to one another in a double-loaded fashion, *lilong* houses are oriented along a

◀ Figure 4.8

Diagram showing the transformational relationship between the courtyard space and morphology of the *shikumen* house (top) and the Anhui rural house.
Drawing by Peter Wong.

North Facing Service Wall

South Facing Public Stone Gate Facade

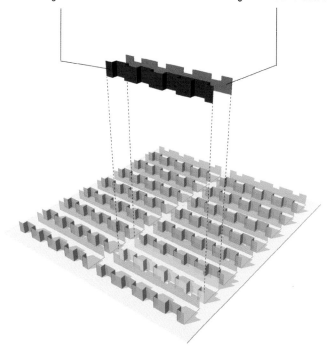

◀ Figure 4.9

Diagram of the difference between the sub-lane façades. The south-facing stone gate façade faces the neighbor's north kitchen façade (and vice versa) allowing for unique and sometimes contrasting social interaction.
Drawing and photographs by Peter Wong.

directional grain where the most public parts of the house almost always face south. This orientation to the alley has its roots in Feng Shui planning, which echoes ancient Chinese philosophy, where the relative position to sun, water, mountains, and wind are an important factor in the siting of the architecture, town, and landscape.[6]

Lilong neighborhoods take advantage of this granular orientation, since the front courtyard of any one house faces the rear kitchen and service façade of another across the alley. Someone leaving the formal side of a dwelling always has the opportunity of witnessing the backside of the house opposite. In turn, the owners of this house, if arriving or leaving via their kitchen, are in view of the formal side of the residence behind. This unique social opportunity can allow a myriad of different scenarios. A person returning from work in the afternoon through her front door may run across a neighbor washing vegetables in the alley as dinner is prepared. Children playing cards or Chinese chess might be

▶ Figure 4.10

Comparison of the *shikumen* and the Charleston "single house." Shaded area depicts the contrast in the use and orientation of open space (courtyards and gardens) of the two house types.
Drawings by Peter Wong.

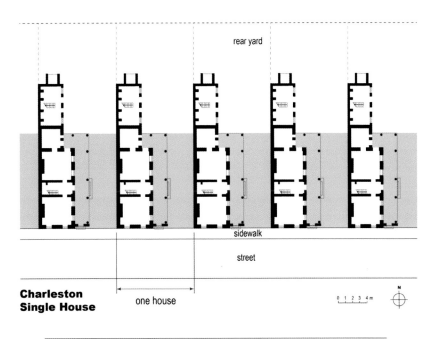

Charleston Single House

one house

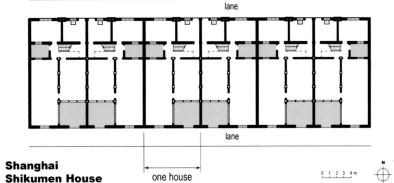

Shanghai Shikumen House

one house

sitting in the alley as the mail carrier arrives with packages. Or freshly washed clothes could be dripping from the rear of a house as a grandmother lounges in the sun shining through the open door of her stone gate courtyard.

One of the housing types that offers suggestive comparisons to the *shikumen* would be the "single-house" form built in Charleston, South Carolina, from 1780 to 1820. In this urban example, houses are lined on one side by a two- or three-story veranda or porch (more typically known as a "piazza"). This porch generally faces the south to catch light and breeze, and is placed adjacent to a small garden. The opposite side of the house sits directly on the property line in such a way that a rhythm of the garden, porch, and body of the house repeats itself as you move down the block. The public character of the porch and garden are oriented against the body of the house on the next lot in such a way that public and private faces must interact with (or screen off) neighbors.

This A:B:C rhythm (garden:porch:house) can be easily seen as one faces the row of houses from the street. One enters the end of the porch, moves to its center, and then enters the house proper at 90 degrees to the street.[7]

The comparison between these two examples illustrates how the shape and form of architecture can guide different social relationships. The Charleston house encourages social manners between neighbors along shared property lines across a garden space. In contrast, the Shanghai house establishes social interaction at the front and back, with neighbors presenting themselves at the stone gate and kitchen door. In both cases, architecture is the stage for rich social exchange.

In Shanghai, these social opportunities are reinforced when the formal meets the informal, public overlaps with private, and sunlight illuminates the shadows. *Lilong* villages, therefore, promoted human interaction as a direct response to neighbors. The social scenarios in the lanes were often positive, but living in these dense quarters could also create conflicts. The morphology and layout of these dwellings presented a rich condition for a particular type of social life that is often lost in contemporary high-rise architecture.

Shikumen Culture

To further understand the cultural space of the *shikumen*, we can turn to the vivid scenes created by Chinese artists, writers, and filmmakers. Some of the first pictures of *shikumen* life were described by Chinese *literati* and dissidents in the 1920s and 1930s who often rented rooms above kitchen spaces in *shikumen* houses. These were the least expensive rooms to rent, harsh in the summer due to the excessive heat from the kitchen below, and chilly in the winter due to the lack of direct sunlight and the cold north wind. These spaces, known as *tingzijian* (small room, cabinet, or cubicle), were frequently inhabited by famous Chinese authors such as Lu Xun and others. Some historians go so far as to claim these rooms as "think tanks" (or political hideouts) for those eager to launch the political interests of the Chinese Communist Party of the 1940s.

Leased spaces, like the *tingzijian*, began a trend that saw most *shikumen* houses change from single-family residences into multi-family structures that housed several Chinese families. Floors or rooms were taken over by entire families as the new Communist leaders attempted to provide housing for new residents to the city. Additional rooms were created by adding floors between the original ones. The south-facing courtyard was enclosed to allow for additional living space. The kitchen and stair became the new foyer and public hall.

The modern fiction writer, Xiaolong Qiu, describes this "flip-flopped" arrangement in his detective novel *When Red is Black*. The story features a Shanghai police inspector who is investigating a murder that takes place in a *tingzijian* room. Qiu, through the eyes of his protagonist, describes a *shikumen* that is occupied by several families, highlighting the public nature of the house's stair:

> In a shikumen house, any usable space was precious. Since no single family could claim the space under the staircase, it became an additional

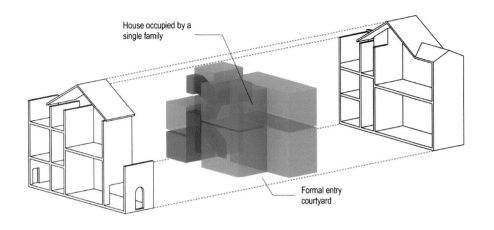

House occupied by a
single family

Formal entry
courtyard

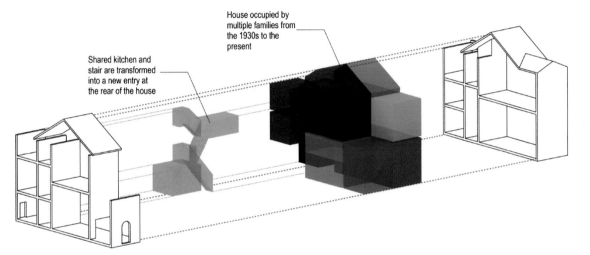

House occupied by
multiple families from
the 1930s to the
present

Shared kitchen and
stair are transformed
into a new entry at
the rear of the house

▲ Figure 4.11

Subdivision of a single *shikumen* house to accommodate more than one family, beginning in the 1930s. The top diagram represents single-family ownership while the lower diagram (multi-colored) depicts the shared use of the kitchen and stair elements as well as the partitioning of the house into separate flats. Often, new rooms were created in the south-facing rooms by inserting additional floors.

Drawings by Peter Wong.

common storage area for all sorts of hardly usable stuff which, in its owner's imagination, still had some potential value—like a broken bike of the Lis, a three-legged rattan chair of the Zhangs, a trunk of coal of the Huangs.[8]

This description accurately portrays how the social arrangement of the typical *shikumen* house was inverted in the 1940s and onward. As more families were crowded into these houses, the northern service side was transformed into the day-to-day entry while the grand stone gate façade became less frequently used. This change also reversed the activities and importance of the lanes as kitchens became the front door of the house and the stair a public meeting place that ascended through the interior to reach individual families.

Life of the Stair

The stair is a wood puzzle at the center of the *shikumen* architectural experience. In all its historical iterations, the *shikumen* contains a tangle of risers, landings, handrails, swinging doors, and screens. This knot-like interior space is a vertical vortex of moving bodies, ascending and descending, going about daily activities, presented in a performance of movement that the static condition of the architecture alone lacks.

The stair is perhaps the most significant element in the *shikumen*, serving as a measure of its historical development. This can be seen over time as the stair acquires new uses that were not original to the building. In early, grand versions of the house, the stair was based on a Western model, and a vertical service hall was buried in the body of the building so that servants and private matters of the house were hidden behind the more formal business of the living areas. Before the introduction of the bathroom in the 1920s, the stair and landings were used to store chamber pots, which were set outside bedroom doors after use, well away from cooking and eating areas. The routine of emptying these vessels occurred in the morning hours, when they were carried out through the rear of the house and into the alley.

In the 1930s and 1940s, as owners began to lease rooms as well as entire floors, the stair gained a new role as the formal entry to the various apartment flats. In this sense, the functional plan of the house was "driven in reverse" as residents entered or exited the building more often at the north face of the house, the service side. This allowed the stair to transform into a public lobby for the flows of people in a different manner than the circulation of a single-family dwelling. Less predictable is how the tenants of the house used these stairs—for example, as a stage for the comings and goings of the elderly, a meeting place for lovers, or the playground for children. The choreography of the *shikumen* stair became increasingly dynamic with people climbing or descending through space under different motivations, changing the flow of forces and therefore the life of the stair.

Ang Lee, the noted filmmaker and director, captures the use of the *shikumen* space in the early 1940s in his film *Lust, Caution* (2007). The film's setting parallels the time in which the function of the stair is changing from a service element to public passage. The sequence features architecture as one of the characters, increasing the tension in the plot. The heroine of the story is a young woman scheming to execute a Chinese spy who is sympathetic to the Imperial Japanese Army's occupation of Shanghai. As the protagonist enters her *shikumen* from the public lane, we are led through a series of filmic cuts that move up and through the section of the house, introducing not only its variety of spaces, but also the residents who dwell there. Entering the kitchen side of the house, the main character is greeted by an old man washing his face; at the same time, she sneaks glances through a window into the brightly lit lane. She moves through this space avoiding a mother with a baby descending a stair before stepping on to the first riser herself; simultaneously, she watches an old woman in prayer in a distant room. The camera cuts to a skewed perspective of the young woman climbing the first run, following her as she switches back at the landing. At this position, she looks up and utters "good morning" to a passing woman. As the camera levels out, following her hand as it slides along the rail, she leaves the frame, and we refocus to a distant view, through an interior window, of a family of four who is seated at a table engaged in a meal. This scene, no more than 20 seconds in length, allows a complex and comprehensive view of *shikumen* space, and, particularly, the space of the stair.[9]

The *shikumen* stair is a knot that binds together the different Chinese families that define post-1949 *lilong* houses. From a purely architectural point of view, these platforms between stairs—i.e., the landings—expand as floors stretch to the edges of each room. By contrast, we could imagine there are *no* landings in these houses, only truncated stair sections reaching to branching floors. The notion of the "free section" comes to mind, recalling the space of modern architects like Le Corbusier or even Adolf Loos.[10] But things are seldom "free" when it comes to the pressures of forced living situations, crowded conditions, and the increase in gravity loads. What can be best taken from the spatial excitement of the Shanghai *shikumen* arrangement is the harsh reality of the Chinese ability to adapt to the availability of space.

▼ Figure 4.12

Encounters while climbing a *shikumen* stair in a house occupied by multiple families. The kitchen and stairwell serve as the public entry; the house's circulation pattern has been reversed.
Images from Ang Lee's 2007 film, **Lust, Caution**.

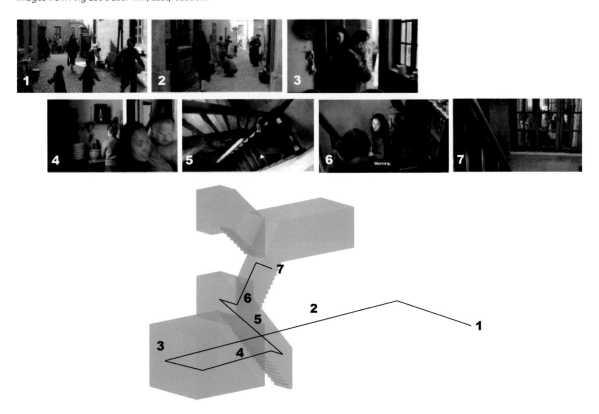

◀ Figure 4.13

Ben Wood and Studio Shanghai's re-creation of a *lilong* block in the commercial shopping district of Xintandi in Shanghai. In this photo, Starbucks Coffee is re-created by imitating the *shikumen* typology.
Photo by Steve Mushero.

The *Shikumen* Today

Some architects and developers are now recognizing the importance of preserving *lilong* morphology through borrowing or re-creating its urban character, as in the retail developments of Xintandi or Tangzifang in Shanghai. However, while such projects have seen commercial success as shopping districts for the internationally affluent, they often re-create the likeness of the original architecture without the social richness or the historical narratives of original *lilong* settlements.[11]

Several modern projects to restore and reinterpret *shikumen* architecture are now being erected in Shanghai. The *Jian Ye Li* Project, completed in 2012 in the French Concession as a joint project of John Portman Associates, the City of Shanghai, and a private developer, is one of the first to combine new housing and historic *shikumen* architecture. The former *lilong* neighborhood was divided into three sections. A portion of the site was left undeveloped in its existing condition, another was demolished and replaced with new housing by Portman, and the final third was renovated by Kokai Studios, a local preservation architect.

The Portman units are based on late-*shikumen* housing, but have grown to four times their size by connecting two units normally found in the standard historic type. Underground parking is provided two levels below street level. Rising above the lane are three floors of living space for a total area of 5,400 square feet of livable space. The size of these dwellings is on par with "super-size" houses we see in Western suburban developments. Such recuperation efforts far exceed the historical standards of the type, and are far beyond the means of most Shanghainese residents.[12]

CHAPTER 4 Peter Wong

▲ Figure 4.14

Kokai Studio's 2011 recuperation of the Jian Ye Li *shikumen* block in Shanghai's French Concession.

The irony of the project lies in the fact that most Shanghainese who experienced the dense conditions of post-1950 *shikumens* cannot understand why the wealthy, many of them Westerners, would wish to live in housing that, in their mind, is associated with overcrowding and a loss of liberties.

A different approach was taken by Kokai Studios. Their focus was to recover the feeling and space of the original single-family *shikumen* house, preserving the original size and layout. Living spaces and service elements are distributed with respect to the building's historic pattern. Accommodations for modern conveniences such as bathrooms, heating, and cooling maintain the original spatial character of the houses. At the same time, the fitting out of these houses is updated with contemporary equipment and finishes. The adaptive reuse of the original *shikumen* masonry shell of this part of the site represents a more sensitive recuperation of the historic type while simultaneously retaining the original sense of the architectural and urban spaces.[13] This kind of historic preservation is less about a strict return to past architectures and more about a modification of the historic type.

Most East and West renditions of Chinese architecture since the 1950s have resulted in grotesque stylistic examples of Chinese Imperial architecture with a modern twist. Instead, a sensitive reading of *shikumen* architecture could provide significant clues on how the physical style of buildings is but one aspect of recognizing architectural heritage. This opens questions about the rich and more authentic means available for maintaining an architectural tradition in the face of necessary modernization in China.

Cultural Continuity

Although it appears that *shikumen* architecture could fade in the face of fast-paced development in China, there are possibilities for new configurations. The test of an enduring puzzle is whether it can be taken up again by new generations and fresh minds. This begins with a quick inspection of what exists, a loosening of parts, and a careful consideration of individual pieces. *Shikumen* architecture was the result of competing interests and making concessions under strict cultural determinants. The Western roots of the type were massaged and modified during its 100-year building history, reimagined and reoccupied by Chinese residents. The building type was adjusted by different patterns of life, cultural traditions, and ethnic preferences. The impact on architecture in this instance is rich, as new forms are found by bending existing canons.

How will the return of foreign interests to China and the rekindled appreciation of Chinese culture and architecture affect *shikumen* housing? How will foreign and Chinese interests in lucrative partnerships influence the unique fabric of *lilong* neighborhoods? Will tomorrow's *shikumens* be subject to erasure by those unable to piece together the complexity of the conditions? Can the architectural type find new adaptations and configurations to meet changes in the cultural, political, and economic conditions of modern Shanghai, while maintaining the inherent quality of the city's urban fabric? Understanding the nature of these houses will require finesse as well as experimentation as pieces are tried, abandoned, and used again.

Discussion Questions and Explorations

Descriptive

1. Sketch a diagram of a typical *lilong* block. Include main lanes and sub-lanes to show the hierarchy and pattern of streets. In addition, note with labels or text where the public, stone gate entry façade would be with respect to the less formal kitchen side of the house.
2. Study the drawings and photographs of the *shikumen* house presented in the chapter. Write a description that portrays the experience of entering and moving through a *shikumen* house when it was occupied by a single family. Then, write an alternative description of this sequential experience for the same house as occupied by six to eight families, each living in a single room of the original house. Consider both the spatial experience and the social experience for the inhabitants.
3. Describe in words to a friend or classmate the urban and architectural characteristics of the following: (a) a Shanghai Concession, (b) the layout and pattern of a *lilong* urban block, and (c) the first floor of a *shikumen* house.

Analytical

1. Compare the plan of the urban *shikumen* house with the plan of the Anhui vernacular rural house. Write a comparison about the similarities and/or differences in the way the courtyard is used in each plan. Compare and contrast the social significance of the placement of these courtyards, as well as the type of light and exposure to weather for each. Debate the connection between these two Chinese house types, keeping in mind that one was imported to Asia by foreigners while the other was an indigenous, rural type. What can be said about the relationship between the two?

2. Find a friend or classmate to debate the colonial influences that are embedded in the Shanghai *shikumen* house type. What consequences or outcomes did this type of architecture create given its importation from a Western to Asian context? What kinds of cultural or ethnic situations arose from this translation of the architecture? Take opposite positions on these and similar issues in order to debate architecture's role in cultural and ethnic change.

3. Comment on and compare the formal and informal (service end) of the *shikumen* house. Using the plan and section drawings of the house shown in the chapter, what can you conclude about the size and location of these rooms with regard to the social and environmental conditions of the house?

Speculative

1. Sketch a series of plan diagrams of a *shikumen* house that imagine a four-step transformation from an Anhui vernacular house to the urban plan shown in the chapter. Do this by drawing simple floor plans that morph from one house to the next. Imagine this transformation as a sequential set of images like a comic strip or animated film sequence. Speculate on the actual possibility of such a transformation of the architectural type.

2. As Shanghai modernizes in the first part of the twenty-first century, *shikumen* architecture is being destroyed so that high-rise residential towers can be built. Outline a three-point argument that promotes the preservation and recuperation of this historic house type. Try to anticipate the counter-arguments by those wishing to replace *shikumen* architecture with these new housing opportunities.

3. What is your opinion of the Ben Wood Xintandi reimagined and re-created commercial *shikumen* district in Shanghai? How do you think this influences our understanding of the original house type? From your perspective, is it a positive or negative re-creation of the *shikumen* house? Write a brief critique or essay about this project and the way it does or does not create an appreciation of the historical type.

Acknowledgment

The drawings and diagrams in this chapter were created in collaboration with graduate students in the Master of Architecture Program at University of North Carolina Charlotte. The author would like to thank Thomas Barry and Lewis Mackey for their skill in preparing the graphics for this chapter.

Notes

1   *Shikumen* or *shi–ku–men* translates roughly as stone, gate, door describing the portals of stone in masonry walls that separate the courtyard of the house from the adjacent lane. The doors in these portals were typically of heavy wood, painted black, and fitted with iron hardware.

2   Article No. 2 of *The Treaty of Nanking*, signed August 29, 1842, states specifically the conditions of the concessions in Shanghai and in three additional Chinese towns.

3   Type or typology in architecture is a way to categorize buildings according to shared physical traits. This is drawn mainly from similarities in the buildings' floor plans. For example, courtyard houses from the Mediterranean, Mexico, and China share similar layouts and plan configurations. These houses have an open space or court in the center or interior of their plans. Hence buildings with a similar type share the same spatial relationships and formal patterns. Architectural typology was important in the nineteenth century during a time when both natural and human-made artifacts were being categorized under taxonomic rules and principles. Architectural typology found renewed interest in the 1980s when architects renewed their interests in historical forms. Urban types in particular are of interest, since such forms are usually inspired by factors that include: the environment, region or locale, parcel size, the social use of space, and other determining factors.

4   See Turpin C. Banister's essay, "Oglethorpe's Sources for the Savannah Plan," *Journal of Architectural Historians* 2, no. 2 (1961): 47–62.

5   Such defensive architecture was important during the Taiping Revolution (1850–1864) and the threat of the Boxer Rebellion (1898–1900) in northern China.

6   *Feng Shui* is the Asian practice of relating buildings and cities to their environs. In simple terms, this ancient practice accounts for both spiritual and physical elements of the land and site to determine the position and orientation of buildings. The practice influenced Chinese Taoist ideas of the relationship between materials, environment, and the energies associated with these elements.

7   For a more complete description of this house type see, Bernard L. Herman, "The Embedded Landscapes of the Charleston Single House, 1780–1820," *Perspectives in Vernacular Architecture: Exploring Everyday Landscapes* 7 (1997): 41–57.

8   Qiu Xiaolong, *When Red is Black* (New York: Soho Press, 2004), Kindle Edition, page 254, Location 1636.

9   Ang Lee based his film on the 1979 novella, *Lust, Caution,* by the author Eileen Chang.

10 Colin Rowe, "Mathematics of the Ideal Villa," *Mathematics of the Ideal Villa and Other Essays* (Cambridge, MA: MIT Press, 1987), 11.

11 Since the commercial success of the Xintandi shopping and tourist district by Ben Wood's office, Studio Shanghai, the architect/developer has also created interest in building similar developments, such as *Waitanyuan* and *Cambridge Watertown* in Shanghai as well as the new *Xihutandi* shopping area in Hangzhou.

12 Yasmine Ryan, "Luxury Project Seizes on Shanghai's Lane Houses," *New York Times*, September 16, 2010. Accessed September 8, 2014. www.nytimes.com/2010/09/17/greathomesanddestinations/17iht-reshanghai.html?_r=0.

13 An interview with the project architect Li Wei of Kokai Studios on December 30, 2011 about the history and execution of the *Jian Ye Li* Project.

Editors' Introduction to Chapter 5

When a person refers to the ethics of a situation, they are generally referring to the set of moral principles that guides one's behavior or actions. Ideally, such principles provide a common basis for social engagement with others, although, in practice, many disagreements still emerge. For example, in democratic societies, an implicit agreement exists between citizens and the leaders that work to preserve citizens' personal liberties and freedoms. When the public good is under direct threat, however, personal liberties have, historically, been sacrificed for the sake of national security. In times of crisis and in the face of threats to national security, personal and civil rights may be seen as dispensable, even necessarily so. What were the conditions and arguments for suspensions of such rights? What were the arguments justifying the denial of such rights for the public good? How do the ethical conflicts in these circumstances become architecturally manifested? These types of questions had real implications for two Japanese American architects living during World War II—Siberius Saito and Hachiro Yuasa.

In this case study, Lynne Horiuchi examines the ethics of architectural practice during wartime. She outlines the effects of wartime hysteria on two Japanese American architects and their more famous white colleagues working for the Farm Security Administration (FSA) in the 1940s. While none of the architects involved were directly responsible for leading troops or establishing military strategy, they were asked to design and construct physical environments for those directly affected by the war. Such people included American soldiers who were stationed at home and overseas, as well as so-called enemy combatants captured by the U.S. military. In an ironic turn of events, the two Japanese American architects that had directly contributed to designing barracks were asked to design prison cities in which they, and other Japanese Americans, would soon been incarcerated.

This situation exposed the racial biases many Americans held toward Japanese American communities during the war, and it shed light upon the professional limits Saito and Yuasa likely faced as nonwhite members of their profession. In order to help us better appreciate the ethical implications associated with designing such military environments, Horiuchi asks us to put ourselves in the places of the FSA architects. For a time, these Japanese American and European American designers had worked together to create innovative solutions for collective housing. In the wake of the war, however, they were placed at odds with one another. Horiuchi asks us, "What would you do as a professional architect if you were asked to design a concentration camp for your colleagues?" Vernon DeMars and Garrett Eckbo, two famous European American architects of the postwar period, had to answer this question, while Saito and Yuasa were confronted with the question: "What would you do if you were a Japanese American architect?"

As you read this chapter, place yourself in the position of DeMars and Eckbo as well as Saito and Yuasa. How might this string of events influence your view of American democracy, or your personal decision to become a professional architect? Also consider one of the ethical quandaries that both groups had to address: whether taking control of, or withdrawing from, the design of military internment camps would do more good in the long run.

Chapter 5

Architects at War

Designing Prison Cities for Japanese American Communities

Lynne Horiuchi

Introduction

Beginning in March 1942, the U.S. government incarcerated Japanese American communities living on the west coast, Alaska and parts of Arizona in concentration camps authorized under Presidential Executive Order 9066 issued by President Franklin Delano Roosevelt (FDR) on February 19, 1942.[1] The incarceration was one of the largest domestic projects for the Western Defense Command and Fourth Army (Western Defense Command) stationed in the Presidio of San Francisco and responsible for the major parts of the Pacific theater during World War II. The planning, design, and construction of the concentration camps for Japanese and Japanese Americans during World War II is generally imagined by the public, the media, and academic scholars as an event managed by the U.S. military with little input on the part of professional architects. The War Department modeled the physical construction of spaces to confine Japanese and Japanese Americans using their standard designs for military camps, including the barracks and guard towers that circulate as the most common visual tropes for representing this incarceration. The U.S. Army used a type of temporary "theater of operations" barracks—cantonment or troop housing designed for rapid construction and for housing troops at the rear of combat zones—for residential housing for civilian families.[2]

 Less well known is the participation the Farm Security Administration (FSA) and its San Francisco Office of the Engineer Region IX and XI, acclaimed internationally for their modernist innovative designs for migrant worker shelters and cooperative communities from the mid-1930s through 1942. Two of the San Francisco Bay area's most socially progressive and pre-eminent architects, Vernon DeMars and Garrett Eckbo, as FSA employees were involved in designing for the incarceration of Japanese American communities.[3] DeMars directed architectural work in the FSA Office of the Engineer from 1939 through 1943.[4] Prior to 1942, the FSA office had employed two young Japanese American architects, Hachiro Yuasa and Siberius Saito. Yuasa, along with several

LOCATION OF ASSEMBLY CENTERS AND RELOCATION CENTERS

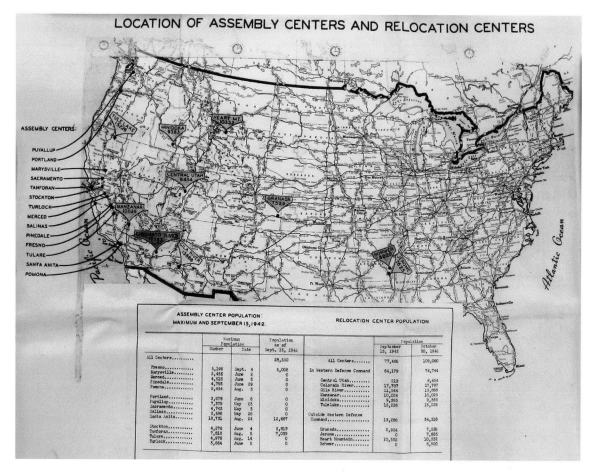

ASSEMBLY CENTERS:
PUYALLUP
PORTLAND
MARYSVILLE
SACRAMENTO
TANFORAN
STOCKTON
TURLOCK
MERCED
SALINAS
PINEDALE
FRESNO
TULARE
SANTA ANITA
POMONA

ASSEMBLY CENTER POPULATION: MAXIMUM AND SEPTEMBER 15, 1942.

	Maximum Population		Population as of Sept. 15, 1942
	Number	Date	
All Centers...........			28,550
Fresno.............	5,199	Sept. 4	5,006
Marysville.........	2,455	June 2	0
Merced.............	4,516	June 3	0
Pinedale...........	4,793	June 29	0
Pomona.............	5,434	Aug. 3	0
Portland...........	3,678	June 6	0
Puyallup...........	7,379	May 25	0
Sacramento.........	4,741	May 3	0
Salinas............	3,586	May 26	0
Santa Anita........	18,781	Aug. 24	12,667
Stockton...........	4,276	June 4	3,819
Tanforan...........	7,816	Aug. 5	7,039
Tulare.............	4,978	Aug. 14	0
Turlock............	3,664	June 5	0

RELOCATION CENTER POPULATION

	Population	
	September 15, 1942	October 30, 1942
All Centers.......	77,465	109,060
In Western Defense Command	64,179	74,744
Central Utah........	213	8,454
Colorado River......	17,787	17,787
Gila River..........	11,544	13,068
Manzanar............	10,026	10,026
Minidoka............	9,383	9,383
Tulelake............	15,226	15,226
Outside Western Defense Command..............	13,286	34,316
Granada.............	2,954	7,539
Jerome..............	0	7,625
Heart Mountain......	10,352	10,352
Rohwer..............	0	6,820

other Japanese Americans, also associated with DeMars, Eckbo, and their associates in the Telesis Environmental Research Group, a prominent West Coast architectural movement.[5]

In the aftermath of Pearl Harbor on December 7, 1941, Yuasa and Saito were removed from their homes and incarcerated at Tanforan Assembly Center in the spring of 1942 and later that year at the Central Utah Relocation Center, resulting in the complete disenfranchisement of their professional lives and all other sectors of their lives. During this same period, FSA architects in San Francisco at the request of the Western Defense Command and the War Relocation Authority (WRA) designed the community facilities, staff housing, and wrote specifications for the ten Relocation Centers or prison cities.

Simply stated, we might ask: "What would you do as a professional architect if you were asked to design a concentration camp for your colleagues?" Alternatively, focusing on the location of Japanese American architects in the internment process, we might ask: "What would you do if you were a FSA Japanese American architect?" This case study of the FSA office provides ways to rethink power relationships of race, racism, and racialization in professional architectural practice at war. It provides some fence posts and benchmarks for

▲ Figure 5.1

Map of assembly centers and relocation centers (tabbed arrows with 1942 populations).
Karl R. Bendetsen Papers; Image courtesy of Hoover Institution Library & Archives, Stanford University.

▲ Figure 5.2

"Living quarters" designed by the U.S. Army Corps of Engineers, Colorado River Relocation Center, Poston, Arizona.
Image courtesy of The Bancroft Library, University of California.

▶ Figure 5.3

Guard tower, Santa Anita Assembly Center.

how designers *compete on the unequal ground* of race, class, gender, or other types of discrimination. It raises questions about the ethics of diversity in professional practice and our knowledge base about architects of color. It allows us to problematize the meaning of state-driven utopian architectural design and planning, if we introduce larger questions about race, racialization, imprisonment, national belonging, and power into the discourse about professional architectural practice.

Racial Identity and Architectural Practice

Professional architectural practice has drawn upon the exclusive models of gentlemen's clubs of nineteenth-century urban culture before academic institutions defined systems of professional accreditation, a legacy that categorically excluded people of color.[6] As Lance Hosey has documented, it has been typically white and male architects who have written and promoted the codes, standards, and normative practices of architecture.[7] Greig Crysler has noted that of the 228 articles he researched in the prestigious *Journal of the Society of Architectural Historians* between 1941 and 1993, all were about white males.[8] This lack of diversity has delayed a concerted and focused effort to engage the impacts of race, racism, and racialization on the profession with little notice of the racial identity of architects, often presumed to be white males.[9]

More recent work in critical race studies and postcolonial studies has moved non-Western and minority viewpoints closer to the center of disciplinary studies. Racial identities are central to recent explorations of architecture and planning in colonial sites under imperial rule.[10] Histories of world fairs and expositions—cultural loci of education, science, and progress—have revealed how racial hierarchies of cultural value were formulated, authorized, and dispersed.[11] For laying out the topography of uneven ground in professional architectural competition, Craig Wilkins has directly engaged personal space and the practice of architects of color in his volume *The Aesthetics of Equity*.

For Wilkins, the naturalized barriers to space and property ownership based on Locke's principles of property ownership constituted privileges only white people could claim, and, as a corollary, the exclusive ability of white people to own property freed them from being owned—from being property.[12] These investments in whiteness, among others that played out in spatial organization, place and property, contributed to the cultural formulation of racial hierarchies and the naturalization of eugenics in design.[13] In the western United States, the investment in whiteness was specifically laid out in the Alien Land Law Acts that prevented aliens ineligible for citizenship from owning land. They were directed at all Asian immigrants who were denied the right to naturalize as American citizens based on their inability to assimilate by reason of their race; corporations with majority stock by such aliens were also prohibited from owning land. The legislation relegated Japanese immigrants to a laboring class to replace the Chinese who had been excluded from immigrating to the U.S. in 1882.[14]

The U.S. military's identification of Yuasa and Saito as "people of Japanese ancestry" was the sole category used for incarcerating them as potential spies or saboteurs and without any formal charges through violence of a global war, reifying the historic privileges of whiteness relative to Asians in the western United States. By racially targeting "people of Japanese ancestry," the American military determined their dispensability and consistently cast them as the "Japanese," obscuring the difference between the enemy they were fighting in the Pacific theater and the prisoners of E.O. 9066. While the people subject to E.O. 9066 were not targeted for extermination like European Jews, dissidents, and other targets of the Nazi government, they suffered disenfranchisement from mass incarceration and ontological violence of an unjust imprisonment.[15] Ethically, we may measure the justice and effectiveness of architectural interventions by professional architects and engineers designing for sites Yuasa and Saito inhabited and in the mirrored role of Japanese and Japanese American architects within the concentration camps.

Architects of the Farm Security Administration Region IX and XI in San Francisco

Vernon DeMars and Burton Cairns, Chief Architect in the FSA Region IX and XI Office of the District Engineer until his death in 1939, had gained recognition in Europe for their modernist "new architecture" designs using adobe building materials for a migrant farmworkers' community in Chandler, Arizona.[16] Talbot Hamlin, the well-respected editor of the architectural journal, *Pencil Points*, reviewed their work in 1941, praising the FSA work as imaginative, extraordinarily creative in the use of building materials. He noted that their work was characterized by "excellent study given to all buildings however modest and the refusal in this study to be bound by stylistic prejudices or conventions."[17] They were well known as American architects of interwar public housing and community planning for migrant workers sensitively attuned to site conditions and local traditions.[18]

The FSA Region IX and XI architectural staff in San Francisco explored their New Deal ideologies in the Telesis Environmental Research Group (Telesis) exhibit at the San Francisco Museum of Art in 1940, *Space for Living*. Resisting scientifically and rationally planned design solutions for low-income housing in standard forms and layouts that could be used anywhere, Telesis devised a design philosophy that was interdisciplinary and environmentally sensitive long before the environmental movement appeared in the national consciousness. Drawing on their working knowledge, FSA architects, including Yuasa, worked on the Telesis exhibit. They associated themselves with European modernist interwar "New Architecture," New Deal ideologies, and major modernist architects with whom they corresponded including Frank Lloyd Wright, Walter Gropius, and Marcel Breuer.[19] Professionally, the group took on ideals that would have a major influence on public projects postwar, exploring holistic environmental designs and progressive planning. Work on this ideal of scientific progress theoretically coalesced in a cross-disciplinary exhibit involving architects, planners, landscape designers, industrial designers, and political activists.

The military assignment of FSA/Telesis architects to design concentration camps for their colleagues went counter to the aesthetic and political ideologies of Telesis and the architectural practice of this small office. The ironies of the concentration camp work for Telesis members Eckbo and DeMars must have been more than single-faceted, since they recognized Hachiro Yuasa as one of their housing experts in the Telesis group. In a Telesis meeting on December 28, 1939, Yuasa was assigned as his work area for the exhibit, "specific living units." DeMars noted regarding his work with Yuasa in the FSA office, "there was enough work on versions of our new housing that this was sort of his specialty, and of course, we were working with him." In describing the work process, he noted that Burton Cairns and he would make the decisions, draw sketches, and carry out the fieldwork. After Cairns and DeMars decided what they wanted, they would then give these sketches to Gerry Milano and to Hachiro Yuasa, an office specialist and competent watercolorist, to draw up.[20]

The Military, War Relocation Authority and the Farm Security Administration

The FSA was a major agency serving the military directly under the operational direction of Colonel Karl R. Bendetsen, representing General John L. DeWitt and Western Defense Command and Fourth Army. A young dynamic leader, Bendetsen took over not only policy direction but all the operational functions of the Army authorized under E.O. 9066 as Assistant Chief of Staff of the Civil Affairs Division Wartime Civilian Control Administration (WCCA). In mid-March

1942, the WCCA set up 48 field stations or Control Centers to which FSA sent representatives. The military by this time had captured nearly all of $88 million in construction contracts for the Assembly Centers and Relocation Centers. They had already initiated construction of the Assembly Centers, using standard protocol modeled on development of internment camps for enemy aliens, Prisoner Of War (POW) camps, and military camps built for American mobilization in preparation for war during the late 1930s. Only after this was the WRA, the primary administrative agency responsible for the Relocation Centers, created through E.O. 9102 on March 18, 1942. The WRA was left directing some of the site selection and construction of the Relocation Centers and making whatever modifications they could.

FSA—Designing for the Incarceration

As a federal cooperating agency of the WCCA, along with many other federal agencies including the Federal Reserve System and the Federal Security Agency, the FSA's primary responsibility was to ensure that there would be no interruptions in agricultural food production and for "fair and equitable arrangements between the evacuees, their creditors and the substitute operators of their property."[21] Although unacknowledged in the FSA Final Report on Evacuation, the Region IX and XI Office of the District Engineer was called in to assist the U.S. Army in designing site plans and recreational facilities for the internment camps. Ultimately, the entire FSA Office of the District Engineer was assigned to work on the planning and design for the concentration camps—work that began in February 1942 and continued through September of 1942 when the construction of the concentration camps was nearly complete.

Vernon DeMars recalls the FSA Office of the District Engineer doing some site plans and layouts and "bits and pieces" of internment projects. These small "bits and pieces" included nurses' housing, a gymnasium, some managers' houses, and theater designs. Having designed innovative site plans for migrant camps, FSA architects appear to have influenced the design of the new prison cities as planned communities through their sensitivity to site conditions and designs for improvements on a limited budget.[22]

Garrett Eckbo was consulted on site planning for which he was considered a national expert.[23] Eisenhower consulted with the WPA and the FSA on "aspects of community organization" and by March 20, 1942, he had set up a Community Planning and Development Division.[24] In consultation with the FSA's Chief Engineer, Eckbo recommended ideal populations of 10,000 for each internment community. As DeMars related it, Eckbo felt that it made sense from a social and management "point of view." Eckbo may also have been following established New Deal methods for neighborhood planning provided by Clarence Stein's ideal model of a "complete, balanced New Town," such as his design for Radburn, New Jersey, and Rexford Tugwell's Greenbelt Towns built to house 10,000 people.[25] In the Radburn plan, neighborhoods were centered within a half-mile radius around elementary schools and playgrounds, and planned for 7,500 to 10,000 according to the best accommodation of students.[26]

In his oral history, architect Vernon DeMars related the circumstances surrounding the removal of Japanese American architects from the FSA Region IX office:

> Then we were brought in to do some planning on the Japanese relocation problem. I think we were pretty much emotionally upset at the whole business since we lost two of our young, talented architects, and longtime close friends to it: "Hachi" and "Si," Hachiro Yuasa and Siberius Saito. We thought we ought to make the best of what we felt was a very unfair and unnecessary proposition. Eckbo was still with us at the time. It was obvious that we were about to wind up, because all the Farm Security building had been completed, and I must have been negotiating to take this job with the National Housing Agency.[27]

DeMars' remarks occlude a great deal of the work carried out by the FSA in planning and designing for the incarceration in which he participated through the near completion of the work in September 1942 as documented in extant plans. Vernon DeMars served as Chief Architect of the Pacific Coast Region from 1939 through 1943, according to Alfred Roth, making him the responsible architect for the FSA's designs for the mass incarceration.[28]

According to the WRA Operations Final Report, the FSA Office of the District Engineer, headed by Nicholas Cirino, was ordered "to prepare plans, specifications and material estimates for the large school building program that was deemed necessary for each of the centers and to prepare plans, specifications and estimates for housing requirements."[29] Staff housing was also added to their tasks. They employed standard planning procedures but took care to adjust to differences in climate. Minimum building became one that could satisfy minimum space and construction requirements for safety and fire protection.

The WRA Final Report for the Engineering Section of the WRA Operations Division noted that the mass incarceration was practically the only task to which the office was dedicated in 1942:

> The Farm Security regional staff in San Francisco used practically their entire organization for the preparation of plans and specifications, field trips were made to all centers to work up site improvements (sic) plans and in order that all requirements such as water, sewage and farm land could be considered, also to prepare landscaping plans to conform with local conditions. They were at that time admirably equipped to handle this kind of job because they had finished an extensive building program of their own that was at least in part discontinued after war was declared.[30]

The FSA assignment to design for the mass incarceration may have been arranged in part through the influence of Catherine Bauer Wurster, a good friend of Vernon DeMars and one of the most important policy makers on housing in the nation. In her March 23, 1942, letter to the WRA Director Milton Eisenhower, she was direct in recommending the services of the FSA Office of the Engineer stating that FSA was already "vitally interested in the problem" and in working to organize "Japanese technicians and craftsmen" and to assist in the project.[31]

Although she responded to the incarceration pragmatically and somewhat belatedly, Catherine Bauer Wurster clearly called out the injustice of the act. In a long letter dated March 24, 1942, addressed to General DeWitt and co-signed by some of the most important intellectual leaders of San Francisco Bay area, she was among the few to question the "segregation of all Japanese residents of the State" and "the doubtful constitutionality of the internment of citizens without due process of law."[32] She called attention for the need to assimilate Japanese Americans into American life "as citizens," noting that many of them were deeply opposed to the military regime in Japan. She addressed the quality of housing to be provided; proposed Japanese American cooperative communities, and drew attention to the reuse of the housing postwar. She suggested, "The planning and construction could be planned under the supervision of some existing agency, such as the Farm Security Administration." Like many in the administration and management of the mass incarceration, she elided the identity of Japanese and Japanese Americans into one category of "Japanese."[33]

Interventions

The evidence that FSA intervened in the design process to provide better conditions for the internees may be found in their actual designs, consultation, and specifications for staff housing and the schools. This archival evidence provides a measure of the contributions of Garrett Eckbo and Vernon DeMars to the mass incarceration project.

Of the extant plans that Garrett Eckbo and Vernon DeMars designed for the Relocation Center blocks, it is clear that both architects were determined to introduce as many community planning amenities as possible into the physical plan. Two of the plans devised by Vernon DeMars and Garrett Eckbo between February 1942 and July 1942 provide examples of designs for the concentration camps utilizing available inexpensive resources to ameliorate difficult living conditions. In a Recreation Layout plan for Manzanar Relocation Center dated June 15, 1942, Eckbo and DeMars clustered adjacent to the elementary school croquet, volley ball, basketball, softball, baseball, and handball facilities and an athletic field. The plan also includes ramadas, picnic tables, and a free play area. Recreational facilities for small children were also designed into a typical block. In contrast to the U.S. Army Corps of Engineers standard plans, these FSA plans consistently show liberal allocations of recreational facilities occupying entire blocks and significant portions of the firebreaks, evidence of the social architecture of FSA's New Deal community planning.

With a limited budget and the same humble materials used for prisoner housing at Relocation Centers, Garrett Eckbo and Vernon DeMars demonstrated how they were able to transform standard plans and units into rational and pleasant living units in a community plan for Manzanar Relocation Center staff housing, bearing their initials dated July 13, 1942. Barrack buildings were

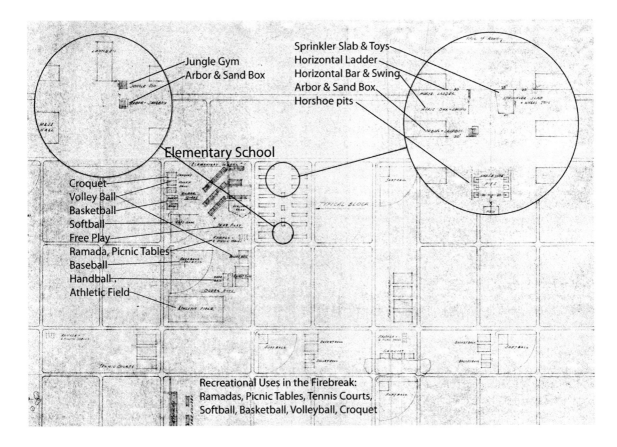

Jungle Gym
Arbor & Sand Box

Sprinkler Slab & Toys
Horizontal Ladder
Horizontal Bar & Swing
Arbor & Sand Box
Horshoe pits

Elementary School

Croquet
Volley Ball
Basketball
Softball
Free Play
Ramada, Picnic Tables
Baseball
Handball
Athletic Field

Recreational Uses in the Firebreak:
Ramadas, Picnic Tables, Tennis Courts,
Softball, Basketball, Volleyball, Croquet

▲ Figure 5.4

Vernon DeMars and Garrett Eckbo: Detail of locations of recreational facilities near a typical block and elementary school. *Manzanar Recreation Layout, June 15, 1942, Farm Security Administration, Office of the Engineer, San Francisco; Collection of the Author and The Bancroft Library, University of California.*

arranged around an asymmetrical plot in imaginatively rhythmic placements. Two units in an L-shaped arrangement are used to close off the pattern, creating an open space that serves as a kind of courtyard fronting a curvilinear drive. Dormitory units diagonally placed on a central rectangular plot as well as single apartment units form part of the community plan. The landscape plan is equally imaginative in creating screening, privacy, and windbreaks.

Yet, such special projects as staff housing at Manzanar demonstrate the funneling of better resources to the administration. Ironically inspired by utopian designs and based on FSA designs for disenfranchised people such as agricultural migrants, the Eckbo/DeMars plans deliver resources to the non-Japanese and non-Japanese American residents of the camps. As the substrata topography of privilege, the utility and infrastructure plans also demonstrate this privileging of space to free persons. The former prisoners and Manzanar Committee members observing the remains of a well-crafted masonry patio wall designed for "Caucasian" or "appointed personnel" wrote, "The structure, built for the pleasure of the WRA staff members, stood in stark contrast to the tar-papered barracks that served as living quarters for the Japanese American internees."[34]

Extant plans for the mass incarceration reveal signs of intervention that are tempting to represent as heroic and negotiations of the limited physical accommodations. Designs survive for "bits and pieces" of the internment

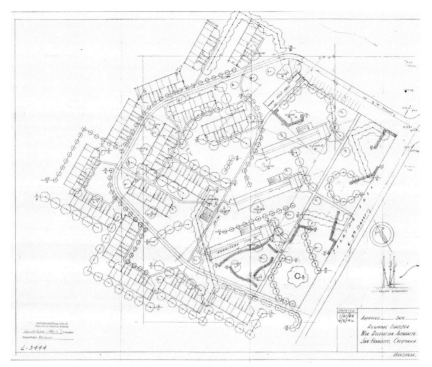

◀ Figure 5.5

**Staff housing, Manzanar
Relocation Center, Garrett
Eckbo Collection.**
*Courtesy of the Environmental
Design Archives, College of
Environmental Design, University
of California, Berkeley.*

environments as Vernon DeMars recalled, such as the typical plans for amphi-theaters. Yet, captured as they are on the standard grid, block and typical plans of prison cities, they exemplify the oppressiveness of the standard plans in the diversion of resources to dominant and "free" persons.

Japanese American FSA Architects

In historical representations, dividing and normalizing practices tend to treat internees and government administrative agents, including architects, as separate groups, leading us to assume that the professional architects employed by the government were white or "Caucasian" in the parlance of World War II government documents.[35] The assignment of "Caucasian" or white FSA archi-tects to design for the incarceration of fellow workers—members of a race-based group who were vulnerable to an unmitigated removal from "white" civil society—created positions of undeniable privilege. Japanese Americans in government positions, including Hachiro Yuasa and Siberius Saito, would have been suspected of sabotage, and it is unclear whether they were retained by FSA after Pearl Harbor, December 7, 1942.[36] Certainly, before World War II, Asian Americans rarely practiced as architects, so the presence of Yuasa and Saito in the FSA office was itself an extremely rare example of Asian American architectural practice in the late 1930s and early 1940s.[37]

Siberius Saito, Class of '34, University of California, Berkeley, Sketches of Tanforan Assembly Center with horse stall barracks on the left and the barbed wire fence on the right.
Courtesy of The Bancroft Library, University of California, Berkeley.

Siberius Saito

Under these conditions, Siberius Saito's achievements and personal journey through the mass incarceration seem remarkable. His personal journey exemplifies his uneven career development and his confrontation with the lack of material resources in the internment camps. Saito graduated with a Masters of Architecture degree from the University of California at Berkeley in 1934.[38] The architectural journal, *Architect and Engineer,* reported the cocktail party on the Lido Porch, Claremont Hotel in Berkeley where he had been honored on December 13, 1941, with other newly registered architects.[39] The same journal recorded his change of address in May 1942 "from 2061 Bush Street, San Francisco to Barracks 88, apartment 3, Tanforan Assembly, San Bruno."[40]

Siberius Saito wrote to his artist friend Bill Irwin about the living conditions within the Tanforan Assembly Camp on June 22, 1942:

> When we got here, we were assigned to an apartment in one of the new barracks. "Apartment" consists of one room 20' x 20' with beds and mattress as sole furniture. The toilet facilities—no running water. Electric light consists of one outlet suspended from middle of room. Average number of occupants in apartment—6 (we're average). The interior finish nor ceilings (*sic*) Partitions, closets, shelves, furniture etc had to be made from scrap lumber left by the carpenters. You know how inadequate that is. There was a mad scramble for wood in which my brother and I were quite successful. ... We managed to achieve a passable degree of privacy and convenience for ourselves but 50% of the people I should judge had neither the necessary planning ability nor equipment to do too much.[41]

His letter, drawings, and notes about housing conditions provide us with a fairly complete record of his vision and thoughts about housing conditions in Tanforan Assembly Center, constructed on racetrack grounds in San Mateo, California.[42] To occupy his time while incarcerated in the Tanforan Assembly Center, Siberius Saito drew sketches of the inadequate housing and taught drafting classes.[43] He returned to the Bay area after the war, but ultimately pursued a successful career in Waterloo, Iowa, opening a studio with Thomas Finn in 1948.

Hachiro Yuasa

Hachiro Yuasa and his family were first incarcerated at Tanforan Assembly Center and later at Topaz Relocation Center. His son, John Yuasa, remembers his father relating his angry response when he was asked to design "for his people."[44] Hachiro Yuasa was able to return to Berkeley and establish a studio designing cooperatives in the spirit of the Telesis movement and his FSA training. He had several important commissions before he left the San Francisco Bay area to live in northern California on the Hoopa Valley Tribe reservation to assist the tribe in cooperative building. His anger at his colleagues' request to design concentration camps seems more remarkable in contrast to his quiet professional comportment related by Doris Maslach, one of his clients, who also spoke to his ability to craft beautiful functional architectural designs.

Comparative Professional Mobility

The inclusion of architects of color in the 1940s in favored circles of valued architects created contradictions played out through the mass incarceration process. Architects could become prisoners, and architects who worked in government agencies could design concentration camps for their former colleagues. The imagined indivisibility of groups racially and professionally separate must be factored into the professional careers of Saito and Yuasa.

Yet, we can see on the FSA plans what might be considered interventions and best architectural practices directing privileged resources to white administrative staff, and we learn from Siberius Saito how he used his architectural skills to remodel the bare resources in his barrack housing. The war provided professional advancement for Vernon DeMars and Garrett Eckbo moving from FSA work to larger projects for defense worker housing, returning to Berkeley postwar to teach and design major commissions in the Bay area and at the University of California, Berkeley. Professional mobility for the FSA Japanese American architects was radically and abruptly derailed by mass incarceration, aborting the promising careers of Saito and Yuasa along with their Telesis associations. Privilege and power bifurcated between upward mobility and incarceration based on race.

In the spirit of the Telesis architectural ideologies, white or "Caucasian" FSA architects might have thought they were ameliorating the conditions of the concentration camps through design interventions, but they do not appear to have been fully cognizant of the ontological conditions that their colleagues experienced within the design office and the concentration camps. The dilemmas of Japanese American architects in this case history challenge the ethics of apolitical design practice and the effectiveness of utopian best practices. The histories of architects Hachiro Yuasa and Siberius Saito as members of the FSA Region IX and XI Office of the Engineer associated with the West Coast Telesis group remain unacknowledged. Their careers as architects may only be understood within the larger context of the U.S. government's forced and racialized incarceration of "people of Japanese ancestry," the abrogation of the American civil rights of citizens, and profound cultural and economic losses and recovery in the movement from elite status into prison camps and release.

Discussion Questions and Explorations

Descriptive

1. Many who were forced to live in Japanese internment camps drew sketches of their homes. Imagine you are just getting off a train that takes you to an internment camp. Using Figure 5.2, describe your new home as if writing a letter to a relative living on the East Coast. Include a sketch of what you describe.

2. Maps can tell us a lot about a place if we take the time to look at them carefully. The map in Figure 5.1 was created by the military to indicate how extensively they would need to collect and imprison Americans of Japanese descent to ensure the safety of the nation. Using the information recorded on this map, list all of the strategies the military employs in locating and designing internment camps.

Analytical

1. Look closely at Figure 5.4. It is a detail of a site plan of a prison city the U.S. government built for Japanese and Japanese Americans during World War II. Site plans are an architect's way of projecting what type of place they would like to create for a potential client. Now examine the list of spaces found on the left side of this image. Based on this list, for what types of clients do you think the architects believed they were designing? Would you assume that this space was a good or bad place to live? Explain the evidence that supports your answer and what facts are needed to be more certain.

2. Figure 5.6 is a sketch of the Japanese American architect Siberius Saito created in an Assembly Center while waiting to be shipped to a Relocation Center. Read the description that describes the types of spaces that were used to house Japanese Americans before being shipped off. Based on the general character of the sketch, how do you think Saito felt about being housed in this space? What message do you think this

environment communicated to the people who were forced to move out of their homes to stay here for an undetermined amount of time? Provide at least two specific details from the image that support your answer.

Speculative

1. Place yourself in the shoes of Vernon DeMars and Garrett Eckbo. After E.O. 9066 was issued, the federal government asked them to continue working on designing prison cities for their colleagues. Do you think that it would be more ethical to continue working on these projects to try to attempt to create more humane environments or would you have decided not to continue working? Use facts from this chapter, other research you have read, and your personal opinion to justify your position.

2. Place yourself in the shoes of Siberius Saito and Hachiro Yuasa. You are only given one week to sell all of your belongings and move to an Assembly Center (or risk being arrested by the U.S. military). Do you think that it would be more ethical for your former colleagues to continue working on internment camps to ensure that they are humane environments, or do you think that it would have been better for them not to continue working on these projects? Use facts from this chapter, other research you have read, and your personal opinion to justify your position.

Notes

1   Karen L. Ishizuka and the Japanese American National Museum, *Lost and Found: Reclaiming the Japanese American Incarceration* (Urbana: University of Illinois Press, 2006), 9. The term "concentration camps" referring to the American mass incarceration has been in widespread use since the 1970s by scholars, government officials, and the media. Tetsuden Kashima has noted that "internment" legally and specifically applies "to the confinement of Germans, Italians, Japanese and other nationals primarily by the Justice, State, and War departments" not held under E.O. 9066. I also defer to discussions with members of American Jewish communities in the Ishizuka volume as well as the findings of the Congressional Commission on Wartime Relocation and the Internment of Civilians. See United States, Commission on Wartime Relocation and Internment of Civilians, *Personal Justice Denied*. Washington, D.C.; Seattle: Civil Liberties Public Education Fund; University of Washington Press, 1997.

2   Carol Lynne Horiuchi, "Dislocations and Relocations: The Built Environments of Japanese American Internment" (Ph.D. diss., University of California, 2005). Sections of this article are drawn from the author's dissertation.

3   See Dorothée Imbert, "The Art of Social Landscape Design," in *Garrett Eckbo: Modern Landscapes for Living* by Marc Treib and Dorothée Imbert (Berkeley: University of California Press, 1997). Dorothée Imbert provides a brief discussion of Eckbo's designs for Japanese American internment but does not mention Siberius Saito or Yuasa Hachiro.

4   Alfred Roth, *La Nouvelle Architecture, Présenté en 20 Examples. The New Archi-tecture Presented in 20 Examples* (Erlenbach, Zürich: Éditions d'Architecture, 1946), 61–70.

5   Vernon DeMars, *A Life in Architecture: Indian Dancing, Migrant Housing, Telesis, Design for Urban Living, Theater, Teaching*, An Oral History conducted in 1988–1989 by Susan Reiss, Berkeley, 1992, 224.

6   Andrew Shanken, *194X: Architecture, Planning and Consumer Culture on the American Home Front* (Minneapolis: University of Minnesota Press, 2009), 6–8.

7   Lance Hosey, "Hidden Lines: Gender, Race, and the Body in Graphic Standards," *Journal of Architectural Education* 55, no. 2 (2001): 108.

8   Greig Crysler, *Writing Spaces: Discourse of Architecture, Urbanism, and the Built Environment, 1960–2000* (New York: Routledge, 2003), 36.

9   Lesley Naa Lorle Lokko, *White Papers, Black Marks: Architecture, Race, Culture* (Minneapolis: University of Minnesota Press, 2000), 14–15.

10 See for example: Sibel Bozdoğan, *Modernism and Nation Building: Turkish Architec-tural Culture in the Early Republic* (Seattle: University of Washington Press, 2001); Anoma Pieris, *Hidden Hands and Divided Landscapes: A Penal History of Singa-pore's Plural Society* (Honolulu: University of Hawaii Press, 2009); Preeti Chopra, *A Joint Enterprise: Indian Elites and the Making of British Bombay* (Minneapolis: University of Minnesota Press, 2011); Brenda Yeoh, *Contesting Space in Colonial Singapore: Power Relations and the Urban Built Environment* (Singapore: Singapore University Press, 2003).

11 Robert Alexander Gonzalez, *Designing Pan-America: U.S. Architectural Visions for the Western Hemisphere* (Austin: University of Texas Press, 2011); Mabel Wilson, *Negro Building: Black Americans in the World of Fairs and Museums* (Berkeley: University of California Press, 2012); P.A. Morton, *Hybrid Modernities: Architecture and Representation at the 1931 Colonial Exposition, Paris* (Cambridge, MA: MIT Press, 2000); Cole Roskam, "Situating Chinese Architecture within 'A Century of Progress': The Chinese Pavilion, the Bendix Golden Temple, and the 1933 Chicago World's Fair," *Journal of the Society of Architectural Historians* 73, no. 1 (2014): 347–371; Lynne Horiuchi, "A Local Global Utopia: The Japan Pavilion at the Golden Gate International Exposition," in *Urban Reinventions: San Francisco's Treasure Island*, eds. Lynne Horiuchi and Tanu Sankalia (Honolulu: University of Hawaii Press, forthcoming 2015).

12 Craig L. Wilkins, *The Aesthetics of Equity: Notes on Race, Space, Architecture, and Music* (Minneapolis: University of Minnesota Press, 2007), 9–26.

13 Cheryl I. Harris, "Whiteness as Property." *Harvard Law Review*, (1993): 1727. In addition to this seminal text, see George Lipsitz, *The Possessive Investment in Whiteness: How White People Profit from Identity Politics* (Philadelphia: Temple University Press, 1998).

14 Frank F. Chuman, *The Bamboo People: The Law and Japanese-Americans* (Del Mar, CA: Publisher's Inc., 1976), 48.

15 See Paul B. Jaskot, *The Architecture of Oppression: The SS, Forced Labor and the Nazi Monumental Building Economy* (London: Routledge, 2000).

16 Roth, 61–70. The *Space for Living* catalogue was dedicated to Cairns.

17 Talbot Hamlin, "Farm Security Architecture, "*Pencil Points* 22, no. 5 (May 1941): 709.

18 Roger Montgomery, "Mass Producing Bay Area Architecture," in *Bay Area Houses*, ed. Sally Woodbridge and David Gebhard (Salt Lake City: Peregrine Smith Books, 1988), 231–241.

19 *Telesis (Group), Organizational, catalogued IA1.1, Begins October 6, 1939,* meeting notes kept by Frances Violich in a small spiral notebook, BANC MSS 99/48c, Series 1: Telesis I, 1939–1940, Box 2, The Bancroft Library, University of California, Berkeley.

20 DeMars, *A Life in Architecture,* 123, 199.

21 U.S. Department of War, *Final Report, Japanese Evacuation from the West Coast, 1942* (Washington: Government Printing Office, 1943), 136–144.

22 DeMars, *A Life in Architecture,* 224. See also Greg Hise, *Magnetic Los Angeles: Planning the Twentieth Century Metropolis* (Baltimore, MD: Johns Hopkins University Press, 1997), 86–89, 115, 225.

23 Garrett Eckbo, "Site Planning," *Architectural Forum* (May 1942): 264.

24 Milton Eisenhower to James Rowe, Jr., Assistant to the Attorney General, Department of Justice, Washington, D.C., March 30, 1942, Japanese American Evacuation and Resettlement Records, 1939–1974, Banc MSS 67/14c, microfilm reel 19:12, The Bancroft Library, University of California, Berkeley.

25 Kenneth T. Jackson, *Crabgrass Frontier: The Suburbanization of the United States* (New York: Oxford University Press, 1985), 195.

26 Horiuchi, "Dislocations and Relocations." See also Clarence Stein, *Toward New Towns for America,* introduction by Lewis Mumford (Chicago, IL: University Press of Liverpool, 1951), 15, 49. A population of 10,000 was commonly recommended for new towns.

27 DeMars, *A Life in Architecture,* 123, 224.

28 Alfred Roth, *La Nouvelle Architecture, Die Neue Architektur, The New Architecture* (Zurich: Verlag für Architektur Artemis, 1975; 1950), 61. See also Horiuchi, "Dislocations and Relocations," 141.

29 C. W. Powers, Final Report, Engineering Section, Operations Division, War Relocation Authority, Washington, D.C., March 25, 1946, BANC MSS 67/14c, Microfilm reel 31:136, The Bancroft Library, University of California, Berkeley.

30 Ibid.

31 Catherine Bauer and Howard Moise, California Housing and Planning Association, to Milton Eisenhower, War Relocation Authority March 23, 1942, Records of the War Relocation Authority, Record Group 210, Entry 38, Box 5, National Archives and Records Administration (NARA), Washington, D.C., LH -P1150664.

32 Catherine Bauer, Ray Lyman Wilbur, Edgar Eugene Robinson, Jessie Knight Jordan (Mrs. David Starr Jordan), Edith Jordan Gardiner, Edward E. Heller, Josephine W. Duvenek, Frank Duvenek, Gerde Isenberg, B.F. Isenberg, Emily Olga Joseph, Walter E. Packard, Edward Moise, Allen G. Blaisdell, Max Radin, Monroe K. Deutsch, Paul S. Taylor, Alexander Watchman, Wilson (CIO), Edward Howden to Lieutenant General DeWitt, March 24, 1942, Records of the War Relocation Authority, Record Group 210, Entry 38, Box 5.

33 Catherine Bauer and Howard Moise, California Housing and Planning Association, to Milton Eisenhower, War Relocation Authority March 23, 1942, Records of the War Relocation Authority, Record Group 210, Entry 38, Box 5, National Archives and Records Administration (NARA), Washington, D.C.

34 Manzanar Committee, *Reflections in Three Self-Guided Tours of Manzanar* (Los Angeles, Manzanar Committee, 1998), 23.

35 I use "white" in place of "Caucasian" in some instances referring to racialized government practices; government documents of the period used "Caucasian" as a normative racial category.

36 The FSA Office records and correspondence from this period remain somewhat elusive, for the most part included in personal archives. I have not found any archival documentation of the removal of Saito and Yuasa from the FSA office. Vernon

DeMars did not remember the details of their removal, although it is likely that they were forced to resign as many Japanese Americans in government positions were.

37 For corroboration of limited opportunities for Asian American architects, see David Rash, "Kichio Allen Arai," in *Shaping Seattle Architecture: A Historical Guide to the Architects,* ed. Jeffrey Karl Ochsner (Seattle: University of Washington Press, 1994), 240.

38 Siberius Saito, "A Modern Glass Research Laboratory," M.Arch. Thesis, University of California, August, 1934.

39 "Cocktail Party" in the section "With the Architects," *Architect and Engineer* 148, no. 1 (January 1942): 47.

40 "Architects Migrate," *Architect and Engineer* 149, no. 3 (June 1942): 52.

41 Siberius Saito to William Hyde Irwin, June 22, 1942, from Tanforan Assembly Center in San Bruno, California, California Historical Society, Augusta Bixler Farm Records, 1879–1970, MS 202B.

42 Siberius Saito to William Hyde Irwin, June 22, 1942. See also Siberius Saito, Drawings of Tanforan Assembly Center, 1942, Bancroft Library, 1979.71 pic. This collection consists of 24 photographs of Siberius Saito's drawings, each given a number that corresponds to notes accompanying them regarding the housing conditions in the Tanforan Assembly Center.

43 Saito, Drawings of Tanforan.

44 John Yuasa, informal interview with author, August 19, 2014.

Part 2 | Gender and Sexuality

Editors' Introduction to Chapter 6

In 1976, *LIFE* magazine surveyed women in the professions and published a special issue that profiled 166 "remarkable American women." The only architect in the group was Julia Morgan, famed designer of the Hearst Castle in California and the first woman to be accepted into *l'École nationale supérieure des Beaux-Arts* in Paris. Remarkably, editors wrote, "None ... is a more exclusively male preserve than architecture."

In 2012, the British *Architects' Journal* published the first "Women in Practice" issue. Findings indicated that women made up over 40 percent of architecture students enrolled in accredited programs in the United States and United Kingdom. While that statistic sounds promising, it is less encouraging to learn that in the UK, only 20 percent of the licensed architects are women, and, in the U.S., that number drops to 16 percent. According to the survey, some of the reasons for the gap include sexism in the workplace, lack of job security, caregiver issues, and low pay. While percentages are higher in a few other countries, the issues that affect women architects in practice are prevalent worldwide.

Because Western society's acknowledgment and acceptance of women in architecture is quite new, we might not fully realize the trials of women pioneers in the field. In this study, Despina Stratigakos focuses on a key place and time, Germany between 1908 and 1920. During this period, Imperial Germany experienced rapid industrial and economic growth. With its great power came progressive social reform, including organizations that promoted women's rights. During the Imperial period, women architects in Germany had remarkable influence. Despite winning the right to vote in 1918, the women's movement in Germany declined during the subsequent Weimar period. Women architects again found themselves struggling to find work, made worse by the devastation of Germany's economy in the years after World War I. Notwithstanding their challenges, these women paved the way for others and served as inspiration for women architects in the attainment of equity in professional education and practice.

The consequences of these early social attitudes have had profound effects not only on the way architecture is practiced today but also on the individual women who have entered or who will enter the field. Gender norms affect professional culture, though they are not always explicitly stated and must be examined in each time period. Learning about early struggles and witnessing vestiges of them today gives us a greater understanding of the dilemmas of women and other underrepresented groups in the design professions.

When engaging this study, think about the ways that social attitudes and cultural norms are means of overt and covert control. What were the barriers for women architects in Imperial Germany? How do social power structures affect women and minority architects and designers today? What are the hidden consequences of these power structures? How is our built environment affected by imbalances in the gender and ethnic makeup of design professions? What can underrepresented groups bring to the professions, and, in turn, what impact can they have in designing more inclusion into our human-made worlds?

Chapter 6

"Should Women Build?"

Debating Gender and Architecture in Germany, 1908–1920

Despina Stratigakos

▼ Figure 6.1

Emilie Winkelmann as a young girl, c.1887.
Source: Author's collection.

In the photograph, the girl is wearing white lace and a bow, her face turns to the side, and she gazes intently at a place beyond our view. What was she thinking in that moment when the photographer depressed the shutter? Is she imagining herself as an architect, like her grandfather? Is she thinking about the drawings she has seen in his office, the blueprints being prepared, the buildings that grow from traces of a pen to masonry? On this, perhaps the day of her confirmation, is her mind on another, prefigured future, that of Christian wife and mother? Or, as her hair slipping its knot suggests, is she simply anticipating the moment when she can escape the photographer's studio, freed of the frills and finery of her portrait dress?

To envision thoughts of destiny and freedom for this girl, the young Emilie Winkelmann, who would grow up to become the first woman in Germany to open her own architectural firm, is to raise questions about dreams and limitations, about what *seemed* possible and what *was* possible in Germany at the turn of the twentieth century. What did it mean for a young woman in this period to imagine her future self as an architect? How might she have envisioned the road ahead of her and its opportunities or perils? To answer this question, I examine German-language publications between 1908 and 1920, varying from professional journals and scholarly books to popular magazines and career guides for girls, which debated the qualities that an architect should possess and whether women were fit for the job. Five interrelated themes surface repeatedly in this literature: (1) the architect's body, (2) the negotiation of the building site, (3) the architect's mind and the female brain, (4) the persona of the architect, and (5) the gender of professional markets. I also consider how women architects practicing at the time adopted or challenged prevailing beliefs about their abilities. I conclude that the idealized masculine image of the architect to emerge from these discourses left women struggling to break into architecture with a seemingly impossible choice: retaining society's approval as a *lady* who did not build or shedding that identity to become an architect and facing condemnation as a misfit.[1]

At the turn of the twentieth century, architecture in Germany was, with the exception of Winkelmann and a few other female practitioners, a male profession. In 1902, a report on women's employment bemoaned the lack of women architects in Germany and the inaccessibility of higher technical education for women. Over the next few years, women challenged the state laws that excluded them from matriculating at Germany's technical universities, which offered, in addition to engineering and science programs, architecture degrees.[2] In 1905, Bavaria became the first state to admit women; Braunschweig was the last in 1909. As these barriers fell, women began entering architecture programs, and while less than two dozen graduated with an architecture degree before 1920, the public and the profession were nonetheless confronted with a nascent generation of female builders.[3] Articles about them appeared in newspapers and magazines, they entered and won architectural competitions, and their work appeared in public exhibitions.[4] The seemingly sudden arrival of these newcomers, who were perceived as different, provoked a rethinking and clarification of the identity of the architect.

As women sought to enter the architectural profession, the human body became a central site where the gendered construction of the architect was played out. Whether arguing for or against women's inclusion, German writers agreed that the architect needed a healthy, strong, and athletic body. So closely were these qualities associated with the male body that some believed that women who became architects would become transgendered in the process. Karl Scheffler, a popular and influential architectural critic, published a treatise on gender and creativity in 1908, *Woman and Art*, in which he claimed that women architects were perverse, that they displayed mannish physical qualities as well as male sexual desires. Women who misappropriated creative energies that rightly belonged to men, he warned, destroyed their femininity, becoming "hermaphroditic creatures."[5] Scheffler's logic was shared by others who wished to discourage and deny professional integration. An engineer named Karl Drews, arguing for the overpowering masculinity of technical fields, insisted that only "male strength and male limbs" could handle the "enormous steel masses" of an industrial workshop. He contrasted the hard physical world of the architect or engineer, who "clothes his thoughts in iron and steel," with the softness associated with a woman's body and with feminine activities, such as baking. Evoking a nightmare of Darwinian evolution, Drews warned that permitting women to enter technical professions condoned the "breed[ing of] a third sex," behavior he considered both reckless and unchivalrous on the part of men.[6] Even supporters of women in architecture feared the weakness of the female body. Margaret Pick, in her 1909 guidebook, *Career Choices for Women*, warned girls considering a career in architecture that they needed to be healthy, free of vertigo, and physically agile in order to climb ladders and scaffolding—activities considered foreign, and perhaps dangerous, to the female sex.[7]

In physical descriptions of the architect, the demands of the building site loomed large. Writing in 1909 on the nature of the modern (and male) architect, Scheffler portrayed him as a rugged worker who "creates in the wind and weather of the building site."[8] Both opponents and advocates of women architects worried about the capacity of the female body to withstand these demands. In 1910, readers of the *Illustrierte Frauen-Zeitung*, a popular fashion magazine, encountered a striking image of a female builder making repairs to the roof of Berlin's Town Hall. The accompanying text introduced her as the first woman to undertake the demanding practical training required for this profession and emphasized the "great deal of courage and self-confidence it takes to stand on a ladder at this height in female clothing and, at the same time, perform a difficult task; in any case, however, this activity should be recommended only to vertigo-free ladies."[9] While depicting the new horizons opening up to women, then, the magazine's editors conveyed a sense of danger pertaining to the female body and its clothing. If her skirt did not snag, the subtext seemed to say, plunging a woman to her death hundreds of feet below, her mental instability (the supposed female tendency to swoon) might lead to a similar ruin. This message, a warning to "lesser" women not to follow in the path of exceptional (and perhaps aberrant) pioneers, was at variance with the calm assurance

▼ Figure 6.2

A woman builder making repairs to the roof of Berlin's Town Hall in 1910.
Source: Illustrierte Frauen-Zeitung 38, no. 2 (1910): 17.

displayed by the builder herself. The attention to vertigo, which did not arise in advice directed toward aspiring male architects, was likely influenced by the contemporary discourse on female hysteria. From the clinical publications of the French neurologist Jean-Martin Charcot to popular novels, images of giddy women were rampant at the turn of the century.[10] On the building site, this presumed female propensity for dizzy spells acquired frightening, deadly consequences.

As suggested by the *Illustrierte Frauen-Zeitung*'s commentary, the "problem" of the woman-architect's female body was nowhere as visible as in the dilemma posed by women's clothing on the building site. Respectable public attire for a "lady" in this period included a hat, long gloves, a skirt to the ankles, and a corset—an outfit hardly conducive to climbing ladders. In her career guidebook, Pick recommended that the woman architect wear "loose reform trousers, high boots, and a smock almost to the ankles, as painters or stonemasons wear."[11] Her solution was thus to cover the body from the neck to the ankles, effectively concealing any signs of female anatomy underneath. Adopting the attire of a male architect, which usually consisted of conventional street clothes covered perhaps by a lab coat, was entirely out of the question. Any woman daring to don trousers in this period risked being attacked as a transvestite, a situation that forced women to wear skirts even on construction sites.[12] Arguing that female workers should be banned from building sites, Fritz Heckert, a government official, wrote in 1912 that women's clothing presented a serious moral danger because men could look up their skirts as they walked across the scaffolding. (It is unclear, however, whether he thought this moral danger threatened men, women, or architecture.) He also contended that female workers were more likely to have accidents because of their clothing than men.[13]

Women architects responded to the challenge of their supposedly frail bodies and dangerous clothing by promoting the reform of women's clothing. In a 1912 photograph, Fia Wille—who, together with her husband Rudolf, owned one of Berlin's most successful design firms—is shown working on architectural drawings. She wears a dress of her own design that exemplified reform clothing, which rejected the corset in favor of loose garments that minimized surface ornament, followed the natural contours of the female body, and promoted freedom of movement. Contemporary male architects, such as Henry van de Velde, also designed reform dresses as part of their interior ensembles, but, unlike their female colleagues, male architects approached clothing design primarily from an aesthetic viewpoint. For supporters of women's rights, by contrast, dress reform was political: it was about liberating women's bodies from the constraints of the corset, and represented the most intimate dimension of a larger process of women seizing space that propelled them across new social, economic, and physical thresholds.[14] By wearing such clothing, women architects presented themselves as empowered, vigorous, and active "new women."

From this brief glance at writings on the architect's body, we begin to see how a physical ideal—an "iron and steel" superman undaunted by nature or machine—was formed and articulated against conceptions of the feminine. The turn-of-the-century discourse about the architect's mind further contributed to

▲ Figure 6.3

Fia Wille hard at work in reform dress, 1912.

Source: "Die Frau in Haus und Beruf," **Die Woche**, no. 8 (1912): 325.

the emergence of a gendered norm. According to Scheffler, man was "the analyzer of life" and objectivity a male characteristic. A woman, by contrast, was locked into materiality, and lived "more in premonitions, drives, instincts, and feelings than in thoughts." Her inability to free herself from this bondage prevented her from ever rising above the immediacy of experience, rendering her incapable of objective analysis or abstraction.[15] But an architect, Scheffler contended, was *ein Denker*, a thinker. For Scheffler, the architect's art was always mediated by his mind, even if it was partly carried out by his skilled and strong hands.[16] Without abstraction, women could not grasp or apply the mathematical laws structuring certain artistic forms: "among the temporal arts, none is so grounded in abstraction and mathematics as music, among the spatial arts, none more than architecture. There has never been, therefore, either a creative composer or an architect of the female sex." Scheffler argued that the mathematical understanding needed for architecture went beyond simple skills to rise to the level of beauty. Since women were unable to grasp this higher "artistic adaptation of gravity," the architectonic remained dead formalism in their hands. Scheffler thus demanded that "woman stay very far away from architecture."[17]

Scheffler was hardly alone in treating women and analytical or mathematical thinking as antithetical. This position formed the basis of Germany's state-mandated school curriculum for girls until the mid-1920s. During the Imperial era, middle-class girls were expected to devote their adult lives to the care of their husbands, children, and households.[18] Employment outside of the home was strongly discouraged; indeed, the visible idleness of wives and daughters provided a measure of the respectability and standing of the bourgeois family. Pursuing a career implied something deeply shameful: a father's inability to support his own daughters. Girls' schools thus trained their pupils for a future within the domestic realm. Their curriculum, which included instruction in religion and embroidery, devoted little time to mathematics or science, subjects considered not only useless for girls who would grow up to be wives and mothers, but also physically dangerous.[19] Medical authorities on both sides of the Atlantic argued that the intellectual exertion needed for rigorous study drained the uterus of blood, potentially rendering girls sterile.[20] And as far as educators at this time were concerned, a womb was a terrible thing to waste.

Opponents of women in architecture harnessed such common views about gender and intellectual ability to bolster their case against the newcomers. Drews, for example, illustrated his contention that women lacked spatial perception by quoting from a well-known novel: "They [women] see everything flat, even an egg, because they do not walk around."[21] So deeply ingrained was this conception that even an article published in a feminist journal in 1920 attributed the success of previous female architects to "an understanding of space relatively rare among women."[22] Paul Klopfer, director of the Royal Building College in Weimar, evoked the image of the tidy housewife who, failing to grasp an underlying order, destroys the well-organized mess on her husband's desk with her petty arranging. In his view, women's "millennial-long practice" of focusing on details had robbed them of an overall architectonic concept. Their inability to grasp the logical structuring that gives order to building (or a husband's desk) explained the lack of female architects.[23]

Wilhelm Wirz, an economist writing on the gendered psychology of taste, evoked women's weakness for baubles and frills as evidence that they were drawn uncritically to appearance over substance and lacked constructive depth. Because building required a feel for the "tectonic," it was best left to men, "who possess the organ for function, for the inner construction of things and for bringing out the anatomy." Women had a role to play in modern design at the level of refinement, which consisted of softening its "hardness" with their feminine flair for intimacy and ornament.[24] Pick countered that women had evolved from decorative to constructive thinking. Specifically, she argued that women's contemporary interest in architecture represented a historical development of the will to give form to one's ideas, finding expression in earlier times in pattern design and later manifested in building.[25]

For most critics, however, the architect's mind represented a state of consciousness that could not be acquired through education or evolution. One possessed the ability to think abstractly and analytically, grasped mathematical or logical sequences, understood spatial relationships, perceived structure, and thought in constructive terms—or one did not. Since male and female brains were presumed to be fundamentally different, one predisposed toward these faculties, the other toward subjective and intuitive forms of reasoning, it followed that women could not be architects. They simply did not have the right brain for the job.

Turn-of-the-century discussions about essential qualities of mind extended to the personality or temperament of the architect. Writing in 1909, Scheffler argued that "grand, masculine characteristics are necessary: desire to produce, will, reliability, intelligence, a sense for the whole, and of personal responsibility."[26] Additionally, an architect was "a man of action."[27] In an article published in 1911, entitled "Should Women Build?" the architect Otto Bartning asserted that healthy architecture could only be produced by "supremely manly men."[28] For these authors, among others, the persona of the architect was defined around a core of "masculine" traits: integrity, authority, willfulness, and creativity or genius. According to the culture of the period, the characteristics of the ideal architect represented the very antithesis of women's expected self-sacrifice, compliance, and modesty. In other words, what made a woman a good wife and mother also made her a bad architect.

Supporters of women architects, including women architects themselves, attempted to neuter some of these characteristics by attributing them to education or experience. In 1913, Winkelmann, by then the owner of a highly successful architectural firm, insisted that a woman architect could earn a client's confidence on the basis of her broad and well-grounded professional and practical knowledge. Indeed, her professional survival—particularly, her ability to obtain private contracts—depended on developing a "thoroughly confidence-inspiring personality, since a woman architect is still an exceptional phenomenon."[29] In other instances, however, adopting a masculine persona seemed the more expedient strategy. Pick, for example, advised women architects to display toughness and authority in their public demeanor. You "must have the strength to keep the coarseness of the workers in check," she warned, and "know how to enforce [your] authority over the couple of hundred workers who are often employed on a building site." While Pick conceded that this requirement was in part to be taken figuratively, since building contractors hired trained technical staff to supervise at the site, there were times when the architect would have to intervene, "and for this [you] must be armed and ready."[30] Being "armed and ready" meant shedding feminine compliance for the armor of masculine authority.

The claim that women architects might possess specifically feminine qualities or talents to offer the profession was made rarely, and always in relation to domestic design. In an article on women architects published in the popular family magazine *Daheim*, a reporter named Fritz Daussig implied that they were needed for the same reasons that female doctors were necessary: women architects were the gynecologists of domestic design, bringing their expertise to the intimate spaces of the home the way a female doctor could best unravel the mysteries of the female body.[31] When women first entered the medical profession in Germany at the end of the nineteenth century, it was assumed that they would limit their practice to female patients and children.[32] Defenders of female doctors maintained that they saved lives by treating women reluctant to expose themselves to male doctors. Additionally, female doctors were expected to be more knowledgeable about female biology and inherently interested in wombs and children. By extending this argument to women architects, Daussig claimed that domestic design, like gynecology, presented itself as the perfect marriage of women's "natural" interests and professional skills. This line of reasoning, while promoting a professional niche for women, reserved the male body for male doctors, and the corpus of monumental architecture for male architects.

Duchess Eva von Baudissin, a writer and cultural commentator, hailed the woman architect as the cure-all to an age-old problem: male architects designing houses for clients whose needs they did not understand. Bedrooms, children's rooms, kitchens, and other domestic workplaces (including those used by female servants) were the spaces that most concerned Baudissin.[33] She thus directed the woman architect's attention away from the public spaces of

the house toward the more intimate spaces associated with the activities of children and women. Assuming an implicit feminine expertise, Baudissin envisioned the woman architect as the pediatrician and gynecologist of the house.

This internalizing outlook represented a further, significant limitation of a woman architect's horizons: not only should she stay close to home but, even there, she should remain indoors. Moreover, as the woman architect was installed within the house, the house was also instilled within her. Pick, who had counseled women architects to abandon certain customary aspects of feminine identity on the building site, nonetheless, held this to be the source of their design strength. A woman, she contended, possessed a deeply innate or instilled feminine sensibility for the interior design of a house. This was the "right place" for the female architect and held the greatest potential for her contribution to the profession.[34]

Women architects both exploited and resisted this attempt at domestication. Therese Mogger, a Düsseldorf architect, seized the possibilities of a niche market catering to women seeking to build a home. In 1913, she created her own design periodical, *Unser Haus* (Our House), published as a supplement to the Düsseldorf journal *Die Frau von heute* (Today's Woman). It featured house-building advice as well as Mogger's pattern-book-style drawings of single-family homes. By contrast, Winkelmann sought to bring attention to the breadth of her work, and was particularly proud of her large-scale projects, which included a theater, factory buildings, exhibition pavilions, and schools. In

▼ Figure 6.5

Emilie Winkelmann, Victoria Studienhaus, Berlin, c.1915. The building, which functioned as a sort of residential college for female students at the heart of the city, still stands today at Otto-Suhr-Allee 18–20 in Berlin. *Source: Postcard Collection of the Zentrum für Berlin-Studien, Zentral- und Landesbibliothek Berlin.*

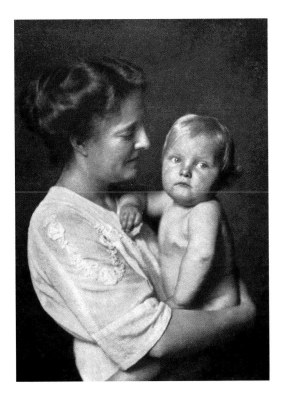

▲ Figure 6.6

Fia Wille holding her son.
*Source: Agnes Harder, "Unsere Kunstgewerblerinnen," **Die Deutsche Frau** 3, no. 20 (1913): 6.*

interviews, she refused to be pegged as a domestic architect, while also insisting that professional standards and skills had no sex.[35]

Given such concerns, it is extraordinary to find a published photograph of a woman architect with a baby. Indeed, I know of no other from this period. Wille is shown gazing serenely at her son, in sharp contrast to her other public guise (see Figure 6.3). Significantly, the photograph of Wille-as-mother appeared in a woman's magazine, in a special issue on female designers.[36] By comparison, the image of Wille as a "new woman" architect appeared in a large-circulation weekly.[37] In the forum of a woman's journal, a woman architect could dare to show herself as artist and mother. Or perhaps she felt obliged to do so, demonstrating that her professional success had not robbed her of cherubic children. In the broader context of discussions about the nature of the architect's creativity, however, this gesture appears less defensive than defiant.

Bartning claimed that women produced feminine or weak architecture because they listened all too readily to the client. A collaborative approach to design, he insisted, undermined the masculine ideal of the architect's autonomy. In particular, Bartning rejected the participation of the housewife in the design process, arguing that her "often troublesome wishes" destroyed the "strict lawfulness" of the plan, and led to the dominance of the "marginal" over the "fundamental," which he termed "feminine" architecture. In his view, strong architecture emerged from a definitively masculine process that was necessarily adversarial: the architect realized and imposed his vision in the face of "struggles, adversity, [and] misunderstandings."[38] Similarly, Scheffler described the architect as a kind of dictator, forcing "thousands of hands [to] serve his creative will."[39] This fanatical will constituted the driving force of the architect's talent. By contrast, Scheffler viewed female nature as static and submissive. Women's reproductive capacity, which he defined as the very essence of the feminine, existed in direct opposition to artistic productivity. Willful and talented women, he contended, violated the natural order and were often unable or uninterested in bearing children.[40] According to Scheffler's gendered division of labor, "normal" women functioned as the reproductive sex and men claimed artistic productivity. The persona of the architect as creator was thus determined along masculine lines. Bartning represented the architect as an all-knowing, almost god-like creator who:

> carries the image of the completed work in his head ... determines the place of every stone [and] the path of daylight ... wrestles the desired form out of the material ... until finally [his vision] stands there dignified, surviving for centuries, giving laws to the other arts and a frame to the life it serves. And this kind of creating is and remains masculine.

The "architectonically talented woman," Bartning continued, "will make an indispensable co-worker for the [male] architect, but never an architect herself."[41] Scheffler echoed this sentiment, stating that a woman could only stand close to genius, not possess it herself. To attempt to do so was contrary to her nature, endangered her femininity, and could never lead to great works of art.[42] In the context of this discourse, Wille's desire to appear as both architect and mother can be interpreted as a challenge to the emerging divide between creative and maternal roles within the field.

Wille's gesture may also have targeted the common assumption, voiced by advocates and opponents alike, that spinsterhood awaited female architects. In defending the latter's right to practice, Daussig maintained that single middle-class women who could not find husbands had the right to support themselves by studying and entering the professions.[43] This argument had been made for female doctors as well and drew on the widely held belief in Imperial Germany that a demographic imbalance had resulted in an oversupply of young women.[44] Others shared Daussig's certainty that women architects, like female doctors, would not wed. The art critic Klara Trost wrote that the architectural profession, "carried out with love and joy, will give the talented woman a life full of inner satisfaction and deep happiness, which will so fulfill her that she will be compensated for all that she will be forced to miss because of spinsterhood."[45] Although framed in a more positive light than Scheffler's theory of sexual degeneracy, this statement reinforced the notion that designing buildings replaced making babies.

While it is true that many middle-class women pursuing professional careers in this period would or could not marry due to cultural prejudices and legal obstacles, the presumption of women architects' celibacy seems to have been based less on reality (like Wille, there were other prominent married practitioners at the time) than on the supposed undesirability of women de-feminized through masculine work. Claiming there was "nothing more unfeminine than the surgical knife," opponents of female doctors "often wondered openly who would marry a woman whose femininity had been corrupted through the study of anatomy and venereal disease."[46] If, as Scheffler, Pick, Bartning, and others maintained, an architect needed to be physically tough, coolly cerebral, and defiantly dictatorial to succeed, a woman architect, too, might be presumed to make poor marriage material.

Returning to the question of what it meant for a young woman to desire to become an architect in early twentieth-century Germany, one could argue that it meant anxiety about the ability to measure up to a professional ideal that differed fundamentally from the gendered social norms according to which she had been raised. In other words, to make herself over in the image of the architect, she would have to dislodge the self that was rooted in cultural notions of femininity. At its most extreme, as expressed in Scheffler's writings, this represented a violent, irreversible, and ultimately futile rupture. Even advocates of women architects, while arguing for a certain continuity with this old self, envisioned a break. Thus, Pick's advice to be "armed and ready" meant shedding a way of being. It involved a physical and psychological transformation, for a "lady" did not climb ladders or face down coarse workers. Becoming an architect meant surmounting the social construction of "a lady." And yet, this feminine identity was also considered desirable by some proponents, a foundation upon which a woman architect could stake her right to exist by claiming special abilities. Designers such as Winkelmann and Wille contested the gendered norms that others attempted to impose upon them, but their voices were drowned out by critics, academics, and officials who espoused more deterministic views of what architecture—and men and women—could and should be. Negotiating these conflicting images and expectations became the inescapable professional fate of the woman architect.

One hundred years later, can we confidently assume that such dilemmas have been left in the past? Despite women's successes in establishing themselves within the profession—thanks in part to the talent and tenacity of these early pioneers—architecture continues to struggle with gender equality. While architecture schools in North America and Europe have almost equal numbers of male and female students, women remain grossly underrepresented among practitioners, academic faculty, and senior partners, leaving the profession in far higher numbers than men.[47] The problem of retaining women has yet to be adequately studied, but preliminary investigations suggest that the hurdle is not, as is still widely assumed, women's biology and their inability to negotiate buildings and babies. Rather, as a 2003 Royal Institute of British Architects study suggested, women leave architecture primarily because they feel unsupported, undervalued, and discouraged by the "macho" culture of the profession and the paucity of advancement opportunities compared to their male colleagues.[48]

In 2013, an international debate that flared over the lack of recognition given to women architects revealed the lingering hidden and often unspoken assumptions about gender and architecture that were explicitly acknowledged and debated in Germany at the turn of the twentieth century. On the website Change.org, two Harvard Graduate School of Design students, Arielle Assouline-Lichten and Caroline James, launched a petition to compel the Hyatt Foundation, which bestows the profession's highest honor, to retroactively recognize Denise Scott Brown after she was excluded from the 1991 Pritzker Architecture Prize that was awarded to her husband and partner, Robert Venturi, in large measure for their joint work. Thousands supported the petition, including Pritzker Architecture Prize laureates, but the debate also exposed biases that many had considered a thing of the past. While, to her supporters, Scott Brown represented a neglected architectural heroine, to her detractors, she remained ever the wifely helper, who, as Bartning and Scheffler had once argued, stood close to genius but could not possess it. As "salvatore" wrote in the comments section of an article about the petition published in the online *Dezeen Magazine*, "Her name is on the door because her husband put it there."[49]

Fortunately, among a younger generation of architects, there is increasingly a desire to confront the stereotypes that have confined not only women in the profession, but men as well. The discourse in early twentieth-century Germany about gender and architecture created restrictions that affected men as well as women: the more that women architects were expected to divest themselves of so-called feminine traits considered dangerous to architecture, the higher the masculinity bar was raised for men.[50] Just as it has for women, this strictly gendered view of architecture has had a long and destructive legacy for men. The popular 2006 film *Click* starred Adam Sandler as an ambitious architect who is forced to choose between family and professional success. The higher his star rises, the more alienated he becomes from his wife and children, until he is left alone and unloved, a broken man.[51] Long before the 2013 petition, Venturi had rejected the idea of the singular, male "genius" creator and insisted that he worked in full collaboration with his partner, Scott Brown. To his frustration, few architectural critics or juries listened.[52] By confronting the deeply gendered premises underlying our understanding of the architect's identity and practice, men and women in the field today have the ability to put an end to the long-lived assertion that architecture is an either/or profession.

Discussion Questions and Explorations

Descriptive

1. Summarize the arguments made in early twentieth-century Germany against allowing women into the architectural profession. What were the qualities or characteristics required of an architect that women were supposed to lack?
2. Summarize the counter-arguments made for allowing women into the architectural profession.
3. How did female architects attempt to conform to or resist gendered stereotypes about women and architectural practice? Cite examples of both.

Analytical

1. How would you describe the professional image of the architect today? What continuities do you see with the gendered stereotypes expressed in early twentieth-century Germany?
2. Are there design professions today that seem intrinsically better suited to one gender over another? For example, would you consider interior design to be a "feminine" occupation, as argued by German writers at the turn of the twentieth century?

Speculative

1. Despite substantial progress in the past century, the architectural profession continues to struggle with gender equality. If you were to encounter gendered biases today, whether in the classroom or at work, how might you productively challenge them?
2. What changes in the architectural profession do you believe would be most effective in promoting gender equality among male and female practitioners?

Notes

1   Portions of this chapter appeared in Despina Stratigakos, "The Good Architect and the Bad Parent: On the Formation and Disruption of a Canonical Image," *Journal of Architecture* 13, no. 3 (2008): 283–296.

2   Vincent Clark, "A Struggle for Existence: The Professionalization of German Architects," in *German Professions, 1800–1950*, ed. Geoffrey Cocks and Konrad H. Jarausch (Oxford: Oxford University Press, 1990).

3   Robert and Lisbeth Wilbrandt, *Die deutsche Frau im Beruf*, Helene Lange and Gertrud Bäumer, eds., *Handbuch der Frauenbewegung*, vol. 4 (Berlin: Moeser, 1902), 376–377; Despina Stratigakos, "'I Myself Want to Build': Women, Architectural Education and the Integration of Germany's Technical Colleges," *Paedagogica Historica* 43, no. 6 (2007): 727–756.

4   For a broader view of the activities of women architects in this period, see Despina Stratigakos, *A Women's Berlin: Building the Modern City* (Minneapolis: University of Minnesota Press, 2008).

5   Karl Scheffler, *Die Frau und die Kunst* (Berlin: Julius Bard, 1908), 91ff. See also Despina Stratigakos, "The Uncanny Architect: Fears of Lesbian Builders and Deviant Homes in Modern Germany," in *Negotiating Domesticity: Spatial Productions of Gender in Modern Architecture*, ed. Hilde Heynen and Gülsüm Baydar (London: Routledge, 2005), 145–161.

6   Karl Drews, "Weibliche Ingenieure: Ein Beitrag zur Frauenfrage," *Die Umschau* 12, no. 4 (1908): 61–62; Karl Drews, "Weibliche Ingenieure: Ein Beitrag zur Frauenfrage: Schluss," *Die Umschau* 12, no. 5 (1908): 90. In addition to physical scale and materials, Drews emphasized the masculine class dynamics of the workshop as an obstacle to women, a concern echoed by opponents and supporters of women in architecture. See Despina Stratigakos, "Architects in Skirts: The Public Image of Women Architects in Wilhelmine Germany," *Journal of Architectural Education* 55, no. 2 (2001): 93.

7   Margarete Pick, *Zur Berufswahl der Frauen: Ratgeber für 35 Berufe* (Breslau: Allegro, 1909), 83–84. Other career guides for girls that mention health or physical abilities as requirements for architectural practice include Josephine Levy-Rathenau, *Die deutsche Frau im Beruf: Praktische Ratschläge zur Berufswahl* (Berlin: Moeser, 1912), 185; and Anna Ramsauer, "Aussichtsreiche und hoffnungslose neue Frauenberufe," *Daheim* 50, no. 15 (1914): 26.

8   Karl Scheffler, "Vom Beruf und von den Aufgaben des modernen Architekten," *Süddeutsche Bauzeitung* 19, no. 13 (1909): 98.

9   "Frauen als Baumeister," *Illustrierte Frauen-Zeitung* 38, no. 2 (1910): 17.

10 Asti Hustvedt, *Medical Muses: Hysteria in Nineteenth-Century Paris* (New York: Norton, 2011).

11 Pick, *Zur Berufswahl der Frauen*, 84.

12 Patricia A. Cunningham, "Trousers: The Rational Alternative to Skirts," in *Reforming Women's Fashion, 1850–1920: Politics, Health and Art* (Kent, OH: Kent State University Press, 2003), 31–74.

13 Fritz Heckert (writing in *Der Grundstein*, no. 14, 1912) quoted by Doris Jindrar-Süß, "Die Männer vom Bau und die Baufrauen," *Frauen in Bau- und Ausbauberufen: Entwerfen—Planen—Bauen* (Berlin: Baufachfrau Berlin e.V., 1990), 13.

14 Despina Stratigakos, "Women and the Werkbund: Gender Politics and German Design Reform, 1907–14," *Journal of the Society of Architectural Historians* 62, no. 4 (2003): 502; Gayle V. Fischer, *Pantaloons and Power: A Nineteenth-Century Dress Reform in the United States* (Kent, OH: Kent State University Press, 2001); see also note 9.

15 Scheffler, *Die Frau und die Kunst*, 35, 68, 27, 42–43.

16 Scheffler, "Vom Beruf und von den Aufgaben," 97–98.

17 Scheffler, *Die Frau und die Kunst*, 49, 57.

18 Ute Frevert, *Women in German History: From Bourgeois Emancipation to Sexual Liberation*, trans. Stuart McKinnon-Evans with Barbara Norden and Terry Bond (Oxford: Berg, 1989); John C. Fout, ed., *German Women in the Nineteenth Century: A Social History* (New York: Holmes & Meier, 1984).

19 Bettina Srocke, *Mädchen und Mathematik: Historisch-systematische Untersuchung der unterschiedlichen Bedingungen des Mathematiklernens von Mädchen und Jungen* (Wiesbaden: Deutscher Universitäts-Verlag, 1989), 55–83.

20 Janice Law Trecker, "Sex, Science and Education," *American Quarterly* 26, no. 4 (1974): 356–357.

21 Drews quoting from *Jörn Uhl* by Gustav Frenssen in "Weibliche Ingenieure," *Die Umschau* 12, no. 4 (1908): 62.

22 Emma Loewe, "Die Frau im Architektenberuf," *Frauenberuf und -Erwerb*, no. 6 (1920).

23 Paul Klopfer, "Die Frau und das Kunstgewerbe," *Kunstwart* 24, no. 15 (1911): 216–217.

24 Wilhelm Wirz, "Frau und Qualität," *Wohlfahrt und Wirtschaft* 1, no. 4 (1914): 197, 200.

25 Pick, *Zur Berufswahl der Frauen*, 82.

26 Scheffler, "Vom Beruf und von den Aufgaben," 99.

27 Karl Scheffler, "Vom Beruf und von den Aufgaben des modernen Architekten: Schluss," *Süddeutsche Bauzeitung* 19, no. 14 (1909): 110.

28 Otto Bartning, "Sollen Damen bauen?" *Die Welt der Frau (Gartenlaube)*, no. 40 (1911): 625.

29 Emilie Winkelmann, "Die Architektin und die Ingenieurin," in Eugenie von Soden, ed., *Frauenberufe und -Ausbildungsstätten*, vol. 1 (Stuttgart: Franckh'sche, 1913), 109.

30 Pick, *Zur Berufswahl der Frauen*, 83–84.

31 Fritz Daussig, "Ein weiblicher Architekt," *Daheim* 45, no. 48 (1909): 11.

32 James C. Albisetti, "The Fight for Female Physicians in Imperial Germany," *Central European History* 15, no. 2 (1982): 109.

33 Eva Gräfin Baudissin, "Die Architektin," *Die Frauenfachschule*, no. 29 (1919): 598–599.

34 Pick, *Zur Berufswahl der Frauen*, 84. For another example of interior domestic design and monumental architecture treated as distinctly gendered professional markets, see "L. D.," "Architektin E. Winkelmann," *Innen-Dekoration* 20 (1909): 154.

35 Klara Trost, "Die Frau als Architektin," *Die Frauenfachschule*, no. 28 (1919): 571–572. On the contrast between Mogger and Winkelmann's strategies, see Despina Stratigakos, *Skirts and Scaffolding: Women Architects, Gender, and Design in Wilhelmine Germany* (Ann Arbor: UMI, 1999), 304–322.

36 Agnes Harder, "Unsere Kunstgewerblerinnen," *Die Deutsche Frau* 3, no. 20 (1913): 6.

37 "Die Frau in Haus und Beruf," *Die Woche* 14, no. 8 (1912): 325.

38 Bartning, "Sollen Damen bauen?" 625–626.

39 Scheffler, "Vom Beruf und von den Aufgaben," *Süddeutsche Bauzeitung* 19, no. 13 (1909): 98.

40 Scheffler, *Die Frau und die Kunst*, 18–19, 29–30, 94.

41 Bartning, "Sollen Damen bauen?" 625–626.

42 Scheffler, *Die Frau und die Kunst*, 31–33.

43   Daussig, "Ein weiblicher Architekt," 11.

44   Albisetti,"Female Physicians," 100–101.

45   Trost, "Die Frau als Architektin," 572.

46   Albisetti, "Female Physicians," 112–113.

47   Ann-Marie Corvin, "Shock Survey Results as the AJ Launches Campaign to Raise Women Architects' Status," *Architects' Journal* (December 1, 2012): 5–9; Kathryn H. Anthony, *Designing for Diversity: Gender, Race, and Ethnicity in the Architectural Profession* (Champaign: University of Illinois Press, 2001). Lori Brown has also raised the question of women's attrition during architectural studies. See Lori Brown, "Introduction," *Feminist Practices: Interdisciplinary Approaches to Women in Architecture*, ed. Lori Brown (Farnham, Surrey: Ashgate, 2011), 1–15.

48   Ann de Graft-Johnson, Sandra Manley, and Clara Greed, *Why Do Women Leave Architecture* (Bristol: University of the West of England, Bristol; London: Royal Institute of British Architects, 2003), 1, 17, 19–21, 25–27.

49   Alexandra Lange, "Architecture's Lean In Moment," *Metropolis* (July–August 2013); "Denise Scott Brown Demands Pritzker Recognition," *Dezeen Magazine*, 27 March 2013, accessed July 21, 2015, www.dezeen.com/2013/03/27/denise-scott-brown-demands-pritzker-recognition/.

50   For more on how hyper-masculinity became an architectural norm, see Stratigakos, "The Uncanny Architect: Fears of Lesbian Builders and Deviant Homes in Modern Germany," 145–161.

51   Stratigakos, "The Good Architect and the Bad Parent," 283–284. *Click*, directed by Frank Coraci and written by Steve Koren and Mark O'Keefe (Columbia Pictures Corporation, 2006).

52   Denise Scott Brown, "Sexism and the Star System in Architecture" (1989), reprinted in Denise Scott Brown, *Having Words* (London: Architectural Association London, 2009), 79–89.

Editors' Introduction to Chapter 7

Dr. John Snow's famous 1854 map of cholera deaths in London is a historic example of information-based visual advocacy. Snow was determined to find the cause of this devastating epidemic and theorized that water, not air, spread the disease. To prove his point, he recorded cholera deaths and found that a significant number of those infected drew their water from the Broad Street pump. His dotted map was so convincing that officials shut down the pump. Once closed, incidences of the disease diminished.

Visual advocacy is a growing component of information design and visual communication. While much (perhaps too much) of our designed visual environments are filled with advertisements for products and services, an increasing proportion are information-based visuals intended to promote social change. Public health, political rhetoric, and public-awareness campaigns are a few examples. Taken together, these are components of advocacy engaged by activists and rights advocates around the world.

Advocacy campaigns pose some of the greatest design challenges. Capturing the audience's attention is difficult amidst competing visuals intended for commerce. Likewise, the subject matter of these campaigns tends to be complex, while the media being used necessitates near instantaneous communication of information. Graphic designers must balance the risk of stereotyping with the challenges of both addressing taboos and not over-complicating information.

Activism takes on many forms and subjects, often seeking to reveal hidden atrocities, concealed practices, or shrouded norms. Similarly, advocacy visuals seek a multiplicity of outcomes—spurring debate, highlighting controversy, sparking curiosity, and/or provoking action.

All forms of visual communication "bend" information in order to capture attention and communicate in a compelling manner, but the ethical and aesthetic challenges of this are particularly significant for social-justice graphics. How can a designer quickly and effectively communicate, through image and text, the heinousness of sex trafficking? How can an advocacy campaign mix humor, empathy, and social criticism to open conversations about sexuality and disability? How can one sensitively, yet powerfully, address genital mutilation and other forms of gender-based violence? How can victimhood be portrayed, while, simultaneously, empowering victims?

Motivating change is the primary goal of the advocacy designer. Communicating data in ways that are clear, compelling, convincing, and conscientious is the main task. Data itself holds biases, which can be overplayed due to the need for efficiency and punch. Visual communications, therefore, must be understood within a cultural context. As John Berger stated in *Ways of Seeing*, "the way we see things is affected by what we know or what we believe." Diverse audiences interpret images in diverse ways. Advocacy designers do not create completed messages, but invite audiences to complete them through interpretation and action. Moving the viewer to question choices, as a mirror reflection of values and interests, is a way to motivate change.

In the following chapter, Maya Indira Ganesh and Gabi Sobliye discuss the challenges and opportunities inherent to activism in communication design. Comparing a variety of examples, they explore how taboos, stereotypes, social conventions, and cultural iconographies are used and transformed to prod dialogues about hidden and not-so-hidden issues in gender and sexuality. As you read, analyze the power relationships in the visuals. Look at how hidden patterns are revealed. Reflect on how the images and data visualizations make you feel.

Chapter 7

Communicating Gender

The Challenges of Visualizing Information for Advocacy

Maya Indira Ganesh and Gabi Sobliye

Here is an image of a control panel that has become popular online.[1] In it, men are characterized as simple, requiring just an on-and-off switch. Women, on the other hand, are shown as complex and confusing, functioning through a variety of switches, dials, knobs, and buttons. There are some common reactions to this image: (1) hearty laughter at a complex relationship cleverly conveyed by a single visual, (2) self-conscious laughter because the image reveals a privately held belief about men and women that is not politically correct to say out loud, and (3) irritation at the essentialist stereotyping of men and women.

Everyone has subjective experiences that result in varied responses to this image. An image like this and reactions to it also signal just how different and specific other people's attitudes about gender can be. From the moment we are born, we experience the world as gendered beings: "It's a girl!" or "It's a boy!" are some of the first words said to us regardless of cultural background. Our

▶ Figure 7.1

Man, Woman, by Miller Levy.
Photo by Barend Jan de Jong.

class, bodily abilities, race, and religion all affect how we experience and perceive gender and sexuality.

The visual acts like verbal language: it is symbolic, idiomatic, literal, and suggestive. It is made of dense accretions of personal and cultural memories. Our cultural contexts give us visual vocabularies with which to recognize and talk about gender and sexuality; film, art, cultural products, advertising, and photography are constantly producing and transmitting gendered concepts. Think about everything around you that might be encoding these ideas: toilets signposted to represent the male and female sexes; products packaged for a particular gender; young, attractive women advertising everything from contact lens solution to cars; and men and women taking on specific roles in movies, video games, and pornography.

Cultures also tend to promote very specific ideas around gender. Some realities can be completely invisible such as toilet signage for a transgender or intersex person and others may be knowingly fabricated like the pink mobile phones that we associate with women. The question is, when no different skill or ability is required to use that phone, why is it coded pink and labeled as a "woman's phone"?

These two examples and the image of the control panel are the sorts of issues with which many gender and sexuality rights activists are concerned: the perceptual and real-world imbalances resulting from negative stereotyping of genders and the politics of visual language. This forms one category of popular advocacy campaigns on gender that encourage a notion of equality based on the idea of *difference* between the genders, rather than similarity, and that all people deserve respect and dignity. Another category of advocacy conveys the injustice and outrage of gender-based violence. There are points of tension in creating these campaigns: (1) giving in to either reinforcing stereotypes or political correctness, and (2) negotiating between the explicit use of detail to inspire sympathy and avoiding the patronizing of victims. Even in an attempt to get it right, things can go wrong. This chapter explores how visual advocacy on gender equality and sexuality rights navigates these issues.

Our work looks at how activists and rights advocates working on gender and sexuality have worked with visual artists and designers to create advocacy campaigns using visuals, data, and information. We use examples of visual advocacy campaigns that take on different formats and forms: some are interactive websites, others are poster campaigns, some are very old, and many are new. Across the formats used in advocacy, we have identified four elements that are used in visual campaigns: information, design, technologies, and networks. The combination of elements determines the communicative power of the images we create and, ultimately, the effectiveness of campaigns. Of course, this is not an exact science but more of an art. Nonetheless, it is possible to become more sensitive to what does and does not work. Each example discussed references the contexts in which they were produced and how the visual works through particular uses of technology. Two aspects of visual advocacy campaigns are the focus of this chapter: the technique referred to as *get the idea*, and its downsides; and how to go *beyond the visual* to tell richer and more nuanced *stories in data*.

Get the Idea

What do you see when looking at these images from a campaign about Female Genital Mutilation (FGM)? What effect does it have on you? Most likely, they create a range of reactions. Perhaps you consider the image to be inappropriate, an unsubtle metaphor trampling over a taboo. Or, perhaps, it inspires discomfort with the contrast between a rose, a clichéd symbol for natural beauty, and what the metaphor, along with the crude stitching, represents. There are others who may think this is a powerful way to signal the brutality of female genital mutilation. The rose is a metaphor for the outcome of an act. This is a way of showing what cannot be said in words, certainly not on a poster. There are three posters in the series, which, to those who know about FGM, are more than a vague metaphorical representation; they refer to the three kinds of FGM that are practiced.

Our organization, Tactical Tech, has used Amnesty's rose image in a number of workshops on visual representation with activists. Most often, there are many responses, ranging from those who think it is powerful to those who think it is an oversimplification or a cliché. Regardless of viewpoint, the approach used in the images illustrates features of visual advocacy that can help an audience *get the idea*.

The dominance of visual techniques is the key characteristic of advocacy products that help audiences *get the idea*. Visuals are the primary vehicles to convey information and to lead audiences to more layers of information. Such

▼ Figure 7.2

Rose, by Yasin Lekorchi and Malin Åkersten Triumf.
Photo Niklas Alm/Vostro, retouch Sofia Cederström/Vostro, Volontaire, Sweden (www.volontaire.se) for Amnesty International, Sweden 2009. CC BY-NC-SA 3.0.

visual tactics borrow from cultural, political, and commercial communications. These forms of expression are often emotive, using shock, humor, subversion and metaphor, and challenge the viewer, in an attempt to create a pivot for their opinions and, ultimately, their actions. When it works, this approach is persuasive because it challenges the values of the audience, breaks taboos, and invites quick and immediate emotional reactions.

While this sort of advocacy is provocative and controversial, it is not necessarily one-sided; it can leave some space for interpretation by the viewer. These kinds of images pass on information about the issue, referring only obliquely to what people commonly think of as evidence, rather than presenting it directly. As provocations, such images mostly work as routes leading into a wider campaign where further information about the issue can be found. They are often designed to appeal to people who have not yet been exposed to the issue or who do not have a clear position. When it works, the effect of such a campaign can be remarkable; it can quickly spread across all media and rapidly bring attention to an issue. In this section, we look at images that help people to *get the idea* as well as some of the downsides of this technique.

Many objects, symbols, and places are associated with certain social conventions or are iconic and vested with authority. Icaro Doria's *Meet the World* uses national flags in an unexpected way to subvert traditional meanings.

I was flipping through the magazine [*Grande Reportagem*], trying to get a sense of it and I saw an article in it about female genital mutilation in Somalia. And there was a picture of the Somali flag right next to the data about how 90% of women there endure FGM and only 10% don't. And I couldn't avoid the fact that the data was very similar, in proportion to the graphic details of the flag: a small white star in a big blue background. I

◀ Figure 7.3

Meet the World—Somalia, 2005. *Icaro Doria/ FCB Publicidade for Grande Reportagem.*

found this very interesting. So I looked through the magazine to see if there were any other such issues from around the world that would be similarly interesting. I was looking for these kinds of patterns between data and their proportions to the images and blocks of color on flags.[2]

Doria produced a series of images of flags and showed them alongside facts that contradict what the flag represents, while making the flag into a proportionate infographic representing the statistics. For example, he added a key to the EU flag showing the yellow of the stars as the number of oil producers and the majority blue background as the number of oil consumers.

"The flags play with people's pride. You take a symbol of national pride and identity and show an aspect of that identity that people are not proud of. It really works."[3] This technique of subversion works because it shows viewers something they recognize and then, on closer inspection, flips their expectations of why the image is there and what it is telling them.

Sexuality and Disability is a website that discusses a wide range of topics and issues about women, disability, and sexuality. Web designers created the image (Figure 7.4) as a positive framing of sex and disability that is revealing and playful. We rarely see images of differently abled people as sexual, and, as a result, we are led to believe that such a person is incapable of desire or pleasure. This image uses provocative humor to send the message that differently abled people are like others in their desire for intimacy. It is hard to get right, but contextualizing and honing humor can be an effective technique. This image uses wit to draw in the viewer, leaving us to reconsider our views around disability and sexuality.

Sometimes, stereotypes become the default and we forget that other realities exist. In 2013, the Lean In Foundation donated money to Getty Images, one of the most widely used stock-photography companies, for a project to change how women are seen.[4] In partnership, they continue to populate stock-photography libraries with images that represent the actual diversity of gender. As a result, online image searches will change. For example, if you search for "a woman working," instead of finding a woman working in a kitchen or smiling in front of an open laptop, the collaboration between Lean In and Getty could result in other possibilities like a woman programming a robot or leading a trade union meeting. By adding richer and more diverse kinds of information, the project confronts conventional ideas of gender and sexual identity.

▼ Figure 7.4

Wheelchair Sex Positions.
Graham Streets, www.streetsie.com, 2010.

I'M PROUD OF MY TRAMP, RAISING TWO KIDS ON HER OWN.

SEX WORKERS ARE DAUGHTERS TOO.
steppingstones.ca

AT MY WEDDING, MY YOUNGER HOOKER GAVE THE FUNNIEST SPEECH.

SEX WORKERS ARE BROTHERS TOO.
steppingstones.ca

I'M GLAD MY PROSTITUTE MADE ME FINISH SCHOOL.

SEX WORKERS ARE MOTHERS TOO.
steppingstones.ca

▲ Figure 7.5

Sex Workers are People Too, 2011.

Stepping Stones.

Stepping Stones, a Canadian nongovernmental organization (NGO) working with women, men, and transgender sex workers and former sex workers, has a campaign that tries to do this in a *get the idea* format. Sex workers experience violence, discrimination, and stigmatization. In 2011, Stepping Stones released a series of posters of smiling photographs of people with captions that invite the viewer to see their children, mothers, and brothers, not as "tramps," "whores," or "sluts," but as people. These posters feel familiar to the viewer, because they are not unlike public advertisements plastered in bus stops or underground stations with high-quality photographs of smiling people. However, the statements alongside the images provoke the viewer to rethink their opinions of sex workers.

As powerful as *get the idea* techniques can be, there is a downside. This approach is difficult to get right. If badly conceived or executed, it can alienate or insult an audience.

In a now-popular TEDTalk, the Nigerian fiction writer Chimamanda Adichie warned of the "dangers of the single story."[5] She was referring to writers' tendencies to fall back on standard narratives, convenient tropes, and set pieces that flatten characters' complex motivations and trajectories. When communicating issues of gender and sexual identity, it is easy to rely on the same visual clichés, tired stereotypes, or misrepresentations. This can be problematic because it tends to transmit certain easy-to-digest narratives that "sell." In attempting to elicit sympathy and support, the single story is actually an incomplete one. This becomes one of the unintended and hidden consequences of designing for complex and nuanced advocacy issues.

An example of this is a video from 2010 titled *The Girl Effect* by the Nike Corporation.[6] Although the video has some compelling visuals and is a good example of the creative use of typography, it fails to adequately capture its audience because it oversimplifies the issue of social development. In trying to show viewers the situation of many girls living in poverty and how they can be powerful agents of social change if investments are made in their futures, the video makes radical generalizations and a simplistic linear equation for how change happens. It discounts many factors affecting girls' development, such as gender-based violence, and assumes that if a girl is given the money to go to school, she will become a thriving, self-sufficient entrepreneur and influence other girls to do the same, leading to a stronger economy for her village, peace, and, finally, "a better world." This video inspired a string of parody videos like *The Idiot Effect*, which not only poke fun at the campaign video but also at the creators. It jokingly suggests that the world's problems can be solved by "buying Nike sneakers" and ultimately implies that *The Girl Effect* is another example of corporate brainwashing.

The danger of the single story is that it can become a tired, overused visual metaphor that becomes a stereotype, and can have the opposite effect on the audience from that intended. One of the ways in which the danger of the single story emerges is when a particular campaign image becomes the default visual language for that issue. Take the example of the Amnesty rose. Online searches reveal that the dominant visual motif that comes up for FGM campaigns is that of flowers, from orchids to desert flowers. While this indicates the popularity of the campaign in creating a way to talk about FGM, the consistent use of the flower metaphor reinforces specific ideas of women's bodies and positions FGM advocacy within limited and conventional narratives.

Stories in Data

Once someone *gets the idea*, what's next? If people have to understand and act on issues, the challenge is much greater than that of representation. There is a need to find concise ways of telling stories that strengthen the information with clear and well-designed presentations that do not dumb down the issues. Helpful shortcuts that increase a viewer's understanding of a campaign's key points orient them within a particular perspective and entice them to further explore the issue. This section looks beyond a provocative image or emotional nudge to inspire a deeper awareness of how language and attitudes about gender and sexuality operate. *Stories in data* examines ways larger and more complex information are used in advocacy campaigns. Using data in interactive, online formats can help amplify and clarify a message.

Addressing linguistic choices is a complicated task because language is often deeply personal and has strong ties to upbringing and value systems. Attempting to shift homophobic language is a challenge taken on by the *No Homophobes* project.[7] It was designed by the Institute of Sexual Minority Studies and Services at the University of Alberta in Canada and led by Dr. Kristopher Wells. Along with the interactive website, the campaign took a cross-media approach with a public service announcement, posters on bus stops with QR codes, and ads placed in the bathrooms around Alberta's campus.

The website captures tweets in real time by scraping Twitter for mentions of four key words: "faggot," "so gay," "no homo," and "dyke." The interface features the number of times these words were mentioned on Twitter each day, week, or since the project's inception. Below this tally of tweets, the viewer can read each tweet in real time and see who tweeted it, thus adding a contextual

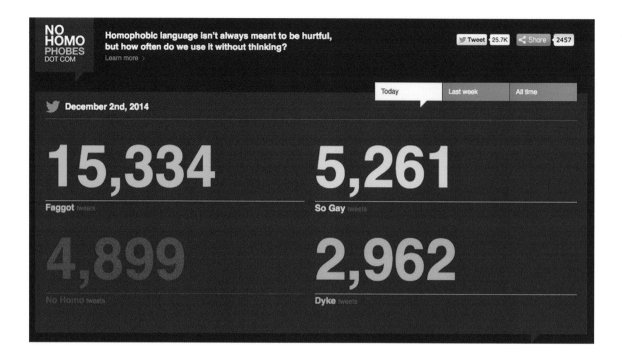

NO HOMO PHOBES DOT COM

Homophobic language isn't always meant to be hurtful, but how often do we use it without thinking?

Learn more >

Tweet 25.7K   Share 2457

December 2nd, 2014

Today   Last week   All time

15,334
Faggot tweets

5,261
So Gay tweets

4,899
No Homo tweets

2,962
Dyke tweets

▲ Figure 7.6

Screengrab from the website www.nohomophobes.org, 2014.

layer. The campaign is designed to encourage people to "think before you tweet," but has larger implications. Framing the information in this way triggers users to consider their linguistic choices and see the scale of the problem. Wells said that this project was successful in "cutting through the noise, going where people are not in a bold, new, innovative way. … This project … might not change the language [people] use, but they are likely to never forget the gravitas of their words."[8]

This site has won various awards and captured the interest of global media outlets. Over the last two years, the site has received 1.7 million unique views, the most coming from *The Guardian* and community-run sites like *Reddit*.[9] Wells recognized that they "tapped into the global conscience at the right time."[10]

At the start of this project, Wells and his team thought about these casual homophobic statements as the most commonly heard phrases that were the least addressed. They started by identifying who they were trying to reach and how they would reach them. Their primary audience was young people for whom these expressions had become shorthand for something "stupid" or "bad." Wells explained that they used social media because it is a popular medium where young people spend time, and it acts as a mirror to social perceptions and attitudes.

The project was not designed to "out" users of Twitter; the tweets, however, are linked to real accounts so the public can engage the tweeters and begin a dialogue if they so choose. Wells said that "giving viewers context was important to the project as context matters, and people can come up with their own conclusions."[11]

What people are saying

Lydia Rose @EsorAidyl   23s ago
@ethanbrady4 @caitlinorman5 Am I the **dyke**? Or...

hi @markl0l   35s ago
@Gunga_Bot fucking **faggot** fuck off

hi @markl0l   35s ago
@Gunga_Bot fucking **faggot** fuck off

idgaf. @CynthiaSilva_Yo   30s ago
@leslievargass y u **so gay**?

idgaf. @CynthiaSilva_Yo   30s ago
@leslievargass y u **so gay**?

Jamela @JaamBam   40s ago
RT @AZEALIABANKS: **Gay** men can call you a bitch, and talk about YA hair and YA nails, but as soon as you call them a **faggot**, all shit breaks...

▲ Figure 7.7

Screengrab from the website www.nohomophobes.org, 2014.

Rights advocates and activists need information that they can use creatively in their work. They also need to think about the best way to get data that is meaningful for the topic they are trying to address. The Egyptian Centre for Women's Rights conducted a survey and wrote a report on how up to 83 percent of Egyptian women and 93 percent of foreign women reported being harassed by men on the streets; 62 percent of men admitted to harassing women.[12] The organization wanted to come up with a way for women to anonymously report on harassment, and, at the same time, collate data that would show how prevalent the problem is in Egypt across different strata of society. This is how they arrived at the idea of *HarassMap*.[13]

HarassMap is a digital mapping platform for women to report their experiences of abuse, as well as where they occurred. It puts the collecting of data directly in the hands of women and does not compromise their identities. It is also a real-time visualization of evidence. *HarassMap* is now a database of information about street-based sexual harassment in Cairo that has resulted in similar sites in 25 cities around the world.

An approach like *HarassMap*, however, is not without its difficulties. It relies on women having mobile phones. But in many societies women have to share mobile phones or have their mobile phone use monitored by spouses or other family members. If you asked another set of questions about harassment, you might gather strong evidence which tells another story about street-based sexual harassment.

I NEVER
ASK FOR IT

P://BLOG.BLANKNOISE.ORG

The Blank Noise Project in India did just this. They started a campaign called *I Never Ask for It* to take on the issue of victim-blaming. In most parts of the world, women are accused of "asking for it" by dressing in a "provocative manner."[14] The campaign invited women to send in photographs of the clothes they were wearing when they were harassed. When Blank Noise assembled the database of photos from women, it became clear that women experience sexual violence despite what they wear. Perpetrators, not victims, cause violence. The evidence challenged myths and created a moving portrait of harassment without divulging identities or resorting to victim pitying. Blank Noise also asked women to send in an article of clothing similar to what they were wearing when they experienced street harassment and used the garments in a public exhibition.

Both *No Homophobes* and *I Never Ask for It* are examples of campaigns that creatively curate data of different kinds—in one case digital and harvested on a large scale, and in the other, visual and collected through individuals—to expose our deeply engrained values and attitudes. In doing so, they have re-fashioned how and what we learn about these issues and ourselves. They started by asking questions about how an issue could be presented for advocacy.

People online are becoming increasingly accustomed to using data visualization to understand, digest, and analyze the world. The next section examines two out of many data visualizations about gender, specifically data visualizations that show the low conviction rate in rape cases. These two examples show how data visualizations can be a powerful tool in conveying large and complex

▲ Figure 7.8

Blank Noise, *I Never Ask for It*, blog.blanknoise.org, 2012.

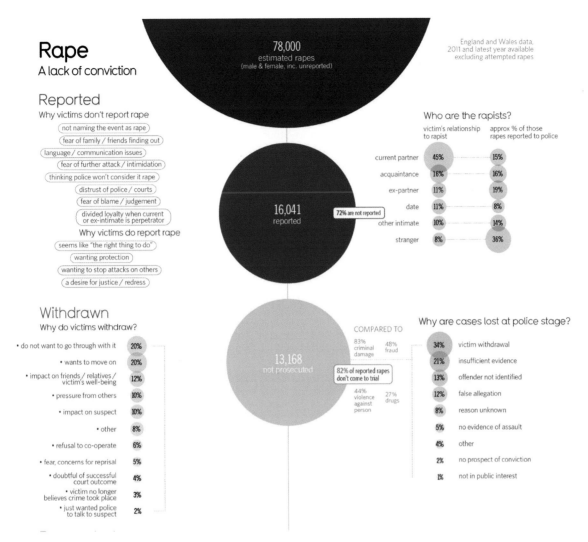

Rape
A lack of conviction

Reported
Why victims don't report rape
- (not naming the event as rape)
- (fear of family / friends finding out)
- (language / communication issues)
- (fear of further attack / intimidation)
- (thinking police won't consider it rape)
- (distrust of police / courts)
- (fear of blame / judgement)
- (divided loyalty when current or ex-intimate is perpetrator)

Why victims do report rape
- (seems like "the right thing to do")
- (wanting protection)
- (wanting to stop attacks on others)
- (a desire for justice / redress)

Withdrawn
Why do victims withdraw?

• do not want to go through with it	20%
• wants to move on	20%
• impact on friends / relatives / victim's well-being	12%
• pressure from others	10%
• impact on suspect	10%
• other	8%
• refusal to co-operate	6%
• fear, concerns for reprisal	5%
• doubtful of successful court outcome	4%
• victim no longer believes crime took place	3%
• just wanted police to talk to suspect	2%

78,000
estimated rapes
(male & female, inc. unreported)

England and Wales data,
2011 and latest year available
excluding attempted rapes

16,041
reported

72% are not reported

Who are the rapists?

victim's relationship to rapist		approx % of those rapes reported to police
current partner	45%	15%
acquaintance	16%	16%
ex-partner	11%	19%
date	11%	8%
other intimate	10%	14%
stranger	8%	36%

13,168
not prosecuted

COMPARED TO

83% criminal damage   48% fraud

82% of reported rapes don't come to trial

44% violence against person   27% drugs

Why are cases lost at police stage?

34%	victim withdrawal
21%	insufficient evidence
13%	offender not identified
12%	false allegation
8%	reason unknown
5%	no evidence of assault
4%	other
2%	no prospect of conviction
1%	not in public interest

▲ Figure 7.9

"Rape: A Lack of Conviction," 2013.
*Concept and design by
David McCandless,
informationisbeautiful.net.*

amounts of information. Data visualizations help contain and simplify a story so that it becomes accessible to a wide range of people. Data itself, however, is not an objective truth; it is carefully and knowingly processed, often containing biases of the owner of the data, the subjects, and the viewer.

David McCandless and his team at his design firm, Information is Beautiful, created a visualization that offered viewers an insight into why there was such a low conviction rate of rape in the UK.[15] "Rape: A Lack of Conviction" is a visualization of male and female rapes in 2011 based on data from the UK Home Office.

There are two ways to look at this data depending on the level of detail that the viewer wants to engage. This enables helpful shortcuts that increase understanding of the visualization's key points, orient viewers within a particular perspective, and entice them to explore issues further. By providing two entry levels, the visualization gives viewers a choice; the slowly diminishing colored circles depict the central story and the grey information surrounding the circles is for those viewers interested in the finer detail of the dramatically small number of convictions. As stated on McCandless' website, "We wanted to go a step further and explore the many complex and sensitive reasons why this figure is so low. Without these reasons, the explanations that circulate are convenient or political. The reality is much more complex."[16]

In the aftermath of the Delhi gang rape in 2012, and state actions in favor of protecting the accused in the gang rape case in Steubenville, Ohio, the *Washington Post* ran an infographic created by *The Enliven Project*.[17] The United States Department of Justice's *National Crime Victimization Survey* and FBI reports show evidence of the abysmally low rate of rape convictions and put false accusations into perspective. This infographic struck a chord with many online who were concerned with how the alleged rapists in the Steubenville case were claiming that they were falsely accused. As soon as it went viral, however, there were posts on forums and major news outlets declaring that the infographic was flawed.[18]

Each figure on the infographic represents one rapist committing one rape. What the infographic should depict is that each icon represents a *rape*, not a

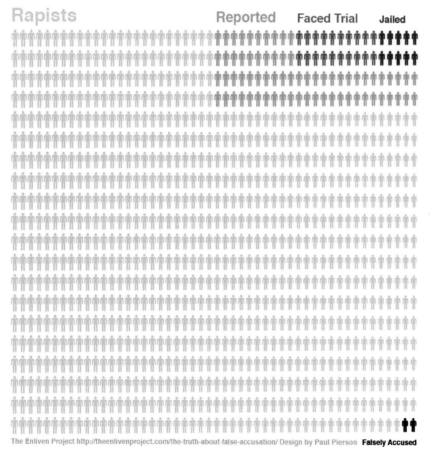

◄ Figure 7.10

"The Truth about False Accusation," 2013.
Designed by Paul Pierson for The Enliven Project. The original graphic can be found on www.theenlivenproject.com.

rapist. According to U.S. statistics, a rapist commits, on average, six rapes, and one in five women is a rape victim. According to this infographic then, one in five men is a rapist, which would make rape something of a pandemic. Additionally, the graphic refers to all men tried, but not found guilty of rape, as rapists. The infographic also overestimates the number of unreported rapes (a number that cannot be established because they are unreported) and conflates false accusations of rape with false reports of rape. If this infographic were to be shown to law enforcement officials, the distinction between a false *report* and a false *accusation* would be extremely significant. In the former, no perpetrator is named and the crime did not actually occur; in the latter, there is a known perpetrator who has been investigated. "According to the document, two to eight percent of reported rapes are false, but the number that are false *accusations* is smaller."[19]

While these might seem like technical details, they do not detract from the point of the infographic; however, the use of this infographic in an actual advocacy situation with people who understand the data and the issues, such as lawyers or law enforcement personnel, could be compromised by misleading or incorrect data.

In contrast with *The Enliven Project*, McCandless made available the data source and supplementary data so that viewers could further investigate the information. Data visualizations are not objective means of scientific discovery, but can be seen as visual arguments. It is easy to "lie" with statistics, and even easier to lie with data visualizations. As a result, we may be consuming easily digestible but false or misleading information. Opening the information-design process to the viewers allows them to assess validity. This includes providing information on how data is collected, how it is interpreted, and how it is presented.

For example, in his blog post, "Disinformation Visualization: How to Lie with Datavis," Mushon Zer-Aviv takes data from a study on attitudes towards abortion in the United States and describes how visual tricks, graphic presentation, and a deliberate set of choices about what parts of the data to emphasize presents the "fact" that Americans have become increasingly pro-life.[20] In summing up that piece of work, Zer-Aviv said, "Rather than seamless design, data visualization should embrace the 'seamful' approach that deliberately exposes the seams of the fallible human process of image making. One that acknowledges the image as an argument, as speech, as a part of visual language, to be debated, questioned … [re]visualized."[21]

Conclusion

In the field of data visualization, there are diverse ways to foster attitudinal and behavioral change. One is to provoke strong emotional responses—shock, anger, or humor—to grab a viewer's attention and stir her/his thinking. A second is about taking a viewer into a deeper exploration of an issue through the presentation of specifically curated data through infographics. These two methods utilize different techniques of representation and narrative, and use various visual media, from photography to interactive data. The examples in this chapter reveal creative ways in which visual techniques can be combined with digital technologies to create a sense of justice, empathy, and advocacy resonate across cultures.

Discussion Questions and Explorations

Descriptive

1. This chapter introduces two techniques: *get the idea* and *stories in data*. Define each concept and show visual examples from the chapter.
2. Examine the Stepping Stone campaign for sex workers (Figure 7.5). What is the hierarchy of each poster? In other words, list what you see first, second, third, and so on.

Analytical

1. Identify a visual that changed how you see a certain group or issue. Verbally describe your original viewpoint, your new viewpoint, and why this image changed your position.
2. Find one visual example for *get the idea* and one for *stories in data*. Describe the techniques used and discuss the strengths and weaknesses of each example.

Speculative

1. Carefully study the infographic entitled "Rape: A Lack of Conviction" (Figure 7.9). How might this infographic be interpreted by various individuals: a partner of a woman who was raped, a rapist, a news reporter, a researcher, and a lawyer?
2. Identify a social issue that has been described visually, for example, the flower representing female genital mutilation. Sketch an alternative visual representation of this issue.
3. Find a small data set about a social issue. Develop a visual that communicates this data in two distinct ways. Deliberately emphasize different components of the data set such that two different messages are communicated.

Notes

1 *Visualizing Information for Advocacy* was published in October 2013 and is a book about how advocates and activists use visual elements in their campaigns. This 170-page guide features nearly 50 case studies from around the world to provide an

introduction to understanding visual information and a framework for using images for influence. It is written and researched by Maya Indira Ganesh, Stephanie Hankey, Tom Longley, and Marek Tuszynski, all of whom have been working on the area of data, technology, and activism for over a decade.

2   Icaro Doria via Skype, July 28, 2011.

3   Ibid.

4   "Lean In," Getty Images, accessed November 9, 2014, www.gettyimages.de/creative/frontdoor/leanin.

5   Chimamanda Ngozi Adichie, "The Danger of a Single Story," *TEDGlobal 2009*, July 2009, accessed November 15, 2014, www.ted.com/talks/chimamanda_adichie_the_danger_of_a_single_story?language=en.

6   Here is one version of Nike's Girl Effect campaign video, accessed early December, 2014: www.youtube.com/watch?v=PouWPaWCdK8. There are a few campaign videos online since the release of the original one in 2010.

7   No Homophobes can be viewed here: www.nohomophobes.com/.

8   Dr. Khristopher Wells via Skype, October 15, 2014.

9   "The No Homophobes Guide to Language on Twitter," *The Guardian*, accessed September 30, 2014, www.theguardian.com/news/datablog/interactive/2012/oct/02/no-homophobes-language-count.

10 Dr. Khristopher Wells, 2014.

11 Ibid.

12 "Sexual Harassment Myths | HarassMap," HarassMap, accessed November 1, 2014, http://harassmap.org/en/resource-center/harassment-myths/; Rasha Mohammad Hassan, "Clouds in Egypt's Sky: Sexual Harassment: From Verbal Harassment to Rape," The Egyptian Center for Women's Rights, accessed November 1, 2014, http://egypt.unfpa.org/Images/Publication/2010_03/6eeeb05a-3040-42d2-9e1c-2bd2e1ac8cac.pdf.

13 "How and Why We Began | HarassMap," HarassMap, accessed March 17, 2013, http://harassmap.org/en/who-we-are/how-and-why-we-began/.

14 "Blank Noise," Blank Noise, accessed April 15, 2013, http://blog.blanknoise.org/; "I Never 'Ask for It,'" Blank Noise, accessed April 15, 2013, www.ineveraskforit.org/about.

15 David McCandless, "Information is Beautiful," Information is Beautiful, accessed early December, 2014, www.informationisbeautiful.net/.

16 David McCandless, "Rape: A Lack of Conviction," Information is Beautiful, 2013, accessed early December, 2014, www.informationisbeautiful.net/2013/rape-a-lack-of-conviction/.

17 "The Truth about False Accusation," The Enliven Project, accessed March 1, 2013, http://theenlivenproject.com/the-truth-about-false-accusation/.

18 Amanda Marcotte, "This Rape Infographic Is Going Viral. Too Bad It's Wrong," *Slate Magazine*, accessed March 15, 2014, www.slate.com/blogs/xx_factor/2013/01/08/the_enliven_project_s_false_rape_accusations_infographic_great_intentions.html.

19 Ibid.

20 Mushon Zer-Aviv, "Disinformation Visualization: How to Lie with Datavis," Visualising Information for Advocacy, January, 31, 2014, accessed early December, 2014, https://visualisingadvocacy.org/blog/disinformation-visualization-how-lie-datavis.

21 Ibid.

Editors' Introduction to Chapter 8

Since at least the 1950s, social scientists have argued that hate speech generates psychological harm to both the speaker and their listeners. This theory played a prominent role in the 1954 U.S. Supreme Court decision *Brown v. Board of Education*, which made state-sponsored segregation of primary schools illegal in the United States. Kenneth Clark, one of the social scientists directly cited by the court, pioneered research on the psychological harm racism produced in both white and black children. In his studies, Clark found that hate speech negatively impacted young people's processes of identity formation; it not only required the speaker to mentally reinforce negative stereotypes of others to elevate themselves but these stereotypes also negatively affected minority groups by lowering their psychological capacity to create a positive sense of self. Using this psychological framework, hate speech was shown to accrue tremendous power over the developing mind. Such insights directly contradict the lessons of the old nursery rhyme "Sticks and Stones may break my bones, but words can never hurt me." Words do, in fact, cause harm.

In this case study, artist and theorist, Mark Addison Smith, directly responds to the negative effects of hate speech directed toward gay men in the form of public restroom graffiti. Like the sociological study of racism in American schools, psychologists have outlined the gendered (male versus female) and sexual (gay versus "straight") stereotypes expressed by graffiti written on the walls of restroom stalls. Building upon this research, Smith theorizes that the power of hate speech can work both ways: listeners do not have to merely act as passive listeners, but can produce utterances that have a positive effect upon their communities. Using the graffiti technique of "overwriting," Smith literally transforms the hate speech written on the bathroom wall into a potential source of positive change. This work on typography visualizes the psychological power embedded in speech that typically remains invisible to everyday audiences. Smith's technique of overwriting challenges the primacy of the speaker of hate speech by creating a conversation between subjects; and, with conversation, this technique constitutes a potential source of dialogue, protest, empowerment, and activism for future audiences.

If the social and psychological lessons regarding hate speech still hold today, then people must be taught to use their speech responsibly. New forms of social media have opened up new horizons of communication, including unforeseen ways of transmitting hate speech to listeners. Studies have found that people feel more empowered to speak their minds online, because it presents an opportunity to speak anonymously. Like the anonymity of bathroom graffiti, digital communications have led to an increase of cyber bullying and other forms of online abuse. Can we defend a person's right to free speech without fostering an environment where hate speech flourishes? The lessons of Mark Addison Smith's art inspire us to navigate these, and other, questions related to the power of speech.

Chapter 8

Overwriting Hate

The Queer Writing on the Bathroom Wall

Mark Addison Smith

In the world of graffiti, writing over another's work is considered the ultimate form of disrespect. In the world of protest, overwriting is a strategy as old as writing itself. Once we, as a community, learned to write (to voice), we also learned to overwrite (to edit, to alter, to censor, to shout, to reclaim). Caleb Neelon, co-author of *The History of American Graffiti* speculated: "I don't have the pics, but it's easy to imagine one caveman drew an animal and someone took over his cave and drew another animal fucking it."[1] While it is difficult to isolate the first instance of overwriting in graffiti, or design for that matter, we can understand the power and value, both artistically and sociologically, that come with one writer's comments being augmented, eradicated, or reclaimed by another.

Overwriting became one of the many operating modes for mass unification during the Stonewall Riots and queer revolution in Greenwich Village. A 1969 image captured by Diana Davies documented the graffiti-laced Stonewall Inn windows awash with a Mattachine Society's plea for "peaceful and quiet conduct on the streets of the Village."[2] Half of the message had been hostilely eradicated by the time Davies snapped her photo.

In an attempt to reclaim land promised to Native American tribes in historical treaties, the Indians of All Tribes (IAT) implemented an eradication of U.S. signage during the 1969 occupation of Alcatraz Island: "United States Property" quickly became "United Indian Property."

In countless examples, it comes down to turf wars, an acrimonious butting of heads between two or more parties over place, space, or influence. Known as "crossing out," "going over," or "X-ing out," a graffiti artist might use big, blocky letters, or blockbuster type, to obscure previous works and reclaim visual hierarchy by covering one writer's name, or tag, with his or her own. Street artist Banksy even named his breakthrough 2003 solo exhibition *Turf War* to claim his king spot in the London art scene.

Textual sabotage is also common in the graphic design world. Designer David Carson established a visual lawlessness within his *Ray Gun* magazine to separate himself from a more manicured, digital style emerging in the 1990s.[3] On his aesthetic menu were practices of illegible overwriting and image layering, horizontally stacked and truncated letterforms, the anti-grid, and hand-rendered visuals. His reverence for graffiti culture can be seen within the cropped photos of his 1999 book *Fotografiks*, while his client work for the National Theatre, Portland's Ace Hotel, and Quicksilver closely emulate graffiti aesthetics of hand-rendered lettering, gritty textures, and textual eradication.

My eradication investigations began at a truck stop in the deep south, Louisiana. In 2006, I was traveling over holiday break with my partner, Erik, and we stopped to refuel our car. I went inside the bathroom, a single-occupancy stall, on what was an average, ordinary pit-stop. When washing my hands, I saw one of my sensitive words—"faggot"—engraved in the basin of the stained porcelain sink.

"Sensitive words" target and silence the recipient. They are words that make you cringe, bite your tongue, scream, or fight when you see or hear them proclaimed in public. They attempt to undermine your core identity by reducing it to a singular word or trait. At one level, the word does not matter so much as the impulse it evokes within you. Words are simply language after all, a mere grouping of letterforms to codify semiotic meaning; no one blames the letter "f" for "fuck" or "faggot." It is the author's intent that is in question.

Semiotics is the study of signs, signals, and sign processes, allowing the viewer to deconstruct and derive meaning from a visual system.[4] Social semiotics examines the long-term impact of cultural or societal power shifts within these initial meanings. Robert Westerfelhaus and Arvind Singhal's social-semiotics study on the generational reshaping of Our Lady of Guadalupe by both the Aztecs and the Roman Catholic Church describe notions of sign appropriation and reclamation by cultures desirous of co-opting a recognizable sign for their own purposes while excluding a sign's undesirable baggage.[5] The English language, for example, is a semiotic code comprised of a set of signs (the basic unit of representation being a letterform) and rules for assembling meaning. This meaning is weakened or charged depending on the author's intent, the audience's analysis, and the location and methods of textual deployment. Bathroom graffiti is a semiotic form of aggression whose meaning gains or loses strength depending on how we, the audience, assimilate or refute its messaging.

In this Louisiana bathroom, however, what was more profound than the discovery of my sensitive word was the word beside it. Rather than carving out a rebuttal word to fight back against the hate exchange happening within this sink, someone had reached for their own sharp tool and blocked out the adjacent word's letterforms to the point of non-recognition. Their impulse had been one of eradication, not supplementation. In reclamation, the sign had been "annexed from one code into another."[6] The scars were still there, even though the original word was gone. So, drawing inspiration from the activist who had eradicated hate speech before me, I reached for my car keys to scratch through "faggot." Then I realized that Erik had the keys with him. "Next time," I thought, "I'll plan ahead."

Because of this experience, my creative work shifted toward investigating bathroom graffiti—specifically anti-gay hate speech—as a typographic means of primal expression and a passageway to queer individuation, space reclamation, and empowerment. It has been a typographic journey of reverse-discourse formation, seeking out and acknowledging wall-inscribed labels, claiming identity, and affirmatively revising negative utterances that try to assign lesser values to members of the queer community.[7] Of specific interest is the men's bathroom, a public space for heterosexual and homosexual users turned immediately private by the nature of what goes on inside the confines of a secured stall. It is a space ruled by bodily necessity, sexual acknowledgment, and self-identity, all of which becomes apparent on the walls.

At the core of graffiti lies the element of reciprocal exchange, oftentimes, escalating to backlash. Graffiti becomes a time capsule unlocking 30,000+ years of history, a form of propaganda and emotional expression, a sociological study of humankind, and a confession. Confession is "a ritual that unfolds within a power relationship, for one does not confess without the presence (or virtual presence) of a partner who is not simply the interlocutor but the authority who requires the confession, prescribes and appreciates it, and intervenes in order to judge, punish, forgive, console, and reconcile."[8] A declaration of one's sexuality is an ever-present example. On a social-semiotics level, the power dynamics within hate speech graffiti heighten when the interlocutor no longer ignores the writing on the wall, but receives it and measures his or her own identity against it.

Months later, on February 19, 2007, in what I anticipated to be a usual afternoon of photographing graffiti within Chicagoland bathrooms, I entered a truck stop at the Illinois/Wisconsin border and discovered the words "gay fagget fucker die you know it's a truck driver" written on the left-hand wall of a dank three- by five-foot stall. The words shared company with a smattering of equally offensive sexual-resistance inscriptions against members of the gay community, women, and young adults—one passage even soliciting children via an anonymous phone number for pornographic videos. Curiously enough, within the two-stall, public bathroom, the stall I occupied on the right focused on homophobia, while the stall on the left focused on racial bigotry. These modern confessionals were divided according to their sins and all those seeking bathroom relief served as the de facto priests bearing witness to every confession. In stark contrast, and true to Alfred Kinsey's prescient 1953 study on the bathroom graffiti–gender divide, the woman's bathroom was marred by one indistinguishable mark: a neutral-colored tag of a woman's name and a corresponding date of 2006.[9]

As a viewer, I was involved in the discourse. Our desire to read the writing on the bathroom walls invites investigation and action: Do we ignore it or do we answer back? Standing in the center of this cramped, darkened stall with my digital camera in hand, I was struck with two questions: Why am I continuing to seek out and document this verbal hatred? What am I going to do about it? Before outlining my solution to the problem, the *what* that led me back to the stall, I will unpack the history and social semiotics of the text in order to explain my hidden fascination, the *why*, within this narrative.

◀ Figure 8.1

On February 19, 2007, I entered this right-hand stall of the men's bathroom inside a truck stop on the Illinois/Wisconsin border.

Prior to this discovery and while archiving bathroom wall inscriptions around the Chicagoland area from 2006 to 2007, I uncovered a system of patterns that could be applied to more universal themes connecting writing and space to gender and sexuality. Male bathrooms are more sexually charged spaces than female bathrooms. Within bathroom graffiti vernacular, men are portrayed as more aggressive (true vandals do two things: say something—anything!—or do damage destroy wreck shit), more sexually explicit (never pull out), and more objectifying against another body (amy k. is fuckalicious completely yeah! she's delicious), as opposed to women who, when writing at all, are more refined and articulate (I'm just really happy about what you did), self-body oriented (just checkin' the tamp), and, in the rare occurrence, self-objectifying as opposed to opposite-sex objectification (have a nice day slut you too biotch).[10, 11, 12, 13, 14, 15] Not surprisingly, Alfred Kinsey found 86 percent of male bathrooms to contain erotic material, 75 percent of a homosexual nature, primarily focused on oral contact, versus 25 percent in female bathrooms.[16] Interestingly, the most popular form of women's bathroom graffiti addressed non-erotic references to lips, curiously paralleling male predilection toward homosexual oral contact.[17]

Kinsey's determination that male-penned graffiti is both more sexually charged and more homosexual in tone suggests that some men are using the "advertising space" on the bathroom walls to attract from within: the homosexual male as both author and spectator. Homosexuality comes into play when you invert the male gaze from a heteronormative setting and lock it up in a bathroom stall with a male-only audience.[18] Homosexuality further comes into play with regard to excretion and childhood. Ernest Jones, in his 1918 behavioral analysis "Anal-Erotic Character Traits," links a child's desire to defecate with anal stimulation—commonly perceived, correctly or incorrectly, with homosexual gratification.[19] Within this bathroom space, we further revert back to our childhood-embedded "primitive smearing impulse," which describes our

The right-hand stall featured layer upon layer of hyper-sexualized and homophobic hate speech graffiti. (For example, the tongue emerging from the hot-pink panther's mouth reads: "high speed clit licker".)

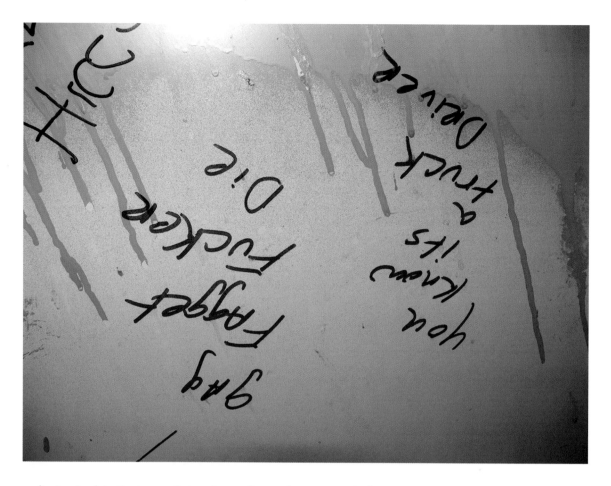

earliest primal instinct to soil the closest flat surface as a voiceless way to command attention.[20] So, when you enter the stalls, use the facilities, read the walls, and, even more, write on them, you are participating in a full-circle discourse connecting public to private, child to adult, function to pleasure, and superego to id.

From both a sensitive-word stance and a research perspective, the "fagget fucker" text engaged and enraged me. It was dirty in language, location, and tone. It reinforced the bathroom as a marked, sexualized space; the text also contained a hot-pink arrow pointing to a solicitation at the base of the stall, reading "tap foot for BJ." The "fagget fucker" text was homophobic while concealing a latent homosexuality. It embodied self-denial and self-contradiction by equating the effeminate male with the stereotypically tough truck driver and condemning this equation to a degree punishable by death. I was engaged because of the duplicitous writing. I was enraged because the words represented hate, aggression against, and danger for my community and me.

A disidentification occurs when a given source (in this case, the graffiti) allows for simultaneous, binary interpretation and that interpretation not only

▲ Figure 8.3

Tucked behind the stall door, and written at seated level, upside down, and in hot pink, I encountered my case study source text. The graffiti writer remains anonymous.

exposes the source's weakness but also ends up empowering the targeted group.[21] Paired alongside "gay fagget fucker die," the words "you know it's a truck driver," penned by the same graffiti writer, provide a hyper-masculine answer as to who is writing, or targeting, while also including this hyper-masculinity within the targeted group. In his text, the writer is chasing his tail and we, the viewer, are allowed inside his head.

This text became my case study, a psychological profile to decode and solve. Desire teaches us that the more something is kept a secret, the more we are driven to uncover or explore it. My desire to unlock another's anonymity by exposing the weaknesses behind their targeted language continues to drive my quest to seek out textual instances of anonymous hate speech.

Upon finding the "fagget fucker" wall text, two things became certain. First, I had to augment the graffiti writer's existing letterforms to generate a new language—a queer language—as a means of "talking back" and reclaiming power over him. A written language, however, is powerless unless received by another; such are the rules with confession. According to ethnographer and folklorist Alan Dundes in his 1966 study on latrinalia, "the sexual exposure no doubt contributes to the bathroom's role as a place of sanctioned license" for confessional inhibitions.[22, 23] Second, I knew I had to return to the original site and write my own confession. A few weeks later, I locked myself inside the same stall at 6 a.m. on a Sunday morning with an answer to the graffiti writer's attack.

I let the letterforms within the text work against themselves, generating a typeface based on the source handwriting. I retraced the graffiti writer's non-repeating, 20 letterforms within and used his strokes and angles to digitally reconstruct the missing 32 letters of a complete uppercase and lowercase alphabet. From a typographic stance, this applied the original strokes, bowls, stems, and terminals from one existing letterform as base anatomical elements in each newly reconstructed letterform. Using a process of mirroring and overlay, I placed his letterforms on top of each other to generate a homosexual uppercase and lowercase alphabet consisting of same-letter ligatures, or same-sex letters having sex with each other.[24]

Within my design practice, both creatively and commercially, I enlist a design-thinking model in which an impulse, or entry point, leads to ideation and iterative design work, and final implementation into the public sphere.[25] At each level comes semiotic analysis. In the early 1970s, designer and theorist Crawford Dunn defined three levels of the human signal—*alphasignal*, *parasignal*, and *infrasignal,* to speak to the nature in which, over the course of a given history, a mark or language unit will accumulate more layered meaning and can, in turn, be subjugated to deeper levels of visual deconstruction. [26, 27]

Alphasignal relates to the hard data of a visual system, that which we see first. Within the truck stop graffiti, the alphasignal is the text on the wall: "gay fagget fucker die you know it's a truck driver." Remember, language is just a mere grouping of letterforms to codify deeper meaning; no one blames the letter "d" for "die." Only after they are read together in a juxtaposed context and mapped onto considerations of author, intention, tone, and messaging does a deeper semiotic meaning emerge.

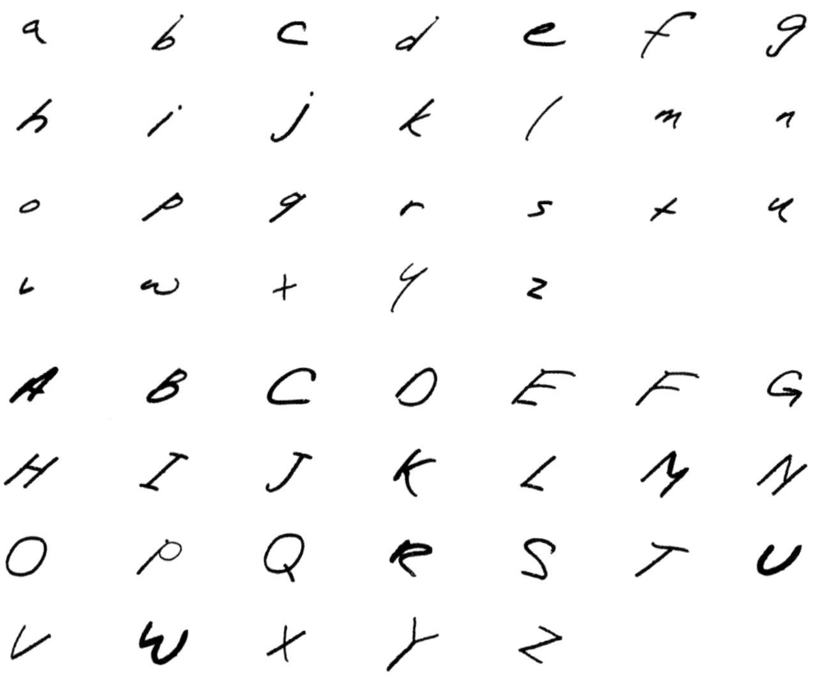

◀ Figure 8.4

My digital interpretation of the graffiti writer's A to Z handwriting as a complete uppercase and lowercase set, as sourced from his original 20 non-repeating letterforms.

Parasignal is a visual system of unmistakable characteristics, deepening the alphasignal's original meaning. In this case, the language—already charged—is amplified by the hierarchically captivating color: four-alarm hot pink. Amongst a sea of graffiti provocations, this color-coding demanded attention. Also, the source graffiti was upside down on the wall, suggesting an imbalance within the graffiti writer and an incongruity of behavior and blame within his circular statement.

Infrasignal is the underlying information, or subtext, which reveals deeper meaning within the initial sign and can often betray the sender's message. When the "fagget fucker" letterforms were doubled and reflected into ligatures, the emerging strokes, counter spaces, and terminals took on a biomorphic appearance, like Rorschach inkblots with a Freudian twist. Largely due to the thick lines and knobby ends generated from the graffiti writer's thick-tipped Sharpie, the new shapes possessed a pelvic-like symmetry, phallic and glandular terminals, ribbed, fleshy strokes, and puckered counter spaces. José Esteban Muñoz states that "disidentification is a step further than cracking open the code of the majority; it proceeds to use this code as raw material for representing a disempowered politics or positionality that has been rendered unthinkable by the dominant culture."[28] My redesigned typography revealed an infrasignal-based disidentification to betray and trump the sender—the graffiti writer's repressed queerness, as exposed by his own handwriting.

To reflect both the graffiti writer's disidentification between body and mind, and my reclamation between language and community, I aligned my language system vertically and with erratic letterform sizing. This evoked both

▲ Figure 8.5

My uppercase queer alphabet set, rooted in the graffiti writer's original handwriting, reconstructed through mirroring and overlay, and imagined as same-sex letters having sex.

▲ Figure 8.6

My lowercase queer alphabet set, also constructed as same-sex ligatures from the source wall graffiti.

the spinal-column support and symmetry of the body (to reference self-identity) and a totem-pole ancestry (to reference the banding together of a larger tribe or community). I generated removable, adhesive transfers spelling out "let's face it we're all queer," a found statement that was first deployed by activists in 1971 as wall graffiti during the post-Stonewall queer revolution on Christopher Street in New York City.[29]

Site-specific, adhesive-based juxtaposition became my overwriting plan for textual eradication. Guerrilla Girls uses adhesive-based signage in site-specific contexts to question cultural roadblocks preventing female empowerment.[30] Shepard Fairey and his following decorated public signage and structures with hundreds of thousands of stickers within his viral, anti-propaganda OBEY Giant campaign.[31] Matthew Hoffman continues to lead a worldwide sticker campaign with simplistically powerful "You Are Beautiful" reminders.[32]

▲ Figure 8.7

A resurrection (and reclaiming) of "let's face it we're all queer," previously used by graffiti activists during the Stonewall-era on Christopher Street in New York City, became my answer against the graffiti writer's hate speech.

▼ Figure 8.8

Adhesive transfer lettering became my weapon of choice for textual deployment. The uppercase, queer K that I am holding became a brand identity for the body of work, as the ligature reminds me of two lovers embracing. (This image is from a 2010 art installation at The ViaDuct Theater in Chicago's Roscoe Village.)

As a design strategy, my medium of choice—transfer letters with an adhesive, transparent film backing—reinforced a binary otherness within my alphabet. I needed a layer of distance and safety between my text and the source text—a design-solution prophylactic to prevent against hate speech infection. This layer of protection, however, needed to convey the illusion of direct intimacy with the source text in a visible, binary juxtaposition. And, removability over permanence was key: the skin of my text felt more elevated to me than the graffiti writer's quick-drawn Sharpie (and more respectful to those who would ultimately be cleaning the walls).

So, at 6 a.m. on a Sunday morning, April 15, 2007, I returned to the stall, avoided eye contact, clandestinely removed the transfer letters from my messenger bag clutched tightly by my side, and applied my text directly on top of the graffiti writer's hot-pink writing, as well as on the toilet seat, and on the wall just above the flush handle. In keeping with the "rules" governing restroom sexualities and "Tearoom Trade," I remained anonymous, not speaking to anyone inside the bathroom, privately planting my confessions on the walls for public readers to view and interpret, and reclaimed the stall as my own, smearing my text over the walls and toilet seat.[33] The installation took around three hours. My partner, Erik, drove the getaway car.

Graffiti, viewed by many as deviant behavior, is stereotypically associated with ne'er-do-wells or counterculturalists. Homosexuality, once commonly diagnosed as deviant behavior, was removed from the *Diagnostic and Statistical Manual of Mental Disorders* (DSM) in 1973. Despite this exoneration, New York City alone reported approximately 70 anti-gay incidents in 2013, a recent high. This included one death: openly gay Mark Carson, who was shot in the face in Greenwich Village after being taunted for his clothing—boots, cut-off shorts, and a tank top.[34] While it is possible that hate speech will lessen as cultures become more tolerant, it will never truly end. Within the queer community, positive strides lead to a sense of empowerment, but can, in turn, lead to an equal sense of subjugation: the more we talk about something, the more real or charged that conversation, or confession, can become. Retribution, oftentimes, surfaces.

To target a specific audience, a language should, to some degree, be impenetrable by others. Traditional Western thinking holds that the ability to reduce, or decode, into complete transparency is essential for understanding another.[35] Édouard Glissant, in *Poetics of Relation*, disagrees: "Opacities can coexist and converge, weaving fabrics. To understand these truly, one must focus on the texture of the weave and not on the nature of its components."[36] Within my queer writing, an instantly decipherable message would have been too easy to access and too easy to dismiss. In reader responses, individuals have picked up on implications of homosexuality and reclamation, even if they are not able to read certain letters. An agenda within the work was to generate such a language system that those open to agreement could learn or *see* the messaging, reading with one's eyes, yes, but also seeing into another's implication. A consequence within the work, and one that surfaces between marginalized groups, is the disorientation one feels when encountering something—language, in this case—that is not native to them. It is not my goal

to ostracize, but, rather, to invite others to linger within this disorientation, decode the letterforms, and absorb this educative agenda. Through disorientation, we learn.

Within sociology, labeling signifies the preconceived ideas that we have against an individual or group, often due to a differentiation in appearance, behavior, social position, or sexual orientation. Within everyday life, labeling draws reference from the physical act of tagging goods or places with textual captions, data, or details. The former, then, becomes a socially derived term, while the latter becomes a design embellishment. The truck stop bathroom graffiti, as well as the coded letterforms that I generated, fit within both categories.

The truck stop bathroom remains a "marked" sexual space and a breeding ground for confrontational messaging. I have returned since my textual intervention, and, while the "fagget fucker" text is no longer visible, new layers of hate speech continue to propagate in its place. Homophobic spaces have the potential to arise anywhere and everywhere; in turn, queer-positive spaces have the potential to arise anywhere and everywhere. The implication lies within the language: "If gay-related graffiti facilitates learning gay men's language and

▲ Figure 8.9

It was imperative that I deploy my queer alphabet directly on top of the graffiti writer's hate speech in order to eradicate his text and provide the viewer with a context for understanding mine.

▲ Figure 8.10

In an effort to reclaim the bathroom space, I applied my queer alphabet throughout the bathroom stall from both a standing and seated perspective. In addition to eradicating the graffiti artist's wall text, I left my mark directly on the toilet bowl rim and at eye level above the flush handle. I carried latex gloves and spray-on disinfectant inside my messenger bag.

culture, then the places where graffiti occur become spaces for learning gay language and culture—and, thereby, become gay spaces in their own right."[37] With a few words and some succinct design solutions, the minority, suddenly, rises to power. From both a design perspective and a queer perspective, language provided my entry for transforming the space.

French philosopher and social theorist, Michel Foucault, might reason that contemporary bathroom behavior links back to the sixteenth-century Counter Reformation, where a strict mandate to confess "all insinuations of the flesh" escalated into our current need to reveal everything.[38] After all, the more something is kept as a secret, the more we are driven to uncover or explore it. Such is the nature of bathroom graffiti, allowing the confessor an outlet to release all "thoughts, desires, voluptuous imaginings, delectations, combined movements of the body" on the public walls for private viewing.[39] Sure, when utilizing the bathroom facilities it is right in our face at eye level, so how can we *not* engage it, take it in, and process it. But, the fact remains that we read it. At least, I read it. And, now, I rewrite it.

Discussion Questions and Explorations

Descriptive

1. Collect a photo archive of text-based provocations within a crowded public space (everything from permanent signs to temporary graffiti). Arrange the text samples into a spectrum: formal to informal, clear to coded, beautiful to repellant.
1. What are your own sensitive words? Consider words or phrases that you feel specifically misrepresent you. These might include stereotypes, a word that you've been called, or a misrepresentation you've witnessed within the media. How did you feel upon hearing or seeing the word? How did you react? What do you wish you had done differently?

Analytical

1. Using two opposing, polarizing words as an entry point, generate typographic explorations wherein the visual expression of each word describes the baggage or charged emotion behind the word. Consider design issues of typographic arrangement, graphic embellishment, and level of clarity. How can you, typographically, generate a tension between what the viewer is familiar with and what is suddenly unexpected?
2. A reverse-discourse occurs when a word or phrase, which was once deemed negative or demeaning to a marginalized group, is reclaimed, owned, and reused—for positive labeling and empowerment—by that group. Consider and discuss ways in which words and phrases have been subverted and reclaimed by diverse communities. How do those instances manifest in the design world and the public sphere?
3. A metasymbol is a symbol—like the peace dove or the swastika—whose contemporary meaning has changed across time and because of cultural influence. What are some examples of symbols that have absorbed new meaning to become metasymbols? Trace the source symbols back to their graphic design origins and discuss their catalyst of change. What historical or socially relevant event(s) occurred to impact the metasymbol's new meaning? Which metasymbols have remained constant across time and history? Which metasymbols have dramatically changed (or even reversed in meaning)?

Speculative

1. Identify and consider non-graffiti instances of hate speech or media misrepresentation and discuss how those instances might be subverted to generate a new narrative. Consider examples within social media, pop culture, advertising, etc. What words or images are charged and why? How could these found instances of misrepresentation or hate be changed into something else (both linguistically and visually)? How would word, symbol, or image substitutions alter the tone and implication of the author's initial statement?
2. Through a lens of authorship, do we have the right, as artists, designers, sociologists, and linguists, to change or modify someone's words or voice?

Notes

1   Caleb Neelon, e-mail message to author, April 15, 2014.
2   Founded by Harry Hay in 1950, the Mattachine Society was one of the first peace-advocating gay rights organizations in the United States.
3   *Ray Gun*, an American alternative-music magazine, ran from 1992 until 2000 and revolutionized experimental typography.
4   Ferdinand de Saussure, Roland Barthes, Umberto Eco, Roman Jakobson, Julia Kristeva, Thomas Sebeok, and Claude Lévi-Strauss are the key figures in this movement.
5   Arvind Singhal and Robert Westerfelhaus, "Difficulties in Co-Opting a Complex Sign: Our Lady of Guadalupe as a Site of Semiotic Struggle and Entanglement," *Communication Quarterly* 49, no. 2 (2001): 95–114.
6   Singhal and Westerfelhaus, "Difficulties in Co-Opting a Complex Sign," 98.
7   Coined by Michel Foucault in his 1976 text, *The History of Sexuality, Volume 1: An Introduction*, a reverse discourse occurs when a marginalized group reclaims and reuses disparaging language, targeted at them, for self-identification and purposeful self-empowerment. Examples from the last half-century include: gay, faggot, and queer, among many others.
8   Michel Foucault, *The History of Sexuality, Volume 1: An Introduction*, Vintage Books Edition (New York: Random House, Inc., [1978] 1990), 61–62.
9   In Alfred Kinsey's *Sexual Behavior in the Human Female* (1953), he concluded that women were less sexually aggressive than men, compiled from interviews with approximately 6,000 women.
10 Men's bathroom, 112 South Michigan Avenue, School of the Art Institute of Chicago.
11 Men's bathroom, 37 South Wabash Avenue, School of the Art Institute of Chicago.
12 Men's bathroom, 112 South Michigan Avenue, School of the Art Institute of Chicago.
13 Women's bathroom, 37 South Wabash Avenue, School of the Art Institute of Chicago.
14 Women's bathroom, 37 South Wabash Avenue, School of the Art Institute of Chicago.
15 Women's bathroom, 37 South Wabash Avenue, School of the Art Institute of Chicago.
16 Alfred C. Kinsey, Wardell B. Pomeroy, Clyde E. Martin, and Paul H. Gebhard, *Sexual Behavior in the Human Female* (New York: Pocket Books, [1953] 1970), 673.
17 Kinsey et al., *Sexual Behavior*, 674.

18   Coined by Laura Mulvey in her 1975 essay, "Visual Pleasure and Narrative Cinema" (*Screen* 16, no. 3 (1975): 6–18), the male gaze forces the audience to view the female object-of-desire from a male-heteronormative viewpoint.

19   Ernest Jones, M.D., *Papers on Psycho-Analysis* (London: Bailliere, Tindall & Cox; Boston: Beacon Press, [1918] 1961), 413.

20   Jones, *Papers on Psycho-Analysis*, 432.

21   José Esteban Muñoz, *Disidentifications: Queers of Color and the Performance of Politics* (Minneapolis: University of Minnesota Press, 1999), 31.

22   Dundes coined the term "latrinalia," in opposition to the folk-inspired "shithouse poetry," to herald bathroom-graffiti analysis as a legitimate means of psychological study.

23   Alan Dundes, "Here I Sit—A Study of American Latrinalia," *Kroeber Anthropological Society Papers*, No. 34, ed. William G. Lockwood (Berkeley: Department of Anthropology University of California, 1966), 98.

24   A ligature occurs when two or more letterforms fuse into a single glyph.

25   Tim Brown, *Change by Design* (New York: HarperCollins, 2009), 16.

26   Crawford Dunn, "Alphasignal, Parasignal, Infrasignal: Notes Toward a Theory of Communication," *Print* 24, no. 6 (1970): 21–28.

27   In my undergraduate *Graphic Design Concepts* course at The City College of New York, I introduce students to the role of semiotics (sign, signifier, signified), graphic signals (alpha, para, infra), and image notation (icon, index, symbol, and meta-symbol)—seamlessly outlined by Philip B. Meggs in *Type & Image: The Language of Graphic Design* (New York: John Wiley, 1992), 1–19—during the first week. These initial vocabulary terms inform the trajectory of the semester, in which an infusion of text and image becomes the crux of narrative construction and project making. When students approach design solutions through a narrative lens and an ethnographic stance, the design work—and their invested thinking—will generate socially relevant results.

28   Muñoz, *Disidentifications*, 31.

29   Robert Reisner, *Graffiti* (Chicago: Cowles Book Company, 1971), 144.

30   Sticker downloads and implementation instructions are available on the Guerrilla Girls website: www.guerrillagirls.com. A 2001 anti-Hollywood campaign, for example, encourages participants to wallpaper movie theatre bathrooms with stickers supporting equal-representation for women within the film industry.

31   Shepard Fairey, interview by Steven Heller, "Interview with Shepard Fairey: Still Obeying After All These Years," *AIGA*, June 4, 2004, www.aiga.org/interview-with-shepard-fairey-still-obeying-after-all-these-year/ (accessed April 6, 2014).

32   Joan Podrazik, "The 'You Are Beautiful' Project: Artist Matthew Hoffman Spreads The Love (VIDEO)," Huffington Post OWN Videos, April 22, 2013, www.huffingtonpost.com/2013/02/22/you-are-beautiful-project-artist-matthew-hoffman_n_2735054.html (accessed April 6, 2014).

33   Laud Humphreys, in his controversial 1970 study on gay sex in public spaces, raised eyebrows with his research in "Tearoom Trade," or, same-gender sex in public park restrooms. Humphreys discovered that the key to public restroom sex is recognizing that silence is golden: it equals private safety within a public space while guaranteeing a stronger level of anonymity and a lesser degree of intimacy.

34   Richard Socarides, "The Murder of a Gay Man in Greenwich Village," *The New Yorker*, May 20, 2013, www.newyorker.com/news/news-desk/the-murder-of-a-gay-man-in-greenwich-village (accessed October 6, 2014).

35   Édouard Glissant, *Poetics of Relation* (Ann Arbor: University of Michigan Press, [1990] 1997), 189–190.

36 Glissant, *Poetics of Relation*, 190.
37 William Leap, *Word's Out: Gay Men's English* (Minneapolis: University of Minnesota Press, 1996), 89.
38 Foucault, *The History of Sexuality*, 19.
39 Ibid.

Editors' Introduction to Chapter 9

Few buildings have a stronger physical and emotional connection to their occupants than housing. Like other buildings, homes provide shelter from weather, while they also provide security from intruders and a safe haven for personal belongings. More than other types of buildings, however, homes often express the identities of the inhabitants—their life histories, personal tastes, physical needs, and aspirations. People purchase homes that they feel best meet their personae and circumstances. They renovate homes to meet their changing needs and desires, and change homes as their lives change.

It is common to think that interior designers and architects design new homes and do home renovations that uniquely match the owner or family. This is a misperception, however, of how most housing markets operate in the United States, United Kingdom, and other post-industrial nations. Developers, home builders, and realtors typically have a much greater influence on housing design than architects and interior designers in a practice commonly referred to as "speculative housing." Speculative, or "spec," housing is designed and constructed in advance of a client/owner, where a developer anticipates (speculates) what spaces, features, styles, and materials will be most desirable to a potential buyer, while balancing other factors, such as construction costs. Given a sufficient supply and an array of options, spec housing can adequately meet the diverse needs and preferences of society. If, on the other hand, supply is low, costs are high, and/or choices are limited, certain social groups may not be able to find or obtain suitable housing, or they may have to settle for less-than-favorable options. This can lead to reduced independence, decreased socialization, diminished self-worth, and an overall dissatisfaction with the home and home life.

During the mid-twentieth century, housing developers and builders in the U.S., in particular, placed emphasis on homes for "traditional" families—newly wedded, heterosexual couples with young children. This mindset has remained largely intact despite major demographic shifts, such as the steep rise in the numbers of single-parent families, widowed older adults, and individuals with disabilities. In short, the spec housing model has not kept pace with changing social structures. This has become particularly problematic for older adults, who experience declining health and ability, and exceptionally problematic for aging lesbian, gay, bisexual, and transgender (LGBT) individuals and couples, who experience similar health challenges plus negative social stigmas and biases in healthcare and housing.

In the following chapter, Carl Matthews, Jennifer Webb, and Caroline Hill discuss both the broad concept of "home"—how a "house" is different than a "home"—and the specific role that home design plays for LGBT older adults. What makes you feel "at home" vs. not at home? How has your sense of home changed over time? What are the characteristics of your ideal "dream" home? What are all of the barriers to achieving this? Comparing several examples, the authors discuss the demographic and economic trends that underlie home design, the unique and not-so-unique needs of LGBT older adults, and the impacts of home design and marketing on this group.

Chapter 9

Designing LGBT Senior Housing
Triangle Square, Carefree Boulevard, and BOOM

Carl Matthews, Jennifer Webb, and Caroline Hill

Before reading this chapter, watch the movie trailers "A Place to Live—The GLEH Triangle Square Story" and "Gen Silent" on YouTube.

Introduction

Art rhapsodizes over his apartment, full of light from the windows opening to the small terrace for his cat. Josie is reserved, but her smile reflects her relief at having a safe place to live, free from abuse. Karen is despondent because she has not been selected for one of the apartments, though she has moved more than 60 times in her life. These are brief glimpses of the new residents of Triangle Square, an LGBT apartment complex on "moving day."[1] These emotions are easy to understand and typical for anyone in the process of moving: anxiety about fitting in and making new friends, excitement about finding just the right place for their possessions, and regret about what is left behind.

Homes, whether they are urban apartments, suburban houses, or rural mobile homes, represent important aspects of who we are and how we feel about ourselves. Our homes fulfill broad social and psychological roles: home is an expression of personal tastes, values, and self-identity; home is defensible and provides safety for self and family; and home is a connection to the greater community where individuals desire to live and participate. Feeling "at home" permits residents complete freedom to talk about their lives, share their histories, and commune with others who understand or are at least sensitive to their unique view of the world. Some LGBT elders struggle to create home when moving into mainstream elder care facilities.[2] In contrast to the current social climate where sexual identity and preferences are increasingly acknowledged, some LGBT elders must suppress their identity to receive fair treatment in traditional senior care facilities. Some feel forced back into the closet when merged with a group that may not understand or accept their identity. This is particularly detrimental to the maintenance of one's personal identity and well-being for older adults where the combination of ageism and homophobia is especially prevalent.[3] Because of a home's critical role in emotional and physical well-being, this chapter explores the concept of home and the process of achieving a feeling of "at home" among LGBT older adults.

A Place to Live: The Story of Triangle Square tells the story of seven LGBT seniors anticipating what may be their final move.[4] The film explores important questions these older adults face as they search for housing. Are there affordable options with space available? Are there places that embody a sense of home and contribute to identity, autonomy, and belonging? Is there a place that will meet current and future physical and social needs? While many older adults confront these issues, some seniors in the LGBT community have experienced a tenuous existence because of their sexual orientation, and many have confronted homelessness or experienced loss of home repeatedly over the years.[5] Though the documentary celebrates the move-in day for several of the individuals featured, not all the seniors can move in, and the difficulty of creating and maintaining a sense of home for LGBT seniors in a variety of conditions is the movie's unifying theme.

> My dream is to live totally out and where I can enjoy the company and comradery of other gay and lesbian seniors. Not in some HUD funded "closet" in Pasadena.
>
> *(Margo)*[6]

Three senior LGBT housing projects serve as case studies for this chapter and were selected for their diverse resident profiles, economic structures, location contexts, and design approaches. Triangle Square, the first U.S. affordable senior housing project targeted to LGBT seniors, is located in Hollywood, California. The Resort on Carefree Boulevard, a lesbian-focused gated community, is located in North Fort Myers, Florida. The high-end BOOM communities have proposed developments in Palm Springs, California, and Malaga, Spain. Within the realm of real estate development, these project types are commonly called niche housing or lifestyle communities. Targeted to specific groups that share common interests and backgrounds (artists, golfers, academics, etc.), Harriet Barovick of *Time* magazine explains that "niche living is the latest step in the evolution of the planned retirement community"[7] and those for LGBTs are one of the fastest growing segments of the senior housing market with more than 20 gay-friendly developments prior to 2009.[8]

A Dramatic Population Shift: Demographic Trends and Older Adults

> It's a shock to find out you're old, being gay, and nobody wants to be with you.
>
> *(Art)*[9]

Baby Boomers, 76 million individuals born between the mid-1940s and the early 1960s, represent the largest generational subset of the U.S. population and they are critical to understanding issues relative to aging and housing.[10] Born into an age of affluence following World War II, Boomers' financial wealth has enabled self-actualization through physical fitness, leisure, and, at times, excess.[11] Compared to previous generations, Baby Boomers (1) will live longer after retirement, (2) will seek out widely varying housing solutions upon retirement, and (3) are more outspoken regarding their preferences. For these reasons, as well as their numbers and financial affluence, Boomers have gained significant attention.

Nonetheless, significant variation within the age group does exist. Economic differences continue to widen as the outcome of the 2008 financial crisis.[12] Cultural differences are profound; there are few other age cohorts with as much diversity inspired by social change. Many in this generation came of age at a culturally volatile time and found their voice in the Civil Rights Movement, anti-war demonstrations, and, for a smaller subset, in the Stonewall Riots, generally recognized as the catalyst for the LGBT rights movement. While current pop-culture seems to embrace LGBT people, many can testify that their fight for equality across minority groups remains unresolved. Laws and institutional systems exist throughout the nation and world that deny LGBT people equal opportunities, rights, and access.

> I get personally excited about housing people that have been shut out of the market or that the market has never really accepted them, sought them out, or saw them as a market. They have the right to a good, decent environment to live in.
>
> *(Tony Salazar, Triangle Square Developer)[13]*

Specific demographics of the LGBT community are particularly difficult to confirm for several reasons. First, there is no question on the U.S. Census that addresses sexual identity. Second, self-report data is unreliable because many respondents fear homophobia and discrimination. Third, because of the complexity of sexual identity, there is no single question able to adequately describe sexual orientation.[14] Nonetheless, it is logical to conclude that a population swell in general means a concomitant increase in the number of LGBT individuals. Estimates of 3.5 percent to 9 percent of the general population identify as LGBT, which suggests there are between 9 and 25 million LGBT U.S. citizens and between 2.6 and 7 million LGBT Baby Boomers.[15] These demographic markers are especially significant now because our understanding of sexual identity is changing so dramatically.

Description of Triangle Square, Resort on Carefree Boulevard, and BOOM

Triangle Square is located in an urban area of Hollywood near a number of LGBT services and cultural activities. Approximately 80 percent of the residents identify as LGBT with an equal distribution of men and women who qualify for low-income housing. The corner-located building is a courtyard complex with 104 units on four floors. It includes a swimming pool, library, media room, art room, fitness center, lobby lounge, laundry facilities, and indoor parking. The building also houses offices for Gay and Lesbian Elder Housing (GLEH), a non-profit organization providing affordable residential communities for LGBT adults. GLEH and the private real estate developer McCormack Baron Salazar received partial public funding to create the facility.

Resort on Carefree Boulevard (Carefree) is located in North Fort Myers, Florida, and is a lesbian-focused, gated community. Carefree is a privately funded, 50-acre development of 278 single-family homes and recreational vehicle (RV) lots appealing to mid- and high-income residents. The houses sell for higher prices than comparable neighborhoods due to the unique target market and overall quality. While there are typical suburban services nearby, there are no nearby LGBT-specific services. The resort features two small lakes, walking paths, a clubhouse, art studios, a dog park, swimming pool, shuffle-board court, bocce court, horseshoe court, tennis courts, putting green, and natural wetlands. There are approximately 130 full-time residents with seasonal residents varying from year to year. Ages range from 40 to 85 and, while most are women, some residents have children or are primary caregivers for aging parents or dependent siblings.

BOOM represents the largest and highest price end of the LGBT senior housing developments. They are planned for popular gay resorts (Palm Springs and Malaga) and cater to a market valuing high design. The projects have yet to break ground, but serve as a vision of what some LGBT seniors seek for their retirement. The communities, designed by well-known contemporary architects, offer a wide range of housing types, assisted living units, full-care facilities, health clubs, lounges, and worship chapels.

Income Determines Housing Options: Economic Diversity within the LGBT Elder Community

The diverse housing choices of Triangle Square, Carefree, and BOOM reflect the demographic diversity of the Boomer cohort. Demand for housing alternatives and economic constraints must be considered in parallel to current economic conditions.[16] Older adults face many challenges exacerbated by limited or fixed incomes such as affordable, supportive, and accessible housing and high-quality healthcare.[17] While working, regular income from employment combined with raises associated with career advancement typically leads to income growth. Following retirement, seniors' incomes, which most often are comprised of social security income, pension benefits, and investments, tend to be stable because additional revenue is not added. For this reason, most older adults live on a "fixed" income.

> Not only is there not affordable housing but many of the seniors we know in that income category have been forced back in the closet.
>
> *(Julia Klisko)[18]*

An increased risk for living in poverty is especially true for older LGBTs, but they may also confront additional barriers.[19] First, as recently as a 2007 study, 68 percent of individuals identifying as LGBT reported discrimination in the workplace, and greater percentages of same-sex households fall below the poverty line.[20] Second, LGBT elders are less likely to be married or partnered, and this negatively affects accrued wealth resulting in fewer resources during later life. Third, income trends of older adults reveal women and minorities are particularly at risk, where women of the Boomer generation earned only 65 percent of what their male counterparts earned, and income iniquities continue today.[21] Finally, existing federal and state laws and workplace protocols frequently deny same-sex partners equal rights to benefits such as social security or pension income, health and life insurance, and family leave.[22] At the opposite end of the status spectrum, some LGBT folks have dedicated more time and energy to their career and financial development rather than to the hegemonic ideals of typical heterosexual families. These financially and socially stable LGBT seniors may have extensive resources to retire exactly how they please.

With acknowledged shortage in affordable, quality housing for older adults, aging Baby Boomers have stimulated the development of alternative housing models.[23] When Boomers began turning 60 in 2005, government agencies, municipalities, and housing developers increased pace to meet the senior housing demand. In addition to traditional nursing homes, there has been an increase in other residential environments such as assisted living facilities, dementia care units, and niche housing, though financial resources remain the primary determinant of one's housing choices.

Location and Design Affects Comfort and Security

> Not everyone will rent to someone they suspect is a lesbian or a gay man.
> *(Ivy Bottini, Civil Rights Activist)[24]*

The sites for these case studies provide diverse contexts for aging. Triangle Square capitalizes on its location in an urban, gay-centric neighborhood while Carefree Boulevard blends into homogenized suburbia and BOOM creates exclusivity in already gay-friendly resorts. Triangle Square, Carefree, and BOOM are only a small sample of the locations and community structures sought by older LGBT adults. Housing theorist Clare Cooper Marcus states, "For most of us, the type of setting we live in is as important as or more important than the type of house."[25] LGBT older adults move into these locations to take advantage of unique characteristics. These communities allow individual and collective identities to be developed in places that are desirable.

> The best part of living in Triangle Square is that I feel safe. I feel that I'm with family. I'm with all these people that I know . . . are old, lesbian, and gay . . . It's something in my life that I never dreamed could happen.
> *(Nancy)[26]*

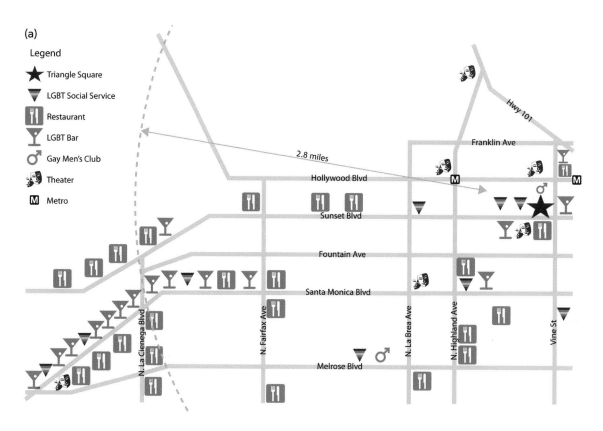

(a)

Legend

★ Triangle Square

▼ LGBT Social Service

🍴 Restaurant

🍸 LGBT Bar

♂ Gay Men's Club

🎭 Theater

Ⓜ Metro

Hwy 101

Franklin Ave

2.8 miles

Hollywood Blvd

Sunset Blvd

Fountain Ave

Santa Monica Blvd

N. La Cienega Blvd

N. Fairfax Ave

N. La Brea Ave

N. Highland Ave

Vine St

Melrose Blvd

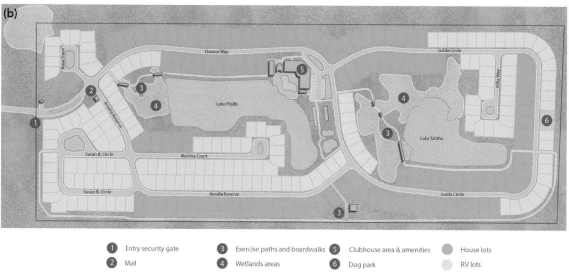

(b)

Eleanor Way

Golda Circle

Rosa Trace

Lake Phyllis

Willa Way

Lake Talitha

Susan B. Circle

Martina Court

Susan B. Circle

Amelia Reserve

Golda Circle

① Entry security gate ③ Exercise paths and boardwalks ⑤ Clubhouse area & amenities ⬤ House lots

② Mail ④ Wetlands areas ⑥ Dog park ⬤ RV lots

▲ Figure 9.1 ▶

Context maps of: (a) Triangle Square; (b) Carefree; and (c) BOOM.
Images courtesy of Carl Matthews, Scott Biehle, and HWKN respectively.

(c)

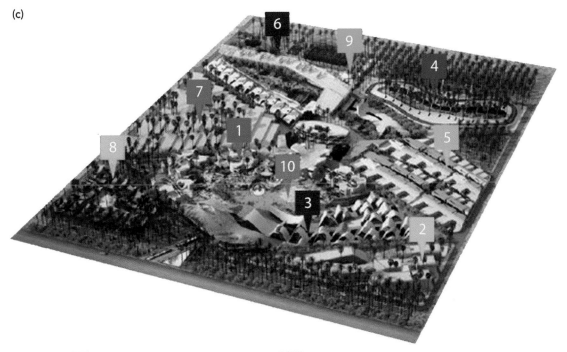

1	J. Mayer H.	6	Joel Sanders Architect
2	L2 Tsionov-Vitkon	7	LOT-EK
3	Diller Scofidio + Renfro	8	Sadar + Vuga
4	Hollwich Kushner	9	Arakawa + Gins
5	Rudin Donner	10	SURFACEDESIGN

While these decisions include aesthetic preferences, they also speak to issues of identity, privacy, and control that contribute to physical and psychological safety. These places ameliorate the potential loss of self-concept/identity by celebrating the commonality of membership in a minority population. Many individuals prefer to age in place as a way of retaining the continuity typically fostered by one's home. All three developments help individuals maintain or heighten self-identity through shared experiences, values, and worldviews. Residents engage in healthy aging through the continuation of important social roles such as spouse/life partner or caregiver.

Triangle Square's gay-centric neighborhood appeals to individuals who have lived in the community and provides safety through like-minded neighbors, businesses, and service providers, effectively buffering the older residents. Carefree creates safety through physical distance and suburban anonymity, and BOOM uses selectiveness. Both Carefree and BOOM use closed boundaries to communicate and enforce safety for residents.

Negotiating a Branded Identity

The physical branding and signage of the three developments forms an important part of their identities. Each community has a strong LGBT identity although their various visual expressions have been debated and continue to evolve. Building signage expresses an LGBT identity at Triangle Square and nearby LGBT services and activities encourage a strong connection between residents and their community. The triangle symbol, once used by the Nazis to label LGBT individuals in concentration camps, has been recast by LGBT activists, and, as such, is prominently displayed in both symbol and word form at the Triangle Square community. While the name Resort on Carefree Boulevard communicates relaxation and freedom, the community adopted a neutral expression in name and signage. This expression is consideration for the comfort of more conservative residents, some of whom were members of military or religious communities where open lesbian identities were not allowed. The lack of LGBT-centric services and activities nearby creates an inward focus at Carefree. Subversively, Carefree streets are named after women iconic to the lesbian community. Casual observers may not understand the references to Willa Cather, Martina Navratilova, and Eleanor Roosevelt on the streets named Willa Way, Martina Court, and Eleanor Way, but community members do.

▼ Figure 9.2 ▶

(a) Resort on Carefree Boulevard street sign; (b) Triangle Square signage; and (c) BOOM graphic identity.
Images courtesy of Carl Matthews, Lisa Pauli, and HWKN respectively.

BOOM uses rainbow-inspired graphics to identify the communities as LGBT-focused and communicates communal power and pride.

This range of comfort with "outness" in community names and signage reflects the range of sexual identity disclosure employed in LGBT senior communities. Some current LGBT seniors marched in the front lines of demonstrations for social acceptance while others hid their identity to maintain jobs and memberships in non-accepting situations (corporations, military, religious communities, etc.). For those who never "came out," anxiety related to LGBT identities is very real, and they fear visible labels such as signage may put them at risk for discrimination and abuse. For other residents, freedom of expression, particularly with regard to their home, is a critical element of their identity, and the public display of rainbow flags and gay pride symbols is empowering. As residents move in and out of the communities, the debate over visible identity markers will continue, reflecting the dynamic relationship between individuals, their physical spaces, and their communities.

(a)

(b)

BOOM
(c)

A BOLD NEW COMMUNITY

Personal Control over Design Influences Satisfaction

The process of moving from one home to another can be a profoundly stressful experience, particularly for seniors who may be moving for reasons of declining health or financial resources. The ability to personalize space, select and display objects symbolizing who we are, or who we want the world to perceive us being, is an important component of how people shape authentic identities.[27] Recreating a previous home through the display of meaningful objects can have a significant impact on whether the move is a positive or negative experience.

Each of the described communities approaches the personalization of living spaces in different ways. Individual modifications of resident apartments at Triangle Square are limited. Interior palettes are gray or beige, and some residents express desire to control the colors of their apartments. Modifications to interior architectural features and other design details (e.g. cabinetry, countertops) are not permitted at Triangle Square because residents do not own the units.

Carefree homeowners have total control over home design decisions and create interior and exterior spaces to suit their preferences. However, it is interesting to note that public display of rainbow flags were banned in the early years (1990s). Fear of attracting undesired attention, possible harassment, and discrimination contributed to an atmosphere some residents described as internalized homophobia. The rainbow flag ban policy has been abolished in recent years, and is concurrent with the increased acceptance of sexual minorities throughout the general U.S. populace.

Spaces Shape Social Interactions

> I live in low income housing right now, but they're all young. It's lonely. And everybody just lives with their doors closed. Nobody talks to each other. Nobody says, "Would you like to have coffee?"
>
> *(Art)*[28]

Triangle Square, Carefree, and BOOM provide communal spaces that are lounge-focused or dedicated to specific activities. At Triangle Square, GLEH organizes a wide range of activities (e.g. cabaret nights, film screenings, potlucks, museum trips, etc.) that are free to all residents and their guests, and strengthen residents' bonds to one another and the larger community. Shared community spaces at Triangle Square provide venues for social interaction and enriching activities. The centrally located swimming pool, entrance lobby, and community room are most active. However, design decisions that isolated the library, art room, media room, and fitness room on separate floors make these spaces less utilized than other shared amenities. At Carefree, the clubhouse is highly utilized; several residents indicated that it is too small to support the way the community socializes. The clubhouse includes an art room that the community quickly outgrew and, subsequently, two freestanding art buildings were added. There has been a recent movement from active pursuits (e.g. running, tennis) to those more sedentary (e.g. art, writing). Personal expression through planting beds around the homes at Carefree also was prevalent. Residents took pride in their gardening, and the well-maintained, attractive yards frequently received positive comments. Creating and maintaining garden and outdoor spaces provides additional outlets for development of interpersonal relationships among residents.

Residents at Triangle Square and Carefree mentioned loneliness in their previous residences, and how the design of the community makes it convenient to find someone to talk to or something to do. Because of the gay-centric setting, finding individuals with shared values and experiences results in greater levels of interaction and support. The gender balance at Triangle Square results in cross-gender support networks sometimes less commonly seen in younger

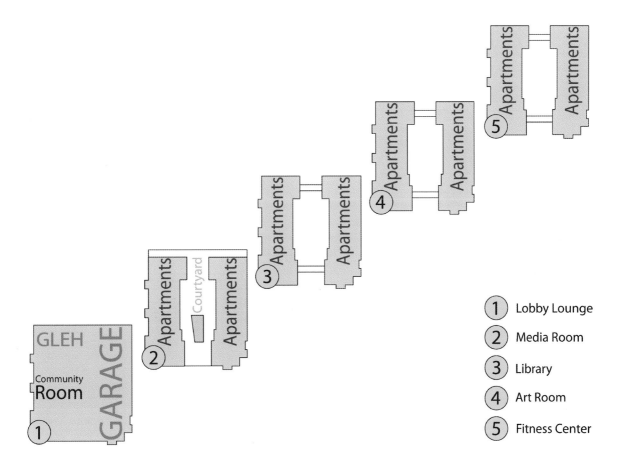

Apartments Apartments

⑤ Fitness Center

④ Art Room

③ Library

Apartments Apartments

Apartments Apartments

② Apartments Courtyard Apartments

GLEH GARAGE

Community Room

①

① Lobby Lounge

② Media Room

③ Library

④ Art Room

⑤ Fitness Center

▲ Figure 9.3

Triangle Square stacking diagram illustrates location of communal spaces.

Image courtesy of Carl Matthews.

gay male and lesbian communities. Residents state they are more familiar with their co-residents and depend upon them not only for socialization, but also for help with daily living tasks. Self-made "family" bonds are strong and include knowing one another's stories, histories, opinions, and idiosyncrasies through conscious effort. These "families of choice" play an important role in the lives of LGBT seniors, and, for many, these neighbors become the people who are expected to care for, assist, and advocate for them.[29] These planned communities are being designed with the desire for community connection in mind. Research has shown that interactions for residents within elder communities increase health, well-being, life satisfaction, and lifespan while decreasing depression.[30] This is particularly relevant for the LGBT community given the social climate and discrimination many have experienced.

> It's nice to be with a bunch of gay old people that can understand each other and have a history together.
>
> *(Art)*[31]

While residents at both developments were interested in social activities, group outings, and utilizing common spaces on site, privacy also was important. Home

(a)

(b)

CHAPTER 9 Carl Matthews, Jennifer Webb, and Caroline Hill

(c)

(d)

Continued overleaf

(e)

(f)

▲ Figure 9.4

Continued

provides the opportunity to practice and maintain physical skills and abilities that are important to identity, self-worth, and feelings of competency. Living environments, therefore, must provide amenities that not only foster a sense of home and desired levels of social engagement, but also facilitate solitary pursuits.

Older adults face many changes in their autonomy as part of the aging process. Health-related changes in functioning necessitate additional support for activities of daily living and transportation through increased reliance on family and friends as well as formalized services. While previous beliefs that all older adults are lonely and live in isolation have been disproved, research findings about the LGBT community suggest increased loneliness in old age. Older LGBT adults report rejection and loss of familial and social relationships leaving a gap in the informal support network.[32] Many of the LGBT community have cultivated chosen families of friends of the same generation, which may reduce the number of individuals able to provide support. Like other older adults, LGBT individuals experience significant life changes when retiring from the workplace. As a result, a sense of connection and community in their domestic world becomes even more important.

Residents at Triangle Square and Carefree Boulevard cited several examples of people having significantly compromised physical abilities prior to moving to the community, and being restored and regaining physical abilities post-move. During a visit to Carefree, a resident shared her story of moving to the development overweight and dependent upon a mobility scooter. Through support and encouragement of other residents, she lost weight, regained her ability to walk, and gave away the scooter. Health status is directly related to autonomy, socialization, mental activity, and physical activity. These stories of marked improvement in an individual's health and well-being upon relocating to a senior living community are supported by other researchers as well.[33] The design of home and community has a significant impact on one's mental and physical well-being. Evans explains, "Personal control, socially supportive relationships, and restoration from stress and fatigue are all affected by properties of the built environment."[34] Admittedly, the reasons for these types of improvements in mental and physical well-being shared by seniors living in these types of communities may or may not be tied exclusively to the experience of living in a supportive senior community. Changes in climate, the release of self-imposed psychological barriers, access to a new healthcare provider, etc. could all be contributing factors.

Conclusion

Ideas of home and our home's reflection of our values and status are tightly tied to our identities. In a series of interviews exploring home, David Seamon found that

> feelings of regeneration and being-at-ease were significant in the experience of at-homeness. The home was seen as a place of regeneration, of repose and refreshment, and renewal of physical and psychological energy. When individuals control space and have privacy needs met, feelings of comfort and freedom are possible.[35]

Niche communities, particularly for those older LGBTs, accept people and the roles they have crafted over time as part of an individual's identity. Triangle Square and the Resort on Carefree Boulevard provide mechanisms to maintain and further develop the identities of their respective populations. Site selection and branding provide for safety and security. Social spaces facilitate interaction, mutual support, and health. Control allows for personalization, privacy, and autonomy. These design features, in turn, nurture and validate the residents as valuable and cherished members of these communities. Are these design features different from those in a more typical, heterosexual senior living community? Certainly these features seem equally important to all older adults, yet there remains an inherent difference. Any population that has endured centuries of oppression and marginalization has unique cultural and emotional needs. Designers must consciously and methodologically examine these needs in order to create a place for optimal health and well-being throughout the aging process. For LGBT seniors, increased attention to spaces for social interaction might be the most important design consideration.

> If I have my way this is not the only building that will be built. We've proven that there is a need. We've proven that there is a will. We've proven that there is a way.

> (Carolyn Dye, Chair, GLEH)[36]

Niche developments reflect the definition of community with shared territories, values, support structures, public realms, and density.[37] The preference for niche housing communities such as Triangle Square, Resort on Carefree Boulevard, and BOOM attest to the desire for some LGBT seniors to age in a place with others who share their values and history. Additionally, "gayborhoods" tend to be some of the most culturally, ethnically, and economically diverse areas of cities accepting all of those who may have found themselves at the fringes of society.[38] Balancing the desire for community identity, increased social interaction, and the need to personalize individual aspects of home represents the ideal senior living scenario.

While the motivation to achieve "wholeness" has been discussed relative to the growing popularity of niche living for LGBT seniors, there are two sides to this coin. McHugh and Larson-Keagy explain, "Retirement communities ... are places rich in meaning and collective identity in aging ... [but] they are simultaneously places of separation and exclusion that speak to the potency of age, social class, ethnicity, and lifestyle as social borders."[39] Many gay men and lesbians have spent their lives being marginalized and some might wonder why they would want to separate themselves in gay-centric buildings or communities. However, the three-year waiting list for an apartment at Triangle Square, and a similar occurrence of 300 applicants for 80 units in a low-cost LGBT senior housing project in Chicago, attest to the fact that LGBT niche housing is in demand. Despite the current popularity, might the desire for an LGBT senior housing community be necessary in the future if we reach a utopic world where all people are treated equally regardless of sexual orientation or gender identity? Might senior communities built specifically for LGBT individuals today follow a similar trajectory of many revitalized "gayborhoods" and become gentrified over time? Existing LGBT senior housing projects and those currently on the design boards may indeed evolve similarly as sought-after places to live by a wider market sector.

Discussion Questions and Explorations

Descriptive

1. Describe the physical differences between Triangle Square, Resort on Carefree Boulevard, and the proposed BOOM communities.
2. Who can live at Triangle Square, Resort on Carefree Boulevard, and BOOM? What are the selection criteria? Who decides? Can anyone be legally excluded?

Analytical

1. Identify another group of older adults you believe face challenges similar to the LGBT community. Discuss three ways in which they are similar to the LGBT community and three ways in which they are different.
2. Who is responsible for ensuring all citizens have a safe place to live? Describe the different groups that you believe should have an active responsibility and explain their roles.
3. Discuss the possible beginning and evolution of "gayborhoods." Why and where did they emerge? Why have many become gentrified over time?
4. What are the positive and negative consequences of segregation, both socially mandated and self-selected? Is the concept of niche housing contradictory to inclusive design?

Speculative

1. In writing and/or sketches, design a sign that identifies one of the communities (or a different market-specific community). Describe the reasoning behind each of your ideas. Address color, material, and other attributes you believe are critical to the community.
2. Examine the stacking/blocking diagram for Triangle Square (Figure 9.3). Propose alternate locations for the Media Room, Library, Art Room, and Fitness Center to encourage more social interaction. Alternately, what other building functions might be relocated to encourage more social interaction?
3. Imagine that you have just moved into Triangle Square, Resort on Carefree Boulevard, or BOOM. Write a letter to your sibling explaining what you believe to be most fulfilling aspects of your new home.

Notes

1   LGBT is a term that means lesbian, gay, bisexual, and transgendered and may include other letters (Q, I, A) or orders. Though limited in nature, this phrase is used to identify individuals who do not consider themselves heterosexual. American Psychological Association, "Lesbian, Gay, Bisexual, Transgendered," accessed April 1, 2014, www.apa.org/topics/lgbt/index.aspx. These individuals are featured in a documentary film as they seek a new home. Carolyn Coal, *A Place to Live: The Story of Triangle Square*, DVD, produced by Cynthia Childs (Westmount, Canada: Filmoption, 2008).

2   Loree Cook-Daniels, "It's About Time: LGBT Aging in a Changing World" (conference report of SAGE National Conference, New York, October 12–14, 2008), accessed April 1, 2014, http://forge-forward.org/wp-content/docs/SAGE_Conference-Findings.pdf.

3   Identity development for gay and lesbian people follows a typical progression of stages though duration varies and repeating earlier stages is common. The stages are: (1) confusion, (2) comparison, (3) tolerance, (4) acceptance, (5) pride, and (6) synthesis. Vivienne Cass, "Homosexual Identity Formation: A Theoretical Model," *Journal of Homosexuality* 4, no. 3 (1979): 2199–2235.

4   Coal, *A Place to Live*.

5   Cook-Daniels, "It's About Time."

6   Coal, *A Place to Live*.

7   Harriet Barovick, "Niche Aging," *Time*, March 12, 2012, 179, and Sally Abrahms, "Finding your Niche Housing in Retirement – or Before!," *AARP Bulletin*, March 7, 2011, accessed April 1, 2014, www.aarp.org/home-garden/housing/info-03-2011/niche-housing-in-retirement.html.

8   Carolyn Said, "Gay-Friendly Senior Housing, Half-Century-Old Idea," *San Francisco Chronicle*, June 26, 2011, accessed March 7, 2014, www.sfchronicle.com/business/article/Gay-friendly-senior-housing-half-century-old-idea-2366764.php.

9   Coal, *A Place to Live*.

10 U.S. Census, "Age and Sex Composition," April 2011, accessed March 17, 2014, www.census.gov/prod/cen2010/briefs/c2010br-03.pdf.

11 "Baby Boomers," Value Options, accessed April 10, 2014, www.valueoptions.com/spotlight_YIW/baby_boomers.htm.

12 Alexandra Cawthorne, "The Not-So-Golden Years," American Progress, accessed April 1, 2014, www.americanprogress.org/issues/poverty/report/2010/09/27/8426/the-not-so-goldenyears/.

13 Coal, *A Place to Live*.

14 Ann Fausto-Sterling, "Dueling Dualisms," in *Sexing the Body: Gender Politics and the Construction of Sexuality* (New York: Basic Books, 2000), 1–29.

15 A variety of credible sources report divergent numbers regarding LGBT population trends. For example, see Gary J. Gates and Frank Newport, "Special Report: 3.4% of U.S. Adults Identify as LGBT," October 8, 2012, accessed March 7, 2014, www.gallup.com/poll/158066/special-report-adults-identify-lgbt.aspx; and Gary J. Gates, "How Many People are Lesbian, Gay, Bisexual, and Transgender?," accessed March 7, 2014, williamsinstitute.law.ucla.edu/wp-content/uploads/Gates-How-Many-People-LGBT-Apr-2011.pdf.

16 Kimberly Johnson and Kathy Wilson, "Current Economic Status of Older Adults in the United States: A Demographic Analysis," National Council on Aging, accessed April 1, 2014, www.ncoa.org/assets/files/pdf/Economic-Security-Trends-for-Older-Adults-65-and-Older_March-2010.pdf.

17 Johnson and Wilson, "Current Economic Status."

18 Coal, *A Place to Live.*

19 Cook-Daniels, "It's About Time."

20 American Psychological Association, "Lesbian, Gay, Bisexual, and Transgender Persons & Socioeconomic Status," accessed July 26, 2014, www.apa.org/pi/ses/resources/publications/factsheet-lgbt.aspx.

21 Income data for 1960 through 2010 were averaged for both men and women and differences were calculated on those means. See "The Wage Gap Over Time," accessed July 26, 2014, http://pay-equity.org/info-time.html.

22 For an extensive review of legislative issues for LGBT individuals, see Nancy J. Knauer, "LGBT Elder Law: Toward Equity in Aging," *Harvard Journal of Law and Gender* 32 (2009): 1–59.

23 S. Robert August, "Baby Boomers and Beyond: Trends for Senior Housing Buyers," North Star Synergies, accessed April 5, 2014, www.northstarsynergies.com/assets/pdf/boomers.pdf.

24 Coal, *A Place to Live.*

25 Claire Cooper Marcus, *House as a Mirror of Self* (Lakeworth, FL: Nicolas-Hays, 1995), 10.

26 Coal, *A Place to Live.*

27 There is extensive research on the role of possessions, identity, and meaning in later life. For one perspective, see Linda L. Price, Eric J. Arnould, and Carolyn F. Curasi, "Older Consumers' Disposition of Special Possessions," *Journal of Consumer Research* 27, no. 2 (2000): 179–201.

28 Coal, *A Place to Live.*

29 Arnold H. Grossman, Anthony R. D'Augelli, and Scott L. Hershberger, "Social Support Networks of Lesbian, Gay, and Bisexual Adults 60 Years of Age and Older," *Journals of Gerontology* Series B 55, no. 3 (2000): 171–193.

30 For an extensive review of literature about the importance of social spaces see Nichole M. Campbell, "Therapeutic Social Space Design for Independent Living Retirement Community Residents" (Ph.D. diss., University of Wisconsin-Madison, 2011).

31 Coal, *A Place to Live.*

32 Cook-Daniels, "It's About Time."

33 Kevin E. McHugh and Elizabeth M. Larson-Keagy, "These White Walls: The Dialectic of Retirement Communities," *Journal of Aging Studies* 19, no. 2 (2005): 241–256.

34 Gary W. Evans, "The Built Environment and Mental Health," *Journal of Urban Health: Bulletin of the New York Academy of Medicine* 80, no. 4 (2003): 536–555.

35 David Seamon, "The Home and At-Homeness," in *A Geography of the Lifeworld: Movement, Rest, and Encounter* (London: Croom-Helm, 1979), 78–85.

36 Coal, *A Place to Live.*

37 Edward J. Blakely and Mary Gail Snyder, "The Search for Community," in *Fortress America: Gated Communities in the United States* (Washington, D.C.: Brookings Institution Press, 1997), 29–45.

38 Manuel Castells, "Cultural Identity, Sexual Liberation and Urban Structure: The Gay Community in San Francisco," in *The City and the Grassroots: A Cross-Cultural Theory of Urban Social Movements* (Berkeley: University of California Press, 1983), 138–169.

39 McHugh and Larson-Keagy, "These White Walls," 252.

Editors' Introduction to Chapter 10

Everyday objects have some of the greatest impacts on our lives, but, because they are commonplace, we often overlook them. Everything from computing devices to transportation systems, from cooking utensils to storage sheds, avoid scrutiny because we use them all the time. As a result, these designed elements of daily life remain conventional. Designers miss the opportunity for more innovative and higher functioning alternatives. And society remains unaware of the potentially negative consequences masked beyond the veil of convention. One such feature, prevalent in classrooms, auditoriums, and public venues throughout the world, is the podium (or lectern).

All designs possess a degree of empowerment and disempowerment: a product might be easily used by right-handed people, but challenging for left-handers; a building might be easily navigated by someone familiar with the place, while a first-time visitor may feel lost; a city or town might seem welcoming to one social or political group, while unfriendly to others. These examples comprise three different realms of empowerment/disempowerment—function (e.g., ergonomics), perception (e.g., wayfinding), and ethos (e.g., social identity). The first two are more straightforward. We can tell if a product, building, or system functions well; and we generally know if those same things are intuitive, providing clues about their use. In complement, we are aware when a device, feature, or service is difficult or confusing, leading to feelings of frustration. The third example, *ethos*, is more complicated. Ethos is the overall character of the design—its look and feel, the value system it communicates, and the user group it implies. What about a building's design causes us to feel included versus alone? What about a city leads us to feel at home versus unwelcome? What about a product's design leads us to buy or overlook it?

The way we feel about a design results from a complex interaction of three things: (1) one's self-concept and personal beliefs (self-identity), (2) the demographic makeup and values of society (social-identity), and (3) the distinguishing material, sensory, and symbolic characteristics of the built environment (aesthetics). When one's self-identity matches the surrounding social-identity and aesthetics, she/he feels satisfaction or pleasure, contributing to what psychologists refer to as self-actualization, the process of achieving one's fullest intellectual, physical, and emotional potential. A perceived mismatch, however, between "self" and "surroundings" produces negative feelings and hinders self-actualization.

In the following chapter, Kathryn H. Anthony discusses the history, hidden meanings, and features of podium design, and presents an alternative proposal. For example, most podia—tall, fixed, and large—are not suitably designed for women of small stature. Typical podia, instead, negatively highlight the body and functioning of the woman, diminishing not only the content of her lecture but also her identity and self-actualization. What are the possibilities for new podium designs? Is it possible to design a podium for short and tall people, for people who are standing or seated, for people with low/no vision or decreased/no hearing? Anthony describes both the design process, which involved a diverse committee of constituents, and the resultant new podium design. As you read this case study, consider how the design process—how the *design* of the design process—affects the outcomes or end product. Likewise, think about how the design of other commonplace products can be reimagined to empower, rather than disenfranchise, diverse users.

Chapter 10

Repositioning Power

An Alternate Approach to Podium Design

Kathryn H. Anthony

Introduction

The podium plays a subtle but significant role whenever someone speaks in a public forum. It establishes distance between the speaker and the audience, conveys a position of power, and acts as a support for the presenter. This chapter examines the podium and its history, concentrating on how podium design empowers or disempowers the speaker. It analyzes how a presenter is perceived when a mismatch occurs between the podium design and the size of the speaker, and how certain body types are advantaged over others. The case study features a women-led design team at the University of Illinois at Urbana-Champaign that developed, constructed, and installed a set of innovative, gender-friendly, universal design podia to help remedy this design bias.

In large lecture halls, students are more likely to be found in the audience rather than on the stage or at the podium. Have you ever thought about what it feels like to be standing behind that podium? Perched behind the podium, professors have a panoramic vantage point from which they can see their audience. For most male speakers of average size, podia work well. Male presenters can be seen from about the waist up, refer to their laptop computer, maintain eye contact with the audience, gesture with their hands, and brace themselves with both arms against the podium. When the podium design fits well with the presenter's body, and the proportional relationship between the two is correct, the audience may not even notice either at all; they blend together as one. In situations like these, the podium recedes into the background. Yet when a mismatch occurs between the podium design and the speaker's size, serious problems ensue.

A wide variety of podia can be found at colleges and universities, convention centers, city halls, houses of worship, and elsewhere—anywhere one gives a public address before an audience.

Some definitions are in order. A *podium* (*podia* for plural) is the raised platform, pedestal, or rostrum where speakers deliver presentations, while the

◀ Figure 10.1

For average size or tall male speakers, most podium designs work just fine.

lectern is a raised, slightly slanted stand where speakers rest their notes or laptop computer. Speakers stand on a podium and stand behind or at a lectern. These terms are often used interchangeably, and their meaning has become synonymous. In this chapter, the term podium refers both to podium and lectern.

Pulpits serve as podia in houses of worship, raising ministers above the congregation to highlight their leadership role. They appear almost hanging in midair, putting them in a position of otherworldliness. Musical conductors stand on podia so that all members of their orchestra can see them. Recipients of prizes and awards are invited to podia to be acknowledged for their accomplishments.

In modern sport, media use the expression "to podium" as a verb, signifying the chances of particular athletes to win in their respective sports disciplines. Winners of Olympic competitions are called to three different types of victory podia for the gold, silver, and bronze medals. Each Winter and Summer host of the Olympic Games produces its own stylized version of the Olympic podium: round, square, rectangular, or octagonal with a color and design concept from its Organizing Committee of the Olympic Games.

But that was not always the case. Starting with the 1896 Athens Olympics, where the King of Greece presented awards to Olympic winners at the closing ceremonies of the Games, to Amsterdam in 1928, where Queen Wilhelmina did

For shorter female speakers, the typical podium design poses problems.

the same, Olympic athletes received their awards in a physical setting located below their dignitary and heads-of-state presenters.

That process was reversed in the 1932 Lake Placid Olympic Winter Games and the Los Angeles Summer Games, such that winning athletes ascended before dignitary presenters. Synchronous with this shift in physical location was a shift in who presented the awards to athletes. No longer did kings, queens, crown princes, and prince consorts present the medals. Instead, Olympic officials had this special honor. Then-International Olympic Committee President Count Henri de Baillet-Latour first ordered organizers to create a raised platform where medals could be awarded to athletes. In 1930, Baillet-Latour had a seat in the first row of the first British Empire Games, now Commonwealth Games, held in Hamilton, Ontario, Canada. There he saw the podium used for a medal protocol that gave him the idea for the Olympics.[1]

Podium design in political debates can prove to be highly controversial. For the U.S. presidential debates, televised before a live audience, political staffers spar over space to cast their candidates in the most favorable light. Presidential candidates have alternated among different formats: standing behind a podium, seated at the same table facing the moderator, or a more informal town-hall or talk-show style, where each moves across the stage. Candidates of shorter stature often stand on hidden stepstools or phone books to match the height of their opponents. The perceived height of candidates is an important factor in how viewers perceive them, as evidence shows that voters prefer their leaders to be tall. In about two-thirds of all U.S. presidential elections, the taller candidate wins the popular vote.[2] And after the election, winners are perceived as taller than before, while losers are perceived as shorter.[3]

Theoretical Perspectives on Podium Design

From a purely utilitarian perspective, the podium serves as a support space, providing speakers with a place upon which to rest their hands. For those who fear public speaking, a common scenario, the podium gives them something to hang onto. It is a place to store water, cough drops, and other emergency supplies for speakers who may lose their voice, feel faint, or start running out of steam. At times like these, the podium and its hidden storage compartments come to the rescue. It serves as both a physical and a psychological aid, a type of security blanket.

From a communications perspective, podia make symbolic social statements, placing the speaker in a dominant position. They convey the message: "Stop, look, listen. I have something important to say."

A complex interaction occurs between the style of the podium and the substance of the speaker's content. The podium design may enable or interfere with communications. At worst, poor podium design may prove so distracting that it can undermine the speaker's message altogether.

Consider the format used in popular "TED Talks, Ideas Worth Spreading," where talks are limited to 18 minutes or less and podia are prohibited. This informal talk-show atmosphere allows a speaker's expertise to stand on its own. Their bodies are visible from head to toe. Absent is the hierarchical nature of the podium that places speakers in a privileged position. Not all speakers are comfortable with this format, but for those who are, it can be a highly effective means of communication.

From an environment-behavior perspective, the podium can be viewed as a type of public territory, much like a seat on a bus or airplane. During the time that you use it, you appropriate the space as your own. You delineate the space with your belongings, be it laptop, notes, or bag. You are highly aware of any territorial invasion that may occur. For instance, it would be taboo if, during the middle of class, a student places his or her backpack atop the professor's podium or a small child runs up to the podium and starts tugging at the professor's leg. Once you depart, you surrender your territory and it reverts to the public; the next speaker, whoever that may be.

The podium can be viewed as a temporary symbol of self. Much like the clothes he or she wears and the bag he or she carries, podia are part of a package that defines the speaker—albeit for a short period of time—when all eyes are focused on her or him as the center of attention.

Many podia are specially engraved with presidential seals, university seals, or other emblems that represent that institution. By standing behind that symbol, speakers are perceived as officials who represent that institution.

Visiting dignitaries, commencement speakers, and award recipients are photographed or recorded on video at the podium. Commemorative photos appear in print and digital media, far outlasting the presentations themselves.

The podium provides distance between the speaker and the audience, what Edward Hall, in his classic work *The Hidden Dimension*, referred to as "public-interpersonal distance." Compared to the "intimate" (less than 18 inches), "personal" (18 inches–four feet), and "social distances" (four feet–12 feet), the "public distance" (12 feet or more) is the farthest.[4]

How well does the typical podium work from the point of view of diversity—specifically gender, body type, or age? For a vast array of individuals, the podium serves as a highly visible example of an inadequate product design, one that is widely used but that works poorly. While we select the watch we wear, the cell phone we use, or the car we drive that makes us feel most comfortable, we rarely have a choice over which podium to use. And yet, we are bonded and branded with that podium whenever we speak before an audience.

From a gender perspective, the podium is a socially constructed, gendered space. Although an unintended consequence, its design accentuates the speaker's gender and body size, often leading to disparate perceptions of men and women, with women being viewed in a less favorable light. It calls attention to a speaker's gender in a way that would not occur had it been properly designed to match her or his proportions. Compared to tall or average-sized men, many women behind the podium may both feel and be perceived as marginalized.

From an accessibility perspective, podia are dysfunctional. Speakers who use wheelchairs can neither see nor be seen from behind the podium. The same is true for young children. The typical podium is not friendly to underrepresented persons, hence a poor example of designing for diversity.

A large body of studies has demonstrated that students tend to be harsher in their evaluations of women professors compared to those of their male counterparts. In many academic disciplines, women are subjected to inhospitable situations, what researchers Bernice Sandler and Roberta Hall first coined as the term, a "chilly climate."[5] Podia designs that cast women speakers in a negative light create an even chillier climate.

Empowerment and Disempowerment at the Podium

No matter what their design, podia convey a position of power. Much of that sensation is from the speaker being situated in an elevated position, with height being a symbol of power, authority, and control.

Public venues feature a variety of podium styles. The podium may be mounted on wheels, making it easy to move around horizontally. Yet the typical podium is a fixed height.

Many podia that house complex audio-video systems are mammoth in size and scale, almost like motherboards on ships. Such behemoth multimedia consoles appear best when accompanied by an oversized body type; behind these, a thin, average-sized male may appear diminished. Technology has driven the size and shape of these podia, rather than body-conscious design.

Yet for many speakers, a highly noticeable, uncomfortable *mismatch* occurs where the relationship between the speaker and podium is out of proportion. For shorter male speakers, for women speakers of average to below-average height, and for speakers with physical disabilities who use wheelchairs or require other assistive devices, this mismatch can be highly problematic. Some speakers may require stepstools. Presenters relying on their laptops may not be able to see much above the top of their screens, forcing them to crane their necks for an occasional glimpse of the audience. Speakers with wheelchairs often have to dispense with the lectern altogether, either setting up a makeshift presentation area from which they can access their laptop computer, or placing their computer or notes on their lap. For many speakers, mammoth podia serve as a barrier that gets in their way, and they have given up on them altogether.

Equally important is the audience's view. When a female speaker of small stature is dwarfed behind a tall podium, her credibility is diminished. When speaking behind a laptop or in a dimly lit space, she becomes even less visible, and her appearance much less flattering. With most of her body hidden behind the podium, and when her laptop is opened for her to review the screen, only a tiny portion of her face can be seen. When a disembodied head is all they see, audiences may find it difficult to take her seriously.

With increasing numbers of women in leadership positions, the podium problem is magnified. Imagine how many women schoolteachers, principals, superintendents, city officials, legislators, and experts in their profession are disadvantaged by the design of podia every day.

During religious services, members of the congregation often participate at the podium for special readings or announcements. This is often the case at special services like weddings, funerals, or coming-of-age ceremonies, such as

▼ Figure 10.3

When a shorter female speaker is hidden behind a tall podium, her credibility is diminished.

CHAPTER 10 Kathryn H. Anthony

UNIVERSITY OF ILI

Campus Announcements   Coll

. Mumps outbreak in the Midwest   Res
  Are you susceptible?

. Register now for the Faculty   Ful
  Summer Institute   Cu

. New website to minimize   Al
  paperwork for researchers   Pa
                                      Fa
                                      V

▲ Figure 10.4

A large podium hides all but a shorter female speaker's head, the only part of her that the audience can see.

bar mitzvahs. Shorter women and children struggle on tiptoe to reach the microphone and, in many cases, they cannot be heard. If they are nervous to begin with, their discomfort at the podium merely makes matters worse.

In situations like these, when a mismatch occurs, the podium design calls attention to itself. It is almost as if the speaker is wearing a set of clothes that do not fit, like a woman with a size-5 shoe wearing a size-12 men's basketball shoe. The podium distracts from whatever message speakers are trying to convey. Instead, it sends a different message: "You don't belong here, this wasn't made to fit you, and we don't care."

And even if special secret measures are taken to help shorter speakers feel more comfortable at the podium, sometimes they backfire. Years ago, I was at an international conference where I had requested a stepstool at the podium. It was placed in an inconspicuous location. The speaker who spoke right before me, a good friend and colleague taller than I am, had no need for it. We had each taken months to prepare our presentations and had just traveled halfway around the globe. As my colleague approached the podium, she failed to see the stepstool, tripped right over it, and plunged onto the stage. Although she was not injured, she was shaken and embarrassed. After she finished her talk, she received a special round of applause. Yet after all that preparation, this was not the way she wanted to be remembered: as the speaker who fell onto the stage. And I, too, felt indirectly responsible for her accident. Had it not been for my need for a stepstool, she never would have fallen.

Designing a Gender-Friendly, Universal Design Podium

The case study presented here provides a gender-friendly experience to all campus speakers. A special podium was initiated, designed, developed, and constructed at the University of Illinois at Urbana-Champaign. A team of women drove the design.

What sparked this project? In the early 2000s, we observed then-Chancellor of the University of Illinois at Urbana-Champaign, Nancy Cantor, at numerous speaking engagements. Described in the *Chronicle of Higher Education* as "a five-foot-tall dynamo with short brown hair and an outsized growl of a laugh" and "a high-energy style," Chancellor Cantor, a distinguished social psychologist, was all too often seen overshadowed by a tall podium.[6] Her relatively short tenure as Chancellor (2001–2004), where she was a steadfast champion of diversity on campus, was rocked by her opposition to Chief Illiniwek, the university's longtime mascot, on the grounds that it was racist and demeaning to Native Americans. The Board of Trustees refused to back her and she soon left to become President of Syracuse University (2004–2013) and, later, Chancellor of Rutgers University (2013–present). During the time that Chancellor Cantor was on our campus, she

▲ Figure 10.5

At this religious service, a tall male and a short female are called upon to read the Epistle. Note how much of each reader can be seen.

had appointed me to serve as Chair of the Chancellor's Committee on the Status of Women (2002–2004). Later (2009–2011), my colleague, Professor Gale Summerfield, and I served as Co-Chairs of the Provost's Gender Equity Council. During that time, we initiated the design, development, production, installation, and use of a gender-friendly, universally designed podium.

Many women serving on our Provost's Gender Equity Council could relate to the uncomfortable situation faced by Chancellor Cantor. Several of us routinely delivered classes and invited lectures from compromised positions behind inappropriately sized podia that were designed for tall men, or behind extremely complex, mammoth podia with dashboards full of controls that seemed to rival those found in a 747 aircraft. As Summerfield put it, "In organizing lectures and symposia on campus, I often had speakers who were too short to be seen over the podium. … Anyone outside that average range, whether male or female, could benefit from the new podium."[7]

Our Gender Equity Council design team was comprised of our two Co-Chairs, our administrative assistant and program coordinator, Anita Kaiser, and our then-graduate student secretary, Kelly Sullivan, from the School of Architecture. Together we worked closely with staff members of the university's Mill Shop, Mark Barcus, Mill Foreman, and Brad Ward. They were enthusiastic about our proposal and contributed technical ideas about how to realize our goals.

The design of the project took just a few months. The project began in January and was unveiled in March. We began by conducting an Internet-based search for existing adjustable podia or lecterns. What we found appeared more like a simple music stand or was aesthetically unappealing, not the type of design on which we wanted our university funds spent.

Nonetheless, we discovered an existing operating mechanism to enable a podium to be adjusted with the push of a button. We needed a design where that push-button mechanism could be installed. At the same time, we decided that, rather than contract out the work, we preferred to make use of our local, on-campus talent. Kaiser and Sullivan contacted our university's Mill Shop to see if the staff there could help. They responded by telling us "design it and we can build it for you." And so we did.

Our design team made several visits to the Mill Shop warehouse in order to oversee the design and construction process. During one of our more entertaining visits, a 6′8″ employee from the university Mill Shop and I (5′2″) tested out the podium and were pleased to find that it worked just fine for both of us.

We brought a mockup on-site to one of our Gender Equity Council meetings so that all council members could try it out and provide their feedback. We also transported the mockup to the School of Architecture, where we tested it out with a number of different individuals of diverse shapes and sizes. One of them, our tallest architecture faculty member, stands over 6′6″ tall. Another architecture colleague uses a wheelchair. As he put it, "This is certainly something I'd like to see after spending many years presenting with my nose resting on various podia,"[8] and he suggested several refinements. We also had an expert from our university's Disability Resources and Educational Services test the design. She, too, recommended a number of revisions. Others who were involved in critiquing the preliminary design included an architecture faculty member with expertise in small-scale architecture and furniture design. In order to determine the ideal size for stowing their bags and purses, several women with varying handbag styles tried the podium.

We also explored different kinds of materials. Many podia are constructed with dark-stained oak and appear very heavy and masculine, as if they belong in an attorney's office or courtroom, a look we sought to avoid. We chose a lighter wood finish, one that could be easily stained to match the décor of the space in which it would be used.

The final design includes the following features:

- push-button operation allowing speakers to raise and lower the podium using two electronic activators
- a microphone
- a flexible light on each side of the podium
- a slide-out for wheelchair access accommodating both left-handed or right-handed speakers
- a power source provided on each side of the podium
- a slide-out cup holder
- space for bag/purse storage
- heavy-duty wheels
- a hidden stool for extra height
- a modesty panel.

microphone

flexible light

slide-out for wheelchair accessibility with modesty panel-accommodates left- and right-handed speakers

power provided on both sides

easy push button operation allowing speakers to raise and lower podium

slide out cup holder

safe storage space for purse or bag

heavy-duty wheels and hidden stool for extra height

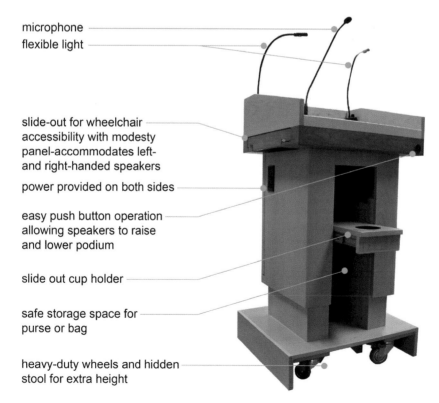

◀ Figure 10.6

The podium's design incorporates several user-friendly features.

CHAPTER 10 Kathryn H. Anthony

▲ Figure 10.7

Our Provost's Gender Equity
Council design team and our new
universal design podium at
Krannert Center for the
Performing Arts, University of
Illinois at Urbana-Champaign in
2011, where hundreds of visitors
tried it out.

Our intention was to keep the design simple in order to accommodate future change in technology. The push-button mechanism allows the podium to be adjusted in height to accommodate speakers ranging in height from 4'2" to 7'0", allowing them to speak comfortably and to be seen by a large audience.

The first podium to be constructed was unveiled at the Krannert Center for the Performing Arts, the university's major performing arts venue, on March 10, 2011, at the same event where several multi-media projects funded by the council were also on display. The event was held in conjunction with Women's History Month. Hundreds of visitors—students, faculty, administrators, staff, and community members—saw the podium. People of varying shapes, sizes, and physical abilities tried it out. The podium received an enthusiastic reception from all who tried it, including University of Illinois alumna Jean Driscoll, American wheelchair racer who has won 12 medals at the Paralympic Games and the women's wheelchair division of the Boston Marathon eight times.

Over the span of just a few months after its unveiling, the Provost's Gender Equity Council funded the design, production, construction, and installation of ten universal design podia at major venues and key lecture halls at the University of Illinois campus (one venue has two of these podia). Recommendations from attendees at the Krannert event, with consultation from location representatives, determined the locations.

Reflection on the Design Process and its Aftermath

In addition to the unusual gender composition of the design team, another aspect that set this design process apart was its user-driven, not client-driven, approach. That is, the university did not initiate the project. Instead, our Provost's Gender Equity Council recognized a glaring deficiency on campus and sought to address it with a design solution.

It was one of the first times that the Gender Equity Council produced a tangible product by working closely with members of the university's Mill Shop. Typically, the council would be conducting campus climate surveys, sponsoring gender-related research, hosting special events, inviting guest speakers to campus, and recommending new policies and procedures.

Yet another unique aspect was the highly diverse, multidisciplinary nature of our Gender Equity Council members, who offered feedback at critical stages of the design process. A wide variety of disciplines were represented on the committee, from philosophy to engineering. Our committee members included diversity of genders, ages, and bodies.

Our graduate student assistant from the School of Architecture played a critical role in helping us to usher the project from design concept to design development to construction. It illustrates the value that architecture faculty and students can add to university committees when financial support is available to spark new design ideas and see projects to fruition.

Summerfield reflected on her experience:

> Sometimes teams are enthusiastic for a few weeks, but people get distracted by other projects and leave the main work to one or two members. However, this was a team where enthusiasm grew at each stage of the project and everyone participated throughout. It was a pleasure to work with the group, especially my co-chair, and was one of the highlights of my career.[9]

One of the first events to use the podium was the 2011 Women and Gender in Global Perspective's Symposium, Gender Equity in Research and Practice, held at the student union building in the center of campus. The podium worked extremely well in this event, where speakers, alumni from several different countries, ranged from 5'2" to over 6 feet tall. Audience members noted that being able to see the speakers' faces was helpful and promoted discussion. Several speakers had issues with being too short or too tall for the traditional podium and were delighted to use the new podium. Often they could not imagine any

▲ Figure 10.8

Since their installation in 2011, faculty, guest speakers, and visiting dignitaries from around the world have used our new podium.

alternatives to the traditional podium and so they were surprised to see the one we had designed. After a few minutes demonstrating how to use the features of the podium, speakers were eager to try it out themselves and relieved to have a closer connection with the audience. Even for those speakers who preferred to walk around during their presentations, the podium served them well.

Since their installation in 2011, faculty members from across campus, guest speakers, and visiting dignitaries from around the world have spoken at these podia. In 2013, these included U.S. civil rights leader Myrlie Evers and Chairman of the Presidency of the Republic of Bosnia and Herzegovina His Excellency Zeljko Komsic.

Here is some feedback received about the podium from Matthew Ando, Professor and Chair of the Department of Mathematics: "The team ... did a remarkable job designing and building the item. In spite of its many features, it is very attractive and compact, and fits very well into our colloquium room, which is heavily used for classes throughout the day. It will be a real help to our faculty and students."[10] A female colleague from the Math Department noted, "The podium is wonderful. Now I just wish I could bring it from classroom to classroom with me."[11]

◀ Figure 10.9

At the 2014 School of Architecture commencement ceremony in Foellinger Auditorium, one of the largest spaces on campus, I announced the names of all masters of architecture candidates from our new podium. It was my first time using it and I could actually see and be seen.

Here are some additional reflections from Summerfield:

> Working on a committee such as the Gender Equity Council takes time and effort. … With enthusiastic participants and some resources, this committee was able to accomplish projects, such as the podium, that made it a unique experience. I really liked the podium because it was a real-world project that supported our academic goals and helped women, men, and those in wheelchairs in their presentations. While my focus was on the University of Illinois, the project has potential well beyond our campus.[12]

Recalling the project, Sullivan said, "I absolutely loved working on that project and working for the council. It was one of the major highlights of grad school for me. I can't thank you enough for giving me the opportunity."[13]

Finally, a personal note: At our 2014 School of Architecture commencement ceremonies, I had the special honor of announcing the names of all graduate students receiving their masters degrees. Our ceremony was held in the Foellinger Auditorium, one of the largest auditoriums on campus facing the university's historic quadrangle. Our commencement speaker was one of our most highly accomplished architects, Cesar Pelli, alumnus of the class of 1954, who had come to Illinois as a graduate student from Argentina.

For the first time, we used the new podium at our architecture commencement ceremony. I am pleased to report that it was a pleasure to do so. At 5'2", I could still be seen and heard by everyone in the crowd. It was a joyous occasion for all, and I didn't even need a stepstool.

Discussion Questions and Explorations

Descriptive

1.   Describe an event where you have seen a mismatch between the podium and the speaker's body size.

Analytical

1.   Find a U.S. presidential debate on YouTube, including debates amongst primary candidates. Examine how each candidate uses the podium.
2.   Stand behind the podium in a large classroom and address the audience for at least one minute. Select two classmates, one taller than you, one shorter than you, to do the same. Take turns watching each from the front, middle, and back rows. What does it feel like for each of you? How visible are you to the audience? Analyze the positive and negative attributes of the podium design.

Speculative

1.   Find examples of 10 different podia. Speculate on the kinds of messages that these podia send.

Acknowledgments

The author especially thanks the Co-Chair of the Provost's Gender Equity Council, Professor Gale Summerfield, along with Anita Kaiser, Program Coordinator, Women and Gender in Global Perspectives Program, and Kelly Sullivan, then-graduate assistant for their critical assistance throughout the podium design and construction process, enabling us to see this project through to fruition. She is grateful to then-Provost Linda Katehi at the University of Illinois, now Chancellor at the University of California at Davis; as well as Barbara Wilson, then-Office of the Provost, now Dean of the College of Liberal Arts and Sciences at the University of Illinois at Urbana-Champaign for providing generous financial support for this project. She also thanks the following members of the 2010–11 Provost's Gender Equity Council for their participation: Jennifer Bernhard,

Electrical and Computer Engineering; Jennifer Hamer, Department of African American Studies; Mona Heath, Office of the Chief Information Officer; Iwona Jasiuk, Department of Mechanical Science and Engineering; Timothy McCarthy, Department of Philosophy; Ann Nardulli, Molecular and Integrative Physiology; Ramona Oswald, Department of Human & Community Development; Madhu Viswanathan, Business Administration; Cindy Williams, College of Law; Lori Williamson, Office of the Vice Chancellor for Institutional Advancement; Mena Pratt-Clarke, Office of Equal Opportunity and Access (Ex-officio); and Peg O'Donoghue, Office of the Chancellor (Ex-officio).

Notes

1   Robert K. Barney, "A Simple Souvenir: The Wienecke Commemoration Medal and Olympic Victory Celebration," *Olympika* 15 (2006): 87, accessed May 19, 2014, www.highbeam.com/doc/1G1-175877031.html; Paul Mayne, "Olympics Detective Uncovers Podium Roots," *Western News: The University of Western Ontario*, January 19, 2006, accessed May 19, 2014, http://communications.uwo.ca/western_news/stories/2006/January/olympics_detective_uncovers_podium_roots.html.

2   Open N.Y., "The Measure of a President Op-Chart," *New York Times*, October 5, 2008, accessed September 8, 2014, www.nytimes.com/interactive/2008/10/06/opinion/06opchart.html?_r=0.

3   Gregg Murray, "It's Weird, Candidate Height Matters in Elections," *Psychology Today* (2012), accessed September 3, 2014, www.psychologytoday.com/blog/caveman-politics/201210/it-s-weird-candidate-height-matters-in-elections. See also Gregg R. Murray and J. David Schmitz, "Caveman Politics: Evolutionary Leadership Preferences and Physical Stature," *Social Science Quarterly* 92, no. 5 (2011).

4   Edward T. Hall, *The Hidden Dimension* (Garden City, NY: Anchor Books, 1966).

5   Roberta M. Hall and Bernice R. Sandler, "The Classroom Climate: A Chilly One for Women?," (Washington, D.C.: Association of American Colleges, 1982).

6   Robin Wilson, "Syracuse's Slide: As Chancellor Focuses on the 'Public Good,' Syracuse's Reputation Slides," *Chronicle of Higher Education* (2011), accessed March 3, 2014, http://imaginingamerica.org/wp-content/uploads/2011/10/Syracuses-Slide.pdf.

7   Gale Summerfield, e-mail message to author, September 9, 2014.

8   Carl Lewis, e-mail message to author, February 3, 2011.

9   Gale Summerfield, September 9, 2014.

10 Matthew Ando, e-mail message to author, September 29, 2011.

11 Alison Ahlgren, e-mail message to Barbara Wilson, October 2, 2011.

12 Gale Summerfield, September 9, 2014.

13 Kelly Sullivan, e-mail message to author, September 11, 2014.

Part 3 | Age and Ability

Editors' Introduction to Chapter 11

It began as a beacon of hope in the early 1950s and ended in an imploded pile of rubble in 1972. In less than two decades, the Pruitt-Igoe public-housing project in St. Louis, Missouri, shifted from a highly praised innovation to an emblem of failed public policy.

Pruitt-Igoe was conceived and built during the postwar period, a time of optimism and prosperity in the U.S. As part of a slum-clearance and redevelopment project, the St. Louis Housing Authority built 33 11-story towers with 2,870 units housing 15,000 tenants. Residents and city officials alike were hopeful, and, in 1957, occupancy rates were 91 percent. That soon changed, however, and, by the end of the 1960s, Pruitt-Igoe was nearly empty, a deteriorated complex plagued with vandalism and violent crime.

What went wrong? Unanticipated public-policy consequences are among the many reasons this project failed. First, the 1949 Federal Housing Act promoted inconsistent policies. On the one hand, it provided incentives for urban renewal projects; on the other, it offered subsidies for those who relocated to the suburbs. The result was an emptying city. In addition, federal policies allowed ample funding for construction of the project, but did not include funding for maintenance, which, instead, was taken from residents' rents. As occupancy declined, so did money for repairs. The result was a broken, unsafe place to live.

Jane Jacobs, author of *The Death and Life of Great American Cities*, predicted what would happen with Pruitt-Igoe. Jacobs supported the idea that public policy, while typically outside the realm of formal design professions, is one of the most impactful areas of design because it has the potential to affect so many people. It is decision making for the public good. Jacobs abhorred public-housing projects such as this, because they lacked the "mixed use" necessary for a thriving urban environment. Instead, Jacobs encouraged the integration of different building types—housing, businesses, recreation, etc.—and a diverse range of people—young and older, wealthy and poor, etc. This mix, she argued, kept neighborhoods active and safe. Storekeepers and residents watched the streets and would ensure activity for many hours during the day and evening. Pruitt-Igoe was the antithesis of this model, a forest of concrete sameness in great need of more thoughtful policy and design.

In this chapter, Mary Jane Carroll shows an example of problematic policy, some 50 years after the Pruitt-Igoe disaster, in another housing project—the redevelopment of Regent Park in Toronto, Canada. The City of Toronto and the Toronto Community Housing Corporation developed a set of policies based on Jane Jacobs' premise that transforming public-housing sites into mixed-income communities would encourage integration and inclusion across socio-economic groups. Carroll documents the differences between political rhetoric and the final built form, and shows who wins and who loses as policies are revised.

Carroll challenges us to consider several questions: What were the multiple agendas at play in this particular case? What, in general, are some of the essential ingredients of effective public-policy design and implementation? What are the dynamics between public policy, regulatory requirements, and commercial interests in architecture? How has thinking about "decision making for the public good" changed since the days of Pruitt-Igoe? Who needs to be involved in decisions that affect "the public good"?

Chapter 11

(Re)forming Regent Park
When Policy Does Not Equal Practice

Mary Jane Carroll

"When I first heard that they were going to build new apartments in Regent Park, I thought, well, finally," said Hazel M., a long-term resident of Canada's largest and most notorious public-housing project, located in downtown Toronto, Canada.[1] At age 68, Hazel has lived there for more than 50 years and has seen the park transform from an award-winning social-housing solution to a neglected, underfunded, and dangerous urban ghetto. When, in 2003, the City of Toronto and the Toronto Community Housing Corporation (TCHC) announced plans to revitalize Regent Park, Hazel and her friends were overjoyed.[2] As members of the urban poor, they were thrilled that their voices and concerns were finally being heard. "We [the residents] had been fighting for better-maintained, safer buildings for some 30 years. When I heard about the plans I thought, 'sounds good.' We all did. But things didn't work out for us like we thought they would," explained Hazel. The original plans for the revitalization (the TCHC refers to the process as "revitalization," but the tenants refer to it as "redevelopment"), as presented to Hazel and her cohort, stipulated that residents of all incomes and ages would be integrated both on the site and in the new buildings. The stigmatization of living in "the projects" would be eliminated. These plans, residents were told, included the razing of all existing buildings, clearing the site, and building new, mixed-income dwellings. The street plan for the area would also be redone. The focus, they were told, would be on building a community.[3]

But somewhere in the process of realizing these goals, plans were changed. With the implementation of Phase One of the project, Hazel and her friends found themselves excluded. In the new Regent Park, they were separated not only by income but also by age, and many of their original community ties were broken in the relocation process. Their optimism had turned to pessimism. As is common for people who live in poverty, their needs were subordinated to more powerful third-party influences. Many residents felt betrayed by the very system that was meant to support them. This case study of Hazel and her friends and their experiences in the redevelopment of Regent

Park exemplifies the negative impact policy changes can have on vulnerable populations when these policies are altered without user input. It also reinforces the need for transparency by housing authorities and politicians in redevelopment projects that involve vulnerable populations. Ultimately, it speaks to the need for commitment by designers, architects, planners, and politicians to embrace user-centered design as a part of their daily practice, with the interests of the most vulnerable groups central to the planning process.

Background

The story of the Regent Park public-housing project resides in the broader story of the development and implementation of public-housing policies in Canada. Public housing for low-income populations has been a challenge in Canada for decades, particularly in the city of Toronto, where housing shortages have been common. Regent Park is the first, oldest, and largest public-housing project in the country. Built in 1950, the Park became a benchmark for Canadian public-housing projects. The 69-acre site, located in the downtown core of Toronto, was originally designed in two phases—the first in the 1940s and 1950s and the second in the 1970s—when public funding for such initiatives was readily available. The site would eventually house a reported 7,500 people of all ages in 2,087 rent-geared-to-income units.[4] Originally, housing was available for families only, and units were available in various sizes, from one-bedroom apartments to five-bedroom townhouses. From 1970 on, tall apartment towers were also introduced to the site and the population density of the Park increased. With changing policies and changing building types, demographics also changed and the population of the Park came to include a greater incidence of single-parent families and people with disabilities.

At the time of its development, Regent Park was seen as the panacea to concentrated urban poverty and social marginalization in Canada. By razing existing slums and replacing them with publicly subsidized housing communities, it was deemed that social regeneration was inevitable. Smaller city blocks were replaced with superblocks. "Worthy" low-income families would occupy clean, affordable housing surrounded by green spaces for children to play. The Park was viewed as a new, "scientific" approach to housing.

At first, the stakeholders were happy. Quality of life was improved. Behavior in the area appeared to have changed and crime diminished. One government official even stated: "A sign might well be erected somewhere on the site: Good Citizens Dwell Here."[5] Regent Park was officially a social, architectural, and planning triumph.

Within ten years, triumph turned to tragedy. What had been labeled a planning success was now a planning failure. The well-ordered community of the 1950s could not be sustained. The area had returned to the squalid conditions, high levels of crime, and long-term, concentrated poverty that the Park had been designed to eliminate. The Federal Task Force on Housing released a report in 1968 that pointed to housing projects such as Regent Park as "breeding grounds for disincentive," encouraging a "what's-the-use" attitude toward work and self-improvement.[6] Over the next 30 years, academics, reformers, and the popular press would solidify this negative image of the Park residents and inhabitants of similar housing projects. Many would brand the people who lived there as the "underclass," and residents were condemned to the same socioeconomic stigmatization, isolation, and marginalization that they had experienced in the slums.

In an effort to find a reason for the failure of this "scientific" solution to housing, much of the criticism focused on the physical, urban plan and on the layout of the dwelling units. To date, few Canadian studies have been conducted on how the physical design of public-housing projects affects occupant behavior. Rather, Canadians have looked to studies of similar projects in the U.S. to find answers. While the demographics differ—for example, African Americans occupy a large percentage of U.S. public-housing units, whereas new immigrants (Somalis, Chinese, etc.) comprise a large cohort of Canadian public-housing residents—the results have been similar. Conclusions drawn by politicians and planners have focused on three key areas: (1) that the creation of superblocks, which eliminate pass-through streets, reduces traffic flow to the extent that areas become dangerous, (2) that buildings on these sites that "turn their backs" on the surrounding neighborhoods also create dangerous areas for residents, and (3) that the concentration of a homogeneous population based on income creates marginalization and stigma. In particular, studies suggest that the inward-looking configuration of these plans created unclear boundaries between public and private spaces, which resulted in disincentive for residents to care for exterior spaces and provoked an increase in criminal activity.[7]

Tenant groups, like the one to which Hazel belonged, had a different perspective. Two problems the community most commonly cited were absent landlords (the housing authority) and a system that did not provide for, and was not interested in, tenant needs. Until 1992, few complaints from tenants in Regent Park had been leveled against the buildings and the plan. Most complaints focused on the management of the site. These complaints pointed to a lack of maintenance provided by the housing authority, safety issues on the site, and underfunding of the projects by government agencies.

Tenants were also concerned with the branding of their community, their home, as a ghetto. From interviews with Hazel and other residents, it became clear that they felt a connection to one another, that they had already established a strong sense of community in the old Regent Park, and that they felt their community was misrepresented in the press. "We all looked after each other," one woman explained. "Everyone knew who belonged and who didn't. And some of us older people would watch the children when their parents weren't around." Studies show that community is very important for people who live in poverty and that these groups generally are more supportive of each other than those in higher-income brackets.[8] People in the middle and upper classes can afford daycare, babysitters, and after-school programs, and, therefore, are less likely to look to neighbors for support. Many residents of the old Regent Park expressed their strong personal connections and their desire to preserve these connections in the redevelopment process.

Of the two different perspectives, it was the shaping of the physical site combined with new ideas for urban planning that became the focus of public and political attention. From 1980 on, politicians and reformers proposed a number of solutions, many of which focused on the reforming of the physical space and the reintegration of mixed-housing types to achieve a new social mix. The problem with the projects, it was argued, was directly related to issues of social isolation and a lack of contact with different income groups. If there was a greater mix of uses and incomes, behavior of public-housing tenants would improve and so would their quality of life. As in the past, the general sentiment continued to be: "Improve the built environment and the lives of low-income residents will improve."

At the same time, significant change had occurred in the funding and management of public housing in Canada. Since the start of the twenty-first century, the federal government has systematically divested itself of much of the responsibility for public housing, pushing the financial burden of administering these sites to the provinces. The provinces, in turn, have passed the responsibility onto municipalities. As a result of this restructuring, on January 1, 2002, the City of Toronto formed the TCHC to manage the more than 2,400 public-housing sites in the Greater Toronto Area. Limited funding for new affordable-housing initiatives, along with poverty trends, led the TCHC to search for both financial and social solutions. At that time, more than 250,000 people lived in poverty in the Greater Toronto Area, while only around 10 percent had a public-housing provision.[9] In 2003, the TCHC commissioned a study to meet the needs of this large-yet-overlooked group.

As a result of the 2003 study, the TCHC made public their decision to "revitalize" distressed public housing, beginning with Regent Park. For the second time in 50 years, the site would be razed and new buildings would be put in its place. The redevelopment proposal closely followed Traditional Neighborhood Design (TND) strategies including the "eyes-on-the-street" theories developed by celebrated urban planner, Jane Jacobs. Jacobs' ideas about diverse, high-density, mixed-use neighborhoods with vibrant sidewalk life are at the heart of TND. It is with these ideas that redevelopments in public housing across North America, including Regent Park, were being rethought. The TCHC proposal was endorsed by all of the stakeholder groups. As Neil Clarke, a resident and vice president of the Regent Park Neighborhood Initiative, stated on the first day of demolition in 2006, "We are thrilled with where we are at today. When we see these buildings fall, it will show that someone listened and understood that we couldn't continue to live in the conditions that we were in."

Inspiration for the revitalization plans was drawn from the success of the Cabrini-Green redevelopment in Chicago, and mixed-income HOPE VI projects in the U.S. These plans called for a new approach to site planning that would provide "seamless integration of market-oriented and TCHC units."[10] Also included in the original proposal was the reconnection of the disconnected streets in the area, restoring much of the original neighborhood plan. Town-houses were to be built to face the street. Traffic would be encouraged rather than discouraged, although different-sized arteries would act as a traffic-calming system. Intentions were that this new community would provide a mix of uses and a mix of housing types to the benefit of low-income earners.

Community Participation

It is important to note that, in gathering the information for the 2003 study, the TCHC and their consultants made the inclusion of the existing Regent Park residents a priority. This is evidenced in the focus groups and design *charrettes* that were part of the feasibility study. Also included in the study was a proposed site plan based on input from the community. Many elements of the original plan remain in the final, as-built environment, including the reestablishment of small city blocks. Key elements that were changed include the reprogramming of buildings based both on income and age.

The inclusion of residents in the design process was remarkable. Before 2003, this user-centered-design approach had never been used in the planning of public-housing projects in Canada. Traditionally, public-housing design decisions had been made by the housing authority in consultation with an architectural team. Design professionals and administrators assumed that they would have the best solutions. This paternalistic approach to design was revolutionized in the late twentieth century with the growing realization amongst design professionals that inclusion of users in design decisions resulted in stronger, more supportive, and more highly functioning design solutions. User-centered design has the potential to acknowledge groups that are often labeled as "special needs," such as the elderly and individuals with disabilities, by including them as a part of the mainstream. The inclusion of tenants in the design process of public housing is particularly important, as these sites have a higher concentration of special-needs groups. Approximately 25 percent of the original Regent Park population had a reported disability and received financial support from the Ontario Disability Support Program.[11]

For Hazel and many other residents interviewed, their inclusion in the design process signified a real change in how officials perceived them. "We were surprised to be asked," remarked Hazel. "It was nice to know that what we had to say about our own homes mattered to administration."

Their inclusion was significant for other reasons as well. First, by including residents as a part of the planning process, public-housing officials were establishing a benchmark for subsequent public-housing projects. It was an acknowledgment that previous planning methods that excluded resident input had not provided satisfactory solutions and had led to some of the failures of the original sites. Second, the approach indicated an increased awareness that sites and buildings must be accessible for an aging population and people with disabilities.

Although, for many years, a portion of the Ontario Building Code included standards for barrier-free environments, Canadian standards do not provide the same rigor regarding accessibility as those provided by the Americans with Disabilities Act. To address this deficiency, the Accessibility for Ontarians with Disabilities Act was passed in 2005. In response to this document, the TCHC produced their own document addressing issues of accessibility for their entire portfolio. This policy, referred to as the TCHC Accessibility Plan, was put in place to guide decisions for improving accessibility for tenants with disabilities, including renovations, redevelopments, and new projects. Even though the original plans for the site were altered, in the end, the inclusion of residents in the process was a positive move toward more authentic user-centered design.

Policy Changes

As the design of Phase One began, city officials were confronted with increasing pressure from special-interest groups to reconsider their original strategy for the site. Commercial stakeholders in the project, including local real-estate agents, prospective businesses, and the site developer, raised three serious concerns about the mixing of incomes in individual buildings: (1) the profitability of units that were in mixed-income buildings, (2) the placement of businesses on the site, and (3) the ratio of affordable housing to market-rate units. To assuage these concerns, the TCHC and city planners altered their policies for the re-development to allow for greater density, taller buildings, and the reprogramming of buildings. This portion of the design process did not include users. The press made no reference to these changes. And, although these adjustments to the original plan would appear minor on paper, the impact felt by low-income residents like Hazel was major. By differentiating buildings and their occupants, these subtle changes served to reinforce the lack of status and relative power-lessness of low-income residents. The following outlines some of the outcomes of these policy changes.

Of the changes implemented, the change with the greatest impact on users was the reprogramming of buildings to separate income groups on the site. Reprogramming, i.e., altering how functions and various user groups are organized in a building, occurred at the impetus of real-estate agents and the developer, who feared market-rate units would be less attractive to buyers if buildings with units for sale also included low-income tenants. The beliefs were that units would be more difficult to sell and that they would sell at a lower price. They also contended that the stigma associated with the site was already harmful enough to potential housing prices.

It is important to note that the sale of market-rate units was the primary funding instrument for this redevelopment project, as government funds for affordable housing are almost non-existent in Canada. In projects such as these, the municipality must look to independent sources for financing, and, in this case, it was the developer who assumed most of the upfront costs of building. This meant that the developer had a vested interest in the sale of units in order to receive a return on their investment.

In keeping with the stated intention to increase affordable-housing oppor-tunities for people with low incomes, Phase One units were marketed as suitable for first-time homeowners by way of a "down-payment advantage plan." This was made available through a joint venture with the developer and the Royal Bank of Canada. Prospective homeowners could mortgage up to 95 percent of the property value, and unit prices were set to attract young urban professionals who might otherwise have difficulty affording their first home. Ironically, many of the units were not purchased by the intended demographic, but were purchased by off-shore investors. This occurred because the TCHC and the developer did not require the purchaser to be a first-time homeowner. The result was that a majority of market-rate units were purchased at this very low price and were, then, immediately leased or resold. Housing prices in the first five years of sales for the area have soared by nearly 300 percent, creating a greater-than-anticipated economic divide among groups on the site.[12]

As a result of policy changes separating income groups into distinct buildings and areas on the site, units sold quickly. Low-income residents were assigned to rent-geared-to-income buildings, and older-adult, low-income residents were assigned to seniors-only buildings.

Problems for low-income residents were not, however, confined to separation alone. At 22 floors, the building designed to house the senior residents is one of the tallest on the site. With the high incidence of disability among the aging population (nearly all residents of the seniors' building will have or already have some mobility issues), tall buildings are particularly challenging. Reasons for this include fire safety and access to egress, maintenance issues with elevators and access to higher floors, and the placement of services within the building. For example, in the seniors' residence at 252 Sackville Avenue, laundry facilities are available on the 7th floor only. As there are no living units on the 7th floor, all residents must leave their residential floor to do laundry. This creates a challenge for many older residents.

The number of market-rate properties on the site also was increased. In the revised plan, the city allowed for a greater ratio of market-rate to rent-geared-to-income units: a 60–40 split. On the positive side, this allowed the TCHC to build new buildings without incurring debt. On the negative side, although the total number of people to be housed on the site tripled, the number of affordable units and low-income tenants remained the same. The new Regent Park, therefore, would not relieve the great need for affordable housing in Toronto.

The composition of tenants also changed from the original plans to the final realization. Original tenants, like Hazel, were assured that they would be given an opportunity to return to the Park and the new buildings when they were completed. This did not happen. Original residents were housed off-site during Phase One, some as far away as 20 miles. Phase One also took more than four years, much longer than expected. This meant that many of the original residents had built new lives elsewhere and did not want to be uprooted again. For those who did return, strong original community ties had been broken, in many instances, irreparably.

Also dramatically altered was a sense of individuality on the site. Many tenants had planted their own urban gardens on the original Regent Park site (Figure 11.1). These gardens, often quite large, helped to provide fresh food for families with a limited income. Community groups planted and tended the gardens for the use of all residents. In an area with abundant green space, the introduction of urban gardens was an efficient and effective solution for many

Gardening on the original Regent Park site.

families and older adults. The new site did allow for urban gardening, but only in fewer, designated and controlled areas, where residents are required to bid on plots.

Finally, the placement of rent-geared-to-income units on the site was also reconsidered. Figure 11.2 shows the position and mix of buildings on the Phase One site and the location of services on the site. Although low-income, senior residents are more likely to have mobility issues than those in higher income brackets; the grocery store, bank, and retail stores are all located in the base of the market-rate condominium building, two full blocks from the seniors-only building. Transit is also at a distance from the seniors' building. Buses run east–west on Dundas Street and north–south on Parliament Street, the main arteries in the area. To catch the bus, older adults must walk a minimum of one city block. This distance can prove daunting to someone with a mobility issue. Services that are commonly frequented by older adults, such as the Tim Horton's coffee shop, are located in market-rate buildings only, also at a distance from the seniors-only building. While having to travel a distance to services and transportation is not new to older residents in Regent Park, many, such as Hazel and her friends, had hoped planners would resolve these issues in the new site.

Impact on Goals

The change to the original plans for the site had a significant impact on the overall goals of the redevelopment in three ways: (1) the relocation of tenants on the site made the possibility of contact between residents with different incomes unlikely, (2) the segregation of residents based on income reinforced the social hierarchy that the original plans sought to remove, and (3) the segregation by age, as well as by income, made the reestablishment of an intergenerational community nearly impossible.

Studies show that the opportunity for contact between people is most likely to occur along main pathways that users travel.[13] In short, walking past a neighbor's door or meeting in the lobby while getting the mail are opportunities that improve the likelihood of interaction between residents. Contact creates connections that can, in turn, lead to friendship. At the very least, residents can identify other residents in their building, thereby improving occupant safety. This was acknowledged in the 2003 TCHC study. Proposed strategies for inclusion focused on the need for improved "at grade" contact between homes, parks, and play areas to provide opportunities for people to meet.

Because of the placement of these building entrances, there is little possibility for daily at-grade contact by most residents, particularly for contact across income levels. Even the townhouses, with front doors that face the street and

▼ Figure 11.2

Map of Phase One Regent Park site with family buildings, seniors' buildings and neighborhood services. The buildings in gold are market rate units, the buildings in red are TCHC units.

that are located directly across from each other, do not provide opportunities for contact as might be expected. Close analysis of the site revealed that market-rate townhouse units include garages accessed from a back alley. On-site observation indicated that front porches and front doors on the market-rate units are seldom used and that access is generally gained from the rear entry. What appears to be an opportunity for contact on paper is not realized in daily life.

The use of "skyparks" also works against the original concept of mixing across incomes. Skyparks, or inhabitable roof gardens, are included in both the market-rate and rent-geared-to-income housing complexes. As Figure 11.3 indicates, these skyparks are inaccessible to each other and to the public. They are self-contained areas that serve only the population of the buildings to which they are attached. What results is a park system that is cut off from the greater community. Access is purposefully restricted. Creating connections between these skyparks would create more equity among socio-economic groups and greater opportunity for inclusion, an original goal of the project.

Segregation of users from the skyparks also reinforces economic differences between occupant groups. Low-income users are not permitted access to the market-rate skyparks and vice versa. Social events in the market-rate buildings are often held in the skyparks, but tenants in low-income groups are not included. The result is that, while green space is still provided around the buildings as it had been in the original Regent Park plan, it is now provided in a much more controlled way.

Finally, the size of the skyparks also matters. The Sackville Avenue skypark, usable by rent-geared-to-income residents only, is very small. The One Cole skypark is very large and more lavishly appointed. The differentiation in size and detailing of these two spaces reinforces the message that one group of users is more important than the other.

▲ Figure 11.3

Map of the Phase One Site showing the Skypark system. The skypark at the top of the image is for TCHC tenants; at the bottom for market rate units.

The original Regent Park was typical of public-housing projects of the 1950s in that it was originally planned as a transitional community to help the working poor to achieve financial stability. The projects were to provide an opportunity for families to get a solid start in clean, safe, affordable housing. This did not happen. Approximately 35 percent of Regent Park residents became long-term residents of the projects, changing the demographics from a community of families with young children to one that spanned all generations.[14] While the failure of families to transition out of the projects is discouraging, the upside is that support systems were developed across generations. Many single-parent families came to depend on these relationships. The segregation of older adults from the families in the new plan interrupts this support system.

While studies show that many older adults prefer to live in controlled, seniors-only communities for safety reasons, there is equally compelling evidence that older adults who live in intergenerational communities stay healthier longer.[15]

Conclusion

Analysis of Phase One of the Regent Park redevelopment project provides important lessons for politicians and planners when considering other projects of this type both in Canada and elsewhere. First, to be truly successful, public redevelopment projects should be resident-driven and not market-driven. Fundamentally, designers and politicians must remember that the real public-housing experts are those who are living in public housing. Projects for vulnerable populations should always consider end-user needs first, regardless of other market factors. In this instance, had Hazel and her friends remained connected to the planning process throughout and not just in the early stages, the risk of repeating the same mistakes would have been greatly reduced.

Second, affordable housing remains an important, but underfunded, issue in many countries, and profiting from the redevelopment of a well-situated, but distressed, site, such as Regent Park, can be tempting to housing authorities. In pursuing a project such as this, financial models should be developed that focus on increasing the number of affordable-housing units rather than maintaining the status quo. Further, controls need to be in place to ensure that units for sale remain affordable and are sold to the appropriate demographic groups. Prop-erties such as Regent Park are owned by the municipality and should, therefore, continue to benefit those most in need.

Third, housing authorities and politicians must ensure that their messages match reality. In the case of Regent Park, public rhetoric indicated a desire for greater autonomy and greater inclusion of all residents. On the final, as-built site, low-income residents experienced greater restrictions and greater segre-gation than on the earlier site, as evidenced in the restriction of urban gardens and strict controls on public spaces.

Social inclusion has been identified as a high priority in the redevelopment of severely distressed public-housing projects in Canada and around the world. Projects such as the redevelopment of Regent Park afford communities the opportunity to remove the stigma associated with living in subsidized housing by providing more inclusive, integrated sites. Yet senior residents and tenants with disabilities still experience significant barriers to accessing the built environment and the site. Issues of segregation were amplified rather than diminished. This case study demonstrates the need for decision makers to understand the populations that they are serving, and to guard against unintended negative consequences for powerless user groups. In Phase One of the Park development, this opportunity has been missed. But with some of the insights gathered from this study and others like it, perhaps new redevelopment projects will be planned differently. Hazel sums it up best: "We had good ideas that would have improved the neighborhood. We were happy to be involved. We had good ideas that would have worked. Maybe they'll take our advice next time."

Discussion Questions and Explorations

Descriptive

Describe what happened to residents of the old Regent Park while the Phase One redevelopment occurred.

Analytical

1. Find two photographs of Regent Park in Toronto: one of the older housing and one of the new redevelopment. Using the images, what you read in this case study, and your own thoughts, compare and contrast the positive and negative aspects of the old and the new versions of housing in Regent Park.
2. Find a photograph of the redevelopment of the Cabrini-Green housing in Chicago, Illinois, and compare it with the redevelopment of Regent Park. How are they similar? How are they different? How would daily life be similar and different in each?

Speculative

1. Read about urban activist and writer Jane Jacobs' opinions on public-housing projects. Redesign the plan of Regent Park using Jacobs' theories on low-income housing and neighborhood design.
2. Think about how various groups are categorized (seniors, low-income, working adults, etc.) in Regent Park. Invent a new set of categories to define Regent Park residents and speculate on how these new categories might affect the ways new housing is developed.

Notes

1. Hazel M. is not a real person. She represents a composite of tenants interviewed for this study.
2. Toronto Community Housing Corporation and Regent Park Collaborative Team, *Regent Park Revitalization Study* (Toronto: City of Toronto, 2003), 107.
3. Ibid.
4. Rent-geared-to-income refers to a type of public housing with a rental rate that is calculated based on tenant income. It is 30 percent of the gross household income.
5. Sean Purdy, *From Place of Hope to Outcast Space: Territorial Regulation and Tenant Resistance in the Regent Park Housing Project, 1949–2001* (Kingston, Ontario: Queen's University, 2003), 396.
6. Ibid.
7. John Sewell, "Public Housing," in *Housing and Homes—Housing for Canadians* (Toronto, Ontario: J. Lorimer, 1994), 132–161; Alice Coleman and King's College (University of London), *Utopia On Trial: Vision and Reality in Planned Housing* (London: H. Shipman, 1985), 92; Lawrence J. Vale, *Reclaiming Public Housing* (Cambridge, MA: Harvard University Press, 2002), 1–36.
8. John David Hulchanski, *Three Cities within Toronto: Income Polarization among Toronto's Neighborhoods, 1970–2000* (Toronto, Ontario: University of Toronto Press, 2010).
9. Ibid.
10. Toronto Community Housing Corporation, *Regent Park*, 107.
11. Statscan, *Census of Canada, Census Tracts, Toronto* (Ottawa, Ontario: Government of Canada, 1971, 1981, 1991).
12. Statistics taken from a comparison of the original TCHC market rate unit prices listed on the Realtor Canada Website, accessed November 11, 2014, www.realtor.ca.
13. Leon Festinger, Stanley Schachter, and Kurt Back, *Social Pressure in Informal Groups: A Study of Human Factors in Housing* (New York: Rinehart and Winston, 1950).
14. Purdy, *From Place of Hope to Outcast Space*, 396.
15. Kristine Bjelde and Gregory Sanders, "Snowbird Intergenerational Relationships," *Activities, Adaptation and Aging* 33, no. 2 (2009): 81–97.

Editors' Introduction to Chapter 12

Public spaces—Rome's Piazza Navona, Mexico City's Zócalo, and Cape Town's Greenmarket Square—are some of the most culturally and politically important parts of cities around the world. According to the American Planning Association, public spaces "promote social interaction and a sense of community." Streets, parks, and squares are common examples of public spaces, but the list also can include certain interior spaces, like major transit hubs, and spaces that are free and accessible to citizens. Public spaces are essential pieces of infrastructure for nations, states, cities, towns, and villages; these spaces allow citizens to meet formally or informally for socialization, commerce, political expression, or philosophical dialogue. There are competing definitions of the term "public" and, therefore, of the definition of public space.

Public space can be defined in opposition to private property. An individual, partnership, or corporation holds the rights to transform or sell private property, whereas a government, municipality, or social group "owns" public space. Public space can also be understood according to use: defined in accordance with the people who—on a regular basis—occupy or utilize a space, regardless of who owns it. Many times, the individual or group that holds ownership is also the primary occupant. In other cases, the group who owns a space and the people who occupy that space are different. Trafalgar Square, the focus of this case study, is governed by the City of London, while a widely diverse group of local citizens, UK nationals, and international tourists occupy the space throughout the year. More particularly, however, a committee of local representatives governs the design of the square and the public art that resides in it—artworks that change year to year. A major question arises: What if the decisions the committee makes do not resonate with needs and preferences of the general public?

The "public" is comprised of diverse groups—children and the elderly, Muslims and Christians, rich and poor. By extension, one might assume that public spaces are designed with all of these groups in mind. Yet this is often not the case, as any given public space may include or exclude various social groups. Persons with disabilities, for example, may use one public space rather than another due to their ability or inability to access the space and its amenities.

Historical and recent events also illustrate that public spaces are not always places of democracy, equality, and free expression. One example is the 1989 Tiananmen Square Massacre (Beijing, China), which resulted in the deaths of hundreds of student, faculty, and civilian protestors. A second example is the tragic irony of Independence Square (Kiev, Ukraine), where activists, police, and journalists were killed in 2014 during what were initially peaceful demonstrations on freedom.

In the following chapter, Korydon Smith utilizes Trafalgar Square in London to discuss concepts and principles of public space; the central theme is the degree to which public space is truly "public"—owned, designed, controlled, and occupied by all. The phrase "public space" implies that places like Independence Square or Trafalgar Square are democratic and free, designed for and open to everyone in society. The case study presented here, however, reveals the competing viewpoints and unequal representations that characterize many public spaces. As you read, consider who designs public spaces and how the designs of public spaces promote or restrict access. Which groups have the greatest and least access to freedom of expression, and what ideas are valued or diminished? And how do public spaces affect the social interactions and perceptions of diverse social groups? Think about these questions in regards to the public spaces you have visited and those that you use on a regular basis.

Chapter 12

Victims and Heroes

Exhibiting Difference in Trafalgar Square

Korydon Smith

In September 2005, crews placed a 12-foot, 12-ton white Carrara (Italian) marble sculpture atop the Fourth Plinth of London's Trafalgar Square. Marc Quinn's sculpture, *Alison Lapper Pregnant*, was a realistic representation of a friend and fellow artist. Upon first glance, the sculpture appears to be a statue from Greek or Roman antiquity, a modern-day Venus de Milo. A deeper reading reveals three key facts: (1) the armless and "un-classically-proportioned" statue is an accurate representation of Lapper, who was born without arms and with shortened legs, (2) Lapper is shown fully nude in her last trimester of pregnancy (her son, Parys, born in 2000), and (3) Lapper is a single mother, herself an orphaned child of a single mother. Controversy over the sculpture ensued.

The presence of this specific sculpture in this specific location and time raised questions about public space and public art; about freedom of speech, citizenship, and ownership; about cultural values and personal boundaries; about the roles of politicians, artists and designers, and the public; and about what types of art are appropriate for public spaces. To resolve these questions, a commission was created to determine what should reside atop the Fourth Plinth, a large masonry pedestal originally designed to display an equestrian military statue. Though crews removed *Alison Lapper Pregnant* (*A.L.P.*) from the Fourth Plinth in late 2007—making room for Thomas Schütte's *Model for a Hotel 2007*, the second in a line of Fourth Plinth Commission unveilings—the debates about Quinn's work did not end. Public discussions surged again with the unveiling of a 43-foot-tall version of Quinn's sculpture in the center of the Olympic Stadium in 2012 at the London Paralympics. Trafalgar Square, the Fourth Plinth, and *A.L.P.*, therefore, illustrate that "public space is the stage upon which the drama of communal life unfolds."[1]

The overarching exploration of this chapter is the degree to which Trafalgar Square fulfills its mission as a public space—a place to facilitate the gathering of Londoners, Brits, and international tourists. According to some scholars, public spaces, to be called such, must fulfill four basic requirements. They must: (1) be "designed, however minimally," (2) afford "everyone … rights

▲ Figure 12.1

Photograph (2006) of artist Marc Quinn's 12-ton marble sculpture *Alison Lapper Pregnant*. *Photo from Daniel Kristensen (Gaellery), (https://flickr.com/photos/gaellery/196512727/, under Creative Commons 2.0 licensing agreement).*

of access," (3) allow for "encounters … between individual users" that "are unplanned," and (4) ensure that users of the space are "subjected to rules none other than those of common norms of social civility."[2] Without question Trafalgar Square meets the first and third criteria; it is the fulfillment of the second and fourth criteria that raises questions. Throughout this chapter, questions are raised about the design of public space in general and the design of Trafalgar Square in particular. These questions are addressed from multiple points of view, leaving room for you, the reader, to explore your own responses.

History and Design of Trafalgar Square

It is essential to understand the importance of Trafalgar Square and its location in central London, the capital city of England and the United Kingdom. With over eight million residents and an international center of commerce, education, arts, industry, sports, fashion, and architecture, London is the fifth-largest metropolitan economy in the world.[3] Trafalgar Square is just blocks from several municipal and national agencies, multiple foreign embassies, and a variety of

▶ Figure 12.2

Aerial view of Trafalgar Square and surrounding area.
Image from Google Earth, © 2014, The Geo Information Group.

tourist destinations, such as the Winston Churchill War Rooms, Buckingham Palace, and the River Thames. The square hosts London's premier New Year's Eve celebration and many other cultural events. It is a gathering place of both locals and tourists, and forecourt to the world-famous National Gallery. The square has been a shooting location for dozens of films and the screening venue of several others, including the world premiere of the final movie in the *Harry Potter* series. Trafalgar Square is the venue for the celebration of English sporting matches and was the site for the announcement that London would host the 2012 Summer Olympics (the only city to host the Olympics three times). The square has also been the site of both political revelry and public protest, referred to as the "foremost place *politique*" in all of Britain.[4] Some even believed that the Nazi SS planned to seize and relocate Nelson's Column, the centerpiece of the square, to Berlin if they had won World War II.[5]

The square commemorates the 1805 Battle of Trafalgar, a British-won naval battle off the coast of Spain during the Napoleonic Wars. Architect John Nash developed initial schemes for the square throughout the first three decades of the 1800s, as part of London's redevelopment. In the early 1840s, architect Sir Charles Barry developed new schemes for the square in order to further establish it as a prominent public space. Planners and designers have continuously transformed Trafalgar Square since that time, including major changes to vehicular and pedestrian circulation as recent as 2003, which closed the northern street to vehicular traffic in order to provide a safer and more direct pedestrian link between Trafalgar Square and the National Gallery.[6]

The National Gallery is the widest and most prominent building in view, fronting the entire length of the north side of the square. The eastern and western sides are asymmetrically bounded, and the southern end is the least defined, as a five-way roundabout sits between the square and the surrounding buildings to the south. One of these streets, a short but iconic route known as The Mall, is an axial link to the famed Buckingham Palace to the west. The southern route out of the square leads to the equally renowned Palace of Westminster (the Houses of Parliament building) and other prominent government offices. A few blocks to the east are the busy Charing Cross and Embankment tube/train stations. These connections further the centrality, visibility, and importance of Trafalgar Square.

The square is symmetrical along the north–south axis and Nelson's Column—a statue atop a Corinthian column erected in 1843 in tribute to Royal Navy Admiral Horatio Nelson, who died during the Battle of Trafalgar—occupies

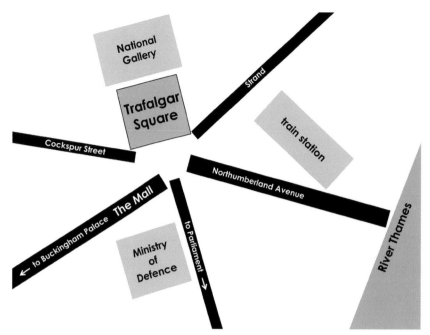

◀ Figure 12.3

Diagram of Trafalgar Square context.
Diagram by Korydon Smith, 2014.

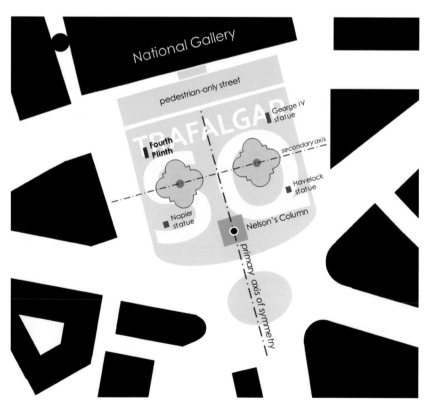

◀ Figure 12.4

Diagram of the design elements of Trafalgar Square.
Diagram by Korydon Smith, 2014.

CHAPTER 12 Korydon Smith

▲ Figure 12.5

Nelson's Column at a Late Blue Hour (Photograph, 2013).
Photo from Harry Ross (https://flickr.com/photos/92680661@N07/9216147268/, under Creative Commons 2.0 licensing agreement). Column designed by William Railton (1840–43).

◀ Figure 12.6

Photograph (2009) of Major General Sir Henry Havelock statue.
Photo from Elliott Brown (https://flickr.com/photos/ell-r-brown/4030007588/, under Creative Commons 2.0 licensing agreement).

◀ Figure 12.7

Photograph (2009) of General James Napier statue.
*Photo from Elliott Brown (https://flickr.com/photos/
ell-r-brown/4030027308/, under Creative Commons 2.0
licensing agreement).*

◀ Figure 12.8

Photograph (2007) of King George IV equestrian statue.
*Photo from Michael Kleinhenz (https://flickr.com/photos/
quendor/1118660807/, under Creative Commons 2.0
licensing agreement).*

CHAPTER 12 Korydon Smith

Photograph (2009) of the "empty"
Fourth Plinth.
*Photo from Elliott Brown
(https://flickr.com/photos/
ell-r-brown/4030076444/, under
Creative Commons 2.0 licensing
agreement).*

the prominent south-center of the square. Four guardian lions surround the column and two large fountains flank it to the north. Most of the square is flat, excluding the grand stairs on the north, and is paved in patterns of stone, with few plantings. A plinth punctuates each of the four corners of the square, three of which hold statues that have been in place since the mid-1800s. These include statues of King George IV, who reigned during the Napoleonic Wars; Sir Charles James Napier, a decorated army general who served during both the Napoleonic War and British conquests in India; and Sir Henry Havelock, an army major-general who served in India shortly after Napier. Occupying the northwest corner is what has come to be known as the Fourth Plinth.

The Fourth Plinth Commission

According to Barry's 1841 plans, the Fourth Plinth was to exhibit an equestrian statue, similar to that of George IV. "Due to insufficient funds," however, "the statue was never completed."[7] Without much explanation, the plinth stood empty for more than 150 years.[8] The emptiness of one of the two largest plinths in one of the world's most important public spaces in one of the world's wealthiest cities for 150 years is nothing short of shocking. Angst about the void and questions about what should be done grew louder at the end of the twentieth century. Should a monument to a military hero or political figure be placed there? If so, should it be someone historic or contemporary; prominent or lesser known; male or female? With the National Gallery close by, is it more reasonable that the plinth be the site of a permanent art piece? If so, should the piece be historic or contemporary, representational or abstract? Should the plinth be removed?

There were proponents and detractors of each proposal. Some Londoners even suggested that the plinth remain empty. Ken Livingstone, the first elected Mayor of London (2000–2008) extended the debate beyond the Fourth Plinth, questioning the works atop all plinths:

▲ Figure 12.10

Ecce Homo on the Fourth Plinth.
(Photograph) © 1999, Roy Hughes. The
Ecce Homo sculpture by Mark Wallinger,
1999, was the first art piece atop the
Fourth Plinth.

▲ Figure 12.11

Photograph of Bill Woodrow's *Regardless of*
History **(2000) after being relocated to the**
Cass Sculpture Foundation.
Image courtesy of the Cass Sculpture
Foundation, 2010.

▲ Figure 12.12

Rachel Whiteread, Inverted Plinth.
(Photograph) © 2001, Walter Rawlings,
courtesy of Fotolibra. Rachel Whiteread's
2001 sculpture, generically titled Monument,
was the largest clear resin cast to that date.

> I think that the people on the plinths in the main square in our capital city
> should be identifiable to the generality of the population. I have not a clue
> who two of the generals there are or what they did. … I imagine that not
> one person in 10,000 going through Trafalgar Square knows any details
> about the lives of those two generals. It might be that it is time to look at
> moving them and having figures on those plinths that ordinary Londoners
> would know.[9]

Livingstone's remarks spurred local and national debates. In turn, a more fundamental question arose regarding who holds decision-making power—city
leaders, planners and designers, an appointed committee, public vote, or some
combination of these? Maybe, for example, artists from around the world could
submit proposals; an appointed committee of representatives could select a
pool of finalists; and a public vote could determine the final outcome (much like
the process of the *Australian Idol*, *Pop Idol*, and *American Idol* music
competitions).

For many Londoners, it remained unclear whether the square and the
plinth shared the same oversight. Maybe decisions about the square belonged
to urban designers, while decisions about the plinth belonged to the arts
community.

In 1998, the Royal Society of Arts, Manufactures, and Commerce (RSA)
developed the Fourth Plinth Project. They conceptualized the Fourth Plinth as
the site for an annual or semi-annual succession of sculptures by contemporary
artists. The RSA commissioned three artists—Mark Wallinger (*Ecce Homo*,

1999), Bill Woodrow (*Regardless of History*, 2000), and Rachel Whiteread (*Monument*, 2001)—to exhibit successive works on the plinth. The efforts of the RSA, along with Livingstone's sentiments, later led to the creation of the Mayor of London's Fourth Plinth Commission, which took over the RSA's Fourth Plinth oversight duties. The commission was dubbed "the UK's most high profile public sculpture commission" with "great national and international signifi-cance."[10] In September 2005, Mayor Livingstone unveiled the first work the Fourth Plinth Commission approved: Quinn's massive sculpture of an armless, pregnant woman.

The Fourth Plinth and *Alison Lapper Pregnant*

Pregnant and nude, Quinn's sculpture clearly depicted femininity. It also portrayed disability. The sculpture was contemporary, but the precious marble figure was reminiscent of the statuary of Ancient Rome or Athens—white and stoic, and armless. As one newspaper columnist wrote, the sculpture was both "womanly" and "warrior-like," both "white" and "dazzling."[11] Likewise, an art critic said that "the work embodies the stereotypes of disability as heroic, tragic, and freakish and functions to make such stereotypes visible, part of public discourse, and open for debate."[12] To some, the sculpture was a display of progress, providing visibility to an often-marginalized issue and bodily state. With her son Parys, age 5, at the unveiling, Lapper said, "It is so rare to see disability in everyday life let alone naked, pregnant, and proud."[13]

To others, it was inappropriate for Trafalgar Square. One newspaper columnist, for example, was critical of Quinn's piece in the context of Trafalgar Square, Nelson's Column, and the other monuments:

> I've grown to loathe the *Alison Lapper Pregnant* statue … [which] captures much of what is rotten in the heart of new Britain. … It shows that we value people for what they are rather than what they achieve. In our era of the politics of identity we seem more interested in celebrating individuals' fixed and quite accidental attributes—their ethnicity, cultural heritage, or, in Lapper's case, her disability—rather than what they have discovered or done in the world outside of their bodies. We prefer victims to heroes.[14]

Regardless of which side one might take—praise or condemnation of the work—A.L.P. became a vibrant talking point regarding the Fourth Plinth specifically, Trafalgar Square more broadly, and public space and public art in general. The most specific issue was that of disability rights and the public's image of disability.

Public spaces play a variety of roles; they *define*, *convey*, *satisfy*, and/or *protect* "significant human rights" and "special cultural meanings."[15] Quinn's work certainly *conveyed* and *satisfied* cultural meanings—such as motherhood, disability, and art history—while public opinion *defined* the work and articulated these meanings. But did the work *protect* any human rights? Did it forge ground in the realm of disability rights or did it depict disability merely as a spectacle? In exploring these questions, it is, first, important to state that disability is a general term within which there is great diversity across the realms of vision and hearing, physical capabilities, cognition, and emotion. In addition, like race, sexuality, and other categories, disability is a human construct and not a natural phenomenon, a way of classifying (naming) things in order to understand, simplify, and control a complex world. According to disability-studies scholar, Lennard Davis,

> We live in a world of norms. Each of us endeavors to be normal or else deliberately tries to avoid that state. We consider what the average person does, thinks, earns, or consumes. We rank our intelligence, our cholesterol level, our weight, height, sex drive, bodily dimensions along some conceptual line from subnormal to above-average. … To understand the disabled body, one must return to the concept of the norm … not so much on the construction of disability as on the construction of normalcy.[16]

The classification of disability has resulted in both negative and positive consequences—stereotyping and repression, on the one hand, and identity affirmation and social supports, on the other. Until only recently, disability was not depicted in fine arts or in mass media. Disability is now portrayed in art or media in one of four ways: "freakish" (as a spectacle), "piteous" (in need of sympathy or charity), "heroic" (able to accomplish titanic feats despite enormous challenges), or "normal."[17] To which of these categories does *A.L.P.* belong? This answer may be dependent upon the viewer's interpretation of the statue. Individual beliefs, values, and life experiences of the observer (you, the reader) affects how one classifies the work. The context of the work also influences one's interpretation.

Public spaces have frequently served as the places for calling out social injustices and promoting women's rights, religious freedom, economic equality, and other civil rights movements. Trafalgar Square, likewise, has been the site of diverse public discourses and demonstrations, including the Million Women Rise event in 2013. Mayor Livingstone also saw the potential of Trafalgar Square in fulfilling this public purpose:

> London is changing rapidly. It is growing fast and becoming more prosperous, but these trends sit side by side with social injustice. Far too many of London's citizens are socially excluded and poorly represented. Culture and creativity have a unique potential to address some of these difficult social issues. They enable people to find a voice, to express themselves, to reach an audience. … Public spaces provide a platform for culture as a place where people can meet and interact, play games, celebrate festivals or set up stalls. London has a wealth of these spaces, from the large public parks and squares, to small local greens, canals, docks, allotments, cemeteries, playing fields and wide pavements. More can be done to protect and enhance London's other public spaces. Trafalgar Square has already undergone a transformation with the pedestrianisation of the north side and addition of new facilities: it is already becoming known as [an] exciting space for cultural innovation.[18]

Public spaces commonly become the repository for markers and monuments of events or periods of advancement in civil rights. It could be argued that *A.L.P.* helped promote cultural innovation, or at least contributed to debates about women's rights, disability rights, and single-parent rights. The presence of Quinn's sculpture in Trafalgar Square, as well as at the London Paralympics, helps concretize, in personal and collective memories, these advancements. The Lapper sculpture changed a heroic-white-male space into a space of disability and femininity, making Lapper "a contemporary heroine of cultural diversity."[19] Nevertheless, it is important to ask if this is appropriate for Trafalgar Square, a space of memorialization of a different sort. More generally, one might ask: What is the role of public art in prominent public spaces? Which is more appropriate, memorializing or provoking, monumentality or subtlety, diversity or uniformity; or does it depend on the context and the culture?

A.L.P., like the statues atop the other three plinths, had monument-like qualities, but, unlike the other figures in the square, Quinn's work did not commemorate a historic event or well-known individual (at least not at that time). There is no doubt that the work was different in scale, material, and subject matter compared to the surrounding monuments, so, one might presume it was intended to be provocative, suggestive, and reflective.[20] Yet public monuments typically have "portrayed political stability and stasis ... rather than reflecting social change."[21] This may be why many citizens held negative views of *A.L.P.*: Trafalgar Square may not have been an appropriate venue for an emerging discourse on disability. The sculpture competed with critic Malcolm Miles' description of public monuments:

> Monuments are produced within a dominant framework of values, as elements in the construction of a national history ... [and] national cultural identity; they suppose at least partial consensus of values, without which their narrative could not be recognized, although individual monuments may not retain their currency as particular figures fade in public memories, and individual buildings may be disliked. As a general category of cultural objects, however, monuments are familiar in the spaces of most cities, standing for a stability which conceals the internal contradictions of society and survives the day-to-day fluctuations of history. The majority in society is persuaded, by monuments amongst other civil institutions, to accept these contradictions, the monument becoming a device of social control less brutish and costly than armed force.[22]

Yet the asserted mission of the Fourth Plinth Commission also counters Miles' depiction of monuments as coercive devices. According to the Greater London Authority, "The Fourth Plinth programme is part of the vision for Trafalgar Square to be a vibrant public space and to encourage debate about the place and value of public art in the built environment."[23] A.L.P. clearly fulfilled this mission, but the larger questions about public space remain. Is Trafalgar Square a space of conformity or debate, a space of unanimity or diversity, or somewhere in between?

Extensive press coverage suggests that the sculpture contributed to the ongoing disability dialogues both internationally and in London, such as the "Designing an Accessible City" initiative. Maybe the sculpture simply brought awareness to people who had not considered disability issues. Nevertheless, no public policies regarding disability rights were implemented or transformed as a direct result of the sculpture, and the design of Trafalgar Square was not changed. The National Gallery, for instance, as of 2014, still does not have an integrated wheelchair- or stroller-accessible entry facing the square, only an accessible secondary entry.

This is an important point of discussion for multiple reasons. First, according to urbanist William Whyte, one criterion for the design of public spaces is "access for the physically disabled."[24] Second, the National Gallery, though an interior space, is an extension of the public realm, an extension of Trafalgar Square. Third, the mayor's office held high aspirations for the design and use of this place. The inaccessibility of the main entry that faces the square breaks the intended spatial continuity between the interior and exterior public realms, requiring people with wheelchairs, walkers, and strollers to travel around the side of the National Gallery and enter at the rear. A public space is supposed to "protect … human rights," but the "accessible" entry to the National Gallery denies this, metaphorically, if not physically, by requiring a certain group of citizens to leave the space of Trafalgar Square. The presence of Quinn's work indirectly calls this into question because there is a reciprocal relationship between public space and public art. The implicit and explicit experiences and meanings of each are set in dialogue. The artwork raises questions about the space; the space raises questions about the artwork.

The National Gallery and Trafalgar Square, nevertheless, are considered important historical architectural works, and many of the current deficiencies result from the historical time periods in which they were designed. The modern services and amenities that the National Gallery offers—to persons with visual impairments, for example—are exemplary. Both the Royal Town Planning Institute (RTPI) and the American Planning Association (APA), the professional organizations in Great Britain and the United States respectively, offer annual awards for well-designed public spaces. The RTPI utilizes nine criteria in judging entries. The last of these criteria regards "how the [project] has addressed equality and diversity issues."[25] The APA identifies eight characteristics of well-designed public spaces, with significant overlap with the RTPI criteria, including the criterion that "a great public space … is safe, welcoming, and accommodating for all users," and, at the same time, "promotes community involvement … and reflects the local culture or history."[26] The struggle between reflecting history and accommodating diverse users is clearly evident in Trafalgar Square.

Conclusion

Public spaces are rarely empty, open areas. They are often comprised of a variety of artworks, memorials, landscape features, paving materials, and other elements integrated into a cohesive design aimed to provide interest, functionality, and a backdrop to socialization. This is certainly the case for Trafalgar

Photograph (2007) of Thomas Schütte's *Model for a Hotel*.
From Lettuce1 (https://flickr.com/photos/53314395@N00/2825619640/, under Creative Commons 2.0 licensing agreement).

Photograph (2009) of one of the participants in Antony Gormley's *One and Other* purportedly performing an act about domestic violence.
From Feggy Art (https://flickr.com/photos/victius/3988929679/, under Creative Commons 2.0 licensing agreement).

◀ Figure 12.15

Photograph (2010) of Yinka Shonibare's **Nelson's Ship in a Bottle.**
From Chris Wilkinson (https://flickr.com/photos/ thewilkybarkid/5025111357/, under Creative Commons 2.0 licensing agreement).

▶ Figure 12.16

Photograph (2012) of Michael Elmgreen and Ingar Dragset's *Powerless Structures.*
From Stew Dean (https://flickr.com/photos/ stewdean/7114967741/, under Creative Commons 2.0 licensing agreement).

◀ Figure 12.17

Photograph (2014) of Katharina Fritsch's **Hahn/Cock.**
From Kate Dahl (https://flickr.com/photos/ katedahl/14089452639/, under Creative Commons 2.0 licensing agreement).

Square. With the diverse crowds that occupy the space daily, the camaraderie that occurs during film premieres and televised sporting matches, and the interspersion of highly contentious protests and debates, Trafalgar Square is a useful example for exploring the relationship between social diversity and the design of public space. The case reveals at least three major concepts regarding the design of public spaces and public art.

First, Trafalgar Square shows us that public spaces are home to a variety of historical, controversial, and mundane events. These events contribute to individual and collective definitions and interpretations of a given public space, leading to what artistic choices or events one deems suitable or unsuitable for those places. Public art and public space affect one another; the history and design of a public space affects the way a society values or devalues a piece of public art, while a public artwork affects the way a society occupies and understands a public space.

Second, Trafalgar Square shows us that diverse groups, with a variety of needs and interests, own and occupy public spaces. Although we think of public spaces as being owned by everyone, usually it is a small group of individuals that makes decisions about them—how they are designed and managed, as well as what and who occupies them. Through law, design, or unspoken codes of conduct, people are included in or excluded from public spaces. This is especially the case for minority groups such as people with disabilities.

Third, Trafalgar Square and the Fourth Plinth show us that the public and the spaces people occupy are reciprocally linked. We see that public spaces and public art provide an important mechanism of dialogue and can be a catalyst for cultural change. *Alison Lapper Pregnant*, in particular, shows us that the design of public spaces affects persons with disabilities, while persons with disabilities affect the design of public spaces. Local and international debates about the Fourth Plinth continue today.

In late 2007, Thomas Schütte's *Model for a Hotel* replaced Quinn's work atop the Fourth Plinth. With the introduction of a more abstract, architectural work, discussions shifted away from the depiction of disability and back to more general questions about the type of artworks that are best suited for the plinth. The discussion took yet a different path with the introduction of Anthony Gormley's *One and Other* in 2009, a performance piece rather than sculpture. From 6 July to 14 October 2009, 24 hours per day for 100 days in one-hour segments, 2,400 people stood atop the plinth. Brian Caploff used his time atop the plinth to advocate for Linda Carty, a black Brit on death row in a Texas prison, believed by many to be innocent.[27] Caploff held a life-sized cardboard cut-out of Carty and a sign that read: "Please don't let me die here." Exemplified with Caploff, social justice was a theme common to many participants, clearly resonant with the civic history of Trafalgar Square.

On May 24, 2010, *Nelson's Ship in a Bottle* replaced Gormley's living sculpture. It was the first commissioned piece to focus directly on the history of the square and the Battle of Trafalgar. Much discussion, however, focused not on the artwork but on the artist, Yinka Shonibare, who became the first black British artist to exhibit work on the Fourth Plinth. We learn that both the artwork and the artist are open to public critique. We also learn that public art can cover a wide spectrum. Mark Wallinger's *Ecce Homo* (1999)—a marbleized-resin, life-sized depiction of Christ wearing a barbed-wire crown—was the first piece to occupy the Fourth Plinth. Bill Woodrow's *Regardless of History* (2000), likewise, brimmed with symbolism—depicting a disembodied head under the weight of a large book and a gnarled tree. In contrast, Rachel Whiteread's generically titled work of 2001, *Monument*, was far more abstract and geometric. A clear resin mirror image of the Fourth Plinth—the plinth atop itself—it pointed to the emptiness of the plinth. Michael Elmgreen and Ingar Dragset's *Powerless Structures, Fig. 10.1* (2012) holds both similarities and differences to all of the afore-mentioned works. A bronze statue of a boy on a rocking horse, the work draws connections to the equestrian George IV statue (and equestrian military statues that exist in public spaces worldwide), yet remains clearly playful. Katharina Fritsch's *Hahn/Cock*, an enormous ultramarine-blue rooster, looked over the square throughout much of 2013–2014, to be succeeded with the works of Hans Haacke and David Shrigley, as well as (at the time of this writing) an indeterminable number of future works.

The first mayor of London, with strong advisory input from the Fourth Plinth Commission, ultimately made the decision to exhibit Quinn's sculpture. Trafalgar Square, however, has multiple stakeholders—diverse individuals and groups—that influence decisions about the design and use of the space. Femininity, disability, motherhood, and a variety of other discussions play out in public spaces like Trafalgar Square. So, how can designers create public spaces that foster such diverse discourses and meet the needs and preferences of diverse members of society? What characteristics would a public space designed for single mothers and their children have? How would this type of space differ from public spaces designed for other social groups?[28] And one final question: Which were the most successful and least successful artworks that have resided atop the Fourth Plinth of Trafalgar Square?

While the ultimate goal in designing public spaces is to meet the needs of everyone, most public spaces likely fall short. Thousands of public spaces are either designed for *someone* or for *no one*, but rarely do we see spaces designed by and for *everyone*. The Mussolini-era Via dei Fori Imperiali was designed specifically by and for the Italian National Fascist Party, while, arguably, Mies van der Rohe designed the Federal Plaza in Chicago, essentially, for no one in particular. But maybe there is a third type of public realm, possibly exemplified in Moscow's Red Square: spaces that are not as much designed as they are appropriated, occupied differently day-to-day and by a variety of social groups. Through this case study and through other examples, we learn that public ownership is an ambiguous concept. Public space, as well, can be tenuous, and not only in war-torn or oppressive nations. In 2014, members of the UK Parliament proposed the Anti-Social Behaviour, Crime and Policing Bill, which would grant local police and authorities "sweeping powers to bar citizens from assembling lawfully in public spaces" due to "nuisance or annoyance."[29] If passed, the London Police would have the greatest power over what events and people occupy Trafalgar Square, furthering the debates about the purposes and entitlements of public space.

Discussion Questions and Explorations

Descriptive

1.   Describe the contextual, organizational, spatial, and material character-istics of Trafalgar Square. Where is it situated; how is the space defined; what are the organizing principles and elements; what are the relation-ships among the elements; and what are the materials used?
2.   Select one of the artworks of the Fourth Plinth and describe the compo-sition of the work. What are the forms, materials, proportions, colors, and other attributes of the work?
3.   Summarize the principles of public space design that are discussed in this chapter. What are the central concepts and criteria designers use in designing public space?

Analytical

1.   Select two artworks of the Fourth Plinth. What are three ways in which they are similar and three ways in which they are different?
2.   Discuss the relationship between Trafalgar Square and *Alison Lapper Pregnant*. How did the square affect the understanding of the artwork? How did the artwork change the use and/or understanding of the square?
3.   Select one artwork of the Fourth Plinth, then, discuss possible intentions of the artist in the context of Trafalgar Square. What is the artist attempting to say through the work and how are these messages connected to the square?
4.   Identify a public space you have visited or with which you are familiar. What are three ways in which it is similar to Trafalgar Square and three ways in which the two spaces are different?

Speculative

1.   In writing and/or sketches, design a new art piece for the Fourth Plinth of Trafalgar Square. Illustrate your intended goals or reasoning, as well as the forms, materials, and other attributes of your proposed design. What new artwork could be done?
2.   In writing and/or sketches, suggest three design changes for Trafalgar Square. Illustrate your goals or reasoning, as well as the organizational, spatial, compositional, and/or material changes you are proposing. What are the most significant modifications that could be made?
3.   In writing and/or sketches, design what you believe is an ideal public space and art piece for a city or town of your choice. Describe the city/town, your goals or reasoning, and the characteristics of the design of the space and artwork. What are the characteristics of the town, of the space, and the art; and how do they relate to one another?

4. Design what you consider to be an ideal public art program—including the governing body, selection process, type of artworks, and location(s) of the work—for a city/town of your choice. What attributes define the majority groups—race, religion, age, gender, etc.? What minority groups are important to include and how do you propose involving them?

Notes

1   Stephen Carr, Mark Francis, Leanne G. Rivlin, and Andrew M. Stone, "The Value of Public Space," in *Public Space* (Cambridge: Cambridge University Press, 1992), 3.

2   Chua Beng-Huat and Norman Edwards, "Public Space: Design, Use and Management," in *Public Space: Design, Use and Management* (Singapore: Singapore University Press, 1992), 2.

3   For population statistics, see the United Kingdom Office for National Statistics, www.ons.gov.uk/ons/dcp29904_291554.pdf, accessed April 18, 2013. For economic statistics, see the Brookings Institute, "Global MetroMonitor," accessed April 18, 2013, www.brookings.edu/research/interactives/global-metro-monitor-3.

4   Rodney Mace, *Trafalgar Square: Emblem of Empire* (London: Lawrence and Wishart, 1976).

5   Norman Longmate, *If Britain Had Fallen* (London: British Broadcasting Corporation, 1972).

6   "Trafalgar Square: A Brief History," accessed June 25, 2011, www.london.gov.uk/trafalgarsquare/history/index.jsp.

7   The Fourth Plinth Commission, "About the Programme," accessed June 23, 2011, www.london.gov.uk/fourthplinth/content/about-programme.

8   Artworks and publicity pieces occupied the plinth from time to time, but for only brief periods.

9   From an October 18, 2000, Greater London Authority meeting, as reported by Paul Kelson, "Mayor Attacks Generals in Battle of Trafalgar Square," *The Guardian*, October 20, 2000, accessed June 22, 2011, www.guardian.co.uk/uk/2000/oct/20/london.politicalnews.

10 Ken Livingstone, "Public Realm in London: An Overview," Sister City Program Public Art Summit White Papers, February 17–18, 2005, accessed June 23, 2011, www.nyc.gov/html/unccp/scp/downloads/pdf/art_london.pdf, p. 9.

11 Rachel Cooke, "Bold, Brave, Beautiful," *The Observer*, September 18, 2005, accessed June 23, 2011, www.guardian.co.uk/artanddesign/2005/sep/18/art.

12 Ann Millett, "Sculpting Body Ideals: Alison Lapper Pregnant and the Public Display of Disability," *Disability Studies Quarterly*, 28 (2008), accessed June 23, 2011, www.dsq-sds.org/article/view/122/122.

13 "Livingstone Unveils Statue of 'Modern Heroine,'" *The Guardian*, September 15, 2005, accessed June 23, 2011, www.guardian.co.uk/uk/2005/sep/15/1.

14 Brendan O'Neill, "Statue of Limitations," *The Guardian*, May 17, 2007, accessed June 22, 2011, www.guardian.co.uk/commentisfree/2007/may/17/statueoflimitations.

15 Carr et al., "The Value of Public Space," 3.

16 Lennard J. Davis, "Constructing Normalcy," in *Enforcing Normalcy: Disability, Deafness, and the Body* (London: Verso, 1995), 23.

17 Davis, *Enforcing Normalcy*; David Heavy, "The Enfreakment of Photography," in Lennard J. Davis, ed., *The Disability Studies Reader*, 2nd ed. (New York: Routledge,

2006), 367–378; and Sharon L. Snyder and David T. Mitchell, *Cultural Locations of Disability* (Chicago: University of Chicago Press, 2006).

18 Livingstone, "Public Realm in London," 9.

19 Millett, "Sculpting Body Ideals."

20 In an interview with journalist Angelica Pursley at Multiplied 2012, Quinn described his approach to art, stating, "I am interested in making art that's about the society we live in and what it means to be a person … themes of identity … embodiment. … Why are we here?" Crane.tv, accessed May 30, 2013, http://blip.tv/cranetv/ artist-marc-quinn-at-multiplied-2012-6394489.

21 Millett, "Sculpting Body Ideals."

22 Malcolm Miles, "The Monument," in *Art Space and the City: Public Art and Urban Futures* (London: Routledge, 1997), 36.

23 As seen on the Trafalgar Square website: Greater London Authority, "The Fourth Plinth," accessed June 22, 2011, www.london.gov.uk/trafalgarsquare/around/4th_ plinth.jsp.

24 William H. Whyte, *The Social Life of Small Urban Spaces* (New York: Project for Public Spaces, 1980), 114.

25 These criteria include: (1) fit with context, (2) social and economic benefit, including happiness, safety, and efficiency, (3) mitigation of threats posed by climate change, (4) social, economic, and environmental sustainability, (5) originality and applicability to future projects, (6) success of the solution in the context given the issues/problems, (7) application of planning concepts and techniques, (8) community involvement, and (9) success in addressing diversity and equality. Royal Town Planning Institute, "RTPI Planning Awards 2011: Categories and Criteria," accessed June 28, 2011, www.rtpi. org.uk/item/4490&ap=1.

26 A "great public space," according to the APA, "(1) promotes human contact and social activities, (2) is safe, welcoming, and accommodating for all users, (3) has design and architectural features that are visually interesting, (4) promotes community involvement, (5) reflects the local culture or history, (6) relates well to bordering uses, (7) is well maintained, and (8), has a unique or special character." American Planning Association, "Characteristics and Guidelines of Great Public Spaces," accessed June 22, 2011, www.planning.org/greatplaces/spaces/characteristics.htm.

27 James Meikle, "Death Row Woman in Texas Uses Gormley Plinth to Plead for Reprieve," *The Guardian*, September 10, 2009, accessed June 28, 2011, www. guardian.co.uk/world/2009/sep/10/death-row-gormley-plinth-carty.

28 Answers to some of these questions appear in Clara Greed, "A Place for Everyone?: Gender Equality and Urban Planning: A ReGender Briefing Paper," Royal Town Planning Institute and Oxfam, accessed June 28, 2011, www.oxfam.org.uk/resources/ ukpoverty/downloads/placeforeveryone.pdf.

29 HM Government, "Block Passage of Anti-Social Behaviour, Crime and Policing Bill," accessed August 11, 2014, http://epetitions.direct.gov.uk/petitions/53083.

Editors' Introduction to Chapter 13

Public restrooms are among the most under-studied and under-designed components of urban infrastructure. Perhaps it is due to the toilet's association with waste and dirt. Maybe it is considered unimportant because it is a culturally unpleasant subject. Consider an alternate point of view. The loo (an informal term for toilet) is essential to urban settings. The challenges of designing the loo make it one of the best opportunities for those interested in improving the public environment.

In large part because of concern about germs, public toilets often are used only as a last option. Loos challenge product designers, architects, and planners to consider criteria that are often overlooked in the design process: sensory experience, equity, identity, cultural appropriateness, psychological/behavioral issues, gender and age issues, timing, flexibility, safety, security, cleanliness, convenience, and comfort.

Public bathrooms are complex and often contradictory elements of cities. They are private spaces in public places. Their primary purposes are for the elimination of urine and feces as well as personal hygiene and grooming, but restrooms serve other functions as well. Sometimes we go there to talk with someone about a private matter or to check cell-phone messages. Some use the public toilet for clandestine sexual activity, and others for drug use. Often the restroom serves as a refuge—a place to hide, be alone, or gather one's bearings. Rather than denying the many uses for public facilities, designers could consider all the possibilities, especially those that do not fit with their own preconceptions.

Design anthropologist Jo-Anne Bichard's case study describes why this commonplace urban element does not work well for many people. Perhaps designers neglected to observe how people use loos or the circumstances requiring their use. Perhaps they didn't consider the wide range of possible users such as older people, women, and those with disabilities. She takes steps to ensure that everyone is considered in the design process, focusing on personal empowerment through multi-sensory and human-centered approaches.

In this chapter, Bichard describes an ethnographic approach to public toilet design in addition to inclusive design. Ethnography, the scientific study of people and cultures in context, incorporates the viewpoints of the people being observed. Typically, ethnographers work with people in their own environments rather than in laboratory settings. Design ethnographers use specific frameworks, processes, and tools to help them detect patterns of behavior that can contribute to improvements in the human-made world. This systematic and immersive way of working gives designers a deeper understanding of how people experience and make sense of their worlds, ultimately leading to more thoughtful solutions.

Bichard suggests several questions for us to consider. How do various groups affect the design of public places, specifically public toilets? How do conflicting interests of users affect the evolution of a design? How do we change attitudes about public facilities that resonate with the broader population? How do we reshape everyday places to transform human values into design?

Chapter 13

ExcLOOsion

How Design is Failing Sanitary Provision

Jo-Anne Bichard

Are You Sitting Comfortably?

Where are you reading this chapter? Are you in school, the office, on the bus or train? If you are reading this whilst away from the place you call home, are you settled and comfortable, perhaps with your favorite beverage? Did you use the toilet before settling down, or do you think you might need to use the "loo" soon?[1] At some point today, you will. Where will you go "to go"? Are you so familiar with the space that you instinctively know where the facilities are? Or are you traveling, and so begins the hunt for a facility that you can access? Is there signage? Is it easy to get to in the time you need to get there? Is the toilet itself in a fit state to use?

For some people, using the lavatory when away from the comfort of the familiar toilet is done without much thought or negotiation. One feels the need to use the toilet, one finds the toilet, one toilets. But for many people, especially when they are in an unfamiliar place, the most natural of acts, the necessity of excretion, becomes fraught with difficulty. For some, a visual impairment may make any signage to the toilet irrelevant, not only on the journey but also in identifying "correct" gender designations. For some, just a few raised steps to the toilet facility may make it inaccessible. For some, the space of the stall may be problematic for themselves, their caregiver, or their mobility aids. For some, there may be problems locking the door, and getting down to or up from the WC pan. There may be no toilet-paper roll, or the roll holder and flush mechanism may be inaccessible to a hand with arthritis. For some, washing hands after using the toilet is a challenge; the sink cannot be reached; the water is too hot or too cold; there is no soap; and the dryers scare children, young people with autism, and older people with dementia. For some, a combination of all these factors make a biologically natural act the equivalent of an endurance test, both physically and cognitively. As Gavin, who is visually impaired, commented:

I was standing in the middle of the station thinking, "I want to go to the loo," hoping there would be a sign saying the loo is at least on the same level. … Well, it wasn't down one flight; it was down four flights of stairs. … It wasn't great. That may well have been the last time I used a public toilet, and I just remember thinking, "God I wish these stairs weren't here," it's just a design thing really.

This chapter gives an overview of nearly a decade's research into publicly accessible toilet provision that formed two United Kingdom Research Council-funded design-research projects and the author's Ph.D. research.[2] The primary method of data collection was user-centered in practice, comprising interviews, focus groups, design participation workshops and letters written to the research groups. In total, 349 informants contributed to both projects' ethnographic data collection.

Participants in the projects spanned a wide age range, with mothers describing the needs of their newborn babies to male and female nonagenarians who were independent or being cared for. Informants within these age ranges also identified as having a disability. These body differences included visible and invisible (dis)abilities, encompassing sensory, cognitive, and/or mobility impairments. In total, some 30 percent of participants identified as having an impairment that restricted their access to the built environment.

Defining the Field

The term *built environment* is used to delineate our human-made environment from that which we designate *natural*. Toilets present a certain disjuncture within this concept, because they are human-made environments for a biological act of necessity. Many people are familiar with the term "public toilet" and, in the UK, these have been traditionally owned and operated by local authorities.[3] In current UK legislature, there is no statutory right for these authorities to offer provisions, and, over the last decade, the British Toilet Association has reported a dramatic decrease in the number of public toilets available.[4]

Whilst there is a decline in *public* provisions, there are many toilets within the private sector including those operated by train stations, motorway services, department stores, shopping malls, hotels, public houses and cafés, and supermarkets—open to customers, and, therefore, serving a measure of the public. To counter the decline in public toilets, many local authorities have partnered with local businesses to offer toilet provisions beyond customer-only use. These Community Toilet Schemes offer the business a payment to cover costs, such as cleaning and maintenance, in return for making their toilets publicly available. However, this further complicates counting and mapping how many toilets there are, since the businesses involved in these community schemes often opt in and out yearly. To ensure that all available toilets, both public (local authority provision) and private (commercial provision), are considered, these studies have incorporated the term "publicly accessible toilet" to denote provision that is both publicly and privately owned and operated and to which the public has access.

Floor plan for BS 8300 Unisex
Accessible Cubicle.

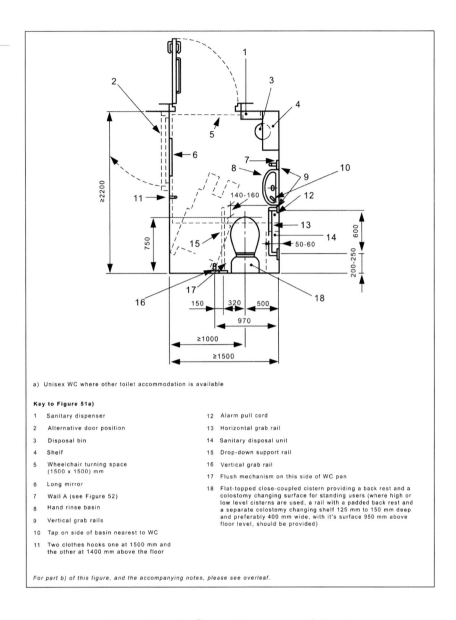

a) Unisex WC where other toilet accommodation is available

Key to Figure 51a)

1	Sanitary dispenser	12	Alarm pull cord
2	Alternative door position	13	Horizontal grab rail
3	Disposal bin	14	Sanitary disposal unit
4	Shelf	15	Drop-down support rail
5	Wheelchair turning space (1500 x 1500) mm	16	Vertical grab rail
6	Long mirror	17	Flush mechanism on this side of WC pan
7	Wall A (see Figure 52)	18	Flat-topped close-coupled cistern providing a back rest and a colostomy changing surface for standing users (where high or low level cisterns are used, a rail with a padded back rest and a separate colostomy changing shelf 125 mm to 150 mm deep and preferably 400 mm wide, with it's surface 950 mm above floor level, should be provided)
8	Hand rinse basin		
9	Vertical grab rails		
10	Tap on side of basin nearest to WC		
11	Two clothes hooks one at 1500 mm and the other at 1400 mm above the floor		

For part b) of this figure, and the accompanying notes, please see overleaf.

Fragmented Provision Reflects Fragmented Design

With so many different providers and no central body overseeing this provision, the management of public toilets is described by Greed as "fragmented."[5] This disjointed approach to provision also is reflected in the design of the publicly accessible toilet despite many guidelines for the design and management of these facilities.

The principle guidelines to the design of the publicly accessible toilet are the British Standard BS 6465 (2006, 2009), for the design of standard toilet provisions predominately catering to the able body, and the British Standard BS

8300 (2009, 2010), which focuses on the needs of the (dis)abled body. BS 8300 is described as a unisex accessible cubicle and is considerably larger than the standard cubicle in order to accommodate a user who requires a wheelchair or a caregiver (who may be of the opposite gender), as well as supporting furnishings such as hand-washing equipment and grab rails. The design template for BS 8300 is also used for the design legislation of Approved Document M (2013) of the building regulations, and therefore has a legislative requirement.

The approved guidelines stipulate minimum design requirements and allow for expansion. This has resulted in many disability groups presenting design recommendations and alternative templates for designers to use. For designers, this abundance of alternative solutions has created a wealth of information and, when implemented, has created a variance in the designs of accessible toilet provision. The resulting variety of toilet design has created a sense of confusion for users, who see a need for more standardization. For many users the inability to access suitable public toilets, including an accessible design, can place people on "the bladder's leash," preventing their access to more distant city spaces, as well as leisure and work opportunities.[6]

A Toilet Audit Tool

To assess the current design of accessible toilet provisions, Hanson designed a Toilet Audit Tool to quantify the design elements of existing toilet cubicles.[7] Analysis of the BS 8300 and ADM templates outlined 50 design features of the unisex accessible cubicle. These included the dimensions of the cubicle and the inclusion and placement of the recommended fixtures and fittings. Using the audit tool, the researchers reviewed 101 toilets in nine English cities and found that none had included the 50 design features as recommended in the design guidance. This highlighted the need to understand how the toilet cubicle was used and showed that incorrectly locating or excluding one of the design features could result in a space not suitable for use. The most commonly observed design feature within the cubicle was the inclusion of lever taps. These were found in 98 percent of accessible toilets. Yet, the researchers noted that, while the guidance recommended taps to be placed on the side of the washbasin closest to the toilet pan for access by seated users, many had the taps installed in the middle or the opposite of the recommended side. Here we see that, although the guidance had been followed with the installation of the correct design of tap, the placement of the tap had not followed the recommendations.

Another common feature of the accessible toilet cubicle is the grab rail to support users whilst transferring on and off the toilet as well as for support whilst toileting. Of the audited cubicles, 95 percent were considered to have sturdy grab rails. Yet only 78 percent of the cubicles had grab rails of the recommended length (600mm), and less than half (from 16 percent to 40 percent) of cubicles had the configuration of grab rails at the correct heights.[8] The misalignment of grab rails makes transferring on and off the toilet difficult for users, especially those who require a wheelchair for mobility. This was particularly problematic for informants who had experienced spinal injury, as the grab-rail configuration

Lever tap in correct position on basin closest to the WC pan.

◀ Figure 13.3

Lever tap positioned incorrectly furthest from the WC pan requiring user to reach further if still seated on toilet.

▲ Figure 13.4

Grab rails in the unisex
accessible cubicle.

determined how they might use the toilet. For users with spinal injury, transfer options for getting onto and off the WC pan are determined during the rehabilitation process, and an incorrect configuration can complicate toileting. It also suggests that the very design intervention installed to aid access can, if not implemented correctly, impede the actions it was meant to assist.

The extended size of the accessible cubicle allows not only for the space of the wheelchair but also assistance from a caregiver. Some 91 percent of cubicles had the correct door width allowing a wheelchair user to enter the cubicle; 71 percent had the correct floor plan width of 1,500mm. However, only 36 percent had the correct depth of 2,200mm. This effectively results in 64 percent of cubicles not following the guidance for the architectural template of the cubicle. Miles, who uses a power chair, illustrates the problem well:

> [In] some [public toilets] you can't turn around to shut the door—might be able to get in head on and use the loo, but can't close the door. Sometimes I can twist round and close the door, but then often I can't open it again. Lots of toilets call themselves disabled, but there's not enough room to turn around.

The design feature found to be lacking in most cubicles was the colostomy shelf. This fixture provides a flat surface for those who use colostomy bags to place the

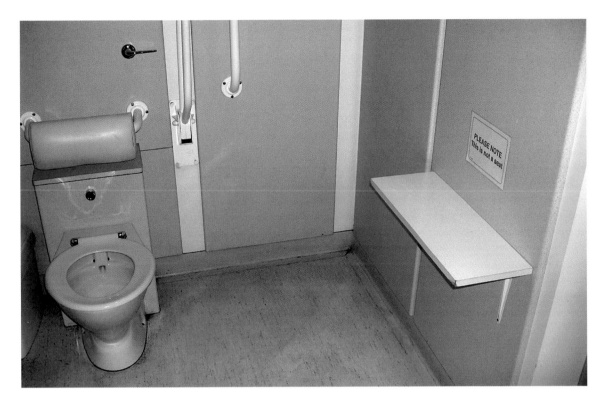

▲ Figure 13.5

A shelf in the cubicle is set in the guidelines to aid users with stomas in the management of their (dis)ability. It is recommended that the shelf is close to the WC pan (see details in Figure 13.1). This shelf does not follow guidance.

equipment they need (new bags, cleaning wipes, medical lotions, etc.). The inclusion of the colostomy shelf was found in only 3 percent of cubicles, and it was noted that the placement of the shelf was not in line with the guidelines.

Non-Toileting Behaviors

The inclusion of the colostomy shelf also highlighted a conflict in the design guidance. Providers had been urged not to include shelves, as this offered a flat surface for the use of illegal drugs. Greed, Hanson et al., and Knight and Bichard have identified how the needs of access are often superseded by the concerns of criminal behavior, a conflict Greed has termed "access versus fortress" and that Bichard has identified as emerging through "secured by design" predominating over inclusive design approaches.[9]

The predominance of the secured-by-design approach, an initiative of the UK police service that focuses on crime prevention in the design outcome, aims to reduce the opportunity for criminal behavior by reducing, in the design, opportunities for the behavior to take place. In many ways, this emphasis focuses on a minority population (those intent on criminal activity) and does not consider the use of public space and facilities by the majority. In the instance of publicly accessible toilets, a secured-by-design approach that seeks to exclude some forms of behavior has often taken precedence over an inclusive design philosophy in which access by the user is one of the primary motivations.

A security approach has been particularly prevalent in the design of publicly accessible toilet facilities, due to their specific cultural association with spaces of anti-social activity, namely the taking of illegal substances and the opportunity of consensual and non-consensual sexual contact. Such an approach has provoked a number of recommendations, such as the removal of the colostomy shelf to prevent drug use and the removal of mirrors to prevent eye contact, an initiate to sexual liaisons, as well as the development of new products, such as the ultra-violet (UV) blue light.

UV blue lights have been installed in toilets to prevent intravenous drug use, by making veins undetectable in the blue light. Hanson found that such lighting also prevented people with visual impairments from identifying contrasting elements of the environment.[10] Caregivers of people with autism reported that those they cared for became distressed in such environments. People with stomas reported the inability to clean their stoma under these lighting conditions.[11] Fred, a wheelchair user who, like many people with disabilities, has other mobility concerns, described his encounter with a toilet illuminated by blue light:

▲ Figure 13.6

A UV "blue light" toilet.

> I have a problem with those blue lights. I have a syndrome where my eyes react to light and where my pupils don't change from dark to bright light rapidly. I'm not visually impaired, but I do find blue lights very disorientating. It would be difficult to transfer and feel comfortable.

Moreover, Cockfield and Moss found that the inclusion of such lights, whilst briefly deterring the use of the facilities by drug users, also created a degree of erotic ambience, resulting in increased opportunities for those seeking sexual contact within facilities.[12, 13] Not only did the light cause exclusion but it also acted to facilitate another form of behavior that these kinds of products aim to design out. Thus the blue UV light has shown that such product development can effectively backfire.

The Experience of Users

Within design, one of the main principles of involving users in the process has been through inclusive design. Extending the process, Knight and Bichard described inclusive design as a philosophy in which end-users actively contribute to the design research process, which gives their needs and voices a central role.[14] In 2005, the management of the inclusive design process was documented in the British Standard BS 7000-6: 2005 as "the design of mainstream products and/or services that are accessible to and useable by as many people as is reasonably possible … without the need for special adaptation or specialized design."[15] It has become a popular method to develop design innovations for public amenities, but can especially meet the needs of older people and people with disabilities. A central tenet of inclusive design is that, by working with "extreme users," namely older and disabled people, the needs of the most challenged members of society are met, and the resulting solutions better serve the majority.[16]

Bichard suggested that it is not only the needs of users that designers can draw upon, but also their experiences.[17] Whilst inclusive design may offer solutions based on users' involvement in the design process, it can still result in design outputs that are tailored to a specific user's needs. In opening up the design focus to the experience of the user, needs can be considered in a comprehensive and holistic way. Experience design has become a popular approach in Human–Computer Interaction (HCI), but has yet to be fully explored by wider design practices, especially architecture, urban design, and the design of products and services that inhabit these spaces. The findings of the Toilet Audit Tool highlighted how a needs-based approach has not met people's requirements and, hence, an approach in design research of toilets may offer more satisfying solutions for users.

One way to incorporate user experiences is to consider the work of environmental psychologist J.J. Gibson on "affordances."[18] Gibson's notion of affordance has proved popular in design research disciplines, including spatial planning, interface and product design, and architecture.

Affordance

Gibson spoke about affordances in the context of not just people but animals in general, proposing that the affordance of an environment is what it offers the animal, what it provides or furnishes—with either positive or negative results. "A surface that is flat, rigid, and horizontal will afford being stood and walked on. Yet, this affordance is only complementary to the animal so that whilst a flat, horizontal and rigid surface affords walkability, it does not afford swim-ability for a fish. The affordance of these surfaces can also afford falling off and bumping into as 'different layouts afford different behaviors and different mechanical encounters.'"[19] Here, we see that the environment can be beneficial for some, yet hazardous for others. Gibson stressed that there is only one environment, and this has been altered by humans. He contended that this has been done "selfishly, wastefully, and thoughtlessly."[20]

Gaver has extended Gibson's concept and suggests that "affordances can provide a useful tool for user-centered analysis."[21] Gaver introduced the concept of the nested affordance. For example, a door handle on its own is merely an independent artifact, yet when attached to the door, it affords the action of opening. Affordances are predominately applied to functional aspects of design resulting in:

- door handle > door > open
- flush handle > cistern > flush.

But what affordances are invoked should these designed functions fail?

Affording Experience

Susan, who uses a wheelchair to aid her mobility, described her experience of not being able to flush a toilet after use.

> In one place I had to go and tell someone I hadn't flushed it. I had to queue at customer services and tell the sales person and everyone not to use the toilet because I hadn't flushed. It was so humiliating—a loss of dignity. I had a choice of humiliating myself or leaving the toilet unflushed.

Susan's experience illustrates that there is more to the product and its context, than the "form-follows-function" ethos of design. For Susan, the inability to use the flush handle prevented her from completing her toileting and resulted in a loss of dignity. This suggests that affordance can be extended to wider experiential concerns.

Another aspect of dignity comes through ritual practice associated with toileting. Zahaa described her preference for the unisex accessible toilet when toileting: "It's embarrassing trying to do ablution in public toilets. That's why the disabled cubicle is so good, as it's spacious and not embarrassing ... not in full view of everyone." For Zahaa, the privacy of a fully enclosed cubicle offered dignity away from others for toileting and hygiene observance that may encompass performative aspects not recognized by other users of the space.

Mothers who participated in the research also shared their experiences of the failure of toilet design to consider the dignity of the user. One mother, sensitive to the dignity of others, described her son:

▲ Figure 13.7

The flush handle should be situated on the "transfer" side of the cistern (not on the wall side as pictured here) so that wheelchair users can flush the toilet after transferring back to their chair.

[He is] fascinated by gaps underneath the door. He tries to crawl underneath especially when I'm on the loo, or he peers under the gap and upsets the person next door. It's an issue at crawling age. I can't put him on the floor; he'll just head for the gap, so I have to go with him on my lap.

For this mother, current partition design infringes on the dignity of others in comparison to a fully enclosed cubicle.

These examples highlight how design needs to consider conceptual themes beyond the mere function of the artifact. Within the design of the publicly accessible toilet, the design brief focuses merely on minimal privacy and the disposal of bodily wastes. The failure to incorporate the correct products, such as the flush handle (on the correct side of the cistern), in the recommended configuration, and the actual experiences of the users, as mentioned by Susan above, highlight that these artifacts serve more than functional aspects. The failure to be able to flush the toilet after use, have somewhere private to conduct personal and cultural observances, and respect the dignity of other users of these facilities highlight a more complex relationship between the users and this space.

A Design Trinity

The broader services within which the products are part are often disregarded as well. In considering the design of the publicly accessible toilet, the architect will have arranged the spatial dimensions, including aspects such as the toilet paper dispenser, within the design template. In turn, the product designer, following guidelines for a toilet paper dispenser that is accessible, will assure the design meets the single-sheet recommendation. Yet, if the toilet paper dispenser is empty and not serviced, the provision of the publicly accessible toilet fails. This suggests that service requirements need to be considered within the design of the whole.

These trinities of design practice highlight how inclusive design must encompass not only the physical projects but also the systems that keep them functional. There is a need for designers to engage with each other *and* the users to understand how their environment, product, and service will work together, in co-design processes with those who will use the space. Bichard and Gheerawoo question if such collaboration is possible given time frames and client expectations within the design brief.[22]

Design Anthropology

Design can be considered an activity comprising many disciplines—architecture, engineering, product design, services, human–computer interaction, and ethnographic research. Within this myriad of activities, there are a parallel variety of frameworks within which the activity is set; it may be sustainable, inclusive, rehabilitative, secure, participatory, empathic, and/or experiential.[23] Given the complexity of these design activities and frameworks, a new theoretical understanding is emerging around what designers do, how they do it, and how their practice fits amongst this multidimensional landscape.

Gunn and Donovan proposed design anthropology as an emergent discipline that "aims towards instigating different ways of designing across different scales, for example products, services, policies, but also working relationships."[24] Their proposition asserted that design anthropology offers a shift from the "problem-driven design question" to one in which the problem may not be there, or at least not obvious on initial investigation. Arguing that the world is "versatile," they suggested the need to move away from one situated context of use, and to consider many contexts and practices that might also consider the unintended consequences of design. Equally, Ingold called for a shift in design's perception of the user from passive recipient of the designed artifact to *user-cum-producer*.[25]

The research and theoretical underpinnings in this field have predominantly taken place under the SPIRE program, and defined design anthropology as a field "not owned by any one discipline or sub-group within a discipline."[26, 27] To help in delineating the possibilities of design anthropology, the program has identified discrete ways of understanding and practice, and suggests a framework composed of three models—*dA*, *Da*, and *DA*—to accentuate the position and influence of anthropology and design in practice.[28]

For work undertaken from a *dA* position, design follows the anthropological lead; design is the object of anthropological study or adopts a theoretical understanding from anthropology. *Da*, in some ways, reverses the relationship between the disciplines and finds fieldwork, a central anthropological activity, placed in the service of design. This positioning tends to follow a more traditional design-as-problem-solving approach rather than an exploration involving a deeper level of engagement with people. Both *dA* and *Da* approaches are well established within university departments of anthropology and design.[29, 30] In contrast, the *DA* approach converges both disciplines, in which design and anthropology inform each other to a position of achieving a mutual knowledge exchange. This shifts anthropology as merely the informant for design, to active re-framing of the wider "social, cultural and environmental relations in both design and anthropology."[31] *DA* can offer a critique not only to the disciplines, but also "towards rethinking what design and innovation could be."[32]

Da dA DA in the Toilet: A Personal Reflection

Situating the work outlined above within the framework of design anthropology presents an opportunity to highlight how the collaboration between social anthropology and design can evolve. Julienne Hanson, architect and professor, first conceived this toilet research, which was informed by my role as research fellow with training in social anthropology and ethnographic studies with people with cognitive impairments. In these early stages of the research, my anthropological training and experience helped frame the questions to be asked and the theoretical underpinnings of the project. These included the recognition of the "body" as a socio-cultural product, socially molded and shaped according to society's norms and goals. This perspective places the body in the environment, which, at this stage of the research, prior to any informant contact, was the object of the study, and, therefore, set the foundations of the project within the *dA* framework in which anthropology informed the initial design research.

As the project progressed and my knowledge of architectural design grew, the project shifted to a *Da* position in which the fieldwork of design audits, observational studies, and in-depth interviews were very much in the service of design. By this stage, there was a clear problem definition that identified the difficulties users were having with the design and layout of the accessible toilet. By highlighting these issues, designers have evidence that helps to avoid current mistakes. Whilst the environment remained the object of the study, the details emerging from informants with a variety of (dis)abilities helped classify how the design had failed to meet their needs.

The *Da* position was also adopted in the second research project that focused on the standard toilet cubicle. This phase included an industrial designer and a now-design-aware social anthropologist. The development of a participatory design game that involved informants in the creative research process, as well as the information gathered from interviews with those responsible for toilet provision, produced a clearer problem definition for the research team. This concerned the difficulty faced by toilet providers in communicating information about toilet availability—such as location, opening times, temporary or permanent closures, and accessibility options—for users to plan their journeys.

Analysis of the research data was completed in collaboration between the designer and anthropologist, and resulted in the development of The Great British Public Toilet Map, a web-based resource that identifies where a toilet is and its features (accessible cubicle, baby changing, etc.).[33, 34] This resource allows people who may have concerns on finding a toilet, to not only plan in advance for future use but also to identify provisions near their current locations. Using open data provided by local authorities to populate the map ensures that information will be updated more frequently.

The project secured secondary funding and the map's development moved on to a stage in which the collaboration has been extended to involve the designer (Ramster), the anthropologist (Bichard), web developers (Neon Tribe), and members of the public. In this phase of the research, all parties have informed each other. The designer has made creative decisions about the map's direction and future possibilities, and these, in turn, were informed by the social anthropologist's evaluation of affordance, along with user engagement that focused on how the resulting design could and would be used. The web developers brought further prototyping tools to the development process to witness how users, specifically older people, would engage with digital technologies and the functions the map would provide. Testing these prototypes with the people who would ultimately use them revealed a resistance amongst some users to such digital applications and the need for the project team to provide opportunities for the map to be printed. This balanced collaboration between design, anthropology, web developers, and users helped improve the design and can be considered to echo the *DA* ethos Gunn and Donovan suggested.[35]

Where to Go "To Go"

Did you find the toilet? How was it? Did it meet your needs or was there nowhere to hang your coat or place your bag? Perhaps you hesitated when operating the door lock—it is, after all, considered one of the more dirty features of public loos. Did you use toilet tissue to open it? For many people, there is an inherent hesitation when using these facilities, especially the unfamiliar ones en route to our destinations—the toilets of the train station, the unfamiliar café, or one of the remaining public lavatories. The apprehension of the unknown can cause hesitation. Will it be safe? Will it be clean? Will there be others in there? These are complex considerations for design to sensitively consider if we are to move away from the access-vs.-fortress paradigm as demonstrated by the Automatic Public Convenience (APC).[36] Continence advisors suggest that good bladder and bowel health is maintained if we are relaxed when toileting. This is hard to achieve if one is fearful of sitting down because of hygienic conditions.

These concerns are equaled, if not magnified, for those who manage sensory, cognitive, and mobility concerns. It is important to recognize that (dis)ability is as equally complex as the context of use and the supporting environment.[37] People may have visual impairments *and* use wheelchairs. To design for (dis)ability from a singular perspective risks excluding others.[38]

Kitchin and Law found that many people tether themselves to areas of familiarity based on their knowledge and experience of the toilet provision in that area.[39] One of the respondents in the research described herself as being like "a little animal," always returning to the same place to use the toilet for fear of not being able to use an unfamiliar provision. For others, the known/unknown becomes the barrier that will not be crossed and they limit the time they are away from home, preferring the safety and sanctity of the toilet in the home. Such active withdrawal from public space can be accentuated as the body ages and becomes frailer. A report by a UK ageing charity found that 52 percent of respondents cited the lack of suitable toilets prevented them from leaving the home as often as they liked. This often leads to a sense of isolation and loneliness, and has been reported to be a bigger health concern than obesity.[40]

Despite these contextual complexities, the one thing all bodies have in common is the need to excrete. What other factors are coming to the fore in preventing satisfactory design solutions for this universal need? Toilets are not necessarily a pleasant subject to talk about—but people do talk about them. Could it also be the toilet's wider cultural association with waste and dirt that thwarts design attention? Is it considered unimportant because it is not pleasant subject matter?

Consider an alternative point of view. The loo is an essential requirement of a public environment. It is used by a wide variety of people. The many challenges of this environment make it one of the best design opportunities for those who are interested in improving the public

▼ Figure 13.8

The Automatic Public Convenience (APC) is illustrative of a "secure" design response to provision.

CHAPTER 13 Jo-Anne Bichard

environment. But, do designers want to be associated with the best toilet roll dispenser, the best grab rail, the best washbasin, or are they avoiding these less glamorous components of everyday life? Perhaps one of the biggest challenges for design is the image of the publicly accessible toilet, its association with dirt and unpleasantness, the associated undervaluing of the usefulness of the facility, and the design within that aids dignified and comfortable excretion for all.

Discussion Questions and Explorations

Descriptive

1. Describe ten features that make a public restroom accessible.
2. What non-toileting behaviors typically take place in public bathrooms? Cite an example of a non-toileting behavior that interferes with the accessibility of the facility.
3. Describe the concept of *affordance* and explain Jo-Anne Bichard's examples of the application of affordance.

Analytical

1. Use the facility yourself, and note the following: Did you have to wait in line to use the toilet? What was the condition of the restroom? How clean was it? Did it have a pleasant smell? Was there enough toilet paper? Were you able to wash and dry your hands? How comfortable did you feel using the toilet? Did people talk inside the loo? List three positive and three negative aspects of the experience.
2. Use the toilet again, this time with a closed fist, and opening, closing, and operating the facility with just your elbow. What could you use? What could you not use? Again, list three positive and three negative aspects of the experience.
3. Spend an hour observing people using a publicly accessible toilet facility. Compare the similarities and differences in behaviors between various groups (parents with children, young men, elderly women, a group of teenagers, etc.)? Consider some of the following: amount of time using facilities, hygiene behaviors, grooming behaviors, conversation, and consideration of others.

Speculative

1. Imagine that you are a design anthropologist who is interested in finding out the levels of social comfort of older people who need to use unisex public restrooms. What methods would you use to gather information?
2. How would you redesign the publicly accessible toilet to be a more socially acceptable and valued space?

3. Design a public toilet of the future to be sited in London in 2040. Keep in mind the increasing diversity of urban users and the changing nature of the city when you develop your proposal.

Notes

1 Loo is an English colloquium for lavatory. The word's origins are not clearly ascertained and believed to come from the French "regardez l'eau" meaning "mind the water," a warning to passers-by in the era prior to sewerage systems when the contents of chamber pots were thrown out of windows *or* as a euphemism for the 'le lieu' the French for 'the place' *or* a shortening of the word 'Waterloo' which was imprinted on many iron cisterns in the toilets of early twentieth-century Britain. WC is an abbreviation of water closet.

2 VivaCity 2020 funded by the Engineering and Physical Sciences Research Council (EPSRC) 2003–2008, www.vivacity2020.co.uk/. TACT3 funded by the New Dynamics of Ageing programme overseen by the Economic and Social Research Council (ESRC) 2009–2012, www.newdynamics.group.shef.ac.uk/tact3.html. Jo-Anne Bichard (2014) "Extending Architectural Affordance: The Case of the Publicly Accessible Toilet" (University College London, 2014).

3 In the United States, 'public restroom' might be more common, whilst in some parts of the UK 'public lavatory' is the preferred term.

4 Currently, no one knows how many public toilets there are for the UK population of 63 million.

5 Clara Greed, *Inclusive Urban Design: Public Toilets* (London: Routledge, 2003).

6 Rob Kitchin and Robin Law, "The Socio-Spatial Construction of (In)accessible Public Toilets," *Urban Studies* 38, no. 2 (2001).

7 Julienne Hanson, Jo-Anne Bichard, and Clara Greed, *The Accessible Toilet Design Resource* (London: University College London (UCL), 2007).

8 There are six recommended grab rails in the accessible cubicle, whose height recommendations range from 680mm to 800mm dependent on their position. Height measurements allowed for a discrepancy of 10mm under or over the recommended height.

9 Bichard, "Extending Architectural Affordance"; Greed, *Inclusive Urban Design: Public Toilets*; Hanson et al., *The Accessible Toilet Design Resource*; Gail Knight and Jo-Anne Bichard, *Publicly Accessible Toilets: An Inclusive Design Guide* (London: Helen Hamlyn Centre for Design, Royal College of Art, 2011).

10 Hanson et al., *The Accessible Toilet Design Resource*.

11 The stoma is a surgical opening used to support the colostomy, urostomy, ileostomy technologies.

12 See Parkin and Coomber for a detailed discussion on how such measures were not only temporary but also had their own health and safety concerns. Parkin, S. and Coomber, R. "Fluorescent blue lights, injecting drug use and related health risk in public conveniences: Findings from a qualitative study of micro-injecting environments," *Health & Place* 16 (2010), 629–637.

13 Colin Cockfield and Kate Moss, "Sex, Drugs and Broken Bowls: Dealing with Problems of Crime Reduction in Public Conveniences," *Safer Communities* 1, no. 2 (2002).

14 Knight and Bichard, *Publicly Accessible Toilets: An Inclusive Design Guide*.

15 British Standard, "7000-6: 2005," *Design Management Systems–Managing Inclusive Design–Guide* (2005).

16   R. Coleman, "The Case for Inclusive Design: An Overview" (paper presented at the Proceedings of the 12th Triennial Congress, International Ergonomics Association and the Human Factors Association, Canada, 1994).

17   Bichard, "Extending Architectural Affordance."

18   J.J. Gibson, *The Ecological Approach to Visual Perception* (Boston, MA: Houghton Mifflin Company, 1979).

19   Ibid.

20   Ibid.

21   William W. Gaver, "Technology Affordances" (paper presented at the Proceedings of the Special Interest Group on Computer–Human Interaction Conference on Human Factors in Computing Systems, 1991).

22   J. Bichard and R. Gheerawo, "The Designer as Ethnographer: Practical Projects from Industry," *Design Anthropology: Object Culture in the 21st Century* (New York: Springer, 2010).

23   This list is by no means exhaustive and does not suggest a frame of one or other but of the possibility of many working together.

24   Wendy Gunn and Jared Donovan, "Design Anthropology: An Introduction," in *Design and Anthropology,* ed. W. Gunn and J. Donovan (Farnham: Ashgate, 2012), 5.

25   T. Ingold, "Introduction: The Perception of the User-Producer," in *Design and Anthropology,* ed. W. Gunn and J. Donovan (Farnham: Ashgate, 2012).

26   Aberdeen University, Swinburne University of Technology, University College London, University of North Texas, Harvard Graduate School of Design.

27   Gunn and Donovan, "Design Anthropology: An Introduction."

28   Ibid.

29   This consideration includes the anthropology of art, which often focuses on the artifact that may be considered more "designed."

30   The working with users within the design process is highly encouraged within design education that incorporates a number of ethnographic-based methods.

31   Gunn and Donovan, "Design Anthropology: An Introduction."

32   Ibid.

33   http://greatbritishpublictoiletmap.rca.ac.uk/

34   Jo-Anne Bichard and Gail Ramster, "Improving Public Services through Open Data: The Great British Public Toilet Map" (paper presented at the Municipal Engineer Proceedings of the Institute of Civil Engineers 165(ME3), 2012).

35   Gunn and Donovan, "Design Anthropology: An Introduction."

36   Alexander Kira did draw on these issues in his groundbreaking work *The Bathroom* but his ergonomic work in this area has been more considered then his wider analysis of the contextual considerations for public bathroom design. Kira, A., *The Bathroom: Criteria for Design* (Ithaca, NY: Center for Housing and Environmental Studies at Cornell University, 1976 [1966]).

37   Rob Imrie and Peter Hall, *Inclusive Design: Designing and Developing Accessible Environments* (Abingdon: Taylor & Francis, 2003).

38   The case of textured paving is one illustration of this. Laid to aid navigation for people with visual impairments, its countenance is that it can make surfaces uneven and difficult to navigate for some users in wheelchairs, and others who use walking aids (I'DGO, "Tactile Paving Design, Siting and Laying" (2010), available from www.idgo.ac.uk/useful_resources/publications.htm (accessed June 9, 2014).

39   Kitchin and Law, "The Socio-Spatial Construction of (In)accessible Public Toilets."

40   www.theguardian.com/commentisfree/2014/feb/17/loneliness-report-bigger-killer-obesity-lonely-people (accessed June 9, 2014).

Editors' Introduction to Chapter 14

Public reactions to tragic events often result in design innovations. Shortages of tires and fuel in World War II prompted the formulation of synthetic rubber and oil. The 2010 earthquake in Haiti drove the advancement of more efficient disaster-communication systems. The 9/11 World Trade Center attack fostered the development of new airport security equipment. The 2011 Japanese tsunami instigated the invention of wave-weakening coastal barriers. The Ebola outbreak of 2014 triggered critical improvements in protective gear.

When designers respond to events, especially those that are catastrophic, they are faced with responding as quickly as possible to big problems. They can, however, become so focused on immediate concerns that they do not consider long-term effects. American sociologist Robert K. Merton, who, in 1936, coined the term "unintended consequences," referred to this phenomenon as the "imperious immediacy of interest."

Addressing pressing matters is an essential part of what designers do. Nonetheless, seeing the big picture—the context, impact, significance, and possibilities—is essential, even in times of emergency.

In this case study, Beth Tauke discusses a tragic event that required "design triage," the 1982 Tylenol murders in the Chicago suburbs, where seven people died after taking tainted medicine. Policy makers and product designers scrambled to prevent more murders. A massive recall was issued. Anti-tampering legislation was adopted. Packaging was redesigned. Because of the pressure of swift action, some design issues were overlooked. These consequences, themselves, became major problems.

Tauke focuses on the unintended results of the design responses generated under extreme duress and the groups who were most affected. She reveals the negative repercussions of over-the-counter medication packaging redesign, which we still live with today. She introduces two related strategies, *design thinking* and *inclusive design*, and presents them as approaches that might help to alleviate unwanted consequences. Tim Brown, president and chief executive of the international design firm IDEO, defines *design thinking* as "a human-centered approach to innovation that draws from the designer's toolkit to integrate the needs of people, the possibilities of technology, and the requirements for business success." According to Elaine Ostroff, founding director of The Institute for Human Centered Design, *inclusive design* is "an approach that honors human diversity, and acknowledges the right for everyone—from childhood into their oldest years—to use spaces, products, information, services, and systems in an independent, inclusive, and equal way." Combined, these two design concepts foster a rethinking of traditional problem-solving modes and offer a more culturally holistic approach.

This case study has lessons that can be applied not only to professional design projects but also to the decisions we make every day. While we can never eliminate all unintended consequences, we can study them for clues to improve design processes—i.e., to more thoughtfully understand our biases and presumptions so that we can reduce systemic errors.

Chapter 14

Packaging Panic

The Design Consequences of the Tylenol Murders

Beth Tauke

Many of you reading this chapter will not remember the 1982 Tylenol murders, even though they generated more news coverage than any other story in the United States between the time of the assassination of President Kennedy in 1963 and September 11, 2001.[1] The Tylenol murders and their attendant consequences have impacted all of us, and continue doing so every day.

On September 29, 1982, Mary Kellerman, a 12-year-old girl from the Chicago suburb, Elk Grove, Illinois, awoke with a cold. Her parents gave her two Extra-Strength Tylenol capsules. Shortly afterward, they found her lying on the bathroom floor. Unbeknownst to them, the capsules were laced with cyanide. She died later that day. Six additional people from the Chicago area died after taking the contaminated medication.

Within a short period, investigators determined the cause of the deaths. They ruled out the possibility that the capsules had been tampered with in production factories. Instead, they determined that someone had purchased the Tylenol bottles, added cyanide to the capsules, and returned the bottles to store shelves for unwitting customers to purchase.

Reaction was swift. The day after Kellerman's death, a press conference warned people not to take Tylenol. In nearby Arlington Heights, Illinois, police drove through the streets and used loud speakers to warn local residents. Chicago police distributed flyers in multiple languages throughout the city. On October 1, Chicago Mayor Jane Byrne ordered the police and health officials to remove all Tylenol products from all stores in the city.[2] News stories on the murders abounded and caused a nationwide panic. To make matters worse, copycat crimes spread throughout the country. The United States U.S. Food and Drug Administration (FDA) reported more than 270 incidents of product tampering in the month following the Tylenol homicides.[3]

On October 5, seven days after the first murder, Johnson & Johnson, the manufacturer, issued a nationwide recall of all Extra-Strength Tylenol capsules, over 31 million bottles at an estimated retail value of over $100 million (nearly

£64 million at that time). The company also offered to exchange all Tylenol capsules that had already been purchased for the safer Tylenol tablets.[4]

To this day, the Tylenol murders, deemed an act of national terrorism, remain unsolved despite leads pointing to extortionist James W. Lewis and less so to the so-called Unabomber, Ted Kaczynski.[5] This tragic event, however, dramatically changed the packaging industry and consumer safety standards in the United States and worldwide.

Background

Like packaging for other products, the packaging for over-the-counter (OTC) medication has several functions: (1) to contain products, defining the amount the consumer will purchase, (2) to facilitate transportation and storage, (3) to carry information, (4) to market the product, and (5) to protect products from contamination, environmental damage, and theft.[6] This case study will focus on the protection aspects of packaging.

Prior to the Tylenol murders, packaging for OTC medication was simple. Typically, pills took the form of a tablet or a two-part capsule, and were stored in a plastic or glass container with a lid. The bottle was offered for sale as is or it was placed into an easy-to-open flapped cardboard box. Consumers simply popped off the cap to get to the pills. The murders changed that; their after effects resulted in tamper-resistant pill bottles and a host of other new packaging reforms.

▼ Figure 14.1

Over-the-counter medication packaging prior to the 1982 Tylenol murders.
Source: Beth Tauke (chapter author and photographer).

Consequence 1: Legislation

On November 5, 1982, the U.S. FDA issued tamper-resistant packaging regulations that covered not only OTC medications, but also products that come in contact with the body, such as cosmetic liquids, oral hygiene products, and contact lens solutions.[7] Requirements included a distinctive barrier to opening and a label explaining the barrier so that consumers could tell if a package had been tampered with or otherwise opened before purchase. In May of 1983, the U.S. Congress approved the "Tylenol Bill," which made the tampering of consumer products a federal crime. In 1989, the FDA set national requirements for all OTC products to be tamper-resistant and tamper-evident.

Tamper-resistant packaging refers to packaging features that are created to resist access whereas *tamper-evident packaging* describes features that make unauthorized access easily detectable to consumers. The phrase "tamper-proof" is not used by regulatory agencies because no packaging design is considered impenetrable.[8]

The International Standards Organization and the World Health Organization both have issued guidelines for the packaging of pharmaceutical products including OTC products; however, these are only advisory. Specific laws and requirements are determined country by country.[9]

Consequence 2: Tamper-Resistant and Tamper-Evident Packaging

▼ Figure 14.2

Pull apart capsules and banded, heat-sealed capsules.
Source: Beth Tauke (chapter author and photographer).

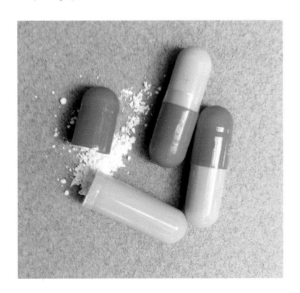

Packaging designers and engineers had to move quickly to develop new solutions that would prevent anything like the Tylenol murders from happening again. On November 11, 1982, just six weeks after the first murder, Tylenol was again on the shelves with safer packaging that included a shrink band, safety cap, overwrap, and safety seal. As such, it was the first product in the industry to use tamper-resistant and tamper-evident packaging.[10]

Examples of tamper-resistant packaging include: film wrappers; blister or strip packs; bubble packs; heat shrink bands; foil, paper, or plastic pouches; container-mouth inner seals; tape seals; breakable caps; sealed metal tubes or plastic blind-end, heat-sealed tubes; sealed cartons; aerosol containers; and cans. In addition to outer wrapping, the capsule itself is considered part of the packaging. The tainted Tylenol capsule had two parts that could easily be pulled apart and put back together. Newer tamper-resistant designs use methods such as sonic welding, banding, and sealing techniques employing solvents and/or low-temperature heating that seal the two halves together.[11] The aspects of the tamper-resistant packaging that make post-factory tampering obvious are considered the tamper-evident components. Warning labels draw attention to the tamper-resistant and -evident packaging to alert consumers even further.[12] For example, a label stating "do not use if safety seal is broken" has become part of the post-Tylenol-murder packaging, and versions of this label are seen on most OTC products.

Consequence 3: Opening Difficulties

The extra tamper-resistant features in post-Tylenol-murder packaging had further unintended consequences. The new packaging added several steps to opening OTC medications, some of which caused difficulties for many people, especially the frail elderly and those with physical disabilities such as arthritis or wrist sprains.[13] Typical problems in the process are (1) opening glued flaps on a box, (2) breaking a thin film wrapper, (3) opening a child-resistant cap, a two- or three-step process, (4) breaking a foil seal, (5) opening a foil packet, and/or (6) opening a blister packet.

In 2005, researchers in Sweden found that,

> among 604 elderly subjects, 14 percent were unable to open a screw cap bottle, 32 percent a bottle with a snap lid, and 10 percent a blister pack. Higher age, living in an institution, Parkinson's disease, rheumatoid arthritis, cognitive impairment, and impaired vision were all associated with a decreased ability to open the containers. Less than half of the elderly people who were unable to open one or more of the containers received help with their medication.[14]

Another recent study from Michigan State University School of Packaging found that "requisite physical actions were challenging along many dimensions. Sometimes packages required too much force; in other cases the size of the package or its features were too small."[15]

Frustration with the inability to open packaging has become so widespread that the term "wrap rage" has entered our vocabulary.[16] Heightened levels of anger and frustration resulting from hard-to-open packaging have spawned websites, blogs, and even awards programs for the worst packaging designs.[17] OTC medication packaging is one of the most maddening for consumers, as these posts garnered from several online forums demonstrate:

- "I am <this>close to getting out a propane torch to crack this baby open."[18]
- "I absolutely detest the packaging of this product!!! My arthritic hands CANNOT open them! My husband has to use his pocket knife to open

▲ Figure 14.3

First re-packaging of the medication by Johnson & Johnson after the Tylenol murders. Original caption: The triple safety-sealed, tamper-resistant package for Tylenol capsules has (1) glued flaps on the outer box, (2) a tight plastic neck seal, and (3) a strong inner foil seal over the mouth of the bottle. A bright yellow label on the bottle is imprinted with red letters warning, "Do not use if safety seals are broken."
Source: Corbis.

▲ Figure 14.4

Older person experiencing difficulty opening over-the-counter medication packaging.
Source: Beth Tauke (chapter author and photographer).

each little tough-plastic covered little bastard pill out of its indestructible #*!%#$@ cocoon. Superman would probably have a tough time opening these little suckers."[19]

- "One word: Chainsaw."[20]
- "Can't open this pill bottle. I might as well buy a cemetery plot and casket, fercryingoutloud; I feel so old."[21]

Consequence 4: Increased Consumer Waste

Another anticipated, but undesirable, consequence of the legislation and industry-designated safer packaging is the increase in consumer waste. The amount of material, especially non-biodegradable material, has dramatically increased since regulations were put in place nearly four decades ago. The recent wave of online purchases of medication and other consumables has intensified this problem due to additional mailing wrappers.

Containers and packaging make up 30 percent of what is buried in U.S. landfills after recycling and composting.[22] Much of this is attributable to *over-packaging*, the practice of using more materials than necessary to protect products. Most of us can recall a product that was delivered in a corrugated box containing plastic air pillows. Inside the box was another cellophane wrapped box. In that box was an injection molded plastic insert. Inside the insert was a plastic bottle with a shrink-wrapped band and a foil-mouth seal. And, finally, inside the bottle was the product itself. In this example, the amount of material used for packaging far exceeded the amount used for the actual product. Very little of the packaging material was biodegradable. Each year, millions of OTC medications are similarly wrapped. Not only does the new packaging use more material, but also it consumes valuable shipping space. This results in enormous waste of materials and energy.

On the one hand, ecology-conscious consumers and manufacturers want to minimize packaging material and move OTC packaging to become fully recyclable, compostable, and made with 100 percent post-consumer content. On the other, safety-conscious consumers and manufacturers want to ensure that products are fresh, contaminant-free, and tamper-resistant. The tension between these two positions has given rise to the new medical-packaging design profession, "an emerging stand-alone field that requires people who are both designers and scientific generalists, that is, people who can combine science, engineering, materials, manufacturing, communications, consumer issues, and societal issues such as environmentalism into packaging."[23] Expertise in balancing these factors is necessary to safely and responsibly bring OTC medicine to consumers.

Consequences of Design

All design actions have consequences, both intended and unintended. According to sociologist Robert K. Merton, who coined the term "unintended consequences," there are three types: (1) a positive, unexpected benefit, (2) a negative, unexpected detriment, and (3) a perverse effect that makes the problem worse.[24]

From the point of view of the Tylenol murderer(s), the intended consequences of his, her, or their actions were the death of several random individuals and perhaps the widespread panic that followed. Unintended consequences included two formally organized actions: legislation and new tamper-resis-tant/-evident packaging, which could be considered positive overall. However, two negative unintended consequences—opening difficulties and increased landfill waste—also followed.

It is impossible to anticipate every design consequence. Nonetheless, what could designers have done to predict a wider range of consequences and thereby reduce some of the negative consequences? Two emerging design processes—design thinking and inclusive design—might have anticipated and avoided the negative unintended consequences to the Tylenol murders.

Design Thinking

Design thinking is a human-centered, team-based, interdisciplinary method for innovation that combines creative and analytical approaches.[25] It promotes ideas that do not necessarily fit with existing models or patterns. Design thinking

CHAPTER 14 Beth Tauke

is, according to IDEO president and chief executive Tim Brown, "powered by a thorough understanding, through direct observation, of what people want and need in their lives and what they like or dislike about the way particular products are made, packaged, marketed, sold, and supported."[26]

Although the term "design thinking" has been in use since the late 1960s, Stanford professor David M. Kelley, who founded the design firm IDEO in 1991, came up with the contemporary definition. Kelley and his colleagues are known for these methods, which now are at the forefront of innovative business practices and educational programs, the most well known being the d.school at Stanford University.[27]

Design thinking differs from typical creative processes, which most often start with a problem to solve. Instead of this reductive approach, design thinking begins with a goal that includes an improved future result. For example, rather than solving the immediate problem of package tampering, design thinkers might start with a general goal of designing safer packages for OTC medications. The differences between these two approaches might seem small, but they can have dramatically different results. By focusing on the goal rather than the problem itself, the design thinking method widens the spectrum of possibilities and relational factors. For instance, the goal of safety not only implies tamper resistance, but also includes other ideas such as environmental protection and use-error prevention. Using this method, designers broaden the scope of their explorations to include production and shipping processes, ergonomic fit, and easily understood instructions for use.

Design thinkers work in multidisciplinary teams where everyone loops through cycles of learning, teaching, and doing. The team goes through a seven-stage, iterative process: *define*, *research*, *ideate*, *prototype*, *choose*, *implement*, and *learn*. The team members study the situation from as many different points of view as possible in order to open "new prospects . . . at each step in the process of design."[28]

This approach expands the array of possibilities. Imagine if the design team for the post-Tylenol-murders packaging had been comprised of product designers, children, environmental engineers, the elderly, chemists, transportation specialists, someone with multiple sclerosis, law enforcement officials, and small-business owners. How would the packaging have changed with this team? What problems could have been avoided with this approach?

Inclusive Design

Inclusive design approaches might have anticipated some of the unintended consequences that resulted from the safer packaging designs brought about by the Tylenol murders as well. This way of working, which embraces many of the concepts of design thinking, enables and empowers a diverse population by improving human performance, health and wellness, and social participation.[29] Inclusive designers put end-users first, and, as a result, they make things that are safer, healthier, and easier to use. The straightforward process involves designing with the following questions in mind:

- Does the design work for as many people as possible in an equitable way?
- Is it safe?
- Is it easy to use?
- Is necessary information perceivable?
- Is it sized right?
- Is it respectful of various cultures and contexts?

While it is impossible to design for everyone, certain groups are routinely overlooked in typical design processes. The groups most marginalized by normative approaches include children and the elderly; those with disabilities—physical, sensory, and/or cognitive; people who do not read the dominant language of a culture; those from lower socio-economic groups; people with various gender identities; and those from various ethnic or religious backgrounds. If the needs of these various groups had been considered in the 1982 Tylenol Bill, some of the negative consequences of the medication packaging could have been avoided. Inclusive designers would have (1) involved a wide variety of users in the design process and product testing, (2) tested the product in a variety of conditions, and (3) considered the sustainability of the manufacturing, use, and waste of the product and its packaging. As a result, they would have witnessed, during the product research and development phases, people with poor dexterity struggling with the packaging, as well as those with low vision, those using the product in low or no light, and those who have difficulty following a sequence. Designers would have noticed that many OTC medications have raised lettering on caps, but that lettering often is the same color as the cap, making it almost impossible to read. Inclusive designers would have observed people reaching for OTC medications from their nightstands, relying on tactile cues to open bottles in very dark environments. By making a few simple changes to the design process, designers would have prevented barely legible instructions, inaccessible foil seals and packets, lids requiring multiple simultaneous actions, and excess waste. Many of the unintended, negative consequences would have been avoided.

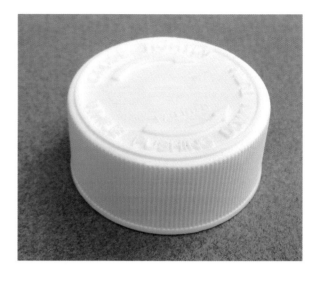

▲ Figure 14.5

Over-the-counter medication lid with opening instructions in white, raised letters on a white background.

Conclusion

The application of design thinking and inclusive design practices to OTC packaging design could have changed the response to the packaging crisis. Both involve collaboration with a broad spectrum of the population to meet a wider range of human needs. Both integrate evidence-based research to prevent errors. While design thinking is more focused on specific processes and inclusive design is focused on human needs, both are enabling processes that lead to better human-centered design. If these practices had been employed early on,

CHAPTER 14 Beth Tauke

packaging might have been not only tamper-free, but also easier for more people to use. Perhaps, if these practices had been implemented prior to 1982, safer packaging design could have prevented the Tylenol murders themselves.

Discussion Questions and Explorations

Descriptive

1. Summarize the principles of inclusive design discussed in this case study, and describe how designers use these principles to evaluate their work.
2. Summarize the action–reaction concepts described in this case study and describe examples using the Tylenol murders.
3. Describe the types of difficulties that people have opening OTC medications. Who experiences these difficulties? What are the causes of these difficulties?

Analytical

1. Purchase an OTC medication and identify the tamper-resistant features of its packaging. What are the positive and negative aspects of the packaging?
2. Which of the inclusive design principles are most important in ensuring safe access to nonprescription medications? Explain your rationale.
3. Identify another historical event that resulted in a design innovation. How did this event trigger an innovation? What improvements were made by this innovation?

Speculative

1. In an annotated drawing, describe how you would redesign tamper-resistant nonprescription medication packaging to ensure both safety and access for the elderly and other adults with cognitive, motor, and/or sensory disabilities.
2. What types of testing procedures would you use to determine whether the designs of tamper-resistant packaging are accessible by the elderly and adults with selected disabilities?
3. Acquire another product (a toy, a kitchen utensil, etc.) in a package and attempt to open it. Think about who might have difficulty opening this package. Write a short synopsis from this person's point of view.

Notes

1   "How Regulation Came to Be: The Tylenol Killings," *Daily Kos*, accessed August 1, 2014. www.dailykos.com/story/2011/06/19/986589/-How-regulation-came-to-be-The-Tylenol-killings#.

2   "30-Year Anniversary of Tylenol Murders: How Would Tylenol Terror or Similar Terror Play Out Today?" *The Cardinal*, accessed August 1, 2014. http://arlingtoncardinal.com/2012/09/30-----------.

3   Dan Fletcher, "A Brief History of the Tylenol Poisonings," *Time*. February 9, 2009, accessed November 26, 2014. http://content.time.com/time/nation/article/0,8599,1878063,00.html.

4   Tamara Kaplan, "The Tylenol Crisis: How Effective Public Relations Saved Johnson & Johnson," accessed August 3, 2014. www.aerobiologicalengineering.com/wxk116/TylenolMurders/crisis.html.

5   Steve Schmadeke, Jason Meisner, and Christy Gutowski, "Investigators in 1982 Tylenol Murders Want Unabomber's DNA," *Chicago Tribune*. May 19, 2011, accessed June 17, 2014. http://articles.chicagotribune.com/2011-05-19/news/ct-met-unabomber-suspect-tylenol-20110519_1_tylenol-murders-tylenol-case-cyanide-laced-tylenol-capsules.

6   Paula Hook and Joe E. Heimlich, "A History of Packaging, CDFS-133," *Ohio State University Fact Sheet*, accessed June 23, 2014. http://ohioline.osu.edu/cd-fact/0133.html.

7   "Inspections, Compliance, Enforcement, and Criminal Investigations," *CPG Sec. 450.500 Tamper-Resistant Packaging Requirements for Certain Over-the-Counter Human Drug Products*, accessed August 3, 2014. www.fda.gov/iceci/compliancemanuals/compliancepolicyguidancemanual/ucm074391.htm

8   H. Lockhart and F.A. Paine, "Packaging of Pharmaceuticals and Healthcare Products," *Blackie Academic and Professional Publication P-1* (New York: Springer, 1960), 98–99,173–178; and Brian Pankratz, "Know Your Terminology: Tamper-Resistant vs. Tamper-Evident," accessed August 3, 2014. http://brianjpankratz.com/2012/07/20/know-your-terminology-tamper-resistant-vs-tamper-evident/.

9   World Health Organization, "Annex 9 Guidelines on Packaging for Pharmaceutical Products," *WHO Technical Report Series*, No. 902, 2002, accessed September 10, 2014. www.who.int/medicines/areas/quality_safety/quality_assurance/GuidelinesPackagingPharmaceuticalProductsTRS902Annex9.pdf.

10 Atkinson, Rick, "The Tylenol Nightmare: How a Corporate Giant Fought Back," *Kansas City Times*, September 12, 1982.

11 "Inspections, Compliance, Enforcement, and Criminal Investigations."

12 Ibid.

13 The Poison Prevention Packaging Act of 1970 (PPPA), 15 U.S.C. 1471–1476, was established to protect children from serious personal injury or serious illness resulting from handling, using, or ingesting hazardous substances, including oral prescription medications. Nonprescription over-the-counter (OTC) drugs were not regulated as a class under the PPPA. In 2001, the Consumer Product Safety Commission issued a rule to require child-resistant (CR) packaging on drugs approved by the FDA for OTC sale.

14 Anna Beckman, Cecilia Bernsten, Marti G. Parker, Mats Thorslund, and Johan Fastbom, "The Difficulty of Opening Medicine Containers in Old Age: A Population-Based Study." *Pharmacy World & Science* 27, no. 5 (2005): 393–398, accessed August 1, 2014. www.ncbi.nlm.nih.gov/pubmed/16341746.

15 Leonard Steinborn, *GMP/ISO Quality Audit Manual for Healthcare Manufacturers and Their Suppliers*, 6th ed. (Boca Raton, FL: Interpharm/CRC, 2003), 53.

16 Megan Griffith-Greene, "Excessive Packaging Dangerous, Frustrating for Consumers: Poll," *CBC News*, January 10, 2014, accessed August 4, 2014. www.cbc.ca/news/business/excessive-packaging-dangerous-frustrating-for-consumers-poll-1.2490047; "Wrap Rage Awards," *CBC News*, April 10, 2013, accessed November 26, 2014. www.cbc.ca/marketplace/episodes/2013-2014/wrap-rage.

17 Consumer Reports launched the Oyster Awards in 2006. "One Step Closer to 'Frustration-Free' Packaging," *Consumer Reports*, accessed May 29, 2014. www.consumerreports.org/cro/news/2008/11/one-step-closer-to-frustration-free-packaging/index.htm.

18 "Can't.Open.RX.Bottle ... Uuuuurrrrgggggghhhhhh!" [Archive] *Straight Dope Message Board*, accessed August 3, 2014. http://boards.straightdope.com/sdmb/archive/index.php/t-287760.html.

19 "Zyrtec-D: Worst Packaging Ever," *Faerey.net*, accessed August 3, 2014. http://faerye.net/post/zyrtec-d-worst-packaging-ever.

20 "Can't.Open.RX.Bottle."

21 Ibid.

22 Edward J. Bauer, *Pharmaceutical Packaging Handbook* (New York: Informa Healthcare, 2009), 511–513.

23 Ibid., iv–v.

24 Robert Merton, "The Unanticipated Consequences of Purposive Social Action," *American Sociological Review* 1, no. 6 (1936): 894–904.

25 d.school, "Our Point of View," accessed June 18, 2014. http://dschool.stanford.edu/our-point-of-view/. Since its inception in the late 1960s, the term "design thinking" has transformed and assumed new meanings, all with iterative and innovative processes at their core. Its roots are in the development of computer problem solving; Herbert A. Simon, noted researcher in intelligent computing, addressed the concept in *The Sciences of the Artificial* (Cambridge, MA: MIT Press, 1969) at the same time that Rudolph Arnheim published *Visual Thinking* (Berkeley: University of California Press, 1969). Shortly after, Robert McKim's *Experiences in Visual Thinking* (Monterey, CA: Brooks/Cole Publishing, 1972) emphasized the importance of imagining and visualizing in abstract thinking. Peter Rowe established the term in design research through *Design Thinking* (Cambridge, MA: MIT Press, 1987). Nigel Cross considered design thinking to be a missing third area of education after the sciences and arts/humanities in "Designerly Ways of Knowing," *Design Studies* 3, no. 4 (1982): 221–227.

26 Tim Brown, "Design Thinking," *Harvard Business Review*, June 1, 2008, accessed July 18, 2014. http://hbr.org/2008/06/design-thinking/.

27 In an e-mail message to the author on November 24, 2014, Sina Mossayeb (IDEO Global Systems Design Lead) revealed that although David Kelley developed the latest version of design thinking, IDEO co-founder Bill Moggridge also was involved in its evolution and implementation.

28 Herbert A. Simon, *The Sciences of the Artificial*, 3rd ed. (Cambridge, MA: MIT Press, 1996), 164.

29 Edward Steinfeld and Jordana L. Maisel, *Universal Design: Creating Inclusive Environments* (Hoboken, NJ: John Wiley, 2012), 29.

Editors' Introduction to Chapter 15

In 1726, 20-year-old Benjamin Franklin designed a system to help him toward his goal of building perfection in his personal character. In a small book, he drew a set of 13 charts, one for each of 13 virtues that he believed were essential for his quest: temperance, silence, order, resolution, frugality, industry, sincerity, justice, moderation, cleanliness, tranquility, chastity, and humility. At the end of every day, Franklin would mark a dot next to the virtues he had violated. At first, there were many dots on the charts, but eventually the number of dots decreased. Explaining the system in his autobiography, he wrote, "I was surprised to find myself so much fuller of faults than I had imagined, but I had the satisfaction of seeing them diminish."

There are a number of contemporary versions of Franklin's system such as Character First, WiseSkills, Values in Action, and the I CAN Character Curriculum, which many elementary and high schools throughout the U.S. have adopted. Imbedded in these systems is an understanding that assuming responsibility for a healthy mind and body is a component of personal character.

With advances in technology, self-monitoring systems and tracking devices, such as mobile apps, fuel bands, sleep monitors, and food intake charts, have become ubiquitous. In 2012, Pew Internet Research conducted its first survey on self-monitoring and found that seven of ten U.S. adults track at least one health indicator.

Most healthcare providers consider the self-monitoring trend to be positive because patients are taking more responsibility for their own health with proactive behaviors. Nonetheless, some have concerns about poorly designed monitoring systems that could lead patients to focus on the wrong data. Others worry that once the novelty wears off, people will get bored with tracking. In addition, being aware of activities and conditions does not ensure that people will change their behaviors. In either case, design tools that support the monitoring and managing of personal health are becoming more advanced and promise to transform healthcare.

In this case study, Craig Vogel, Linda Dunseath, and Lori E. Crosby trace the collaboration between designers, healthcare workers, and patients in the development of new patient–provider and self-monitoring tools. As a newly emerging field, healthcare design focuses on ways that design intervention can significantly improve life quality. This case study looks at Sickle Cell Disease (SCD), the most common genetic disorder in the U.S. It describes the difficult transition that teens experience as they move from pediatric to adult care, just as the disease worsens. Preventative medical support systems such as this are essential components of healthy lifestyles for children and adolescents. Yet, the first evidence-based practice Leadership Summit that focused on children and adolescents was held just seven years ago. Vogel, Dunseath, and Crosby stress the importance of promoting healthy lifestyles that enable younger people with SCD to achieve their full potential.

As you read this case study, think about the many people involved in the healthcare design process and the roles that they play. Consider the transition process that patients go through, and the many things that can go wrong. Reflect on the ways that these types of support systems might change our healthcare culture. Most important, identify the social structures that underlie these types of initiatives.

Chapter 15

iTransition

Promoting Healthcare Independence for Teens with Chronic Illness

Craig Vogel, Linda Dunseath, Lori E. Crosby

Introduction

For the past decade, a shift in healthcare research and practice has created an opportunity for design at all levels. The concept of patient-centered and empathic healthcare is re-centering the relationship between doctor and patient. Researchers are attempting to better understand the needs of patients and adopting *co-design* approaches, which "allow users to become an active part of the creative development of a product by interacting directly with design and research teams."[1] Co-design works in concert with *translational research,* which is focused on converting research into practice thereby "ensuring that new treatments and research knowledge actually reach the populations for whom they are intended and are implemented correctly."[2] The primary goal of translational research is to increase the speed and sophistication of ideas as they evolve from the lab to the patient. Designers can now bring their research, visualization, and conceptualization methods into research teams to complement scientific research approaches and methods of validation. In this case study, co-design and translational research methods were engaged in a project conducted with multidisciplinary teams from Cincinnati Children's Hospital Medical Center (CCHMC) and the Live Well Collaborative (LWC).

The Cincinnati Children's Hospital Medical Center is one of the top hospitals for children in the United States. The Live Well Collaborative, a nonprofit organization co-founded by the University of Cincinnati (UC) and Procter & Gamble, initially focused on the needs of consumers 50 years and older. Live Well is led by the School of Design in the College of Design, Architecture, Art and Planning at UC and has several corporate members. Each LWC project is unique and involves faculty and student teams from colleges across the university. CCHMC learned about LWC's design thinking interdisciplinary approach and became interested in exploring this model as a way to expand their research and clinical experiments. After an initial project to test the relationship, CCHMC agreed to join the LWC. The board of LWC agreed to expand

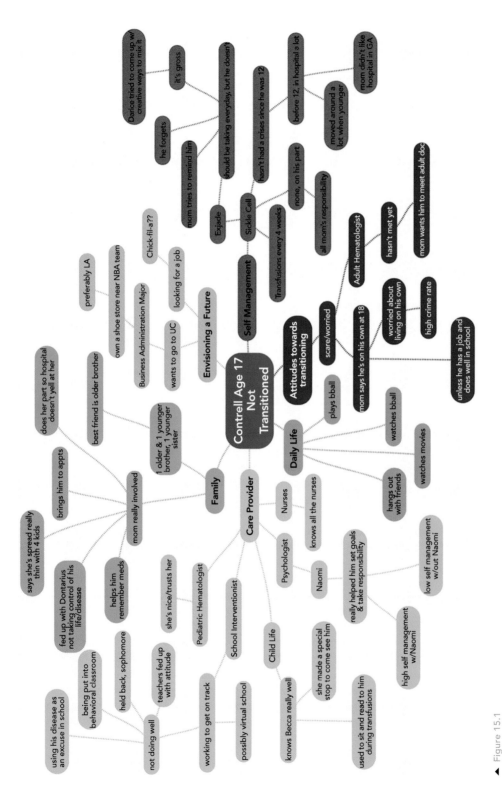

◄ Figure 15.1

Network diagram of factors that could affect transition into adult care.

Source: Lori E. Crosby, PsyD: Cincinnati Children's Hospital Medical Center & Live Well Collaborative.

the mission of the nonprofit to "living well across the life span." One of the first projects that CCHMC brought to the LWC was focused on Sickle Cell Disease (SCD) in adolescents.

Ideally, the teen years are a time of good health, without the illnesses that can affect older people. Unfortunately, there are chronic diseases that can affect teens—diabetes, asthma, schizophrenia, and epilepsy to name a few. Sickle Cell Disease is one that worsens during teen years.[3] Through the CCHMC and LWC project, the design team built awareness of childhood diseases, their symptoms, and the social side effects. Medical professionals, researchers, and patients working on the project learned that there are many ways to benefit those dealing with SCD.

Sickle Cell Disease

Most of us don't know much about Sickle Cell Disease, but it is the most common genetic disorder in the United States. Some argue that it has been 'under the radar' because SCD often is thought of as a disease affecting African Americans. The reality is that it "affects people with ancestors from Africa, India, Central and South America, the Middle East, the Caribbean and Mediterranean nations like Italy, Greece, France and Turkey."[3] So while we might not realize it, SCD affects us all either directly or indirectly.

SCD is an inherited, serious condition that causes red blood cells to become sickle-shaped instead of disc-shaped. These harder, sharp-edged cells can get stuck, especially in smaller blood vessels. This prevents proper blood flow resulting in severe pain, anemia, infections, organ damage, and even stroke.[4]

During most of the twentieth century, SCD was thought of as a children's disease. Thirty years ago, less than half of all children with the condition lived beyond the age of 14. Today, "because of earlier diagnosis and more effective treatments, nearly 86% of all patients—and more than 97% of those with mild forms of the disease—live until at least 18 years of age."[5] The current average lifespan of SCD patients is 42 years for women and 48 years for men.[6]

The improved survival rates create their own challenges, however. During childhood and teen years, a pediatric healthcare team manages treatment of SCD. In their teen years, patients undergo a transition process into adult-centered care. This transition requires that young patients assume much more responsibility for their own healthcare. They have to learn more about SCD, be proactive during medical appointments, monitor symptoms, take medications regularly, make medical decisions, and become a self-advocate. Often this transition is difficult because it occurs at a time when the disease typically becomes worse—mortality rates between 19 and 25 years are high.[7] Young people with SCD are afraid of the unknown and often do not know what to do or where to turn.

Project

CCHMC researchers and medical staff asked, "How can the transition process be managed for these patients so that they feel prepared for an adult clinic and are able to manage their disease in a real-world setting without feeling abandoned or confused?"[8] The medical team partnered with LWC, who brought in an interdisciplinary team of faculty, researchers, and students to address this question through a sponsored-project research design studio. The studio, which is known for using a design thinking model, focused on the goal of developing "patient-oriented solutions to enhance the transition from pediatric to adult care."[8]

The project team included four students from graphic, digital, and industrial design; two faculty supervisors; and a psychologist, psychology fellow, and three to five psychology research assistants. The co-designers included the SCD Transition Team (hematologists, nurse practitioners, nurse care managers, social workers, and school intervention staff), as well as several SCD patients.[9]

Phase 1: Qualitative Research

To begin, the team conducted background research and literature reviews to understand Sickle Cell Disease and its impact on child, adolescent, and adult bodies. They also studied the pediatric care required for young children with SCD (including daily doses of penicillin until age 5); the difficulties of the transition process; and how stakeholders (patients, family members, a pediatric hematologist, a care manager, a nurse practitioner, a psychologist, an adult hematologist, a social worker, a primary care provider, a school interventionist, and a vocational educator) become involved in the transition.

To understand the experiences of providers administering care, the project team conducted focus group interviews with the caregivers responsible for the patient's transition to gather additional information about how the process might be redefined, modified, and improved.

To understand the patient experience of care, team members conducted interviews with SCD teens, and asked questions about the transition process. They shadowed patients' appointments at the adult and pediatric clinics, and observed their interactions with care providers. (Because students who were close in age to the patients were doing the shadowing and asking the questions, the patients were comfortable enough to share personal experiences.) Subsequently, the team created patient maps in order to identify design opportunity areas and insights.[10] In addition, they developed profiles of each patient and outlined the unique steps required for his or her transition.

Phase 2: Concept Ideation

Using Live Well's ideation tools, the team held sessions with SCD care providers where all of the steps of the transition process were first analyzed and then challenged. The co-designers reorganized the steps of the transition process (dividing, subtracting, combining, etc.) to explore possible new structures and to identify openings for improvements. They also listened carefully to patients' feelings and perceptions to find ways to rethink the transition process.

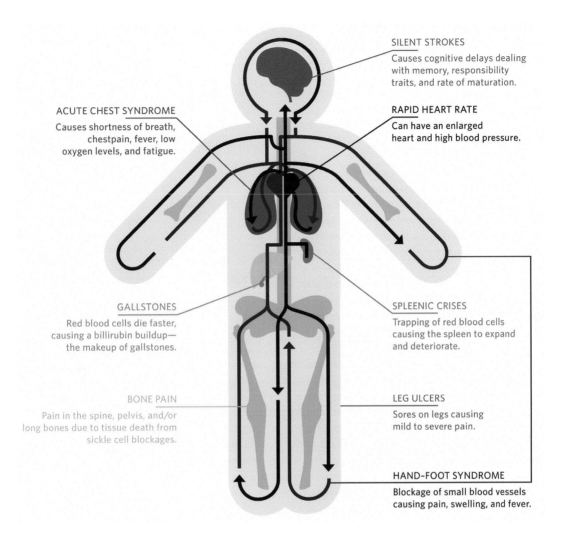

SILENT STROKES
Causes cognitive delays dealing with memory, responsibility traits, and rate of maturation.

ACUTE CHEST SYNDROME
Causes shortness of breath, chestpain, fever, low oxygen levels, and fatigue.

RAPID HEART RATE
Can have an enlarged heart and high blood pressure.

GALLSTONES
Red blood cells die faster, causing a billirubin buildup—the makeup of gallstones.

SPLEENIC CRISES
Trapping of red blood cells causing the spleen to expand and deteriorate.

BONE PAIN
Pain in the spine, pelvis, and/or long bones due to tissue death from sickle cell blockages.

LEG ULCERS
Sores on legs causing mild to severe pain.

HAND-FOOT SYNDROME
Blockage of small blood vessels causing pain, swelling, and fever.

▲ Figure 15.2

Effects of Sickle Cell Disease on the body.
Source: Lori E. Crosby, PsyD: Cincinnati Children's Hospital Medical Center & Live Well Collaborative.

According to project director Dr. Lori. E. Crosby, three main concepts emerged from the ideation process:

> (1) the transition process should be standardized, but flexible enough to meet individual patient needs, (2) patients and providers need a shared vision around transition and a way to communicate throughout the process, and (3) patients need a way to tie transition goals to more general developmental milestones, as they generally did not see the connection between healthcare management tasks (for example, scheduling medical appointments) and other life tasks (for example, scheduling meetings at work/school).[11]

Live Well team members used these three concepts to develop a design solution that they termed "iTransition."

Phase 3: Concept Refinement

The design team proposed a simple, inexpensive management system that could be individualized to address each patient's needs, and included a patient and provider interface. Essentially, the tool is (1) a booklet for each patient with a set of cards that address: Patient Profiles, Transition Steps, Milestones, Power-Up incentives, and (2) a Patient–Provider Interface in the form of a journal.

The Patient Profile summarizes the primary areas that affect the patient's transition into adult care: daily life habits and issues, self-management skills, attitudes toward transitioning, relationships with care providers, and future goals. It also contains cards with infographics on the physical effects of SCD, pain experiences, and management strategies, all individually tailored for each teenager with SCD. These profiles can be customized by the patients themselves and are intended to help them understand their own symptoms. According to Dr. Crosby,

▲ Figure 15.3

Patient booklets.
Source: Lori E. Crosby, PsyD: Cincinnati Children's Hospital Medical Center & Live Well Collaborative.

> The SCD clinical team and patients found these profiles to be useful because they: (1) concisely provided relevant information about where patients were with respect to the key domains affecting transition, (2) could serve as a self-management tool and help patients and providers understand the impact of SCD on an individual patient quickly (at a glance), (3) identify areas where the team could provide more support or education to enhance self-management and transition readiness, and (4) allow for comparisons across patients with respect to pain experience, management strategies, and level of support.[12]

◀ Figure 15.4a

Folders that identify patient attitudes about transition: i continue.
Source: Lori E. Crosby, PsyD: Cincinnati Children's Hospital Medical Center & Live Well Collaborative.

Folders that identify patient attitudes about transition: i prepare.
Source: Lori E. Crosby, PsyD: Cincinnati Children's Hospital Medical Center & Live Well Collaborative.

Folders that identify patient attitudes about transition: i postpone.
Source: Lori E. Crosby, PsyD: Cincinnati Children's Hospital Medical Center & Live Well Collaborative.

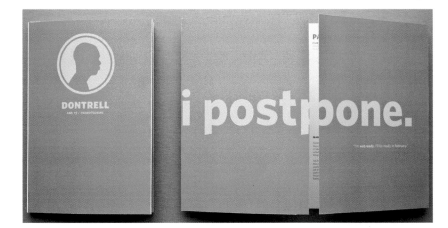

Folders that identify patient attitudes about transition: i transition.
Source: Lori E. Crosby, PsyD: Cincinnati Children's Hospital Medical Center & Live Well Collaborative.

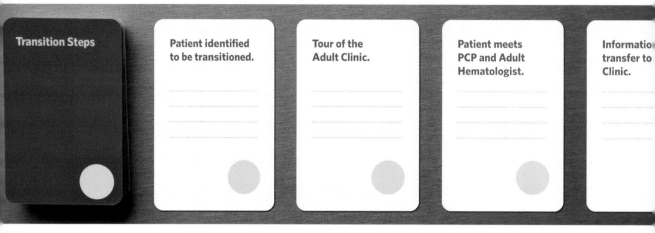

▲ Figure 15.5

Transition cards that are used to envision individual scenarios, which are then discussed and evaluated.
Source: Lori E. Crosby, PsyD: Cincinnati Children's Hospital Medical Center & Live Well Collaborative.

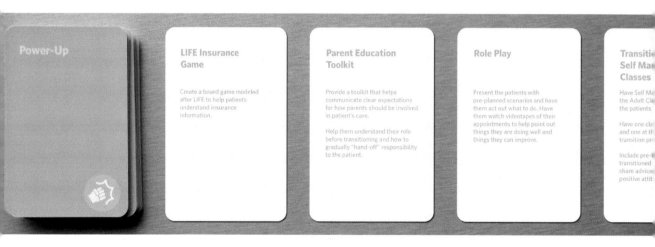

▲ Figure 15.6

Power-Up cards that suggest current or new interventions that could benefit a transitioning patient.
Source: Lori E. Crosby, PsyD: Cincinnati Children's Hospital Medical Center & Live Well Collaborative.

▲ Figure 15.7

The iTransition card set helps both patients and providers keep track of where they are in the transition process.
Source: Lori E. Crosby, PsyD: Cincinnati Children's Hospital Medical Center & Live Well Collaborative.

An action-based card set with three categories was developed to help patients with the transition process. The Transition Steps cards specify for each patient what is needed to advance to adult care. Examples include: "Patient meets Adult Hematologist," and "Patient goes to first appointment." The Milestone cards address goals for a patient going through the transition process. If, for example, a patient has self-management challenges, the Milestone card might read: "Get to an appointment on my own." The missions (or tasks) necessary to reach that goal would be added to the Milestone card. Examples might be "Schedule the appointment," and "Set up transportation." Power-Up cards identify interventions that are needed to ensure transition success. Examples range from "Develop a buddy system" to "Provide a parent education toolkit."[13]

Finally, the Patient–Provider Interface journal was established as a simple, focused way for patients to keep track of their progress, and receive feedback for their achievements from their healthcare providers. In addition, the journal has storage areas for important items such as medication and insurance information, and pockets for the card sets. Part of the journal is set aside for the display of rewards such as iTunes gift cards for fulfilling goals on the Milestone cards. This journal is the valise that contains all of the important items necessary for the journey into adult care.

Conclusion

Children's Hospital and Live Well partnered in an "integrated way to achieve the desired outcomes of developing a solution that empowers young people to manage their own healthcare and teaches CCHMC staff to integrate design methods into their everyday healthcare approach."[14] The success of this project demonstrated several things that became the foundation of the relationship between the two organizations.

- Design thinking methods can have a significant positive impact on the process of medical research.
- Design faculty and students can become functionally literate on research-related information and, working with research doctors and staff at CCHMC, can form successful cross-functional teams.
- Design ethnography has been integrated into the process in order to gain deeper insight into the needs, wants, and expectations of patients.
- Designers can visualize research information for team interaction and shared knowledge, and can also develop multiple concepts to test and evaluate with all shareholders.
- Finally, the results of the project can yield more sophisticated and contemporary solutions than medical researchers can conceive on their own.

For designers, the positive factors are equally powerful. Designers working with CCHMC researchers are working in a context with clear constraints and variables dictated by the research protocols. By co-designing with the research team, results are integrated into the research framework, and validation of concepts and results can be achieved.

The iTransition project is one of many that indicate a change in attitudes about the role of design and the power of patients in their own healthcare. Design is becoming more valuable in the development of systems for daily care as patient/provider partnerships increase. More than ever before, healthcare designers have the opportunity to rethink faulty systems, methods of administering care, and patient empowerment. This long overdue integration of thoughtful design into healthcare is a positive indicator of how our cultural values are changing.

Discussion Questions and Explorations

Descriptive

1. Describe the transition process for someone with Sickle Cell Disease, and discuss what health difficulties that person might have during the transition.
2. Describe the design process undertaken by the Live Well team in attempting to improve the transition process.
3. Summarize the basic elements of the iTransition patient booklets, and how they improve the transition process.

Analytical

1. Compare the Live Well team's findings of the patients' and providers' perceptions of the transition process. What were the most important differences in their perceptions?

2. How did the Live Well team specifically apply design thinking methods to the challenge of improving the transition for SCD patients?
3. Is the iTransition a product? A process? A service? A system? How would you describe this type of design?

Speculative

1. Identify other diseases that were once considered childhood diseases, but, because of medical/scientific advancements, have evolved into adult diseases as well. What are some of the complications of these diseases? How might design intervention improve life for those coping with these conditions?
2. Identify a non-medical transition in young adults' lives. Use the iTransition as a model, and design a system that improves the transition process.

Notes

1 Catalina Naranjo-Bock, "Creativity-Based Research: The Process of Co-Designing with Users," *UX Magazine,* article 820, April 24, 2012, accessed November 29, 2014. http://uxmag.com/articles/creativity-based-research-the-process-of-co-designing-with-users.
2 Steven H. Woolf, MD, MPH, "The Meaning of Translational Research and Why It Matters," *Journal of the American Medical Association (JAMA)* 299, no. 2 (2008): 211–212. http://jama.jamanetwork.com/article.aspx?articleid=1149350.
3 "Sickle Cell Disease," *Genetics Home Reference,* U.S. National Library of Medicine, November 1, 2014, accessed November 30, 2014, http://ghr.nlm.nih.gov/condition/sickle-cell-disease.
4 Mayo Clinic Staff, "Sickle Cell Anemia," *Diseases and Conditions,* Mayo Clinic, June 11, 2014, accessed December 2, 2014. www.mayoclinic.org/diseases-conditions/sickle-cell-anemia/basics/definition/con-20019348.
5 Harry S. Jacob, MD, FRCPath(Hon), "Lost in Transition: Care for Adults with Sickle Cell Disease 'Complex Puzzle'," *Healio: Medical News, Journals, and Free CME,* March 25, 2013, accessed December 2, 2014. www.healio.com/hematology-oncology/hematology/news/print/hemonc-today/{e7295a0a-f481-4f2c-8c01-23b3ef9cfa07}/lost-in-transition-care-for-adults-with-sickle-cell-disease-complex-puzzle.
6 Orah S. Platt, Donald J. Brambilla, Wendell F. Rosse, Paul F. Milner, Oswaldo Castro, Martin H. Steinberg, and Panpit P. Klug. "Mortality in Sickle Cell Disease—Life Expectancy and Risk Factors for Early Death," *New England Journal of Medicine* 330 (1994): 1639–1644.
7 Charles T. Quinn, Zora R. Rogers, Timothy L. McCavit, and George R. Buchanan. "Improved Survival of Children and Adolescents with Sickle Cell Disease," *Blood* 115, no. 17 (2010): 3447–2452.
8 Lori E. Crosby, Naomi E. Joffe, Linda A. Dunseath, and Rachel Lee, "Design Joins the Battle against Sickle-Cell Disease," *Design Management Review* 24, no. 2 (2013): 48–53.
9 Ibid.

10   For a full description of the design process, see Lori E. Crosby, PsyD, "Case Studies,"
      Live Well Collaborative RSS2. January 1, 2012, accessed December 1, 2014. http://
      livewellcollaborative.org/portfolio/itransition.

11   Crosby et al., "Design Joins the Battle."

12   Ibid.

13   Ibid.

14   Ibid.

Conclusion

Prospects for the Future of Diversity and Design

Beth Tauke, Korydon Smith, and Charles Davis

> *The poor have the right to be beautiful, too.*
> (Dr. Ivo Pitanguy, forefather of Brazilian plastic surgery
> and founder of the Pitanguy Clinic in Rio de Janeiro)

The aesthetic treatment of the body is one of the simplest and most long-standing forms of design in the world. Practices have ranged from grooming to dressing, hair styling to dieting. The reasons for body design vary from culture to culture, and often center on issues of beauty (as diversely as that is defined), yet nowhere is body design more directly connected to social mobility than in contemporary Brazil. Despite widespread poverty, as of 2013, Brazil has had more plastic surgeons and more cosmetic surgeries per capita than any country in the world. Not merely for the wealthy, a large percentage of people obtaining breast implants, facial surgeries, the famed "Brazilian butt lift," and other procedures—or *plástica*—are from middle and lower income groups. Many used privately financed credit (or public subsidies/donations) to purchase the surgeries. Since its beginning in 1960, the Holy House of Mercy Hospital in Rio de Janeiro, affiliated with Dr. Ivo Pitanguy, "the world's most renowned plastic surgeon," and his clinic, has performed more than 50,000 plastic surgeries for "members of underprivileged communities."[1] While many of these surgeries were for "congenital or traumatic deformities," a large number were purely cosmetic.

This peculiar story of cosmetic surgery resides alongside one of the world's largest informal ("squatter") settlements, home to around 1.4 million urban poor. Systemic poverty, poor sanitation, diminished health and well-being, and scarce opportunities for social or economic mobility characterize what are termed the *favelas* of Rio. Body modification is one of few options available to Brazil's poor. "In Brazil's *favelas* many dreams for social mobility center on the body." This is particularly so for working-class women who "face long lines at public hospitals to have cosmetic surgery" and who, otherwise, are "excluded from other means of social ascent, such as education or entrepreneurship. For the poor, beauty is often a form of capital that can be exchanged for other benefits, however small, transient, or unconducive to collective change."[2] Thus, the need is met in the reduced-fee clinics that, in the words of Francesco Mazzarone, president of the Pitanguy Clinic, provide not simply tummy tucks but "equality ... equal rights to everyone. The patients come here to get back something they lost in time. We give to them the right to dream. ... What we do here is altruism."[3]

It is a nearly unimaginable concept to outsiders: equality through plastic surgery. Each piece of this story gives us pause. Mazzarone's remarks leave us wondering: Is it truly altruism or is it veiled entrepreneurism? The Pitanguy Clinic is involved in research and education, along with philanthropy, but we cannot deny the fact that cosmetic surgery is the focus.

Deeper explorations reveal how Brazil's cosmetic surgery industry and the Pitanguy Clinic are featured on the website *Patients Beyond Borders*, a site whose name casually sounds like the reputable Doctors without Borders but whose true purpose is to provide information about medical tourism. Brazil, for instance, is highlighted as a premier destination for cosmetic surgery for pets.

Furthermore, the notion of subsidizing (or borrowing money for) elective cosmetic surgery is puzzling. Exemplified in Brazil, the number of people living in informal settlements is expected to double to two billion within a generation, while the resource disparities between wealthy Western cities and impoverished cities of the Global South (as well as the disparities within these cities) grow wider.

Wouldn't cosmetic-surgery investments be better spent elsewhere— housing, education, or *real* healthcare?

On the other hand, maybe it *is* an appropriate use of resources, so culturally specific that it is difficult for outsiders to understand. And, maybe, it won't be so unusual in the near future in countries throughout the world.

In any case, this modern-day allegory illustrates that the limits of body design push well past the social norms and laws of most nations. The anecdote, distant or near to one's own life experiences, tests one's worldview and ethics; it gives us a small glimpse into the possible futures of society—how, in 10, 20, 50 years, conversations about diversity and design might evolve. Who will be seen as the most marginalized groups? Will children, for example, remain under-represented in design and society? Which design professions will have the greatest impacts on society? Will large-scale systems design be most important or will it be nanotechnology, or body design? Is it likely that race will disappear as a category—no longer tracked in census data or medical records—possibly replaced by DNA codes or other data points? We have witnessed the emergence of gene therapy and "genography" (DNA mapping), and we have seen the faceting of racial identity into nearly infinite permutations of multiracialism/ multiculturalism; the case is similar for sexual identity.

This future seems not only plausible but also quite near.

Possible Futures for Diversity

It is clear that the rise of multiracial marriages and nonwhite immigration across the world will be a major factor in redefining what diversity means in the near future. These demographic trends have been especially important in the U.S., which has seen a dramatic increase in the immigration of Asian and Latino groups since 1965. Such changes have led many to believe that America has finally reached a "post-racial" phase of development where race is no longer a factor in everyday social relations. However, the future social and economic status of immigrants raises more questions than answers.

In the face of such constant change, it is reasonable to ask the question that Jennifer Lee and Frank D. Bean posed in their book, *The Diversity Paradox: Immigration and the Color Line in 21st Century America*: "If race is declining in significance, as many have claimed, is it declining equally for all nonwhite groups?"[4] To answer this question, one has to simultaneously keep track of the legacies of migration and racial discrimination in various parts of the world. In the U.S., one part of this question is answered by keeping track of African Americans' progress toward assimilation and equity, particularly regarding its poorest and most marginalized members. While there is room for optimism, sociologists have continued to point to "persistent and glaring disparities between blacks and whites in educational attainment, income, wealth, and residential segregation" as obvious obstacles to future change.

When considering the role of immigration, the popular use of labels like "Asian American" and "Hispanic" often masks a great deal of ethnic and economic diversity within these and other groups. For example, in the U.S., Filipino, Vietnamese, and Hmong immigrants have not reached the same levels of social and economic success that their Japanese, Chinese, and Korean peers have experienced. The same disparities are true of the struggles that many Mexican and Puerto Rican families face in comparison to other Hispanic groups. This illustrates the need for a more sophisticated approach to diversity than a mass, homogeneous assimilation of all minorities.

A positive trend in the future study of diversity seems to be the broadening scope of this term's meaning in recent years. One of the populations previously overlooked during the canon and culture wars of the 1980s was people with disabilities. The passage of the *Americans with Disabilities Act* in the 1990s prompted a host of changes to national and local building codes, and, thereby, the design of buildings and cities. Similar legislation has been passed and initiatives begun throughout Europe and Asia as well. Universities have followed suit by establishing academic departments and research laboratories dedicated to disability studies—expanding the historical narratives, scientific research, and public policies regarding physical, cognitive, and sensory (dis)abilities.

Another area of diversity that will have a tremendous impact on future populations is the rising importance of class and socio-economic status. While W.E.B. Du Bois declared the problem of the color line to be the major issue of the twentieth century, U.S. President Barack Obama declared wealth inequality as a primary challenge of the twenty-first century. While gross domestic product (GDP) and corporate profits have reached record highs, the income of the average worker has stagnated, if not decreased, around the world. The implications for designers are both economic and ethical, and the future of design will depend on the worlds in which we dwell.

Possible Futures for Design

For a Syrian refugee family, design will focus on basic survival needs—food, water, and shelter—in temporary and hostile conditions. For the adolescent immersed in video games, the role of design might involve the development of digital worlds not possible in physical space and the exploration of alternate identities and role playing. For a Tokyo-based couple expecting the birth of a child, design interventions could give them a healthier (or more desired) baby. For the London dialysis patient seeking a kidney transplant, biological design— "living product design"—will be an important area of innovation. For a farmer confronted with pests in West Java, Indonesia, ecosystem design will be the key.

As dissimilar as they are, these worlds share commonalities that have implications for the future of design. They all illustrate design-in-transition. The examples push boundaries—physical, virtual, biological—and radicalize the contexts, processes, and outcomes of design; they challenge and blur current concepts of design, the ways it is practiced, and who is involved; and they raise ethical questions about the nature of design itself.

The very nature of design presupposes a desire to push the boundaries, to make new things. From humans' early existence, we have continually attempted to erase limits—to perfect and extend, through tools and technologies, our capabilities. Because of widespread technological advances and cultural shifts, today, we are experiencing changes more rapidly than at any time in history. This acceleration promises to continue. For example, in this volume, we have addressed issues facing people during their lifetimes. But design is moving towards other possibilities. Not only will design address birth-to-death, but design will extend to pre-birth and after life, including the design of death itself. The expectant Japanese couple might choose to alter certain genetic codes to prevent inherited diseases. The adolescent gamer might develop a virtual second self with a digital lifespan beyond his or her own. And any of these examples may, with the assistance of a doctor (or designer) whose practice focuses on end-of-life care and death, choose how and when they die.

If life-to-death is one continuum, scale is another. Design is moving further in to the micro level and out to the macro level. Designers working at the nano-scale already can purify contaminated water and reassemble garbage, molecule by molecule, into a variety of items including building materials, food, and energy. Because of these advances, the basic needs of Syrian refugees could be met. In parallel, designers working at macro levels already have delivered networked systems that track weather, earth resources, and navigation, and provide worldwide communication, which could give the West Java farmer the information he needs to more successfully manage crops. Macro-scale and micro-scale design innovations could also add to the before-birth and after-death options we have yet to imagine.

Another trajectory is the degree to which design has become integrated with the human body, rather than independent from it. The first lenses, developed by the ancient Assyrians, were large pieces of polished quartz or crystal. Ancient Greeks and Romans filled glass spheres with water to magnify objects. Subsequently, "reading stones," glass spheres cut in half, were used by medieval monks to read manuscripts.[5] Next, handheld magnifying glasses enlarged text, and eyeglasses soon followed. Contact lenses were developed in the late 1800s, and by the mid-1900s, intraocular lenses were introduced.[6] By 2013, lab-grown lenses were developed, and, just recently, gene therapy has been used to restore poor vision, and "smart lenses" have been developed to manage diseases.[7] The evolution of products to improve eyesight shows how we have moved from large to small, from synthetic to organic, from external (outside the body) to internal, from material to systemic, and from restoration to extension. What other external design might be internalized in the future? What can move into networked rather than physical form? What are the non-negotiable aspects of life that cannot take on non-material forms? How will these smaller, organic, internal, systemic, and extending developments affect design and the recipients of design?

The distinct silos of the traditional design professions are also disintegrating. Some authors in this book discussed design practices that address cultural fragility. Others debated fractures between signifier and signified in the designed world. Still others considered practices that merge the statistics-driven "cloud" with social advocacy. Some revealed the increasing research component of design practice, while others exposed the fusing of science and design. And several authors addressed the redesign of design processes themselves. Design paradigms are morphing, shifting, and merging such that some categories are disappearing and new ones are emerging—ways of designing that do not, as of yet, have names.

The definitions and roles of design are rapidly changing. All of us, as designers, need to carefully consider how we act as catalysts and how we respond to these changes. And we need to think about the implications and consequences. As we contemplate possible futures of design, ethics is of paramount concern.

Already, design interventions impact societal and economic structures. Already, synthetic replacements of organic matter question our current notions of the biological body. Already, nanotechnology is giving us "god-like" powers, but with hidden, tenuous consequences, such as how nano-particles flushed into waste water might affect ecosystems, farms, and human health.[8] The ethical dilemmas of design lead us to ask: How are emergent design fields changing social and individual identities? Will design advancements lead to a greater divide between those who can afford it and those who cannot, or will they shrink the gap? What ethical obligations do designers have to expand or limit design innovations and their implications?

As such, we are asked to be thoughtful, socially conscientious designers who consider all the possible consequences and implications of this intriguing time in which we live.

The Project of Diversity and Design

Body modification—piercing, tattooing, etc.—has existed throughout human history and across cultures. Body design may be one of the oldest design practices. Taken in incremental steps, then, it is not surprising that, as technologies, techniques, and customs evolve, body modification evolves. In complement, it is not surprising that some members of society choose to participate in the newest forms and fashions of body modification, while others—based on everything from religious convictions to social conventions—contest their use. Yet this binary leaves out two other groups: those individuals or groups who desire body modification but are denied access, and those individuals or groups who are coerced or forced into body modification. To one group, circumcision is a religious rite of passage; to another group, circumcision is a simple medical procedure to improve health; to a third group, circumcision is a violent act done without the consent of the individual on whom it is being performed. A parallel dialectic is playing out in Brazil's plastic surgery industry, as well as emerging design fields across the globe.

As we have seen throughout the case studies in this book, there is a complex relationship between design and society. Design has the ability to empower or to disenfranchise. Design can promote or hinder identity development. Design has unintended consequences. And, reciprocally, the desires, values, and needs of society influence the trajectory of design. The relationship between diversity and design will only grow more multifaceted and complex. Designers have always had to deal with technological and material limitations, laws and regulations, and social conventions. Environmental sustainability is a newer concern. Social justice—more commonly discussed in regards to education, employment, and healthcare than in design—will, likely, sit side-by-side with issues like sustainability, possibly even integrated with the design professions' historical and popular kinship with beauty and aesthetics.

From product design for children to urban planning for Chinese immigrants, or from gender-focused media to elder housing, ethical (and economic) debates will increase, even for projects that seem innocuous. Hidden consequences will also exist, *especially* for innocuous projects. Through experience and research, however, designers can learn to better anticipate these consequences; and through improved design processes—processes that include diverse perspectives and voices—designers increase the likelihood of improving physical, emotional, and social well-being. Design cannot overcome systemic poverty, nor can it eliminate racism or ageism, nor can it undo political oppression or genocide. Design cannot save the world, but designers cannot afford, even amidst skepticism and debate, to abandon it either. At the core of design are optimism and persistence. Architects draw buildings that do not yet exist. Product designers imagine objects that we do not yet know we need. Urban planners craft policies that impact citizens not yet born. All three envision future societies that, through the tools of design, are better off than the current one.

Notes

1   The *Patients Beyond Borders* website, a source for medical tourism, described Pitanguy as "the world's most renowned plastic surgeon" on their Brazil page: www.patientsbeyondborders.com/brazil, accessed November 17, 2014. The Holy House

of Mercy Hospital is described on the Ivo Pitanguy Clinic website: http://pitanguy.com.br/pitanguy/en/index.php/o-instituto/santa-casa/, accessed November 17, 2014.

2   Alexander Edmonds, "A Necessary Vanity," *New York Times*, August 13, 2011, accessed November 17, 2014, http://opinionator.blogs.nytimes.com/2011/08/13/a-necessary-vanity/?_r=0.

3   Lourdes Garcia-Navarro, "In Brazil, Nips and Tucks Don't Raise an Eyebrow," National Public Radio, October 7, 2014, accessed November 17, 2014, www.npr.org/blogs/parallels/2014/10/07/353270270/an-uplifting-story-brazils-obsession-with-plastic-surgery.

4   Jennifer Lee and Frank D. Bean, *The Diversity Paradox: Immigration and the Color Line in 21st Century America* (New York: Russell Sage Foundation, 2010), 9.

5   "History of Optics and Lenses," Museum of Vision Exhibits RSS, accessed December 1, 2014, www.museumofvision.org/exhibitions/?key=44&subkey=4&relkey=29.

6   "A Brief History of Contact Lenses," *GP Contact Lenses,* accessed December 1, 2014, www.contactlenses.org/timeline.htm. Also see R. Belluci, "An Introduction to Intraocular Lenses: Material, Optics, Haptics, Design and Aberration," in *Cataract*, ESASO Course Series, ed. J.L. Güell (Basel: Karger, 2013), vol. 3, 38–55.

7   Rachael Rettner, "Gene Therapy Improves Vision for Some with Rare Disease," *LiveScience*, January 15, 2014, accessed December 1, 2014, www.livescience.com/42617-gene-therapy-eyesight-blindness-choroideremia.html; and Leo King, "Google Smart Contact Lens Focuses on Healthcare Billions," *Forbes*, July 15, 2014, accessed December 5, 2014, www.forbes.com/sites/leoking/2014/07/15/google-smart-contact-lens-focuses-on-healthcare-billions/.

8   Andrew Chen, "The Ethics of Nanotechnology," January 1, 2014, accessed December 1, 2014, www.scu.edu/ethics/publications/submitted/chen/nanotechnology.html.

Contributors

Kathryn H. Anthony (Professor, University of Illinois at Urbana-Champaign School of Architecture). The author of *Designing for Diversity: Gender, Race, and Ethnicity in the Architectural Profession* (2001, 2008), *Design Juries on Trial: The Renaissance of the Design Studio* (1991) and over 100 publications, Dr. Anthony has served as a spokesperson about gender issues in architecture on *ABC World News with Diane Sawyer, National Public Radio (NPR), The Chicago Tribune, The Economist, The Los Angeles Times, Time.com, The Wall Street Journal, The Washington Post,* and elsewhere.

Megan Basnak (Research Associate, Center for Inclusive Design and Environmental Access (IDeA), University at Buffalo—State University of New York). Megan is an architectural designer and researcher whose interests include investigating forms of architectural practice that aid typically underserved populations and understanding how universal design initiatives impact users of various abilities. At the IDeA Center, Megan collaboratively works on designing home modifications for clients with varied levels of ability and assists with design consults for local and regional organizations. In addition, she assists with an ongoing initiative that seeks to better understand the state of universal design education in various design fields in the United States.

Jo-Anne Bichard (Senior Research Fellow, The Helen Hamlyn Centre for Design, Royal College of Art). Dr. Bichard's dissertation "Extending Architectural Affordance: The Case of the Publicly Accessible Toilet" focuses on the experiences of users when finding and accessing toilet provision. Jo-Anne has led and worked on a number of research projects in the area of toilet design that is inclusive and user centered. She worked with designer Gail Ramster in the development of *The Great British Public Toilet Map*, the UK's largest database of publicly accessible toilets and a location-based resource for users to locate the nearest facilities.

Mary Jane Carroll (Professor, Sheridan College and University of Toronto). Mary Jane is an architect and interior designer who has been teaching and researching person-environment fit for the past 12 years. Current research focuses on inclusive design and public housing, with a particular focus on accessibility; the development of federal standards for the home modifications industry in the U.S., in conjunction with the IDeA Center; and an aging in place certificate program for working professionals. She has authored many journal articles and has presented at conferences both in Canada and abroad.

Lori E. Crosby (Professor, Cincinnati Children's Hospital Medical Center). Dr. Crosby is a pediatric psychologist, co-director of Innovations in Community Research and Program Evaluation and the director of training for the Community Engagement Core of the Cincinnati Center for Clinical and Translational Science and Training. As a director and collaborator on more than 15 federal grants, Crosby has emerged as a leader in conducting research to transform the healthcare system for adolescents and young adults with sickle cell disease (SCD). In 2012, she was elected as Fellow of the American Psychological Association (APA) Division 54 for her work with individuals affected by SCD.

Charles Davis (Assistant Professor, University of North Carolina). Dr. Davis teaches history, theory, and criticism in architecture. His research examines the historical integrations of race and style in modern architectural debates. Charles' scholarly work has appeared in peer-reviewed journals including *Architectural Research Quarterly* and *Journal for the Society of Architectural Historians*, as well as the interdisciplinary journals *APPX* and *VIA*. He is working on a book manuscript that surveys the influence of race science on architectural movements in France, Germany, and the United States.

Linda Dunseath (Executive Director—Live Well Collaborative, University of Cincinnati). Live Well Collaborative (LWC) is an innovation incubator that partners with the University of Cincinnati (UC) and member organizations to develop products and services for living well across the lifespan, with an expertise in the 50+ consumer market. Since joining LWC in 2007, Linda has strategized with industry partners and UC to facilitate over 40 projects that have exposed more than 500 students and 30 faculty to multidisciplinary teamwork using design-thinking methodologies.

Maya Indira Ganesh (Director, Applied Research, Tactical Technology Collective). After leading the Evidence & Action program for the past three years, Maya is in a new role as the Director of Applied Research at Tactical Tech, Berlin. Current research projects examine digital security pedagogies and the flip side of technology for transparency and accountability. Maya's role also involves "field building" to convey Tactical Tech's work with its peers and partners as contributions within the information-advocacy sector. Before joining Tactical Tech, she worked as a researcher and activist with women's rights organizations in India and internationally. Maya holds an MA in Applied Psychology from Delhi University, India, and another in Media and Cultural Studies from the University of Sussex, UK.

Caroline Hill (Associate Professor, Texas State University). Professor Hill's research areas of interest include design psychology and sustainability issues, particularly as they relate to professional practice. Her creative and scholarly work has been published in the *Journal of Interior Design*, *Interiors & Sources*, and other periodicals. Professor Hill is a registered interior designer in the State of Texas and an active member of the International Interior Design Association (IIDA) and Interior Design Educator's Council (IDEC).

Walter Hood (Professor, University of California, Berkeley). Walter is an artist, designer, and educator engaged in architectural commissions, urban design, art installations, and research for almost 20 years. He regularly exhibits and lectures on professional and theoretical projects nationally and internationally. The work of his studio features landscape, architectural, urban design and art installation projects, including the gardens at the new De Young Museum in San Francisco, Splash Pad Park in Oakland, CA, the Sculpture Terrace for the Jackson Museum of Wildlife Art in Wyoming, the Powell Street Promenade in San Francisco and the Baisley Park/50 Cent Garden in Queens, NYC. Many of his works are regarded as transformative designs within the field of landscape architecture. Recently, Hood won design competitions for the Center for Civil & Human Rights in Atlanta, GA; Garden Passage, a public artwork in Pittsburgh, PA; and a 1.1 megawatt photovoltaic array within the campus landscape at the University at Buffalo. In 2009–10 Walter Hood received the Cooper-Hewitt National Design Award for Landscape Design, in 2010 was bestowed the title, Master of Design, by *Fast Company* magazine, and was recently appointed as the inaugural holder of the David K. Woo Chair in Environmental Design at Berkeley.

Lynn Horiuchi (Visiting Scholar, University of California, Berkeley). Dr. Horiuchi is an architectural historian who researches the planning, design, and construction of Japanese American concentration camps. She currently is writing a book, *Dislocations and Relocations: Building Prison Cities for Japanese and Japanese Americans during World War II*, and editing a collection of essays with Tanu Sankalia on Bay Area development, *Urban Reinventions: San Francisco's Treasure Island*. She has published a number of articles on urban planning, low-cost housing, and community project development.

Maggie La Rochelle (Ph.D. Candidate, University of California, Davis). Maggie La Rochelle's current research focuses on the theory and practice of situated relationships to place, especially through experiential learning. Her work is informed by critical nature theory, the movements for social and environmental justice, sustainable agriculture, poetry and creative writing, and community development at the local and regional scales.

Carl Matthews (Professor/Head, University of Arkansas). Carl Matthews is the department head of the interior design program in the School of Architecture. He has served on the leadership group for the Interior Design Educators Council and on the board of directors of the Council of Interior Design Accreditation. His research focuses on the relationship of education and practice, as well as issues of gender, identity, space, and design.

Jennifer L. McHenry (Ph.D. Candidate, University of California, Davis). Jennifer McHenry's research focuses on place-making, the way people create and function in places, and how identity is shared between people and their physical environment with a particular interest in urban geography.

Sina Mossayeb (Global Design Lead in Systems Design, Co-Founder/Co-Lead of Victoria Labs). Sina designs for change at IDEO, where he leads projects addressing complex problems and organizations. He combines his social science background with design thinking to advise on projects involving movement design and behavior change. Prior to IDEO, Sina worked as a director of innovation, researcher and university lecturer, and practitioner across the education, development, and government sector. His doctoral research at Columbia University addressed movements and designing strategies for collective behavior.

Patsy Eubanks Owens (Professor/Chair, University of California, Davis). Patsy Eubanks Owens is a Professor in the Landscape Architecture + Environmental Design program and currently serves as Chair of the Department of Human Ecology. Her research focuses on the relationships between people and place including the analysis of landscape use patterns, understanding user preferences, and identifying the needs of specific client groups. In addition to her research presented in this volume, she is examining the role of the physical environment in the development, health, and well-being of youth, and methods for youth and adult engagement in design and policy development. Her research has been published in *Landscape Journal*, *Urban Geography*, *Community Development*, *Children's Geographies*, *Journal of Development Processes*, *Child and Adolescent Social Work*, and *Children, Youth and Environments*.

Korydon Smith (Associate Professor/Associate Dean, University at Buffalo— State University of New York). Dr. Smith teaches courses in architectural design, theory, and methods. His primary research investigates the roles that design plays among marginalized groups, while a second line of scholarship investigates alternative models of design education. Smith is the lead author of *Just Below the Line: Disability, Housing, and Equity in the South* (2010), co-editor of the *Universal Design Handbook*, 2nd ed. (2010), and editor of *Introducing Architectural Theory: Debating a Discipline* (2012).

Mark Addison Smith (Assistant Professor, The City College of New York). Mark Addison Smith's design specialization is typographic storytelling: allowing illustrative text to convey a visual narrative through printed matter, artist's books, and site installations. With his ongoing, text-based archive, *You Look Like the Right Type*, he has been illustrating fragments of overheard conversations every day since 2008 and exhibiting them as larger-scale conversations in venues including A+D Gallery in Chicago, Brooklyn Artists Gym, and MAGMA Brand Design's

Slanted Magazine. He has spoken about linguistics and letterforms—specifically as they relate to gender dynamics within bathroom graffiti—at American University and Manchester Metropolitan University. Permanent collections include the Kinsey Institute for Research in Sex, Gender and Reproduction at Indiana University and the Leslie-Lohman Museum of Gay and Lesbian Art in New York City. He holds a Master of Fine Arts from the School of the Art Institute of Chicago (SAIC).

Gabi Sobliye (Program Coordinator, Tactical Technology Collective). Gabi works on a variety of data representation projects for groups looking to tell stories with their data. In particular, she focuses on visual persuasion areas central to Tactical Technology's book *Visualizing Information for Advocacy.* Prior to joining the team, she worked at Transparency International, contributing to data projects such as the Global Corruption Barometer, and for *The Guardian* in London. Currently, she is working on a visualization of housing collapses in Egypt.

Despina Stratigakos (Associate Professor, University at Buffalo—State University of New York). Dr. Stratigakos is an architectural historian with an overarching interest in gender and modernity in European cities. She is the author of *A Women's Berlin: Building the Modern City*, a history of a forgotten metropolis and winner of the German Studies Association DAAD Book Prize and the Milka Bliznakov Prize. Stratigakos has also published widely on issues of diversity in architecture and in 2007 curated an exhibition on Architect Barbie at the University of Michigan to focus attention on gendered stereotypes within the architectural profession. In 2011, she collaborated with Mattel on the development and launch of the doll in the Barbie I Can Be series. Her current book project, *Hitler at Home*, investigates the architectural and ideological construction of the Führer's domesticity.

Beth Tauke (Associate Professor/Associate Dean, University at Buffalo—State University of New York). Beth Tauke's research focuses on design education and inclusive design's relationship to the senses. She was co-principal investigator of the Universal Design Identity Program and Bridging the Gap: Increasing Access to Universal Design to Meet the Needs of African American Communities, both sponsored by the National Endowment for the Arts. She co-edited *Universal Design: New York* with G. Scott Danford, and has written numerous chapters and articles. Professor Tauke is a co-founder and current editor of *Universal Design Education Online*, the primary website for Universal Design education.

Craig Vogel (Professor/Associate Dean, University of Cincinnati). Professor Vogel is Associate Dean for Research and Graduate Studies and teaches industrial design. He is a Fellow, Past President Elect and Chair of the Board of the Industrial Designers Society of America (IDSA). He is co-author of *Creating Breakthrough Products* and *The Design of Things to Come: How Ordinary People Create Extraordinary Products.* During the last 25 years Professor Vogel has been a consultant to over 20 companies, and has advised and managed dozens of research projects and design studios collaborating with industry. He was recognized in the 2008 and 2011 *Design Intelligence* publication listing the best design and architecture schools as one of the most admired design educators in the U.S.

Jennifer Webb (Associate Professor, University of Arkansas). Jennifer Webb's research and pedagogical interests focus on the well-being of humans across the social, psychological, and physiological continuums. She collaborated with faculty in architecture and rehabilitation education to produce *Just Below the Line: Disability, Housing, and Equity in the South* (2010). As a professional interior designer, Webb has worked in the field of corporate and healthcare design. She has served on the Arkansas State Board of Registered Interior Designers as the Southwest Chair of the Interior Design Educators Council and as a member of the *Journal of Interior Design* Board.

Peter Wong (Associate Professor, University of North Carolina at Charlotte). Peter Wong teaches courses in architectural design, history, and theory. He is a recipient of a 1996 Design Excellence Award given by the National Organization of Minority Architects (NOMA) and was recognized with a Merit Award in 2004 by the Charlotte AIA Chapter for a workshop and guest house completed in 2003. His written scholarship includes a translated edition of Vittorio Gregotti's essay, "Inside Architecture" (1996), as well as journal writing that explores the meaning and use of architectural drawing techniques. He recently received an honorable mention with his colleague Jeff Balmer for "Writing Architecture in Six Genres," an undergraduate writing seminar, as part of the ACSA's Creative Achievement Award Program for 2010.

Index

Page references in *italics* indicate a figure.

Californian Alien Land Act (1913) 59, 60, 104
Canada, public housing policies 210, 212
Canada community, University of Virginia: burial ground 36, 43, 47–8, *49*; gentrification of 43–4; history of 42–3
canon wars, USA 9
Cantor, Nancy 198–9
Carefree Boulevard, Florida *see* The Resort, Carefree Boulevard, Florida
Carson, Clayborne 26
Carson, David 153–4
children: exclusion from the design process 268; historical narratives of 1–2; inaccessibility of podia 195, 197; underrepresentation in design 1
Civil Rights Movement: anonymous volunteers, role of 20, 26, 27; Martin Luther King Jr. (MLK) Memorial 25–7; in Nashville 40; as ongoing struggle 30–1; peaceful protest movement, 1960s 19–20; role of the National Mall and 19–21; *Witness Walls*, Nashville 40, *40*
Clay, Grady 56–7
co-design 273
cognitive biases 38
commemoration 39–40
Cordier, Charles 23; *African Venus 23*
critical race theory 5
Crosby, Dr Lori E. 272, 277, 278
Crysler, Greig 103
cultural histories: alternative resource research 57–9; and body aesthetics, Brazil 286; critical landscape analysis 75–6, *75*; and experiences of gender 138; of immigrant populations 55; impact on design 19; incorporation of in abstract modernism 24; and material forms 78; methodology for reading 56–9; narratives of, culturally focused design 38–42; observation 57; reading in a landscape 54; slow, measured travel through a site 56–7; ties with community histories 56, 75
culturally focused design: commemoration 39–40; the everyday and the mundane 38–9; life ways 41–2; recognition of cognitive biases 38; triad of investigations 38–42; use of multiple histories 50

Davis, Lennard 232
DeMars, Vernon 101, 104–5, 106, 107, 112
design: decision-making process 36; defining 5–7; design trinity 253;

diversity within 6; empathic design 3; inclusive processes 7; innovation and tragic events 260; and the other, considerations of 3, 5; possible future directions 288–9; relationship with society 290; sociodemographic impact of 1–2, 286–7; unintended consequences 8–9, 13, 260, 266
design anthropology 253–4
design professionals, characteristics of, USA 6, 103–4, 110
design thinking 260, 266–7
Diderot, Denis 3
disability: accessibility issues 213–14; and accessibility of public bathrooms 243–4, 246; and accessibility of public spaces 234; as a construct 232; and difficulties opening tamper-resistant packaging 264–5; and exclusion from the design process 268; input into user-centered design 213; non-depiction of in fine art 232; public dialogue on, *Alison Lapper Pregnant* statue 234, 237; public image of and public spaces 231–2; Trafalgar Square, London as space for 233; visual advocacy. *Sexuality and Disability* (website) 141, *141*; and withdrawal from public spaces 256
diversity: awareness of 12–13; as core mission in education 13; defining 3–5; within design 7; re-defining 286–7; and self-identity development 4
Donavan, J. 254
Doria, Icaro 140–1
Dragset, Ingar, *Powerless Structures 236*, 238
Dramov, Boris 25–6
Dunn, Crawford 159

Eckbo, Garrett 101, 104–5, 106, 107, 112
education: canon wars, USA 9; diversity as core mission 13
Elmgreen, Michael, *Powerless Structures 236*, 238
empowerment: and design considerations 41–2; ethos 191; function 191; perception 191; power dynamics and hate speech 155; and retribution for homophobia 163; social process of 10–11; of speakers, podia design and 195–7; through design 191
environmental justice 38
experience design 251

Farm Security Administration IX and XI (FSA): design interventions